RELIGION AND CREATION

Religion and Creation

KEITH WARD

CLARENDON PRESS · OXFORD
1996

Oxford University Press, Walton Street, Oxford OX2 6DP

Oxford New York

Athens Auckland Bangkok Bombay
Calcutta Cape Town Dar es Salaam Delhi
Florence Hong Kong Istanbul Karachi
Kuala Lumpur Madras Madrid Melbourne
Mexico City Nairobi Paris Singapore
Taipei Tokyo Toronto

and associated companies in
Berlin Ibadan

Oxford is a trade mark of Oxford University Press

Published in the United States
by Oxford University Press Inc., New York

British Library Cataloguing in Publication Data
Data available

Library of Congress Cataloging in Publication Data
Religion and creation/Keith Ward.
Includes bibliographical references and index.
1. Creation—Comparative studies. 2. Cosmology. 3. God—
Comparative studies. 4. Trinity. I. Title.
BL226.W37 1996   291.2'4—dc20   95–44774
ISBN 0–19–826393–7 (cloth)
ISBN 0–19–826394–5 (pbk.)

1 3 5 7 9 10 8 6 4 2

Typeset by Cambrian Typesetters, Frimley, Surrey
Printed in Great Britain on acid-free paper by
Bookcraft (Bath) Ltd., Midsomer Norton

ACKNOWLEDGEMENTS

I owe so much to so many people that it would be impossible to acknowledge them all. In finalizing this volume, however, I would like to record some particular debts of gratitude. The Bornblum Judaic Studies Department in Memphis, Tennessee sponsored my work on Heschel. The Teape Lectureship at Delhi and Calcutta in 1989 focused my attention on Aurobindo. Teaching for the Ismaeli Institute in London led to a study of Iqbal. Arthur Peacocke, Director of the Oxford Ian Ramsey Centre, and Peter Hodgson, the head of the Nuclear Physics Theoretical Group at the Nuclear Physics Laboratory at Oxford, kindly read sections on science and biology. David Ray Griffin and Brian Davies took a great deal of time to discuss process and Thomist thought, respectively. Part of Chapter 12 was published as 'God as a Principle of Cosmological Explanation', in *Quantum Cosmology and the Laws of Nature*, ed. Robert John Russell, Nancey Murphy, and C. J. Isham. Finally, I would like to thank my colleagues and graduate students at Oxford, who have been a constant source of inspiration.

K.W.

CONTENTS

PART I

Four Scriptural Traditions

I
The Hebrew Bible

INTRODUCTION

Theology is an enquiry into the being of God and the relation of God to the universe. In a comparative theology, one seeks to conduct such an enquiry in the context of a global understanding, taking note of various religious traditions which have exercised an important influence on human thought on these matters. Naturally, no one person can consider all religious traditions, and no one can honestly claim to be outside of or uninfluenced by all traditions. What one can do, however, is to locate one's own judgements within a historical and global context which may place them in a wider and perhaps a deeper perspective.

My own tradition is Christian, and I write from within a specific twentieth-century strand of that tradition. In *Religion and Revelation*, I gave an account of how such a tradition could reasonably appeal to revelation as a major source of its judgements, and of the sense in which revelation might be taken as a source of theological beliefs. I also argued that a study of the forms revelation takes in a number of main religious traditions is an important factor in building up a more comprehensive view which will be rooted in, but not limited to, its own historical tradition.

The same is true of the doctrine of God—or, to take a wider description, the doctrine of a supreme or absolute reality. The twentieth century has seen a rethinking of this concept, in the light of changes in scientific, ethical, and philosophical thought, in a number of traditions. I propose to discuss four such traditions, which are all basically theistic in form: the Jewish, Muslim, Hindu, and Christian traditions, and the way in which one major twentieth-century theologian of each faith interprets them in his own time. I think it is better to attempt a fairly detailed study of a small number of roughly contemporaneous thinkers than to try to generalize across a vast range in an unspecific way. I have therefore, with some regret, omitted non-theistic traditions, like Buddhism, entirely, though that is not at all because I think them unimportant.

The reason I have selected the concept of God is, of course, because it is central to my own Christian belief system. My aim is not, however, to demonstrate the superiority of my beliefs. It is, rather, to articulate and reconceptualize my beliefs by a positive interaction with those of others. In the enterprise of comparative theology to which this is a contribution, others from other traditions will continue the conversation from their own perspectives. In Part 2 of this volume, I consider the general question of how one may speak of God as an objective reality, in the face of much twentieth-century scepticism about that possibility. In Part 3, I go on to develop a specific idea of God which draws on the traditions considered in Part 1, but does so from a Christian viewpoint. Then, in the final part, I relate this idea to recent discussions of cosmology and of the nature of the physical universe, seeking to place a Trinitarian idea of God in the context, not only of other faith traditions, but also of recent conceptions of the nature of the cosmos which suggest a particular view of it as the creation of God. In this first part, however, my aim is to explore what some major twentieth-century theologians from four main religious traditions have said about God, and the extent to which what they say reflects distinctive viewpoints.

I did not have any preconceived plan in selecting theologians for consideration. I went to Jewish, Muslim, and Indian scholars, asking whom they thought were the most reputable, influential, or widely respected theologians. Any such choice is slightly invidious, and all I would say is that Abraham Heschel, Mohammed Iqbal, and Aurobindo Ghose were agreed to be certainly among the most respected twentieth-century thinkers in their own traditions. It transpired, however, that there were some similar themes running through their work, which correlated with similar themes present in the work of many Christian theologians of this century. So this volume turns out to be, not just a consideration of differing images of the Divine Being, but an exploration of a number of similar themes which suggest a revision of some traditional images.

One such theme is the way in which God is felt to have a much more dynamic and responsive relation to the created universe than has been presented in the classical statements of each tradition.[1] For each of the theologians considered here, it may be said that the God

---

[1] I have given an account of the main classical statements in *Images of Eternity* (Oxford: Oneworld Publications, 1993).

who is known to humans through revelation is a God who is in some sense essentially creator. The central theme of this volume, then, is an exploration of the idea of creation in four religious traditions, and of the nature of the God who is known as creator in these traditions. I shall seek to elaborate a positive conception of God from a Christian point of view, taking into account both some of the insights of modern physical theories of the nature of the universe and the writings of non-Christian theologians. One of the things I shall emphasize and try to clarify is the distinctively Trinitarian nature of the Christian image of God. Nevertheless, I hope it will become clear that the relations between such an image and the more unitarian views of Jews and Muslims, and the more non-dualist view of Aurobindo, are more complex than may at first be supposed, and offer many opportunities for constructive interaction.

This is, then, a work of Christian theology, offering a constructive doctrine of God which is meant to be distinctively Trinitarian. But it is also a contribution to comparative theology, seeking to broaden its horizons beyond a purely Christian tradition, to promote a positive interaction between diverse traditions, and to seek inspiration, so far as is possible, from the whole religious history of the human race.

THE HEBREW PROPHETIC TRADITION

The concept of God is not dreamed up by philosophers or invented anew in every generation. It is a concept with a long history of uses in a number of religious traditions. One of the oldest of these is the Jewish tradition, from which the Christian and Muslim views later sprang. To trace the history of the concept is not to reject all subsequent developments or to discover what the concept 'really means', as some early anthropologists thought. But it should give a greater understanding of some of the strands of belief which continue to be embedded in much later formulations, and which may well exert an important influence upon them. Thus it forms an important part of the analysis of the idea of God as it is used in religious discourse.

The *Tanak* or Hebrew Bible, called by Christians 'the Old Testament', is a valuable source of information about early theistic beliefs, even though its documents have been edited and rewritten for particular religious purposes. Most biblical scholars would regard the books of Samuel, Kings, and Chronicles as giving the

earliest reliable information about historical events in world literature. In these documents one can find information about the social
institutions of religion and about early beliefs in the God of Israel.
Even if, as may plausibly be supposed, the documents tidy the
accounts up to suit the theological theories of the editors, they
convey valuable information about widespread religious beliefs and
practices, often whilst trying to play down their importance, in the
case of heterodox beliefs.

The feature of religious life which is most important in Jewish
history is the existence of prophets. The editor of 1 Samuel relates
that the prophets used to be called 'seers',[2] people who have visions
and who can foretell the future or provide oracles of success or
failure. There were bands of prophets, with musical instruments,
who would dance and proclaim in frenzied speech, under the
influence of the spirit.[3] Of the prophet Elisha it is said 'when the
minstrel played, the power of the Lord came upon him',[4] which
gives an insight into one form of prophetic inspiration. Three main
ways of making enquiries of God are specifically mentioned[5]—by
dreams or visions; by the casting of lots, like the Urim/Thummim,
which apparently gave yes–no answers to questions put to it;[6] and by
asking for a prophetic oracle or inspired utterance. There seem to
have been huge numbers of prophets, who often operated under
royal patronage—400 are mentioned as prophesying in the presence
of the King.[7] They clearly disagreed in the oracles they gave. In the
case just mentioned, the 400 are said to have been possessed by
'lying spirits' sent from God, while only Micaiah told the truth. This
passage, like a number of others in the Hebrew Bible, gives a picture
of God seated on his throne, surrounded by spirits who can lie or
dissemble,[8] put humans to the test,[9] or drive them mad.[10] They
argue among themselves about what should be done, but they all
carry out God's orders in one way or another. Some of these spirits,
sometimes in the form of angels or in human form, appear to
prophets in dreams and visions and possess them in oracular
utterance. A divine spirit was also believed to be able to lift up
prophets and carry them away to mountains or far places.[11]

---

[2] 1 Sam. 9:9. All Old Testament quotations are taken from the Revised Standard
Version (New York: Collins, 1973).   [3] 1 Sam. 10: 5.
[4] 2 Kgs. 3: 15.   [5] 1 Sam. 28: 6.   [6] 1 Kgs. 22: 19.
[7] 1 Kgs. 22: 19.   [8] 2 Sam. 24: 2.   [9] Job 1: 6-12.
[10] 1 Sam. 16: 14.   [11] 2 Kgs. 2: 16.

Prophets commonly possessed miraculous powers, in confirmation of their God-given authority. Elijah and Elisha caused lions or bears to eat those who crossed them, called down fire from heaven, produced food out of nowhere, and brought the dead back to life. Like all holy things, their close contact with God made them dangerous sources of spiritual power, walking 'containers of Spirit', which could break out in destruction as well as in healing acts.

From a history of religions point of view, the prophets are holy figures, familiar in many religious traditions, who are susceptible to spirit-possession in trance and ecstatic speech, who divine the future, who have dreams and visions, often by 'incubation' or sleeping in a holy place. They are believed to possess paranormal powers, and are often consulted at moments of crucial decision in the life of a tribe or city. The eighth-century BCE Hebrew prophets are distinguished by their clear perception of an overriding demand for social justice, for their interpretation of the chaotic Middle Eastern wars as judgements upon injustice, and for their formulation of an intense hope for the liberation of the poor and righteous in a peaceful and just land. This change of emphasis from foreseeing the future to moral proclamation is what perhaps underlies the difference referred to in I Samuel between a 'seer' and a 'prophet'. In developing these insights, the prophets develop the idea of God, the source of the spirit who inspires them, as the one and only creator of heaven and earth, who has a right to make demands of creatures, who has the power to punish injustice, and whose plans for creation are ultimately bound to be realized.

PROPHETIC VISIONS OF GOD

It seems as if there is an early stratum of thought in the Hebrew Bible for which the God of Israel is viewed as one god among many, or perhaps as the Father of the gods. Psalm 95 asserts that 'The Lord is a great God and a great King above all gods,' which implies that there are other gods. Psalm 82 says that 'God has taken his place in the divine council; in the midst of the gods he holds judgment.' This general view is confirmed by the fact that, even as Solomon proclaimed that 'there is no God besides thee',[12] he was able to worship other gods and build hill-shrines for them. Micah 4: 5 states

[12] 2 Sam. 8: 22.

that 'All the peoples walk each in the name of its god,' which suggests that each people has its own god, and Jahveh is the God of the Israelites.

Nevertheless, even if such strands of what has been termed 'henotheism'—belief in a single god, without the assertion that there is only one god—do exist in the Hebrew Bible, there is no doubt that monotheism was soon firmly established in Israel. 'I am God, and there is no other,' says Isaiah 45: 22, and the idea that God is the creator of heaven and earth is central to the whole Bible. The edited texts as we have them suggest that prophetic experience of spirit powers was first of all centred on tribal spirits, without defining their theoretical status precisely. Critical study of the texts suggests a subsequent development of the idea that there is only one causal power behind all the varied phenomena of nature, though it often works through spirit intermediaries of various sorts.

Thus the prophet Micaiah sees, in a vision, God seated as a king on his throne with all the host of heaven surrounding him, ready to obey his commands.[13] This sort of vision of God is repeated in a number of recorded prophetic experiences. The cryptic appearance of God on Mount Sinai to seventy of the elders of Israel[14] seems to have been an appearance of God seated on a throne with a pavement of sapphire under his feet. The great vision of the chariot-throne in Ezekiel 1 pictures God as a humanlike figure of bronze and fire. Isaiah's vision[15] is of God as an enthroned king, surrounded by cherubim, his train filling the Temple. All these are clearly stated to be visions of a reality not apparent to normal human perception. All that most people can see is thick darkness[16] or a dazzling light, so that no man can see God's face and live.

This King may perhaps begin as the tribal god of the Israelites, but in the canon of Scripture he is presented as a visionary appearance of the one and only creator of the heavens and the earth. He does not really live on Mount Sinai or in Jerusalem or even in heaven (the sky), for he creates all these things, and therefore exists beyond them—'heaven and the highest heaven cannot contain thee.'[17] As Creator, God brings about the whole universe through the divine word, that is, by thought and intention. He brings it

---

[13] I Kgs. 22: 22.   [14] Exod. 24: 9.   [15] Isa. 6.
[16] Exod. 20: 21.   [17] I Kgs. 8: 27.

about because of its goodness, and creates humans 'in his image'—to share the divine creativity and enjoyment of that goodness.

The Genesis account seems to suppose the existence of a dark and formless deep (*tohu-va-bohu*), over which the spirit of God moves. God creates light and divides the deep, bringing form and order to the universe. This is reiterated in a more overtly mythological fashion at Isaiah 51: 9, echoing other Middle Eastern origin myths: 'Was it not thou that didst cut Rahab in pieces, that didst pierce the dragon? Was it not thou that didst dry up the sea, the waters of the great deep?', suggesting the bringing of order out of a primeval waste or chaos.

There is nevertheless no suggestion that God was impeded in the divine purpose by the character of this primal chaos. On the contrary, he brings the universe into being by his mere thought. The doctrine of God as Creator clarifies the metaphorical nature of much biblical language about the Divine. God does not really cut a primeval monster in two, and God does not really have his throne in the sky. God says, 'Heaven is my throne and earth my footstool,'[18] but the language here is clearly symbolic. Such symbols are common, and are deployed freely by the prophets. 'Look from heaven and see, from thy holy and glorious habitation,' prays Isaiah.[19] 'O that thou wouldst rend the heavens and come down, that the mountains might quake at thy presence,'[20] 'Who is this that comes from Edom, in crimsoned garments . . . marching in the greatness of his strength?[21] 'The Lord is coming forth out of his place, and will come down and tread upon the high places of the earth. And the mountains will melt under him.'[22]

God is often pictured as a storm and war god who is worshipped because he liberated Israel from Egypt, destroys her enemies in Palestine, and establishes a kingdom in Israel and Judah. In the poem of 2 Samuel 22, God is pictured as riding from his temple on the backs of the cherubim, breathing fire, clothed in dark clouds, flashing lightning, cleaving the sea, to deliver the poor and humble the mighty. 'Thou didst exalt me above my adversaries . . . for this I will . . . sing praises to thy name,' the poet writes. And the prophet Habakkuk says, 'Thou didst strip the sheath from thy bow, and put the arrows to the string . . . thou didst bestride the earth in fury, thou didst trample the nations in anger.'[23]

---

[18] Isa. 66: 1. [19] Isa. 63: 15. [20] Isa. 64: 1.
[21] Isa. 63: 1. [22] Mic. 1: 3. [23] Hab. 3: 9, 12.

These images leave little doubt that God is depicted in metaphorical terms, as the Warrior, the King, the Storm God. It seems to be sheer naïvety to hold that the Old Testament seriously regarded God as a male person who lives in the sky and comes down to interfere in earthly affairs from time to time. The prophetic visions are appearances of a reality which has no visible form (it cannot be seen by normal sight), and the poetic images are precisely imaginative depictions of the ultimate spiritual reality which underlies the world the Israelites encounter in their historical experience. That reality gives a moral shape to history, bringing judgement on evil and liberating the poor and righteous. It does not *interfere* in earthly affairs; it *is* the ultimate causal principle which brings about all those affairs, ordinary and extraordinary, harmful and providential.

Many people may think that there is no such spiritual causal principle at work in the universe, and that there is no moral structure to and purpose in history. There is plenty of room for serious dispute here. But the argument should not be wholly skewed by supposing that the biblical writers were misguided literalists who thought there was a man in the sky who kept interrupting the ordinary course of events in whimsical and apparently arbitrary ways. The proper question is whether there is a spiritual causality underlying human history which works to destroy evil and to establish justice. That is the reality to which the visionary metaphors of King, Judge, and Warrior Saviour claim to refer.

God does not only appear in visions as the Warrior King and Storm God. God appears in the cloud of fire, which moves through the wilderness, and in the thick darkness which fills the Temple of Solomon and covers the Holy Mountain. God appears in the burning bush and the flaming torch. God appears in human form, wrestling with Jacob, eating with Abraham, and ascending to heaven in flame. The conclusion is inescapable that God appears in various forms—in human form, in a shining body of glory, in a form of flame and thick darkness. But as creator of all forms, God is beyond them all. So, central to the biblical tradition is the idea of a God beyond all images. The 'still, small voice' that Elijah heard in the cave[24] is the voice that thunders from Mount Sinai and commands through Moses the obedience of the people of Israel. In the innermost Sanctuary of the Temple, the covenant chest contains the words of

---

[24] 1 Kgs. 19: 12.

God, but no visible image of God, and the First Commandment forbids the making of any visible image. The Creator is a God without visible form—'To whom then will you liken God, or what likeness compare with him?'[25] God appears to the prophets in visible forms, but the divine being is not confined to them, and they are only fleeting and finite appearances of his unlimited glory.

It is as Word and Spirit that God is most intimately known by the prophets. The Spirit inspires them to ecstatic utterance and empowers them with insight, just as it fills Samson with strength and Bezalel with creative power. The Spirit is a divine energy which raises human faculties to a new height and imparts paranormal power. The Word of the Lord is the teaching enshrined in Torah, setting out the way of life, which is a way of wholeness, justice, and inner renewal. The Word is the Divine Wisdom which orders human life to its intended goal and initiates God's covenant with humanity.

Through this creativity and wisdom God interacts with the prophets, not just as an external being, but as an inner power which penetrates the depths of the mind and heart: 'The word is very near you; it is in your mouth and in your heart, so that you can do it.'[26] God is not only an external causal power. God is a dynamic power within human minds, inspiring them with creativity and wisdom. God is concerned with the fulfilment of the goal of human life, a society of justice, mercy, and love.

This goal is not a purely moral or political goal; it is a goal which involves creative loving relationship to God himself. Most importantly of all, perhaps, for the Hebrew Bible, God is represented as a being 'in whose presence is the fulness of joy'. He is the Shepherd, Bridegroom, and Father of Israel, merciful, patient, loving, and kind. 'As the bridegroom rejoices over the bride, so shall your god rejoice over you.[27] '[Israel,] I will betroth you to me in faithfulness.'[28] 'My beloved is mine and I am his.'[29] These, too, are obviously poetic symbols, but they represent a relationship of passionate love, in which God is spoken of as delighting in Israel and as being 'grieved' when Israel rebels.[30] The great commandment to love God with all one's heart, mind, and soul only makes sense when the full and conscious realization of such a loving relationship is seen

[25] Isa. 40: 18.   [26] Deut. 30: 14.   [27] Isa. 62: 5.
[28] Hos. 2: 20.   [29] S. of S. 2: 16.   [30] Isa. 63: 10.

as the goal of human life. It is this set of images which gives rise to
the view that the biblical idea of God is of a person. For what else
than a person can be filled with passionate love or sadness?

The multiplicity of these images for God should, however, make
one hesitate before classifying God too readily. The visionary image
of the King is a finite temporal manifestation of a being which, as
Creator, is beyond the time of the world itself. It therefore seems
that the images of the Bridegroom, Shepherd, and Father, based on
experience of liberation from oppression and a felt sense of an
empowering spiritual presence, are also manifestations of a reality
which is beyond all images humans can form. God is not a
bridegroom, though this metaphor expresses something of the soul's
joy in the presence of God, as being in some respects like that of a
bride on her wedding day. It is natural, then, to say that God is not a
person, though personal images of God express the soul's conscious
relation to God as being in some respects like the relation to a
respected and loved person.

In other respects, however, the relation is rather different. One
can relate to God as to a trusted and loving friend, in a very intimate,
almost familiar way—'I led them with cords of compassion . . . I
bent down to them and fed them.'[31] Yet God is also a remote king, to
be feared—'Behold, like the clay in the potter's hand, so are you in
my hand, O house of Israel.'[32] God may seem to be clearly
known—'He will gather the lambs in his arms, he will carry them in
his bosom.'[33] Yet God 'has said that he would dwell in thick
darkness'.[34] God is a charismatic power who works within the
prophets to give them insight and discernment. God is the absolute
source of moral law, whose being does not permit the questioning
that would be appropriate for any person who promulgated law. God
is the creator of heaven and earth, and thus God thinks and acts. Yet
no person thinks as God does, without hesitation, deliberation, or
inference. No person acts as God does, calling up human beings out
of the dust, to exist with their own reason and responsibility.
Perhaps the most appropriate thing to say of the biblical God is that
there are many ways in which it is proper to relate to him as, and
thus to think of him as, a personal being. But this can only be so if
one is careful always to insist that God is a being infinitely greater

---

[31] Hos. 11: 3, 4.   [32] Jer. 18: 6.   [33] Isa. 40: 11.
[34] 1 Kgs. 8: 12.

than humans can conceive—'I am God, and there is none like me.'[35]
It might be better to say that the biblical God is anthropophanic, not
anthropomorphic. God manifests the divine in human form, but that
is not a form which defines the essential divine being.

THE POWER OF GOD

Once monotheism was established, there is no suggestion of any
power opposed to God which might thwart the divine will.
Throughout the Hebrew Bible there is no notion that any power
exists that can finally frustrate God's purpose. Satan is viewed as a
messenger of God who job it is to test humans or incite them to
rebellion. A comparison of the accounts of 2 Samuel 24 and 1
Chronicles 21 shows that the Satan who incites David to take a
census in Chronicles is doing no more than God's work, and 2
Samuel attributes the incitement directly to God. Similarly in Job,
Satan is the tester appointed by God, not a spirit who disobeys the
divine command. Sometimes God not only sends a tester, but
actually sends lying spirits to deceive people: 'If the prophet be
deceived and speak a word, I the Lord have deceived that
prophet.'[36] God is unequivocally seen as the cause, even if indirect
cause, of the misfortunes as well as of the good fortunes of humanity.
'The Lord kills and brings to life.'[37] There is no evil power in
conflict with God, and no power which acts without the permission
of God.

However, the Hebrew Bible often suggests that things happen
which God does not will. 'The prophets are prophesying lies in my
name. I did not send them, nor did I command them or speak to
them.'[38] A number of passages, however, do suggest that God
delegates power to created beings. According to Micaiah's vision in 1
Kings 22: 19–24, God asks the assembled hosts of heaven who will
entice Ahab, and by what means. After a discussion, one spirit
comes up with a suggestion, and God accepts it, assuring the spirit
that his ruse will succeed. Similarly, in the Book of Job, God asks
Satan where he has been, and Satan suggests that he might put Job
to the test. God agrees, and gives Satan permission to do so.
However primitive these accounts are, they suggest that, while

---

[35] Isa. 46: 9.   [36] Ezek. 14: 9.   [37] 1 Sam. 2: 6.
[38] Jer. 14: 14.

nothing happens without God's permission, created spirits have a certain autonomy to make suggestions and implement courses of action on their own initiative.

Such accounts suggest that God is responsive to the actions of creatures, though never allowing them to get out of control. Some things happen, however, that God does not directly decide, though they cannot frustrate God's purpose. Such responsiveness is a feature of many passages concerned with prophecy, where God seems to make the fulfilment of prophecy dependent upon human action. 2 Kings 20 records the prophecy of Isaiah that Hezekiah is to die. But when he repents, God says, 'I have heard your prayer, I have seen your tears; behold, I will heal you.'[39] Repentance brings a remission of judgement to King Rehoboam,[40] and at Jonah 3: 10 God is said to repent of the evil he had intended for the Ninevites, when he saw that they turned from evil.

Classical commentators like Maimonides often claim that when God prophesied punishment in such cases, he always meant it conditionally—unless repentance occurred. Moreover, they say, God knew repentance would occur, and so always knew he would not do what he threatened. This is the only reasonable account a believer in the total immutability of God can give of these passages. However, on the face of it this is a strained reading, which should only be adopted if there is no alternative. The straightforward reading is that God intended to punish Hezekiah, but that when Hezekiah repented, the mind of God changed—in response to a human act. Even if God always knew that this would happen, the divine action is in response to a human action, and so entails change in God. God leaves the decision to a human will, and the divine response is different than it would have been if that decision had been otherwise. This means that what God does depends partly, and by divine will, upon what humans decide. It must therefore be said that God changes from what God would have been if no human decision had been made, or if the decision had been made differently. God permits humans the possibility of obedience or disobedience, and may adapt some plans accordingly. That does not destroy God's possession of omnipotence; but it entails that God does not always exercise the power to determine that things should happen exactly as God wants. God allows particular things to happen

[39] 2 Kgs. 20: 5.   [40] 2 Chr. 12: 7.

which God does not will, precisely because God does will that such creaturely freedom should exist, and therefore that God should not determine absolutely everything.

The Bible is fairly clear that God wills human freedom to exist, in order to allow the existence of human responsibility for choosing righteousness or sin. Ezekiel 3: 16–21 shows God charging the prophet Ezekiel to warn people of judgement, so that, taking heed of the warning, they shall repent and live. Jeremiah 18: 7–11 makes the same point, that prophetic warnings are given in order to turn people to repentance, not because God wants to destroy them. It is a consistent theme of biblical teaching that God sets before people a way of life and a way of death and invites them to choose. God will then treat them in accordance with their choice, which entails responsive change in God and a real moral freedom on the part of human beings.

For the biblical view God is omnipotent—'Behold, I am the Lord, the God of all flesh; is anything too hard for me?'[41] This is spelled out, not in terms of a technical analysis, but in terms of God being able to do whatever God wants. It does seem, however, that divine power is often delegated to spirits, and that it is responsive to human choices, towards which God reacts passionately in delight or sadness. Given the extensive use of metaphors in biblical language, it is hard to say how much of this is metaphorical, but the most obvious interpretation is in terms of a responsive and impassioned divine interaction with relatively free creatures. This is even taken so far that God can say, 'I did not command them, nor did it enter into my mind, that they should do this abomination.'[42] Creatures may apparently take God by surprise—though this may be a figure of speech for saying that creatures again do what God does not wish them to do, rather than that God did not even foresee it.

DIVINE PROVIDENCE

The biblical doctrine of God is underdetermined. That is, one cannot tell, from the text alone, how far God is spoken of literally and how far what is said is a figure of speech. Thus, interpretations of God in Judaism vary from an almost complete agnosticism about the divine being in itself to a near literalism which thinks of God as

[41] Jer. 32: 27.   [42] Jer. 32: 25.

spatial as well as temporal. None of these views are wholly ruled out by the scriptural text; so the principle of interpretation must come from elsewhere. Nevertheless, some beliefs about God are fairly clear in the Hebrew Bible.

What is clear in the final biblical view is that God is the one and only Creator; that God calls the descendants of Abraham into a special relationship of loyalty and love; that God teaches through the prophets a way of justice and mercy; that God judges evil and promises to deliver the humble from oppression; and that God wills all humans to acknowledge the divine power and glory. It is clear that God is believed to have sufficient power to accomplish the divine purposes, and to have sufficient knowledge to judge rightly the hearts of human beings. God is stern in judgement, but above all merciful and gracious, willing good to those who obey the divine law and do what is right. Further speculation on the exact nature of the divine being, its power, knowledge, and goodness, is absent. The whole force of Jewish reflection is focused instead on the requirements of Torah, the fostering of justice among humans and of a relationship of love and joy with God. In this sense, biblical thought remains intensely practical, and its theoretical content remains largely at the level of metaphors or images for the relationship of the creator, judge, and saviour to human creatures.

There are nevertheless a number of theoretical problems which have to be faced. Two main problems are the nature of the relationship between creaturely freedom and divine power, and the relation between the existence of evil and divine goodness. These are, of course, closely related, since they both concern the extent to which states may exist which are not desired or intended by the Creator. It may seem sometimes that God is the author of everything that happens, and so must intend everything. Amos says, 'Does evil befall a city, unless the Lord has done it?'[43] Again, 'The Lord of hosts has sworn: As I have planned, so shall it be.'[44] Yet God also says on one occasion, 'If any one stirs up strife, it is not from me.'[45] And, 'When I looked for it [the vineyard—Israel] to yield grapes, why did it yield wild grapes?'[46] These passages can seem to be straightforwardly contradictory. It is easy, however, to avoid contradiction if one set of passages is interpreted in a restricted

---

[43] Amos 3: 6.   [44] Isa. 14: 24.   [45] Isa. 54: 15.
[46] Isa. 5: 4.

sense, so as to apply to some but not all, relevant occasions. There is a natural inclination to seek an interpretation which preserves the total sovereignty of God. But if this is taken to entail that God actually wills everything, this leaves the problem of why so many things happen that God is said to hate, disapprove of, and condemn.

However one decides to resolve these conflicts, some statements will have to be taken as hyperbole. This will hardly be surprising, given that prophetic speech is filled with hyperbole. It is, I think, fairly clear which set of statements is more likely to be hyperbolic. The Amos quotation is immediately followed by the verse, 'Surely the Lord God does nothing without revealing his secret to his servants the prophets.'[47] It is obvious that God does many things which he does not reveal to the prophets; so the statement cannot be taken literally. It means, rather, that the prophets are often, but by no means always, given insight into what God is doing. So, that the Lord always makes evil befall cities is most naturally taken as hyperbole, meaning that often, but by no means always, the Lord raises up armies to destroy cities. Similarly, the Isaiah quotation refers to a particular purpose which God has, the divine purpose to destroy the power of Assyria. It should not be applied to every detail of human history.

Taking these statements as prophetic hyperbole, one can consistently say that God makes plans which he will carry out, and raises up armies in judgement. But things happen which God does not will, indeed which he forbids, and these things too will be woven into the divine plans, though not as he had at first intended. It would be much more unnatural to take the passages condemning human disobedience as hyperbole, as though God condemned some disobedience but not all, or as though God causes people to disobey but condemns them when they do so. The latter interpretation would introduce moral inconsistency into God, whereas the former simply states that human disobedience will not ultimately frustrate God's plans, and can often be used by God to further good purposes.

This interpretation can be reinforced by a consideration of one main prophetic book, that of Isaiah. The constant theme of the book is God's declaration, through the prophet, of judgement on evil and the divine purpose of final redemption. The whole book only makes sense if one thinks of humans as free to rebel against God and to

---

[47] Amos 3: 7.

frustrate the divine plan, for which they incur judgement, in the form of defeat, oppression and plagues of various sorts. 'They have rebelled against me';[48] 'they have brought evil on themselves.'[49] Humans disobey God's commands, and it is hard to give sense to this unless they can do what God does not intend them to do. Not only that, but God is saddened by their actions: 'I drench you with my tears, O Heshbon and Elealeh.'[50] What they do causes God sadness.

It follows that many things that happen in the world are not what God intends. 'Woe to the rebellious children . . . who carry out a plan, but not mine.'[51] Such plans will often affect others, bringing suffering on other people that God does not intend: 'If anyone stirs up strife, it is not from me.'[52] Suffering comes on guilty and innocent alike, and it is not what God wills: 'O that you had hearkened to my commandments, then your peace would have been like a river.'[53] Nevertheless, much suffering *is* willed by God, as punishment for evil: 'I will turn my hand against you.'[54] God has a plan for salvation which cannot be defeated: 'I planned from days of old what now I bring to pass' (in this case, that Assyria would punish Israel, but would then be punished in turn).[55] The divine purpose is inexorable: 'The Lord of hosts has purposed, and who will annul it?';[56] 'I am God . . . declaring the end from the beginning . . . I have purposed and I will do it.'[57] God plans to reign on Mount Zion and bring in a kingdom of peace and justice, and God will do it, for that is the divine plan from the beginning. Nevertheless, not everything has been planned from the beginning. 'From this time forth I make you hear new things . . . they are created now, not long ago.'[58]

The meaning seems plain, that humans can frustrate the divine intentions, but not for ever. They will be punished and destroyed, and God will ensure the salvation of those who turn to God in repentance and righteousness. This God is known in prophetic vision and oracle as a God who commands righteousness, who permits rebellion and weeps over it, who will punish evil and who will ultimately bring salvation to the earth, even though now the innocent suffer oppression. God has a power which none can resist:

---

[48] Isa. 1: 2.   [49] Isa. 3: 9.   [50] Isa. 16: 9.
[51] Isa. 30: 1.   [52] Isa. 54: 15.   [53] Isa. 48: 18.
[54] Isa. 2: 5.   [55] Isa. 37: 26.   [56] Isa. 14: 27.
[57] Isa. 46: 9.   [58] Isa. 48: 6–7.

'I work, and who can hinder it?'[59] But God permits evil to rule, until 'in that day . . . he will slay the dragon that is in the sea'.[60]

Why should the creator of all permit rebellion and suffering? How can one who allows such freedom ensure redemption and a kingdom of peace and justice? These questions are not answered by the prophet, but what is quite clear is that creaturely actions frustrate the intentions of the Creator, though the final purpose of the Creator is not frustratable. In sum, there does seem to be a consistent idea of God in the Hebrew Bible, and it is the idea of a creator who leaves creatures free to choose justice or self-will, who punishes injustice, and who promises fulfilment in relation to him for all who turn to God. God is a dynamic, responsive, passionate God who continually does new things and weaves human decisions into his larger purpose, a purpose symbolized by the image of a marriage of God and the people of Israel. God is the Power which makes for justice, the Presence which empowers justice, and the Perfection which places the demands of justice upon human beings.

THE PASSIONATE GOD: A JEWISH VIEW

For Jewish thought, God is rarely an object of theoretical enquiry, and a quasi-philosophical approach to questions of the divine being and nature can even be considered as irreligious. Nevertheless, distinctive and profound insights into the character of God have been provided by twentieth-century Jewish theologians. Martin Buber emphasized the personal nature of God in his poetic masterpiece, *Ich und Du*. Abraham Heschel, in his study of the prophets, develops Buber's thought, writing that 'To the prophet, God is always apprehended, experienced, and conceived as a *Subject*, never as an object.'[61] God is not a proper object of dispassionate investigation, and one can say nothing of the divine essence. All that one can say of God is founded on prophetic experience, which is of how God relates to humans in 'pathos and relationship'. Thus 'The prophets experience what he [God] utters, not what he is . . . not the mystery of God's essence, but rather the mystery of his relation to man.'[62]

---

[59] Isa. 43: 10.   [60] Isa. 27: 1.

[61] Abraham Heschel, *The Prophets* (New York: Harper, 1962), 485.

[62] Ibid. 484.

In Judaism, there remains a strong sense of the ineffability of the divine being, of which no image can be made, whether in physical matter or in thought. Maimonides, in the classical tradition, takes this thought to its furthest extent when he denies that any true positive statements can properly be made about God, except on the pure basis of revelation. Heschel reiterates this: 'No image must be fashioned, no concept formed.'[63] This is a difficult doctrine, hard to interpret. It could mean that one knows nothing whatsoever about God. But that would make reference to God impossible, and speech about God vacuous.[64] It could mean that we know positively that God is wholly unlike anything of which one has knowledge. It is not clear how one could know this. Appeal to revelation is no help, since if one thinks that God reveals, one is committed to the belief at least that God acts and communicates, so that one knows God is something like a personal being in some respects. Even if one did know that God was wholly unlike anything else, that would entail that God is not good or wise or loving or just, in any sense we can understand. That seems wholly unacceptable to a theist, and it is hard to think that Maimonides really believed it.

A more subtle interpretation therefore seems to be required. The traditional course is to distinguish between God as related to creatures ('what God utters') and God in essential nature, beyond all relations to space and time. It may then be said that one can know that God truly relates, as Creator, Judge, and Saviour, to creatures. It is unequivocally true of God that God creates and judges, and therefore is a personal reality, a subject. However, it may well be true that God is not only that. 'The secret things belong to the Lord our God; but the things that are revealed belong to us and to our children for ever.'[65] Beyond the commands of God lies the will of God for creatures. Beyond the will of God lies the wisdom of the divine nature, related to created reality in loving-kindness. Beyond the wisdom of God lies the mystery of the divine being in itself, of which one can say no more than that it is the source and foundation of wisdom and will. The form of divine reality, however, is wholly beyond our understanding, which can only dimly grasp its actions and effects. The reality of God is not exhausted in God's works. While we truly see what God is, in the divine acts, God is infinitely

[63] Abraham Heschel, *The Prophets* (New York: Harper, 1962), 274.
[64] This topic is treated in more detail in Ch. 6.   [65] Deut. 29: 29.

more than that, and we cannot begin to conceive that infinity. The vast immensity of God which has not been revealed cannot be described. It is this ultimate divine nature of which no concepts must be formed, since its infinity defeats all attempts to encompass it with the abstractive and generalized concepts of any finite mind.

In the classical apophatic tradition, this led to the idea of God as wholly immutable and impassible. Being beyond time and space and all their limitations, God must be beyond change, and therefore beyond any influence from finite things. Heschel neatly turns the apophatic tradition upon itself. If God is beyond all images and concepts, one must be careful not to conceptualize the divine as 'really' a static being without feeling. That would be to impose our concept of impassibility upon the unknown divine essence. It would be a false move to say that because the divine nature is inconceivable in itself, it is therefore not true that God feels or truly relates to the world. If one can speak truly of God on the basis of revelation, one must attend to the prophetic witness, and affirm it as containing truths about God's real relation to the world. What the apophatic tradition leads one to add is that the divine being in itself is far greater than one can conceive, so that it is not limited by God's real relation to the universe. Nevertheless, that such a relation is real is not deniable simply by appeal to belief in God's unlimited and inconceivable perfection.

If one attends to the prophetic witness as conveying a real if limited truth about God, Heschel claims, one finds that God 'is moved and affected by what happens in the world, and reacts accordingly . . . this notion that God can be intimately affected . . . basically defines the prophetic consciousness of God'.[66] Thus Heschel wants to speak primarily about the pathos of God; that is, about the affective attitudes of God towards humanity, since 'prophecy consists in the inspired communication of divine attitudes to the prophetic consciousness'.[67] The idea of divine pathos may easily be misunderstood to connote some sort of weakness in God, some inability of God to control what happens, some vulnerability to something beyond the divine will. The pathos which the prophets communicate is nothing of that sort. 'Pathos must be sharply contrasted with the theme of divine passion . . . in passion, the divinity is thought of as a martyr . . . in pathos, God is thought of as

---

[66] Heschel, *The Prophets*, 224.　　　[67] Ibid. 223.

the supreme Master of heaven and earth, Who is emotionally affected by the conduct of man.'[68] Pathos is not something which afflicts the divine will, making God powerless. Pathos in God 'is a willed, transitive feeling'.[69] It 'results from a decision, from an act of will',[70] and is not thrust upon God against the divine wishes. God remains wholly in control, but wills to be related to creation in such a way that God is related to it in righteous anger, in sorrow, and in joy. 'God looks at the world and is affected by what happens in it.'[71] At least that is how the prophets unanimously depict the situation; and how can any purely philosophical speculation then explain it away?

I entirely accept Heschel's distinction between a God who wills to relate to the world affectively and a God who, out of weakness, is hurt by the world. It seems to me, however, that one can speak of a 'passionate God' while fully allowing that distinction, whereas there is no other term that will quite do. Certainly, to speak of a 'pathetic God' would be no improvement. Hoping for Heschel's understanding, I shall therefore construe his book as a defence of divine passion, not in the sense of vulnerable weakness, but in the sense of freely willed affectivity. In this sense, Heschel seeks to restore to Judaism the sense of a passionate God, whose 'anger is voluntary and purposeful, motivated by concern for right and wrong'.[72] That sense has always been there in devotion, in the singing of the Psalms, and in the reading of *Tanak*. But it has sometimes been interpreted by a classical tradition of speculative philosophy, which has mitigated or even entirely undermined the sense of divine pathos.

Heschel claims that 'The static idea of divinity is the outcome of two strands of thought: the ontological notion of stability and the psychological view of emotions as disturbances of the soul.'[73] That ontological notion is a misrepresentation of the ultimate mystery of the divine being, an essence which is unreachable by thought, even by the thought of stability as logical immutability. Of that mystery one can say nothing. Thus one must not say that it is impassible, as if we knew for certain what it was not, or what words did or did not more or less apply to it. The mystery must always be preserved, but it needs no philosophical concepts to do so; just the reminder that all speech, even prophetic speech, given by God, is about 'what he [God] utters, not what he is'.[74] As for emotions being disturbances

---

[68] Heschel, *The Prophets*, 320.   [69] Ibid. 258.   [70] Ibid. 298.
[71] Ibid. 483.   [72] Ibid. 282.   [73] Ibid. 260.
[74] Ibid. 484.

and imperfections, one must simply say that sympathy is not imperfection or disturbance. If it is God's will to be related to the world in *chesed*, in loving-kindness, then such a relation is divinely willed, and no disturbance in the unbounded love of the Creator.

Heschel thus proposes that we think of God as a being whose essence remains hidden in the mystery of 'deep darkness', but who chooses to relate to us, and to make that relation known through the prophets, in pathos, in mercy and compassion, in anger and forgiveness, in sympathy and delight. What these things mean in God is not for us to say; but that they mean something which cannot be put in any other way, or cannot be interpreted better by any philosophical concepts, is part of the prophetic revelation. If God 'utters' and 'chooses', something is being said of the divine nature. That nature may be beyond our intellectual grasp, yet it is correct to speak of it as choosing, speaking, and loving, i.e. as personal. The proper sense of divine mystery is not enhanced by denying feeling and real relation to God, but rather by affirming the unutterable transcendence of the One who relates thus to creation. What is unutterable cannot be described, even by negations. If God *in se* does not change or feel as we do, it is not that God lacks such properties. Rather, the essential being so far exceeds them that even our denials, in so far as they give rise to any positive ideas at all, must be denied. Denial of feeling cannot be allowed to give rise to an idea of utter unaffectedness or unchangeability. For one must also deny lack of feeling in God. God feels, and one must think of such feelings by analogy with one's own. But one must never suppose that such feelings in God really are like the feelings—so qualified by weakness and irrationality—common to sinful human beings.

Abraham Heschel provides one twentieth-century Jewish expression of the view that the God of Judaism is a passionate, responsive God, and that philosophical theology must come to terms with this, not subordinate it under some allegedly more adequate classical schema. God is the unbounded, infinite Lord of the world; but He encounters humans as personal. 'The outstanding feature of a person', says Heschel, 'is his ability to transcend himself, his attentiveness to the nonself . . . it is in this limited sense that we speak of God as a personal Being.'[75] God is personal, in being concerned for non-divine being; but one can only assert this on the

[75] Ibid. 486.

basis of prophetic revelation, not as some speculative statement about the divine essence. In prophetic experience, two sides of the divine being must always be balanced against one another: the aspect of absolute mystery, and the aspect of personal address and relationship. It would be wrong to think that God does not relate personally and intimately, in pathos, to creation. That, for Heschel, is the error of the classical theologians. It would be wrong to think that God can simply be understood as such a personal, passionate, responsive being. That is the error of of idolators, who make God into a being like others. God is that beyond all finite forms which relates to creation in the most intimately relational of forms, the form of passionate concern. When God gives *Torah*, God's personal teaching, what God gives is a way of relating to the Divine which is the discovery of ourselves as objects of the divine concern. We find ourselves grasped by the divine attentiveness, the divine love; but its ultimate source remains always and necessarily beyond our grasp.

PROBLEMATIC ASPECTS OF THE BIBLICAL TRADITION

This basic idea of God remains central to the Jewish, Christian, and Muslim traditions, and, as Heschel indicates, it is firmly rooted in the prophetic teachings. Yet the biblical idea of God contains elements which are alien to later Jewish and Christian thought. First of all, God is sometimes seen to act in very destructive, seemingly indiscriminate, and disproportionate ways. Given the belief that God is the ultimate spiritual cause of everything that happens to humanity, it is natural that God should be seen as the destroyer, acting in plague, earthquake, and storm to destroy his enemies. The prophetic perception is that these destructive acts are, whether directly or indirectly, judgements on human evil and presumption. The power of God breaks out upon those who disobey the laws of justice or who are careless of the taboos which protect the divine mystery and sovereignty. God is indeed to be feared, for the hearts of humans are inclined to evil, which God destroys.

As a god of storm and war, God is utterly ruthless towards his, or his peoples', enemies. He requires blood-vengeance, and punishes Saul for not completely destroying all the Amalekites, men, women, children, animals, and property.[76] God sends a famine because of

---

[76] 1 Sam. 15: 17–19.

unavenged blood-guilt.[77] God kills 70,000 men because David took a census, which God incited, or tempted him to do.[78] God kills David's son because of David's sin.[79] God demands of Abraham the sacrifice of his son,[80] which presupposes that he had a right to command such sacrifice—though this again was a 'test' of faith, and so might well have been (though it was not) ascribed to Satan, as God's servant.

All this is well summarized in the core description of Exodus 20: 5–6: 'I the Lord your God am a jealous God, visiting the iniquity of the fathers upon the children to the third and the fourth generation of those who hate me, but showing steadfast love to thousands of those who love me and keep my commandments.' God destroys evil, but that is not the dominant aspect of God for the prophets. Much more important are the attributes of steadfast love and mercy. At Exodus 34 God proclaims, 'The Lord, the Lord, a God merciful and gracious, slow to anger, and abounding in steadfast love and faithfulness, keeping steadfast love for thousands, forgiving iniquity and transgression and sin, but who will by no means clear the guilty.'[81] God is the deliverer from oppression, the one who brings peace to those who love the Lord, who will establish Jerusalem as the place of God's steadfast love. God's purpose is to restore the world to fellowship with the Divine Being, and Israel is chosen as a holy priesthood to accomplish this purpose.

One traditional attitude to this—found, for example, in Maimonides—is to say that, as Creator, God can do whatever he wishes with human lives. Since they are all evil anyway, to will their destruction is perfectly just. Nevertheless, it would be morally unacceptable nowadays for anyone to punish children for their parents' sins. Such views of divine retribution and blood-vengeance reflect contemporaneous tribal ideas of morality, rather than being ideas which truly derive from God. Thus Achan, in Joshua 7, is burned with all his family for his personal theft. Later prophetic thought, as in Ezekiel 18: 20, advances a very different view: 'The soul that sins shall die. The son shall not suffer for the iniquity of the father.' In Torah itself, Deuteronomy 24: 16 states forthrightly that 'children are not punished for the sins of their fathers.' Jesus is speaking from within the Jewish tradition, not in contradiction to it,

---

[77] 2 Sam. 21: 1.   [78] 2 Sam. 24.   [79] 2 Sam. 12: 14.
[80] Gen. 22.   [81] Exod. 34: 6.

when commenting on the doctrine of an eye for an eye: 'Do not resist one who is evil.'[82] From these passages, it appears that the early view of God as demanding blood-vengeance is superseded by the perception that goodness requires love of enemies and not their destruction. The story of the sacrifice of Isaac teaches that God did not really desire the sacrifice of the first-born son, though this practice was apparently widespread in Canaan, and though Torah even enjoins it.[83] Of course, in Torah it is essential that first-born sons are to be redeemed, usually by the payment of money, but the presence of the theoretical requirement to offer them to God suggests an earlier practice of child sacrifice. By the time Torah was codified, however, it had become clear that God demands respect for all human life, not only for one's kin.

If these early ideas of divine goodness seem harshly retributive to those familiar with the teaching of the later prophets, one reason is the early belief, common to many primal traditions, that sin is a form of ritual contagion. Wrongdoing, whether it is oppression of one's fellows or the breaking of cultic taboo, brings an impurity on the people which must be expunged before relationship with God can be restored. So seventy men are killed by God for looking at the Ark,[84] and Uzzah is killed for touching it.[85] The King of Egypt is stricken with plague for lying with Abraham's wife, though he thought she was his sister. These beliefs see God as a source of dangerous power which works automatically to destroy those who do not fear or respect it. In these ways the God of Israel is very like the other gods of the Middle East at that time, a sacred force capable of erupting into human life, particularly in storms, plagues, and military conquests, a liberator and protector of his people, but a dangerous one, to be treated with careful respect.

The moral world of the early Israelites is a world in which God is a dangerous power who liberates and protects the Hebrew tribes as long as they obey divine law, but who ruthlessly destroys all those who impede the divine purposes for his people. Any disobedience or infringement of law, even if not intentional, brings impurity on the people. Like an infectious disease, it must be wholly expunged, with all those whom it may have contaminated. However, for those who repent and humbly turn to God, there is a promise of restoration.

---

[82] Matt. 5: 39.   [83] Exod. 22: 29.   [84] 1 Sam. 6: 19.
[85] 2 Sam. 6: 7.

This is the primary sense in which God is good—God will be merciful to the penitent, and give good to those who turn to the Lord. However, God's destructive power is inexorable against those who ignore divine commands. In the chronicles of the history of the kings of Israel and Judah, destruction comes to those who turn from God to the worship of idols, and prosperity and happiness come to those few kings who turn back to God. It is in the events of history that the judgement and liberating power of God are shown, and the prophets are those who interpret this history in moral terms, who warn of impending judgment and promise the possibility of repentance.

One basic reason why the early biblical view of God seems morally difficult to most believers of later times is that it has, at best, an ambiguous view of human freedom and responsibility. If evil is a contagion which needs to be eliminated, then it is understandable that men, women, and children who are implacably hostile and whose influence is dangerous should be exterminated.[86] But if one thinks, as later biblical thought does, of persons as bearing responsibility only for consciously intended acts which they know to be wrong and are free to avoid, then wholesale extermination will seem both disproportionate and indiscriminate. If one further thinks of God as desiring the welfare of every human being, extermination will be hard to square with such a desire.

A strong belief in divine omnipotence, which has not yet come to a clear view of individual human responsibility or of the universality of the divine love, may drive one to believe that God can dispose of human lives as God wishes, so that God can rightfully destroy evil that God himself has created, or bring to prosperity whomsoever God will. Any difficulties one feels about such a view must simply be referred to the mystery of the divine will, which is neither to be understood nor questioned by human presumption.

It is not surprising that early biblical views see God as remorseless in judgement, and as enjoining a vengeance morality, to enable evil to be exterminated completely. The biblical records are culturally influenced responses to a sense of divine demand, presence, and promise. They show a changing and sometimes developing apprehension of what these demands and promises are, and of what the

---

[86] Deut. 20: 16–18.

divine presence effects.[87] Thus one will not be surprised at the occurrence of views which take sin to be a contagion and often a matter of cultic error, responsibility to be a communal matter, and the action of God to be catastrophically destructive as well as liberating and protective.

Such a general view of the Hebrew Bible in terms of a developing apprehension of the divine nature is supported by the realization that many of its stories seem to be hugely exaggerated. Samson's killing of one thousand men with an ass's jaw-bone, the 700 left-handed marksmen who never miss, and the standing still of the sun at Gibeon to allow further slaughter by the Israelites—these and many other accounts are most plausibly understood as legendary accretions to tribal victory stories. It is irrational to accept that such accounts are legendary, and yet insist that every moral or spiritual statement about God in the same Scripture is exempt from error of any sort. The reasonable course is to expect beliefs about God to be influenced by the sorts of factual limitations and moral unclarities which affect most tribal societies struggling for existence in a hostile environment. Yet one may find in the Hebrew Bible a developing perception of the divine nature which has inspired a commitment to social justice and to intellectual investigation which has changed the face of the earth.

THE MYSTERY OF EVIL

If a genuine human freedom to obey or disobey God is allowed, then some of the puzzles about the occurrence of evil in the world can be resolved. The Israelites were oppressed in Egypt because of the immorality of the Egyptians. God did not desire their oppression, which is why God liberated them. Yet it could be said that God did foresee their oppression and plan their liberation, since God foresaw what evil choices would do, and could use them in planning what would ensue.

In such a world, it nevertheless cannot be the case that God will always punish the evil and reward the good, for the evil oppress the good, against the desire of and in contradiction to the command of God. This entails that the good must sometimes be oppressed, however little they deserve it. For freedom to exist, in any world in

---

[87] Such a view of revelation was expounded and defended in my *Religion and Revelation* (Oxford: Oxford University Press, 1994).

which evil choices are freely made, the wicked must flourish, at least for a time, and the good must suffer.

But there is a deeper mystery here. Why should there be any evil to be chosen, and why should anyone choose it? On this the Hebrew Bible is silent, except that it unequivocally refers evil as well as good to God. Even though it is admitted (especially in the book of Job) that not all particular cases of evil are due to individual sins, a connection between suffering and sin is clearly asserted. Deuteronomy 30 records the setting before Israel of God's blessing and God's curse, and makes it clear that obedience to Torah will bring blessing, while disobedience will bring the curse of suffering and death. The way of life is the way of loving God, but the way of death is the turning of the heart to other gods.[88]

This could be interpreted in a rather crude fashion, to say that if the Israelites worship the God of Abraham, God will reward them, whereas if they worship Chemosh, Abraham's God will punish them—which sounds intolerant and narrow-minded. The point, however, within the context of the biblical narrative, is that these are people with whom God has made a particular covenant, whom God has liberated from oppression and to whom God promises knowledge of the divine presence for ever. For them to turn to other gods is not conscientiously to decide that some other religion is preferable to Judaism. That interpretation is wholly anachronistic. It is to renounce the covenant, to break the ancestral promise, to forget the liberation, to ignore the moral law, and to worship fertility and power instead of a just and holy God.

Evil exists because the possibility of a breaking of trust, of ingratitude and lack of concern for others, is an essential component of any form of humanity, which has not been transfigured by the unitive power of divine love. This created universe is such that there is a particular importance in the existence of human persons whose unitive transfiguration is to be accomplished in part by their own unconstrained response to the divine love. Until that unconstrained response has been made, resentment, ingratitude, and contempt remain possible existential attitudes for any self which values its own existence and happiness more than the realization of goodness for its own sake. What the Hebrew Bible points out is that the choice of self

---

[88] Deut. 30: 17.

is a choice of self-destruction, whereas the way to life is a self-abandonment to the source of all goodness.

The savage judgement of God is a dramatic portrayal of the way in which those who hate goodness bring self-destruction and disaster upon themselves and upon those generations who follow them. The mercy of God is a promise that goodness remains a possibility for all those who turn back to God. For the Hebrew Bible, instances of divine judgement are great natural disasters. Floods, earthquakes, and storms are all ascribed to divine judgement, as are defeats by the enemy in war, famine, and drought. God is directly involved in events, sending manna, causing women to conceive miraculously, determining the way lots fall, making sundials go backwards, consuming sacrifices with fire, dividing seas, and moving in a cloud or column of fire.

This way of thinking is alien to scientific understanding, and few seriously expect God to act in these ways today. The natural way to interpret these records is to see them as mythologized accounts of events recalled from a fairly distant past, poetically heightened to make a spiritual point or bring out a spiritual meaning. In this respect, they resemble accounts from many primal religious traditions, which recall ancient times when heroes and gods roamed the earth, and when the elements were directly controllable by spirit forces. In such accounts, historical remembrance and mythic imagination work together to produce myths of tribal origin and ancestral history. Their real basis is the mediation with present spiritual reality which they express, though this in turn has been formed by historical remembrance of great events in tribal life.

THE INTERPRETATION OF BIBLICAL NARRATIVES

If the Hebrew Bible gives mythicized history, then it cannot be taken as providing historical evidence for justified beliefs about God. It cannot be *evidence*, precisely because it has already been reshaped by mythical imagination and reflection. What it does is to present the view, in mythical form, that history has a moral and purposive character, that it expresses the relation between an underlying spiritual reality and human actions. Once one sees that the view cannot be accepted by us just as it stands, the major problem becomes one of interpretation—of determining what is true in such accounts.

The most hopeful interpretative approach, quite widely adopted both in modern Judaism and Christianity, might be to see the biblical records as constructed from contemporaneous beliefs about God retrojected onto an idealized past history, and to ask what sorts of prophetic or devotional experiences, in what sort of social and historical context, might give rise to such myths. One would then be seeing the experiences of God recorded in the Bible in mythic form as not wholly different, given their different social and cultural contexts, from possible experiences of those who read the accounts in the present. At the same time one will not wish to discount in advance the possibility of genuine revelations that are unique to specific times and cultures, and that have a unique and unrepeatable place in human history.

If one adopts such an approach, the first major aspect of the biblical God that emerges as distinctive in the history of religions is that God is a judge and deliverer. Events that happen in history have a moral and salvific dimension, so that evil is self-destructive and the possibility of deliverance from evil is always present. In the Indian religious traditions, the law of karma was introduced to give a moral dimension to history. Suffering is a direct result of past evil deeds, probably in a previous incarnation, and deliverance from suffering is possible by learning non-attachment. The Hebrews had a very sketchy doctrine of an afterlife, and no doctrine of reincarnation, so this solution did not occur to them. Consequently, God was introduced in a much more directly active way, punishing evil by plague and disaster and intervening to liberate the Israelites from oppression and lead them to a country of their own. The moral aspect then comes, not so much on a purely individual level, but on the social level, where consequences affect future generations for good and evil, rather than individuals in some personal future life.

For the prophets, there is a spiritual basis to the natural order. The natural world exists to realize values, but selfish choices frustrate such realization and increase forms of suffering and destructiveness. The possibility of destructive choice is a necessary part of the natural order of things. One might speak of the prophetic knowledge of God as knowledge of the demand to realize values, a demand implicit in the structure of possibilities before one. The prophets feel an assurance that such values will be realized and they claim to experience a power helping to realize them. The Torah is the way in which this moral demand, rooted in the nature of things, is apprehended. The promise of the Kingdom is a discernment of the inner purpose of history. Experience of the Spirit as a creative and liberating energy gives participation in the divine creativity. The Covenant is an experience of a vocation to realize value, to mediate the divine life in one's own society. Judgement is experience of the frustration of value which results from one's self-will, and salvation is experience of the power which continues to work, transforming even evil into good.

The Biblical myth reports that, for instance, on one occasion God sent a plague because of idolatry, as a direct responsive action to human sin. One may take the view that the account was never based on a literal experience of such a thing. There was an underlying belief that God sets up the structure of the world so that selfishness, the root of injustice, leads to personal and social destruction. This is expressed as a specific divine action in direct response to injustice. When the people were penitent, the plague stopped. Real history is not quite as neat as that. Professions of penitence will not stop a plague. But the underlying insight which the narrative expresses is that altruistic acts will lead to the alleviation of destructive forces. One might suggest that what the Hebrew Bible often reports as particular direct acts of God can be reinterpreted as general structures set up by God to lead to specifiable general outcomes.

In the evolutionary process, for example, God will not act directly and specifically at a particular point in time to introduce a new set of chromosomes and thus create a distinct species. Rather, God sets up the evolutionary process so that, by stochastic (probabilistic) variation and environmental interaction, rational agents will eventually come into existence.

This does not mean that, having set up the structure, God is then not involved in it. God continuously supports the structure and works within it to strengthen good outcomes and impede bad ones. That is divine 'deliverance' and 'judgement'—empowerment of the good, creative aspects and frustration of evil, destructive aspects (often by permitting destructive consequences to operate freely and self-destructively).

The prophetic sense of calling is founded on a belief in a liberating empowerment which is also a demand for self-transcending moral effort and an assurance of ultimate realization. The prophets sense the self-destructiveness of injustice and the necessity of a turning to the divine source, and express this in terms of specific, catastrophic events and promises of extraordinary deliverance on condition of repentance. Forged in the political maelstrom of Middle Eastern politics, these insights are projected in the literary form of earth-shaking or even cosmic events, both backwards into primeval history and forwards into an apocalyptic end of all things.

The clue to interpreting the Biblical records is, first, then, to see them as products of a culture as alien from post-scientific society as that of ancient Greece, Rome, or Scandinavia. They are products of a wholly pre-scientific world-view, emerging from a polytheistic animism with its beliefs in direct spirit influence on all natural events. Second, one can recover, by a process of imaginative reinterpretation by analogy with present spiritual experience, a sense of the prophetic experiences of vocation, demand, judgement, deliverance, presence, empowerment, and promise which were centrally formative in creating this religious tradition. Third, one can gain a feeling for the mythico-symbolic character of religious concepts, by a study of the symbols and myths of many religious traditions. Mythic speech expresses, in terms of cosmic scope and discrete specific actions (acts of the gods or of God), beliefs about the inner structure of the world, in its general relation to suprasensory or spiritual reality. What are represented as the acts of God, either in speech or in calling up storms and earthquakes, are in fact discernments of a morally oriented interactive creativity in nature, as prophetically divined in the history of a nation feeling itself called to a special relationship with and loyalty to the creative power.

It is noteworthy that the eighth-century BCE prophets and literary editors with whom the early Biblical narratives originate report clear and cataclysmic acts of God long ago in history or in the apocalyptic future. The more sober accounts found in the court histories of David and Solomon give a more accurate view of historical realities. Both the Patriarchal history and the eschatological visions of redemption have the character of myth, rather than of accurate historical record, and the spiritual insights underlying them have to be teased out by a process of sympathetic recontextualization and reinterpretation.

The Hebrew myth or 'founding narrative' is that God chose Israel as his 'son'; freed the people from Egypt and gave them Canaan; taught them the Law and made a covenant of love with them. They rebelled, so God punished them by pestilence, drought and defeat in war. In the end, however, God will save a remnant from destruction, establish a perpetual kingdom in Jerusalem, and all nations will acknowledge God, worshipping together in a renewed Temple. What underlies this myth is the struggle to find some meaning in the historical experience of a nation which believed itself to be bound in relationship to a God of righteousness, loving-kindness, and mercy. Feeling the intensity of the demand of righteousness, the prophets also felt the intensity of their failure and rebellion. So they could construe the disasters which befell their people as judgements on sin. Yet they still experienced the divine as a loving presence, and so looked for forgiveness, for deliverance from oppression, and for a fulfilment of the divine demands in a renewed society. Sometimes, even or especially in the latest books of the Hebrew Bible, this fulfilment is still thought of in a very nationalistic way, as the political triumph of Israel and the enslavement of her enemies. But there is also the more universal theme of a return of all nations to God, with Israel as the priesthood of a renewed earth. The prophets believed they stood in a long tradition of people who had been called to a knowledge of and loyalty to God. This God was experienced as both demanding and forgiving, both majestic and loving, both righteous and gracious, and the divine nature was disclosed as the Israelites responded to these experiences. Thus the prophets viewed their history in terms of relationship to a holy and compassionate being on whom they depended for their existence, and the scriptures record their struggle to understand that relationship.

The fundamental prophetic experience is that of an encountering reality of holiness, power, deliverance, and compassion, mediated in and through the events of Jewish national history. The divine reality manifests itself to the prophets in four main aspects. As Perfection, it is experienced as the supremely holy being, which requires justice and mercy, as it orders the world justly and mercifully. As Power, it is taken to be the underlying cause of all that happens in history, for good and ill. As Promise, it inspires hope that goodness will flourish and evil will be finally defeated. And as Presence, it is encountered as a sustaining, loving personal reality.

The prophetic tradition builds a cumulative store of concepts and images, refined by testing against hard experience. Gradually the warrior tribal god becomes the one source of glory, power, and loving-kindness, though still bound to this nation by a special tie. One way of making sense of the Hebrew Bible is to see it as a reflective and imaginative working-out of the idea of a Holy Creator. Such reflection is founded on a cumulative tradition of historically contextualized experience of the Divine. It begins from a basis of tribal shamanistic experiences and goes on to develop the idea of one universal spiritual presence, willing justice and mercy.

This myth needs reinterpretation in different cultures which can still receive it as expressing an authentic discernment of the inner character of human existence. Such reinterpretations have often been given, although they were, as is common in religious traditions, usually said to be 'recoveries of original meaning'. Some major reinterpretations were provided after the Exile, in early Christianity, in Islam and in Rabbinic Judaism, in post-Enlightenment Christendom and in post-Shoah twentieth century Judaism. In each revision, the fundamental theological problems remain very similar. Can a divine providence be discerned in the apparently chaotic events of human history? How can a God of *chesed*, loving-kindness, allow such suffering to exist in the world? How can a redemption from evil be effected by God without simply destroying human freedom? Will redemption come in history? And what is the part that Israel has to play in such a redemption?

These are not speculative questions about the origin of the universe, or about what is the best explanation of how things are. They are questions about the authenticity and plausibility of the fundamental prophetic experiences of a loving and morally demanding God, in a world wherein God seems to be hidden and silent. Such problems do not exist without acceptance of the prima-facie claims of the prophets to experience divine reality. Given some disposition to give credence to such claims, no reflective theologian can act as though these problems did not exist and were not severe. Part of any adequate account of religious faith, in the Semitic tradition, must be an explanation of the problematic nature of faith and of the sort of commitment such prophetic experiences can license.

Abraham Heschel has been mentioned as a twentieth-century Jewish thinker who suggests that such problems might best be approached by a modification of the classical doctrine of God accepted by Maimonides. Heschel attempts to revive within the Jewish tradition what he sees as the biblical view of God as a dynamic God who is affectively related to creation, and takes personal form in relating to creatures as others capable of fully personal relationship with the Divine. For such a view, the prophets of Judaism do not present an exclusive religion from which others are barred. They do insist that God calls the Jewish people into a covenant relationship; but this is seen as a special case of the relationship which all creatures should have with God, as the subject who responds to creatures in judgement and in mercy, and above all with loving-kindness. These insights have been taken into account by some Christian and Muslim theologians in the twentieth century, and developed in ways consonant with their own distinctive traditions of revelation. In working towards a fuller presentation of an idea of God, I shall show how, in these traditions also, the older classical concepts are being challenged by views which claim both a more scriptural basis and a rather different philosophical vision. To what extent these views help to resolve the genuine problems of Semitic theism remains to be seen.

2

The New Testament

THE INCARNATE GOD

The Christian idea of God is rooted in reflection upon the New Testament, and upon a specific sort of theistic experience which is believed to be mediated through the person of Jesus, by the power of the Divine Spirit. Classical expositions of this idea were, as in the Jewish case, deeply influenced by a Greek philosophical tradition, deriving from Plato and Aristotle. The twentieth century, however, has seen attempts on the part of theologians to reconceive the classical tradition and interpret the biblical sources in a different way. Just as, within the Jewish tradition, Abraham Heschel gave a dynamic, affective, and relational view of God, rooting it in his interpretation of prophetic experience, so a number of Christian theologians have reinterpreted their own classical traditions, claiming thereby to return to a more biblical basis for a doctrine of God. Since this volume itself provides a Christian delineation of the idea of God, I will not consider the work of a particular Christian theologian in great detail. I will, however, take the work of Karl Barth—considered by many to be the outstanding twentieth-century Christian theologian—as representative of attempts to provide a more dynamic and relational doctrine of God. I will point to some aspects of his writings which illustrate the way in which the classical doctrine of God has been revised and is capable of further revision. My main aim, though, is to bring out the distinctiveness of the idea of God as Trinity which developed from reflection on the New Testament, and at the same time draw attention to some possibly surprising affinities between major modern theologians working in very different religious traditions.

The Christian God is undoubtedly the God of Abraham, Isaac, and Jacob. Yet the basic Hebrew idea of God as a providential moral will, interacting with created wills to establish a community of justice and peace, has to be modified considerably to take account of the role and person of Jesus. The main orthodox tradition of

Christianity rejects the view that God interacts with Jesus as an external will in relation to a free created will. It holds that, though Jesus had a free created will, it does not have the sort of relative existential independence possessed by other human wills. It is the human will of God the Son, and that makes it unique in the form of its relation to God.[1]

The Synoptic Gospels give Jesus an authority which is virtually that of God. They see him as the Son of God, who will reign as King of Israel and take on the divine prerogatives of forgiving sins and judging human lives.[2] But it is in the prologue to John's gospel that Jesus is identified with the Word who 'was with God, and was God', and 'was made flesh'.[3] The startling idea of God, the supreme spirit, becoming flesh, or 'taking' a human mind, intellect, and will, is bound to modify the idea of God as quite other than any created thing. If the idea of incarnation makes sense, then God is in some sense identical with at least one created thing, the body and soul of Jesus.

Everything depends on what sense is to be given to this identity. The main orthodox tradition denied that God *changed* to become human, to turn into a human being. Rather, the humanity of Jesus was 'assumed' by God, without any change in the Godhead itself.[4] Such a view is not formulated in the New Testament, and New Testament views of the relation of God and Jesus are suggestive rather than clear. In the earliest documents of the New Testament— some of the letters—God the Father and the Lord Jesus Christ are linked together as objects of praise and worship. In what is often regarded as the earliest extant letter, 1 Thessalonians, Jesus is represented as one who taught the love of God and the Spirit-filled life;[5] as one who was killed, and whose death was for the sake of his followers;[6] as one whom God had raised from death, defeating the powers of evil;[7] and as one who was to return with the angels and saints in glory to judge the world and gather his chosen followers to be with him for ever.[8]

---

[1] Defined at the Third Council of Constantinople, CE 681; J. F. Clarkson *et al.*, *The Church Teaches* (St. Louis: Herder, 1955), 188.

[2] Luke 1: 32; 5: 20. All New Testament quotations are taken from the Revised Standard Version (New York: Collins, 1973).   [3] John 1: 1, 14.

[4] Cf. Tertullian, *Against Praxeas*, 27, in M. Geerard, (ed.), *Corpus Christianorum*, Series Latina (Turnhout and Paris: Brepols, 1953–), i. 1198.

[5] 1 Thess. 4: 2.   [6] 1 Thess. 5: 10.   [7] 1 Thess. 1: 10.

[8] 1 Thess. 4: 17.

Jesus' role in human history is represented as being unique and his authority is taken to be absolute. His teachings reveal the truth about God. His death is a voluntary sacrifice which succeeds in freeing humans from the rule of evil. His power is sufficient to overcome even death. And he is destined to reign as King over all people. When he is raised to the right hand of God, he takes precedence over all angels and spiritual powers, as one before whom all in creation should kneel.[9] If he is a man, he is a man with a unique relationship to God, a relationship variously characterized as the relationship of son to father, of word to thought, of visible image to invisible essence. It would not be absurd to see him as the 'dayspring from on high' of Luke, or even, as Paul saw him, as the one through whom all things were created and who was equal with God before becoming human.[10]

Some New Testament scholars see in these documents a progression, from seeing Jesus as a wholly faithful man who was declared Son of God by his raising from death, to seeing him as one who had lived with God before his human birth. That there was such a progression cannot be established, and can be asserted only as a matter of likelihood, by looking at allegedly parallel cases of the divinization of human beings. What one can say with some degree of assurance is that the earliest sources we have regard Jesus as having a unique relationship to God and a unique authority.[11] He was believed to have appeared after his death to the Apostles, who looked for his return to judge the world and save his followers from evil, both being divine prerogatives in Jewish thought. Thus he had the closest possible association with God, being seated at God's right hand, above all spiritual powers. It took some time to work out just what the 'closest possible association with God' might be for a human person.

The idea of a human agent of divine eschatological action is distinct from many other Jewish ideas of the Messiah as a purely political deliverer who would put Israel in her rightful place among the nations. It is a Messianic idea, but it has already taken on the Hebrew Biblical themes of heavenly Wisdom,[12] the Suffering Servant,[13] and the triumphant Son of Man.[14] Jesus is given a cosmic

---

[9] Phil. 2: 10.   [10] Luke 1: 78; Col. 1: 15–16.

[11] A helpful account is given in James Dunn, *Christology in the Making* (London: SCM Press, 1980), esp. the final chapter.   [12] Prov. 8: 22–31.

[13] Isa. 52: 13–15.   [14] Dan. 7: 13.

dimension, as the instrument of God's final purpose, which is also God's eternal plan. Perhaps, then, he is that Wisdom which is the first-born of creation. Or perhaps his creation, being before time,[15] is not, properly speaking, creation at all, but an eternal generation from the Father, which shares in the divine being and is not a product of the divine will.

These ideas were worked out over many years, until Chalcedon adopted the generally normative view, for Christians, of the incarnation of God in Jesus. Though the details of development cannot be ascertained, it is undeniable that there was a development, at least in the formulation of the doctrine. From the extent and intensity of the arguments in the early Church, it is also clear that there was no generally agreed explicit view on such matters among the Apostles themselves. If there had been, their authority would have been used to silence debate at once, whereas the Fathers vacillated and argued for many years before coming to a decision.

The question is not whether there was a development of understanding, since there certainly was. The question is whether it can be seen as an articulation of what was implicit in Jesus' own life and work; whether it is the only such articulation which is plausible; and whether it is an adequate one. It may be thought that there is not necessarily a huge distinction between seeing Jesus as God's eschatological agent and seeing him as an incarnation of a hypostasis (a 'person') of the Trinity. There is rather a whole continuum of cases from seeing Jesus as a merely human prophet to seeing him as the omnipotent and omniscient God in human form. Orthodoxy has always rejected the former extreme, and though it has sometimes come near to the latter, in my view it lies at roughly a middle point on this continuum. Chalcedon is remarkable, in its historical context, for its insistence on the full humanity of Jesus and its implicit rejection of the view that his humanity was simply a form or appearance the divine took.[16] Jesus' humanity is not omnipotent or omniscient, since human nature is not capable of such things. It forms 'one person', one unified reality, with the divine nature of the Word. This unity is of a unique kind, bridging the gulf between finite and infinite being, but it seems clear that the infinite cannot be

---

[15] Ecclus. 24: 9.

[16] The definition states that Jesus is 'truly man, consisting of a reasonable soul and body': H. Denzinger, *Enchiridion Symbolorum*, 23rd edn. (Freiburg: 1963), no 302.

allowed to swallow up or wholly overpower the finite, making the humanity merely an instrument of the divine. Any adequate account must be more complex than that.[17]

THE RELATIONALITY OF BEING

The history of Christian thought about God has been expressed in an effort to see Jesus as the human manifestation of God, a direct expression of God's will, and to see Jesus as a fully human being, with moral freedom and responsibility. Christians have wished to assert that God is manifest and expressed in Jesus, which entails a doctrine of God as truly expressed in finite form. The idea of a finite appearance of God does not as such transcend the horizons of the Hebrew Bible, which often depicts God as manifesting the divine being in human form.[18] The crucial difference from the Hebrew understanding is that Jesus was a fully human being, who was born, suffered, and died. He was not a visionary apparition or one who took human form without being fully human. It is the identification of a human life with the divine that is often shocking to the Jewish understanding.

The most plausible way to render such an idea comprehensible is to develop a view of the human which sees its destined fulfilment as lying in union with the Divine, and to develop a view of the Divine which sees it as naturally and properly expressed in and through a finite personal being, or a community of such beings. Then the human would not be set in necessary opposition to the Divine, as a wholly self-determining will, doomed always to exist in heroic isolation or, at best, in freely contracted relationships with others. The Divine would not be set in necessary opposition to the finite and contingent, as a self-sufficient, wholly blissful, and immutable reality, finding no possibility of real relation to beings other than itself, or of temporal self-expression.

The root of the conceptual problem of incarnation lies in the basic concept of self-sufficiency or self-determination which the classical tradition took as the defining concept of divinity, and which much post-Enlightenment thought takes as the defining concept of

---

[17] One attempt to present such an account is in my *Religion and Revelation*, part 4, sect. D (Oxford: Oxford University Press, 1994).

[18] For example, the story of Jacob wrestling with God at Peniel (Gen. 32: 30).

humanity. Suppose, however, that the self is construed as being most truly itself when it is directed to what is not itself, to an other in which it can find fulfilment. This is perhaps the most fundamental revision which Karl Barth makes to the classical idea of God in the Christian tradition. He first of all roots the idea of God firmly in God's act of self-revelation in Christ. This is a life of self-emptying love,[19] which 'means that so far from being contrary to the nature of God, it is of his essence to possess the freedom to be capable of this self-offering'.[20] Since God's revelation is truly of the divine being as it is, such a freedom of self-offering is of the very essence of God: 'God loves because he loves . . . this act is his essence.'[21] God constitutes himself as love, by an eternal and free decision which is identical with the divine essence: 'God exists in his act. God is his own decision.'[22]

If God is in essence a free act of love, then God is so from all eternity: 'in his Son he has otherness in himself from eternity,'[23] and he relates to that otherness in fellowship and self-giving: 'the knowing subject, its object and the seeking and creating of fellowship with it, are one.'[24] Thus Barth sees the Trinitarian being of God as self-constituted by a willed act of fellowship and self-giving relation to an otherness which is at the same time a unity of love.

It is not my purpose at this point to examine the sense in which God may contain love and fellowship within the Trinitarian being itself; I will do that in Part 3. What is noteworthy is the way in which Barth stresses that God's own being, as love, requires some form of otherness and fellowship, of community and self-giving, as constitutive of the divine being. This is a very different starting point for a doctrine of God than the traditional scholastic procedure of beginning with proofs of a changeless First Mover. That procedure later has to try to make a doctrine of the Trinity cohere with the concept of the simple and self-sufficient being for whom self-giving is an ontological impossibility, since there is no otherness in the wholly simple Prime Mover. Barth begins, on the basis of the life of Jesus taken as the self-manifestation of God, with a much more

---

[19] Phil 2: 5 ff.
[20] Karl Barth, *Church Dogmatics*, ed. G. W. Bromiley and T. F. Torrance (4 vols.; Edinburgh: T. & T. Clark, 1936–37), ii/1: 517.   [21] Ibid. 273.
[22] Ibid. 272.   [23] Ibid. 317.   [24] Ibid. 285.

dynamic idea of God as the one who 'is who he is in his works'.[25]

Indeed, Barth presses this principle so far that the whole of time and history seems to be included in the eternal divine decision. At least, it is not possible for us to think of one, eternal aspect without thinking of the other. Since 'we know God in Jesus Christ alone,'[26] and since 'God is actually and unreservedly as we encounter Him in His revelation,'[27] we must say that 'in the beginning, with God, i.e. in his decree which precedes the existence, possibility and reality of all his creatures, the primary element is . . . Jesus Christ.'[28] Thus God eternally, though freely, wills to create fellowship with creatures through Jesus Christ. That is part of God's eternal nature. Thus time and creaturely existence are already constituted as real in the eternity of God. It is in this sense that God is essentially not self-sufficient, but self-giving, and related in love to finite beings.

For Barth, if the divine self constitutes itself as love—and Christian revelation testifies that it does—it manifests its nature in calling other selves into being, to whom it can impart love, with whom it can share love, and from whom it can receive creative co-operation in love. Those selves, in turn, are fulfilled by receiving being as gift, by sharing their lives freely with one another, and by giving themselves wholly to the God who is the source of their being. The freedom of the finite will then might be said to consist in its ability to relate to others in attentiveness and love. However, finite wills do not, like God, have the essential nature of love. They are free, and 'freedom means to . . . be determined and moved by oneself.'[29] It is open to finite wills, therefore, to empty themselves in relation to God or to be closed in upon themselves in egoistic isolation. True fulfilment for a finite will only comes when it attends to the supreme value which is the source of its being and which has the power to instil this value into the one who attends to it. That is the authentic choice of the will, though the inauthentic can be chosen, and will turn out to be a way of self–destruction in the long run.

It is not that the will is poised neutrally between love of the other and its rejection, as though the choice was an arbitrary matter. The will by nature inclines towards the good, as the object of its attention

---

[25] Ibid. 260. [26] Ibid. 318. [27] Ibid. 325.
[28] Ibid. ii/2: 171. [29] Ibid. 301.

and striving. However, there is a discipline of self which is necessary to achieve the good. The self which can relate itself in trust and commitment to others can also seek to possess its own being and happiness. Then, in a world which is insecure and interdependent, the self will try to achieve an impossible security and independence. Others will become objects of fear or contempt, competitors to be defeated or appeased. All threats must be destroyed before they become too strong; all others must be regarded as means to one's own enjoyment or frustrators of it.[30] Thus the ego-centred self becomes immersed in the passions of lust, aggression, and hatred, which it cannot master.

Freedom can only be regained if one can overcome fear, anxiety, and selfish desire. Such freedom can only be achieved by a love of God so strong that it drives out all fear, by a trust in God so whole-hearted that it eliminates anxiety, and by an obedience to the divine will so complete that it destroys egoism at its root. Such love, trust, and obedience are gifts of grace. It is God who fills us with faith, hope, and love. Christians have traditionally claimed that in Jesus such gifts exist to their fullest extent, so that he has perfect love of, trust in, and obedience to God the Father. Jesus Christ is the fully human being whom God elects to fellowship with the Divine. Indeed, 'Jesus Christ is the electing God,'[31] the one who chooses humanity as well as the one who is chosen by God. In his person the self-giving of God and the self-surrender of humanity find their uniting and consummating point.

For the main Christian tradition, through the life of Jesus, God enters the world in grace, to reorient human wills, to destroy selfish desire and unite humans to the divine life. Such inner transformations are often expressed, in mystical Jewish thought, in the form of cosmic occurrences connected with the 'end of all things', the final goal of divine creation. In the light of such traditions, Christianity may be seen as a development of one form of mystical Judaism, expressing its beliefs in standard apocalyptic imagery of cataclysmic destruction and the appearing of a cosmic Saviour in the clouds with the hosts of God and the risen dead. The spiritual meaning of these symbols is given by interpreting destruction as the destruction

---

[30] One of the most effective presentations of such a view of human life is to be found in the play *Huis Clos* (*No Exit*) by Jean-Paul Sartre.

[31] Barth, *Church Dogmatics*, ii/2: 110.

caused by desire, whose flames spring from itself and destroy itself. The Son of Man is the fulfilment of humanity in God, when all good will be retrieved and transfigured by the divine presence. Jesus is the foreshadowing of that hope for all creation. For Christian faith, he is seen as a humanity renewed by divine initiative, not as a man who by supreme effort has achieved union with God. It is as such that he is able to lead us from the fear, anxiety, and passion of our alienated humanity, as the Spirit incorporates us into his divinely transfigured humanity.

What difference does a doctrine of incarnation make to the Biblical concept of God? It relates God in a very interior way to human personhood, involving the Divine in human suffering and taking human nature into the Divine. 'He is not impassible,' says Barth,[32] but participates in the distress of the poor. The flesh becomes the manifestation of Spirit, through a process of dying to self and being born in the power of the Spirit into a new creation. The cosmic process comes to be seen as one of estrangement from God and return to God through a divine act of renewal. The world is not as such and in its entirety the self-expression of God, since it falls into self-destructive disharmony. In that important sense the world remains other than God, in its alienation. That alienated world, however, is an essential possibility in the being of God. It is a possibility which, as a pure possibility, cannot be eliminated from the nature of God itself. With the actual existence of this universe, the possibility of its alienation springs from God as part of the unfolding of finite being from its infinite source. Within this universe, new sorts of goodness and of divine relationship can be created. As such, the universe can become a vehicle of God's self-expression in the temporal process, which returns to its source in a new form of relationship, a newly actualized potential in the life of God. However, the possibility for alienation, always being possible, has been actualized through the free choice of creatures in this universe. That corrupts the nature of the universe as a full self-expression of the Divine, and means that the history of this cosmos must be the history of a divinely effected reconciliation of alienated being to the glory of God. On this planet, Jesus is the focal point at which the universal process takes on a consciously recognized and particular form. The Spirit makes present and applies the redemptive

[32] Ibid. 370.

power of God which took form in Jesus, and thus the idea of the Trinity takes shape.

The Hebrew Bible saw God as a interactive, morally purposive Will. The New Testament does not deny this idea at all. But it adds the belief, already implicit in much Jewish thought, that God does not only stand in relationship to humans as a relatively external Will, shaping history to its purposes. God enters into the historical process to include humanity, and thereby ultimately all creation, in the divine being. The controlling model is not so much of an external Will as of an inward and unitive Love, an infinite Divine Life in which all created things can share.

So God includes time in the divine being: 'Time is not excluded from his duration but included in it.'[33] As with Heschel, God is not simply made temporal, as if inhabiting and subject to the same time in which humans exist. Yet God is not wholly non-temporal, as in the classical traditions. 'True eternity has the power to take time to itself,'[34] but when time is taken into God it is transfigured: 'Eternity lacks the fleeting nature of the present, the separation between before and after.'[35] Barth can speak of the *simul* of eternity as something transcending time as we experience it. The idea of divine eternity as including and transfiguring time and history expresses a much more deeply incarnational view than the classical tradition. It encourages a more dynamic and affective concept of God, and one which begins not from reflection on Platonic essences but from the particularity of Jesus Christ. Sharing some of these concerns with Heschel, it yet seeks to explore more deeply what is implied in the core Christian perception of God in Christ as unitive love.

THE DOCTRINE OF ELECTION

The vehicle of this unitive love of God, which makes present the renewed humanity which was in Jesus, is the Church, as the community of the Spirit. In the New Testament, the attempt to understand the role of the Church, the 'New Israel', gave rise to a greatly increased emphasis on the doctrine of divine election, sometimes construed as predestination. In the Hebrew Bible, Abraham and his descendants were seen as elected by God to a

---

[33] Barth, *Church Dogmatics*, ii/2: 110.   [34] Ibid. 617.
[35] Ibid. 613.

special vocation, to obey him, to be a kingdom of priests, and to receive his promise of a society of peace.[36] Yet the early followers of Jesus felt that the people of Abraham, even though chosen by God, had seemed to reject God and crucify the designated Messianic King. Had they then lost their vocation for ever? Paul, struggling with this idea in his letter to the Romans, asserts that the vocation of saving the world has passed to the Church; but the old Israel retains a special place in God's providence. It still has a role to play; and, in the end, 'all Israel will be saved.'[37] As the Church comes to be seen as the New Israel, it is seen as called to obey God in Jesus Christ, to be a kingdom of priests and to receive the promise of eternal life. The problem this raises is whether God, who calls some but not all into the Church, the vehicle of salvation, is now seen as predetermining the destinies of human beings, regardless of their merits, saving and damning whom God wills.

This problem becomes much more severe in the New Testament than it was in the Hebrew Bible. The calling of the Jews is a calling to a specific vocation in this world, which many of them fail to respond to. But it can easily come to seem that the calling of Christians into the Church is a saving from eternal hell and original sin, which is effected solely by the elective will of God. The consequences of this calling are infinitely more important, and do not seem to allow of human refusal or co-operation. The problem could be eased if one could see a calling into the Church as a specific vocation which one could refuse (at least in the heart and perhaps temporarily), and which would not erect an eternal difference between being damned and being saved. Those who are not so called are not as such damned. On the contrary, they may be led to salvation precisely by the vicarious priesthood of the Church.

The two key New Testament texts are Ephesians 1: 4 and Romans 8: 29. The former asserts that 'he chose us in him before the foundation of the world . . . he destined us to be his sons . . . according to his purpose, we . . . have been destined to live for . . . his glory.' This sounds as though God, at the foundation of the universe, knew that God would call specific individuals to be God's sons and daughters. So God must have known these specific individuals would exist, and chose them to become sons of God.

The famous passage in Romans says, 'Those whom he foreknew

---

[36] Isa. 61: 5–7.   [37] Rom. 11: 26.

he predestined . . . he called, justified and glorified.' Again, God knows who will exist, and God chooses, from the beginning of time, to glorify them. There is here a strong doctrine of divine foreknowledge and foreordination. God knows even the specific individuals who will exist in the future of the universe, and what their destiny will be. Moreover, God decides on this destiny. This does not sound like a God who waits to see what humans do before responding to them, or who leaves humans free to reject God if they wish. More subtly, they may reject God if they wish, but God determines what they wish for.

A strong doctrine of omniscience and predestination leads naturally to the idea of a timeless God; for the willing of the universe, in all its details, must be conceived as completed 'before' the beginning of time. It does not therefore have to wait for temporal events to occur before it responds freely to them. It rather orders all temporal events in one determinate act of will. Such a completely determining God is best conceived as creating in one single timeless act. The omnipotent God is the all-determining God. This is a considerable strengthening of those strands in the Old Testament which speak of a divine calling and purpose, but it requires abandoning those elements of divine responsiveness and creative innovation which are also present in the Old Testament.

One might, however, interpret the texts in this way: God, in creating the universe, determined that there would be some creatures who would share in the Divine Life. Perhaps all would, eventually, or so God willed. But some God purposed to share in it in a specific way, by being conformed to the image of perfect humanity which would be manifest in a divinized human life, and made present in the community of the Church. God determined that God would bring such creatures to be; that God would call some of them to unity with the Divine through the Church; that God would justify them if they responded, and glorify them. God foreknew, because God had so decided, that there would be some such creatures, that some of them would respond affirmatively, and so would be glorified. But God did not know who, in particular, they would be. Then we might construe the passage in Romans as follows: 'I foreknow (i.e. I envisage and intend) that there will be some, and I determine (*pro-orizō*) that there will be some, whom I will conform to the image of the Son. To ensure this, I will call many to discipleship. I foreknow and determine (i.e. I will ensure, by repeated and patient preparation and assistance) that some will respond affirmatively, though I do not know exactly whom. Them I will justify and glorify.' Here, 'some' would not refer to specific individuals, but to a group of individuals, the specific membership of which is undetermined. This interpretation would fit with the Gospel saying: 'Many are called, but few are chosen.'[38]

In considering the idea of predestination, one might stress that the calling of Israel was not a calling to exclusive salvation. It was a calling to a specific priestly vocation, intended to bring the whole world to God by Israel's fulfilment of its intended role.[39] Israel was bound to God by a special love, but one that is intended to spread into the whole world through Israel. So one might think that the New Israel is not a community intended for exclusive salvation. Its calling is to reconcile the world to God, through its own service and praise. God always intended the Church to exist and to have this special calling. The Church is the means by which the whole world returns to God. The glorification of the faithful (or some of them) in Christ is a foreshadowing of and a model for the glorification of the whole creation in God, and the means to it for all. Such a view of predestination mitigates the exclusiveness which has often characterized Christian thought, while retaining a stress on the divine calling to membership of the Church and on its centrality in God's purpose for the whole of creation.

TWO NEW TESTAMENT PICTURES OF GOD

It would, of course, be inconsistent with my general view of Scriptural revelation to let a basic and vital doctrine depend upon a strict interpretation of one or two isolated sentences from the letters of Paul. One can perhaps best account for these sentences by the sense of overwhelming grace that marked the early Christian experience. As God had chosen Abraham and his descendants, so now it seemed that God was choosing a new Israel, from among the poor and marginalized people of the Roman Empire. God's choice came first, through the preaching of the Gospel and birth in the Spirit. If people responded, they felt that they were privileged to be united to the Son by an eternal divine decree, not by their own efforts or merit.

[38] Matt. 22: 14.　　　[39] Isa. 60: 3.

Karl Barth emphasizes this sense of the overwhelming grace of God to a marked degree. He writes that ' "In Christ" means that in him we are reconciled to God, in him we are elect from eternity . . . that is why the subjective reality of revelation as such can never be made an independent theme.'[40] Salvation is objective in that it has taken place solely in Christ. It does not depend upon our assent of faith (the 'subjective aspect') to any degree. It is wholly a matter of God's eternal decree, and all faith can do is to acknowledge this unconditional divine choice with gratitude. Barth does not give human freedom any strong co-operative role in the process of salvation, and in this respect his view follows the Reformed Calvinist tradition of accepting total divine sovereignty.

In the history of Christian reflection on these matters, two different pictures of salvation, which carry with them two different pictures of God, are discernible. On one interpretation, the New Testament seems to darken the biblical picture of human nature, introducing the idea of original sin, which was foreign to Jewish thought; of Satan as a fallen angel existing in opposition to God; of hell as a place of unending misery and pain: and of the Last Judgement as the purchase of the elect in Christ from the mass of damned humanity. This is all part of the apocalyptic picture which emerged from some strands of inter-testamental Judaism. The Hebrew Bible on the whole stressed the goodness of the created order, the natural goodness of human beings, however weak they might be, the positive role of Satan as God's tester, and the relative unimportance of life after death. Apocalyptic Judaism, however, presented a different picture. The world became an order opposed to God, bound to the rule of Satan, now seen as a fallen angel, and destined to punishment. The faithful are taken out of the world, which hates them, and they are saved from coming destruction by the heavenly Messiah, who selects them for no merit of their own, but by his own good pleasure.[41] The book of Revelation carries strong elements of this view, even though it is mitigated by other traditions, present alongside but not integrated satisfactorily with it.

For such a picture, human moral freedom is not of any great importance, since no one can be saved by moral effort or moral success. It becomes virtually incomprehensible why such a huge amount of evil should exist, since it is seen both as rebellion against

---

[40] Barth, *Church Dogmatics*, i/2: 240.   [41] I Thess. 4: 17; 5: 3.

God and as directly caused by God, the only determiner of all things. It is morally incomprehensible why creatures should be punished for their sins, which God causes them to commit, when God could equally well have determined everyone to salvation. One can only account for the picture by sensing the pessimism of a culture dominated by imperial tyranny, with no apparent prospect of political success for Israel any longer. Thus the old hope of a society of peace in Israel became transmuted into the hope for a resurrection of the justified, the poor of the earth. The whole world order, instead of being seen as finally joining with Israel in the praise of God, was consigned to destruction by fire. Only the elect would be saved, through no merit of their own, solely because of their reliance on God. Of course, the final irony is that such reliance becomes itself a sort of merit, if it is within human power to rely on God and repent, or to reject God's offer of grace. More consistently, divine grace was seen to be irresistible; the last vestige of human freedom was eliminated, and God becomes responsible for both sin and its punishment.

Fortunately, this is not the only picture present in the New Testament. It can be seen how a rigorously predestinarian view could develop from these strands of New Testament thought, which represent a hardening of an apocalyptic Judaism. Nevertheless, the dominant picture of Jesus in the Gospels is of the Good Shepherd, who goes in search of sheep which are lost, to bring them back to safety.[42] Jesus eats with outcasts; he forgives sinners; he heals the sick. The picture is not that Jesus walks among the damned, arbitrarily selecting a few to be saved from the wrath to come. Rather, Jesus walks among those who have lost their way, who have squandered their inheritance, who are burdened by guilt, and he calls any who will hear him to find freedom in following him. He does point out the terrible consequences of greed and selfishness, the loneliness and self-destruction they bring. But his good news is of the power and rule of God which he makes present, the gift of eternal life which he freely offers. The cross upon which he dies is seen as a ransom, the expression of a divine suffering and self-giving which frees humans from the bondage of self.[43] This is not God as stern Judge, who saves a few from destruction by mere whim. It is God as Saviour, who enters into the suffering of creation to bring

---

[42] Luke 15: 1–7.   [43] Mark 10: 45.

creatures back to the divine presence and to eternal life. This is not an all-determining God, but a God who seeks to persuade by love, giving freedom to creatures to follow the goods that they choose, however destructive to self and others such choices may be, but always placing before them the goal of that supreme goodness which can alone satisfy them finally. On this picture, God is much more of a participant in the struggle and suffering of creatures. God's passionate involvement, already pictured in Hosea and the later Isaiah,[44] leads God to share in the suffering of creation and to work actively in love to turn it to good. Here a different strand of Jewish thought is developed in a distinctive way.

Barth's view, while not withdrawing an inch from its insistence on divine sovereignty, is much nearer this second picture. Drawing on his fundamental insight that love is the essential nature of God,[45] and his belief that God 'is free from all origination, conditioning or determination from without',[46] Barth concludes that nothing can prevent God's love from achieving its goal. It cannot be God's will that anyone should be lost, and it is God's will that all should share in the divine love. Thus 'there is no one who does not participate in him [in Christ] in this turning to God . . . There is no one who is not raised and exalted with him to true humanity.'[47] The problem of why God should only elect some to salvation is resolved by declaring unequivocally that God elects all, without exception, to salvation.

Of course, this leaves the slightly different problem that not all seem to accept salvation, and that many biblical passages speak of the possibility of hell. Barth's response is once again to root everything in the particular life of Jesus Christ as the whole revealed truth about God. Christ does declare divine condemnation on sin; but he also takes divine judgement upon himself on the cross, and thereby annuls it. 'God's wrath is not separate from but in his love,'[48] and it is God's universal love, declared in Christ, which annuls the wrath of God against sin. Barth accepts that 'we cannot venture the statement that it [salvation] must and will finally be coincident with the world of the human race as such.'[49] There is

---

[44] Hos. 11: 8; Isa. 43: 4.
[45] 'God's loving is necessary' (Barth, *Church Dogmatics*), ii/1: 280.
[46] Ibid. 307.   [47] Ibid. iv/2: 217.
[48] Ibid. ii/1: 363.   [49] Ibid. ii/2: 417.

always the 'impossible possibility' of a human rejection of grace. Yet we cannot venture the opposite statement either; and it seems clear that Barth's position on the sovereignty of grace really commits him to a doctrine of universal salvation, or at least commits him to denying the belief that God condemns anyone to perdition. My own view, to be developed in Part 3, places much more stress on the 'subjective' element, on human freedom, than does Barth's account. Nevertheless, there is a welcome and unequivocal stress in Barth on the universal salvific love and will of God, and on the way in which God freely enters into the suffering of a sinful world, to reconcile it to the divine being.

In the previous Chapter, I drew attention to the way in which Abraham Heschel, as a twentieth-century Jewish theologian, distanced himself from the classical theistic tradition of an impassible and self-sufficient God. Drawing on the prophetic tradition, he strongly affirmed the idea of God as a passionate God, though not a weak or limited God, in freely willed personal interaction with creatures. Although some would argue that the Trinitarian God of Christianity is quite different from the unitarian God of Judaism, it might rather seem that the Christian view results from drawing out certain strands of Judaism to a natural, if at first surprising, conclusion. If God truly involves the divine self in the pathos of the universe, it is a natural extension of this idea to see God as actually entering into the suffering of creatures, to share in their suffering in an even more comprehensive way. If God wills to save all creation by bringing it into fulfilling relation with the divine self, it is natural to think of God as constituting such a relation from within, as it were, by setting the Divine Spirit within the hearts of those who love God, to renew and re-create them. If God expresses the divine glory in the beauty of the heavens, might God not express the divine love for humans in a human life which embodies the Divine Wisdom, the Torah, itself? And if God wills the salvation of all beings, is it out of the question that one might see that salvation as a taking up of creatures into the very life of God itself?

In these ways, one might see the Christian idea of God as a development of certain strands of Jewish thought, which was prompted by the Apostles' acceptance of Jesus as Messiah. Such acceptance modified the idea of what a Messiah was, and thereby also modified the underlying idea of God. The Messiah as embodied in Jesus was clearly not a political saviour, but one who introduced a new way of relating to God through the Spirit which he sent.[50] The implication is that God is not a God who is known in power and worldly triumph, but one who is known in the apparent weakness and obscurity of love. Heschel protests at any imputation of weakness to God, and at any thought of a real union between God and creatures.[51] A Christian might respond that this divine 'weakness'—which the Christian would call '*kenosis*' or self-emptying—and this divine-creaturely unity—which the Christian would call '*theosis*'—represent the highest possible degree of the divine pathos and will for relationship which Heschel perceives as the prophetic insight into the divine nature.

In the end, differences remain in the way God is conceived. But it is clear that the idea of God as a passionate, responsive, personal reality, concerned to be attentive to creatures, is not a purely Christian idea. Similarly, the idea of God as self-expressive, suffering, and reconciling love is deeply rooted in the Hebrew Bible. The Trinitarian concept of God, however, takes these elements and weaves them into a new pattern, focused on the person of Jesus as a decisive revelation of what God is. In that sense, the Christian idea of God is distinctive, and leads in turn to a distinctive view of the origin and goal of creation.

GOD AS TRINITY

The idea of God as Trinity emerges with the thought that God, as the creator and Father of the universe, the only source of its being, is also the Spirit who enters into created, alienated being to reconcile it to the divine life. This God, utterly transcendent in creative power and utterly immanent in reconciling love, takes particular and paradigmatic form in a human life, the exemplar of the union of all things with God and the origin of the process of the sanctification of the world through the community of the Spirit. Jesus is a man who is filled with the Spirit and wholly obedient to the Father;[52] whose humanity is transformed by inward power and open to the supreme perfection of the unconditioned source of all. As the Spirit reconciles creation to the Father, it transforms created being into participation

---

[50] John 18: 36.
[51] Abraham Heschel, *The Prophets* (New York: Harper, 1962), 320, 356.
[52] Luke 3: 22.

in the divine.[53] In Jesus, this transformation is effected fully in a human life, and so the at-one-ment of alienated creation and perfect Creator is realized. Jesus, as the Spirit-filled human, is raised to the throne of the Father, with whom he is inwardly united. This man becomes the mediator between Creator and creation, the matrix from whom the Spirit works to unite the world to God and the goal towards which it helps the world to strive. One might say that Christ is the form of the reconciled world, the pattern on which it is to be shaped.[54] Jesus is the human exemplification of the cosmic Christ, and the pattern for reconciled humanity. The Spirit is the shaper, the reconciler.[55] The Father is the one from whom pattern, persuasive power, and cosmos flow, and to whom all return.[56]

It can hardly be claimed that such a view is explicit in the New Testament. On the contrary, this is just one development which is possible from its rich array of varied materials. Yet it is clear that in the New Testament Jesus is placed on virtual equality with God, which requires some theory of an intimate union between God and humanity. The Spirit is experienced as uniting believers to God through Jesus in a special way, which requires some theory of the inner working of God in human lives. Christian doctrines of the Trinity are in the end based on the witness of the Apostles that Jesus is the Messianic King, the supremely authoritative teacher of the nature of God, who was raised from death and showed God in his own glorified person. They also witness that the Spirit has been poured out upon them in a new and living way. If the early believers waited for Christ to return in glory, it was because in him they had seen the purpose of God fulfilled, and they shared the experience of seeing this fulfilment at least partially realized in their community, too. The central Christian doctrines are based on new and vital experiences of a particular community. As the Hebrew prophets had felt the moral demand and providential presence of God, so the Apostles felt the power of the love of God in Jesus and the promise of resurrection and new life in the community which Christ was believed to indwell.

If experience of oppression by military powers and the overwhelming character of God's grace led to predestinarian theories, experience of the extraordinary growth of the Church in the Gentile

---

[53] 2 Thess. 2: 13.   [54] Col. 1: 15.   [55] 2 Cor. 3: 18.
[56] 1 Cor. 8: 6.

world, of the selflessness of Jesus and the saints, and the free forgiveness of sins led to theories of the universal salvific will of God. Christianity has contained from its beginnings this ambiguity; it can be interpreted as a way of salvation for the few from the doomed corruption of the world, or as a power to heal the world's corruption and infuse it with the divine love. These interpretations are very different. Yet they both acknowledge that the character of God is redemptively loving and supremely just; that Jesus offers forgiveness and reconciliation with God; and that the final goal of human life is participation in the love of God. It was the life, death, and resurrection of Jesus which generated the apostolic insight that God is redemptive love, which enters into suffering and unites human lives to the Divine.

Of course, one must trace the source of this insight to the life and experience of Jesus himself. According to the Gospel accounts, which it is mere speculation to probe behind, Jesus understood himself to be appointed to a Messianic Kingship, which was of decisive significance for the judgement and redemption of the whole world.[57] In his proclamation of the Kingdom, he assumed an intimate knowledge of the divine purpose and of the fulfilment of the prophetic promises which presupposes uniquely authoritative access to the divine mind. In his power over disease, the forces of nature, and evil spirits, he assumed a unique access to divine power. In his freedom from sin, he assumed a moral authority which presupposed a unique access to and empowering by divine grace. Jesus was a man appointed to a unique vocation and given a unique form of relationship, a form of access which can most properly be called 'union' with the Divine, as filled with divine wisdom, power, and righteousness. It is only as such that he could be plausibly seen as the judge of the world and the saviour of those who turn to follow him.

This particular life, occurring at a crucial transitional point in the historical and cultural experience of Israel, mediated a complex of images for the Divine, which are susceptible of many ways of development, but which always circle around the central idea of a human life of forgiving, suffering love as a decisive disclosure of the divine nature. It is not just that one sees in Jesus such a disclosure, as in an object over against one, a separate and individual person. Rather, that quality of love was felt as a power within the

[57] Cf. Matt. 26: 64.

community, so that the Spirit which was in Jesus also empowers his disciples. The God who discloses the divine nature as love does so in a particular time and place, and mediates that love in and through the lives of creatures, as they turn to God. So God must be conceived as self-expressive, active, and reconciling. God does not remain serene and unmoved by the world. God does not simply judge or approve of it. God expresses the divine being actively within it, in a particular human life and in the community which continued to embody the Divine Spirit, to unite what is alien to the divine being. Any Christian notion of God must take seriously this revelation of the activity and transforming power of God in creation. It must take seriously the creativity of God, the importance of otherness, and the reconciliation of the other to the one, through the self-expression of the divine nature as love.

The doctrine of God as Trinity, which is distinctive to Christian faith, has its experiential basis in worship of the Creator, discipleship of Jesus, and indwelling by the Spirit. If the doctrine moves too far from this experiential basis, it is in danger of being transmuted into abstract speculation which may detract from the practical and transforming impact of Christ. As the classical theologians held, the Trinity is indeed a revealed truth. But it is not revealed as a proposition which can be found explicitly formulated in the Bible or which was uttered by Jesus himself. It is revealed by reflection on the life of Jesus as a disclosure of God and as the origin and pattern of a new experience of the Spirit in the community of the Church.

The New Testament inherits the problems of theism which the Hebrew Bible bequeaths to it, problems of providence, suffering, and redemption. In addition, the central distinctive question for Christian theism is whether God is a God of self-expressive, redeeming love, who includes the finite in the divine being by costly self-sacrifice. Much Christian piety has depended upon such a view of God. Strangely, much Christian theology has been uncomfortable with it, and has preferred a more monarchical view of complete divine sovereignty, with its implications of strict immutability and impassibility. It is only in the twentieth century that the monarchical view has been strongly and consistently challenged at the level of theological debate. Part of the force and attraction of Barth's theology is the way in which he sees a Trinitarian, dynamic, and time-including notion of God as a direct implication of God's true self-revelation in Jesus Christ. Barth's God remains monarchical in one sense, that the divine will seems all-determining—'Our will is. . . foreordained by God in all the possibilities of its choice.'[58] The importance of history and creaturely freedom is in the end only ambiguously stressed by Barth. Yet his emphasis on the divine love as real self-giving, and on the divine will to enter into fellowship with creatures, implies a much stronger challenge to monarchical theism than even he makes.

What I have tried to suggest, in this chapter, is that the scriptural materials provide many resources for such a challenge. There are strands in Scripture which suggest a total divine foreknowledge, foreordination, and determination. It is those strands which combined with Greek philosophical reflection to provide the classical tradition of Christian thinking about God. If one is now to reinterpret that tradition, it is not enough simply to reject it. One must attempt to show how it can be reinterpreted more fruitfully within the different and more fundamental strand—of divine suffering, responsiveness, and real relationship to creatures—that has undoubtedly always been present in Christian piety.

[58] Barth, *Church Dogmatics*, ii/1: 585.

3

The Koran

MOHAMMED IQBAL: A MUSLIM VIEW OF GOD

If the Trinitarian concept of God is distinctive to Christianity, then Islam exists, at least in part, as a decisive rejection of that concept. Islam is a clear and insistent proclamation of the unity and uniqueness of God (the unitarian thesis), and of the impossibility of identifying any finite thing with God (the transcendentalist thesis). In that respect, its basic idea of God is a return to the perspective of the Hebrew Bible, without admitting the view that God enters into a specific covenant relation with a particular group of people. In medieval times, Muslim philosophers took the lead in constructing an articulated concept of God, a task which they executed with the aid of the philosophy of Aristotle. Since that time, however, philosophical analysis of the concept of God has not been a feature of Muslim theology. In the twentieth century, the Pakistani philosopher Mohammed Iqbal attempted a reconstruction of the concept of God in a non-Aristotelian framework, a reconstruction which he claimed to be truer to the spirit of the Koran itself. A consideration of his view will provide an example of some of the creative possibilities open to Muslim theology, and may also suggest the need for qualification of a strictly unitarian and transcendentalist concept of God within Islam itself.

Iqbal is one of the most respected poets and philosophers of Islam in the twentieth century. He has been described by Fazlur Rahman as 'the most serious Muslim philosophical thinker of modern times'.[1] Iqbal set out to construct a Muslim doctrine of God and creation which would be free of the 'classical', Greek philosophical influences which had marked the work of the great medieval Muslim philosophers. They had attempted to interpret the Koran in terms of Aristotelian philosophy. Indeed, it was through them that Aristotle was introduced to Western Europe in the twelfth century and became the basis of Thomistic theism. It is not surprising, therefore,

[1] Fazlur Rahman, *Islam* (London: Wiedenfeld and Nicolson, 1966), 225.

that the philosophical articulation of the doctrine of God in Islam is fundamentally identical to the classical Christian doctrine. Both accept such basic Greek ideas as that of the ontological superiority of the timeless to the temporal, the supreme value of contemplation, the self-sufficiency of the Supreme Being, and the simplicity of the divine nature. These ideas may seem naturally much better adapted to the central Koranic doctrine of the unity and transcendence of God than to the Christian doctrines of the Trinity and a divine incarnation in time. Nevertheless, Thomas Aquinas' doctrine of God is similar in all basic respects to that of his philosophical predecessors in Islam, and part of Thomas's virtuosity lay in his merging of Christian revealed truths with a fundamentally unitarian idea of God. In *Images of Eternity*, I have discussed the work of the two most generally acknowledged major theologians of Islam and Christianity in medieval times, al-Gazzali and Thomas Aquinas, so as to spell out the common classical influences which they both accepted, and which became characteristic of their traditions.[2]

Iqbal argues, nevertheless, that the Greek influence on Islam, which in fact hardly survived the medieval period, was always an alien intrusion. 'The spirit of the Koran was essentially anti-classical,' he claims.[3] By this he means, partly, that the Koran is concerned with the particular, with observation and experiment, rather than with abstract thinking about universals. But he also develops a particular interpretation of the Koran which is, possibly, unique to him. He speaks of 'The essentially Islamic idea of continuous creation which means a growing universe', and says that 'All lines of Muslim thought converge on a dynamic conception of the universe.'[4]

He cites a number of verses from the Koran in support of this view, most notably 35: 1: 'God adds to His creation what He wills,' and 29: 19: 'Hereafter will He give it another birth.' But most fundamentally, what impresses him is the concern of the Koran with time (*Dahr*), with its reality and purposive character. 'We have not created . . . in sport . . . but for a serious end.'[5] Whereas for the

[2] Keith Ward, *Images of Eternity* (Oxford: Oneworld Publications, 1993).

[3] Mohammed Iqbal, *The Reconstruction of Religious Thought in Islam* (Oxford: Oxford University Press, 1934), 122.   [4] Ibid. 131.

[5] Koran 44: 38. Quotations from the Koran and transliterations of the Arabic are from the text and translation by Yusuf Ali, *The Holy Koran* (Leicester: The Islamic Foundation, 1975).

Greeks (or at least for Plato), time was finally unreal, for the Koran it has the true reality of a created order; and whereas for the Greeks it had no purpose or end, for the Koran it has a purpose, it is directed to the unfolding of its inherent potentialities. The universe is growing towards perfection: 'From state to state shall ye be surely carried onward.'[6] Humans have a divine commission to subdue and perfect nature: 'It is He who hath made you His representatives on the earth.'[7] So, Iqbal claims, the Koran teaches that God creates the universe for a purpose which is to be realized in time, and humans have a positive part to play in realizing this purpose. That is their destiny, to participate in the dynamic transformation of creation.

Iqbal denies that the idea of destiny (*Taqdir*) is fatalistic in any way. 'The world process is certainly devoid of . . . a far-off fixed destination to which the whole creation moves . . . nothing is more alien to the Koranic outlook than the idea that the universe is the temporal working out of a preconceived plan.'[8] He thinks of destiny rather as a free realization from among the potentialities of a created self or ego. Thus he rejects what he sees as the Greek view that time is either unreal or a mere succession of mutually exclusive moments, to be run through by the self as if on a sort of pre-determined path. In its place he puts what he calls the Koranic view that time is a real progressive change, so that the whole universe is 'a free creative movement'.[9]

GOD AS THE INFINITE EGO

In all this, his claim is that the central message of the Koran is the spiritual nature of reality, coupled with an urgent insistence upon the unitary nature of reality. 'He begetteth not, and He is not begotten.'[10] That is, Iqbal claims, God does not produce an 'other', over against God. 'All things depend on Him,' in the intimate sense that they have no subsistent being of their own, from which it follows that God is the only subsistent being they have. So one can say that 'Reality lives in its own appearances.'[11] There is not a God who exists alone and a world which exists separately. There is only the world, as directly expressing the will (and, since God is one, therefore the being) of God. One can best conceive of God as 'an

---

[6] Koran 84: 20.   [7] Koran 6: 165.   [8] Iqbal, *Reconstruction*, 48.

[9] Ibid.   [10] Koran 112: 3.   [11] Iqbal, *Reconstruction*, 14.

immanent Infinite in whose self-unfolding movement the various finite concepts are merely moments'.[12]

God is infinite, but this infinity does not exclude the finite. 'The true infinite . . . embraces the finite without effacing its finitude.'[13] God includes the finite: 'He is closer to you than the vein of the neck,'[14] not distant and wholly transcendent, but so close that God's will is the only true subsistence of creatures. Iqbal presses this so far that he can say, 'A self is unthinkable without a character'[15]; and 'Nature is to the Divine Self as character is to the human self.'[16] The universe is the self-unfolding of the Infinite, or the Ultimate Ego, as Iqbal terms it. 'Nature must be understood as a living, ever-growing organism whose growth has no final external limits'; and God is 'the immanent self which animates and sustains the whole'.[17]

It may sound as if Iqbal is wholly subordinating finite selves to some Absolute, which endlessly pursues its own self-realization. But this is far from his intention. 'From the Ultimate Ego only egos proceed',[18] but those finite egos have an enduring reality. 'He [the finite ego] shares in the life and freedom of the Ultimate Ego who, by permitting the emergence of a finite ego, capable of private initiative, has limited this freedom of His own free will.'[19] Even though finite egos have their subsistence in the Ultimate Ego, they nevertheless have a creative freedom of their own. They have inner possibilities of creative activity, and they will live for ever as individuals. However, their individuality is to be enlarged by a sort of unitive experience. 'In the higher Sufism unitive experience is . . . the Infinite passing into the loving embrace of the finite.'[20]

One's destiny is to be a willing instrument of the divine creativity. Immersion of the self in greed, hatred, and delusion is clearly possible, and its ultimate outcome is hell. Yet 'Hell, as conceived by the Koran, is not a pit of everlasting torture . . . it is a corrective experience which may make a hardened ego once more sensitive to the living breeze of Divine Grace.'[21] Finite selves can follow many limited, superficial, and finally unsatisfying paths. Yet they never exist as isolated psychic atoms. They are essentially bound together in an 'Ultimate Reality as pure duration in which thought, life and

---

[12] Iqbal, *Reconstruction*, 14.　　[13] Ibid. 28.　　[14] Koran 50: 15.
[15] Iqbal, *Reconstruction*, 53.　　[16] Ibid. 54.　　[17] Ibid.
[18] Ibid. 68.　　[19] Ibid. 102.　　[20] Ibid. 104.
[21] Ibid. 116.

purpose inter-penetrate to form an organic unity'.[22] They are parts of 'an all-embracing concrete self'. What Iqbal means by 'pure duration' is a form of temporal being in which the past is not lost as a set of unknown, mutually exclusive moments, and the future is not somehow there, waiting to be traversed in an unchangeable way. The past is taken up into a perfectly conscious dynamic present which is always creatively realizing itself in new ways.

God has the purpose that the universe should proceed to endless creative fulfilment, through the actions of the finite egos which unfold at least a small part of God's own infinite nature ('Nature is only a fleeting moment in the life of God.'[23]). Finite egos may deviate from the straight path. But, as in the case of Adam, 'Afterwards his Lord chose him for Himself and was turned towards him, and guided him.'[24] So 'the world-life intuitively sees its own needs, and at critical moments defines its own direction . . . this is called prophetic revelation.'[25] In the end, each finite ego will be sensitive to the Ultimate Ego on which it depends, and then 'In this process of progressive change God becomes a co-worker with him.'[26] The purposes of the Ultimate Ego, whose behaviour is the universe, will be realized, even though the finite egos may immerse themselves in the evil of self-regard for long ages.

IQBAL AND THE CLASSICAL TRADITION

Iqbal does not work out his views in any great detail. He refers to the work of Bergson and Whitehead, in particular, as suggestive and important, though he is not seeking to be a disciple of theirs. What he seeks to do is to give a broad, rather impressionistic vision, which may reorient Muslim thought about God in the light of some of the new trends in science and philosophy. His references to the Koran may strike one as requiring rather forced interpretations on occasion, though it is hardly for me to comment on that. What is clear is his rejection of the early Muslim philosophical traditions, which used Aristotelian categories to develop speculative interpretations of the Koranic concept of God.

It is probably fair to say that since al-Gazzali, philosophical speculation on the nature of God has not been a feature of Muslim

[22] Ibid. 53. [23] Ibid. [24] Koran 20: 114.
[25] Iqbal, *Reconstruction*, 140. [26] Ibid. 11.

thought. The general situation is well summed up by Abul-Kalam
Azad: 'The attributes [of God] are to be treated as figurative. So, the
Koran considers intellectual effort to comprehend them as fruitless.
Indeed, they will open the door for doubts and misrepresentations.
Tafwid is the only attitude appropriate to the situation, the attitude
of affirmation and belief in them and suspension of judgment. All
the philosophical disquisitions, which our dialecticians have indulged
in, are not in conformity with the teaching of the Koran.'[27] On the
one hand, one must take seriously the injunction, 'Coin no
similitudes for Him',[28] and the often-quoted verse, 'Nothing is like
Him, the all-hearing, the all-seeing.'[29] On the other, one must take
seriously statements such as, 'Nay, both His hands are spread out',[30]
ascribing hands to God. Muslim scholars have tended simply to
accept the descriptions of God in the Koran, and refuse to offer any
interpretation of them, except to say that, while they do apply to
God, they cannot apply as we understand them. God has a face and
hands; God has a place, above His throne in heaven. These are not
mere metaphors; they are literally true of God. Yet we cannot liken
God to any created thing, so we cannot in our present state say what
their literal meaning is.

Iqbal is dismissive of this tradition. He states bluntly that 'During
the last five hundred years religious thought in Islam has been
practically stationary.'[31] Recognizing that the Aristotelian interpretation was not suited to the inner spirit of the Koran, he aims to
set out, as a programme for future research, a different form of
philosophical interpretation which may inspire a reconstruction of
religious thought for our own age, giving it a new vitality in its
encounter with modern scientific knowledge. He is not seeking to
state the one finally true interpretation. Indeed, he is at pains to
stress the elasticity of Islam, pointing out that in the first three
hundred years of its history no fewer than one hundred systems of
theology appeared. He is content to offer his interpretation as a
contribution to that creative process, in the hope of revitalizing the
study of theology in the Muslim world.

His view of God is not, however, wholly novel in Islam, and it
bears some affinity with the Sufi doctrine of *Wahdat al-Wujud*, the

---

[27] Abul-Kalam Azad, *Tarjuman al-Koran*, tr. A. Husain as *The Quintessence of
Islam* (London: Asia Publishing House, 1960), 133.   [28] Koran 16: 74.
[29] Koran 11: 42.   [30] Koran 5: 64.   [31] Iqbal, *Reconstruction*, 6.

Oneness of Being. This was probably first formulated by Ibn al-Arabi, the thirteenth century Spanish Sufi, and most Sufis have accepted it in some form. The Sufi argument is that there can be no reality outside of God, for then there would be somewhere from which God is excluded. God is infinite, and it is in that sense that there is nothing like God, yet other than God, and that God does not beget another, who is outside the divine self. All finite realities must therefore be modalities or manifestations of the Infinite Being. A key text is: 'Everything (that exists) will perish except His own Face',[32] which is taken to mean that 'there is only one true Self, and that is God'.[33]

One of the major problems for such a view is to spell out in a satisfactory way the relation between the one true Self and the many finite selves, which fall into ignorance and evil, and come under judgement. Clearly, some sort of 'otherness' must be asserted between finite and infinite selves, since God is not capable of being either ignorant or evil. Yet the total dependence of all things upon God seems to undermine any ultimate otherness. It is possible that Iqbal's vision of a nested array of egos, included in one another at various levels, would provide a resolution of the basic problem. If the reality of the Supreme Ego is essentially that of a realization of creative potentiality, and if the being of an ego is such that it overflows from itself into a form of community (as Iqbal puts it, a growing organic unity), then the place of the Supreme Ego may consist in giving general rational direction to the striving for mastery of many finite egos, the ultimate goal being 'to convert it [the universe] into itself and to illuminate its whole being'.[34] That is to say, the production of finite egos is a production of true creative centres, with their own potentiality and capacity for evil as well as good. But, since 'the ultimate Reality is a rationally directed creative life',[35] these will all be brought into union with the one Ego, when they become its consciously obedient instruments. While it is true that 'the Absolute Ego is the whole of Reality',[36] it is not an all-determining being. It contains within itself a community of co-operating and competing selves, bound together in a 'living, ever-growing organism'.[37] The ultimate reality is a community of selves,

---

[32] Koran 28: 88.
[33] Ali, *The Holy Koran*, 1027.
[34] Iqbal, *Reconstruction*, 9.
[35] Ibid. 57.
[36] Ibid.
[37] Ibid. 54.

included in one Supreme Self, which will finally achieve in this universe one expression of its endless creative purpose of self-realization.

MODELS OF DEITY

There seem to be three models of God at work in Iqbal's thought. First, there is the model of God as the inclusive 'immanent Infinite', of which the universe is but a small part.[38] This idea of God as the Unconditioned is the vaguest, and could perhaps be taken as pointing to the ultimate ineffability of the divine being and to its transcendence of any of the categories of human thought. Nevertheless, it is said of this Infinite that it includes the universe and that it unfolds in the universe, so that at least part of its life is conditioned. Or perhaps one might say that its unlimitedness is such that it includes all limited beings in itself without being limited by them. This whole universe, though revealing only a tiny aspect of the divine being, does unfold it as creative and self-expressive power.

The second model is that of the universe as an organism or organic unity,[39] which is construed as the 'behaviour' or character of the cosmic Self, which is God.[40] For this model, God is the Ultimate Ego and the universe is its body, through which its character is expressed. God might be thought of as the Cosmic Mind or even as the World-soul, which gives a rational direction to the universe, unfolding its inner possibilities in a purposive way.

The third model is that of God as a creative co-worker with many finite selves,[41] generating other egos to help in the realization of the divine purposes. It is difficult to see the universe as the body of God on this model, for many things may happen in it which are the results of finite willing, and which are not under the direct control of the Ultimate Ego. This is a more communal model than that of the self-realization of the one Ultimate Ego, and both are much more personal models than that of the Infinite which unfolds itself in space-time.

Iqbal could simply be dismissed as having three conflicting models of God, and therefore as having an incoherent concept of

---

[38] Iqbal, *Reconstruction*, 9.   [39] Ibid.   [40] Ibid. 54.
[41] Ibid. 104.

God. It would be a more constructive and a more sympathetic view, however, to say that he is articulating three models of the divine being which may each be necessary to illuminate some important element of what God is. It might seem unhelpful to suggest that there is something like a Trinitarian view of God at work here, since there is hardly anything which would seem more unlikely for a Muslim thinker. Yet as long as one is careful to stress the utter unity and uniqueness of God, there may be a sense, especially for Muslims sympathetic to Sufism, in which God is manifold even in unity. A Christian theologian can point without undue strain to resonances with a certain interpretation of Trinitarian views.

In this vein, one might want to speak of God as the Infinite, the self-unfolding source of all things, who is not remote from them but present at the very heart of their life, yet whose being so far transcends human thought that one may wish to speak of the glory and hiddenness of God as an aspect of the divine being one would ignore at the cost of a loss of proper understanding. Some Christian understandings of the Fatherhood of God, as ineffable source of all being, who is yet intimately present to all things, would resonate well with this thought.

One might also want to speak of God as the Self of the World, the rational pattern of its being and the spiritual reality in which the physical universe exists, which can be characterized in some sense as a personal reality, in which all things are to be united, 'illuminating all things and converting them into itself'.[42] Some Christian understandings of the Sonship of God, as the *Logos* or eternal Wisdom of God, through which the universe is created, upon which it is patterned, and in which it is to be united and completed, would resonate well with this thought.

Finally, one might want to speak of God as a reality which co-operates with finite wills, guiding them towards harmonious creativity and a community of life in which creativity can be more fully exercised. Some Christian understandings of God as Spirit, as the creative energy which works within and between human spirits, guiding them into truth, creativity, and co-operative community, would resonate well with this thought.

My intention is not to represent Iqbal as a quasi-Christian or to prove the 'superiority' of a Christian idea of God. Iqbal's threefold

[42] Ibid. 9.

God, who is the Infinite, the Cosmic Ego or Self, and the creative co-worker with and guide of finite selves, by no means reflects the Christian doctrine of the Trinity exactly. There is no notion of God as Father, of incarnation, or of the interior action of the Spirit. I do not wish to stretch or compress the theologians of all faiths on one Procrustean bed, especially a covertly Christian one. Nevertheless, it may be important to note that the sorts of opposition which have sometimes been said to exist between Muslim and Christian doctrines are not as straightforward as may at first seem. There can be a complex, developing, and productive interweaving of Christian and Muslim strands of thought on the question of God, in which each can illuminate and enrich the other. It may turn out, and I have tried to show that it does turn out, that the idea of God as Trinity is not, on every interpretation, as far from the Muslim idea of the unity of God as might have been imagined. The idea of God as uniting the universe to the Divine (*theosis*) is not as far from Sufi interpretations of the Oneness of Being as is sometimes assumed. Just as the medieval philosophers of Islam and Christianity largely agreed in their ideas about God, so one can discern a common movement, in Iqbal and in Barth, for instance, to rethink the idea of God in a more dynamic, temporalist, and non-Platonic way. Christian and Muslim theology do not develop as distinct and unrelated wholes, unless political forces make them think they should do so. They develop by common responses to general historical changes and influences, and by unfolding their own inner resources in creative ways, which always generate new possibilities of understanding and co-operation, as well as of conflict and disagreement.

GOD IN THE KORAN: UNITY AND POWER

It is hard, especially for a non-Muslim, to say how far Iqbal's views are implicit in or fully compatible with the Koran. It can be said that he is a widely respected scholar among Muslims, and he would not usually be accused of unorthodoxy. If I may attempt an assessment, it seems to me that the Koran permits views like those of Iqbal, while it does not entail them. Many descriptions of God are given in the Koran, and their general meaning is entirely clear, though they do leave open the possibility of many specific interpretations.

Sura 112 describes God as 'the One and Only'. Above all, Islam insists upon the unity and uniqueness of God. There is only one God and there is nothing else at all which is like God. Thus God is unique in kind: 'There is none like unto Him.' 'He is above all comprehension', and 'no vision can grasp Him.'[43] Anthropomorphism is ruled out, and even visions of God do not begin to grasp what God really is. Further, God is '*samad*', which Yusuf Ali translates by two terms, 'the Eternal' and 'Absolute'. The meaning is that God is wholly independent in existence; perhaps that God is the only one who absolutely exists, whether or not anything else exists. God is self-existent. Then, in a phrase which naturally causes great difficulty to Christians, 'He begetteth not, nor is He begotten.'[44] This is often taken to repudiate the Christian doctrine that God begets a Son, and that the Son is begotten by the Father. It could, however, be taken as repudiating the idea that God is brought into being by any other and that God, like Zeus, has divine children who are separate gods, worthy of worship on their own account. As has been seen, Iqbal interprets it to mean that God does not create another being or even a universe which is completely autonomous, over against the divine being itself. Naturally, Christians have no difficulty with that interpretation.

With regard to the Christian doctrine, a Christian would undoubtedly say that the begetting of the Son by the Father is not any sort of procreation of a separate being (*ousia*) of the same sort. It is, rather, an assertion that within the unbegotten being of God there are eternal, uncreated relationships, which do not compromise the proper unity and simplicity of the divine being. Christian and Muslim can entirely agree that God is begotten by no other god, and God begets no other god. God remains one and unique, the only self-existent and the only being worthy of worship. So the Koranic phrase may properly be taken as a denial that there are two or more gods, related causally to one another. This reading can be supported by reference to 6: 100: 'Yet they make the Jinns equals with God, though God did create the Jinns; and they falsely, having no knowledge, attribute to Him sons and daughters'. The reference here is most naturally to those pagan Arabs who worshipped created spirits, or who worshipped the sons and daughters of God, the many gods of Arabian polytheism. If this is so, the condemnation of divine Sonship is unlikely to refer to orthodox Christian views, although it

---

[43] Koran 6: 103.   [44] Koran 112: 3.

may have some reference to heterodox views of the Trinity which were present in the Medina district at the time of the Prophet. The phrase is a reminder to Christians not to lapse into tritheism, even inadvertently, but it does not rule out most traditional Christian accounts of the Trinity or of the Sonship of Christ, as they have been propounded by major theologians like Thomas Aquinas.

One of the best-known verses on the nature of God is the *Ayat-ul-Kursi*, the Verse of the Throne.[45] God is described as 'the Living, the Self-subsisting, Eternal', to whom belong all things and who 'knoweth what (appeareth to His creatures as) before or after or behind them'. God guards and preserves all things, and is 'the Most High, the Supreme (in glory)'. The word translated as 'Eternal' is '*Qaiyum*', which carries no particular implications about timelessness. It refers to the self-existent nature of God, upon which all other existents depend. God is one who has power over all things, who cherishes and preserves them, who has knowledge beyond that of any creature, and who is supreme in being. God is certainly omniscient; God is 'the Knower of all things, hidden and open'.[46]

Belief in divine power is reinforced at 3: 6: 'He it is who shapes you in the wombs as He pleases.' This power, however, is always exercised in supreme wisdom, for God is 'the Wise'. 'He created all things, and He hath full knowledge of all things.'[47] God is also the Judge of all things—'In the end will (all affairs) go up to Him,'[48] but God judges with mercy; 'He is oft-forgiving, most merciful.'[49] God 'forgiveth sin, accepteth repentance, is strict in punishment, and hath a long reach'.[50] 'To Him shall ye be brought back.'[51] As God was the beginning and source of all things, so God is the goal of all things, and all will be brought back to God.

'He is the First and the Last, the Evident and the Immanent (*Batin*).[52] God is within, at the root of heart and soul, as well as without, known in the glorious signs of the world's beauty. God is 'the Sovereign, the Holy One, the Source of Peace (and Perfection), the Guardian of Faith, the Preserver of Safety, the Exalted in Might, the Irresistible, the Supreme'.[53] God is 'the Creator, the Evolver (*Bari-u*), the Bestower of Forms'.[54] God is a living and dynamic

[45] Koran 2: 255.
[46] Koran 32: 6.
[47] Koran 6: 101.
[48] Koran 32: 5.
[49] Koran 25: 6.
[50] Koran 40: 3.
[51] Koran 43: 85.
[52] Koran 57: 3.
[53] Koran 59: 23.
[54] Koran 59: 24.

power, who works all things in accordance with the divine wisdom and perfect knowledge of the secrets of every heart. '*Bari-u*', the Evolver, is the term which best supports Iqbal's claim that the Muslim concept of God is a dynamic one, who calls the universe gradually to unfold its powers in co-operation with the divine purpose. As merciful Judge, God holds all rational creatures responsible for their own acts; and if God brings all to the divine being at the end, it will be through their repentance and because of God's mercy, which will not allow judgement to be the last word. God may indeed be all-powerful, but leaves creatures free to choose good or evil, to obey or to repent, and divine power is exercised in such a way as to bring all things into the unity of being which is the Lord's will, by their free repentance and consent.

DIVINE DETERMINISM AND FREEDOM

Much popular thought regards Islam as a faith with a strong degree of fatalism. God's eternal decree (*qadar*) is absolute, and all humans can do is submit to it. A number of verses in the Koran can be brought forward in support of such a view, all of them stressing the certainty and unchangeability of the divine plan for creation. 'All that hath been promised unto you will come to pass: nor can ye frustrate it (in the least bit).'[55] 'Nothing will happen to us except what God has decreed for us.'[56] 'No misfortune can happen on earth or in your souls but is recorded in a decree before We bring it into existence.'[57] Taken in isolation, or interpreted within a tradition which stresses the completely exercised sovereignty of God, these verses suggests that God has foreordained everything that will happen. An eternal decree governs everything that comes to be in time. There is, however, a long history of debate about the degree of human freedom allowed by the Koran, and there are other verses which suggest a rather different account. 'Whatever good, (O man) happens to thee, is from God; but whatever evil happens to thee, is from thy (own) soul.'[58] This suggests a degree of personal causality which is not to be identified or even to be coincident with the divine causality, which wills only good. Moreover, at the Last Judgement, people receive what they deserve, because of what they themselves,

---

[55] Koran 6: 134.   [56] Koran 9: 51.   [57] Koran 57: 22.
[58] Koran 4: 79.

and no others, have done. 'Ye shall indeed taste of the grievous penalty; but it will be no more than the retribution of (the evil) that ye have wrought.'[59] Each individual soul will receive the reward of its own works: 'It will be the Day when no soul shall have power (to do) aught for another.'[60] Such verses emphasize personal responsibility for evil and the justice of its punishment. And of course the whole message of the Holy Koran supposes that human beings bear the responsibility for responding in faith to the message of the Prophet and repenting. When the Day of Judgement comes, every person will be rewarded or punished for the deeds they alone have done, and God is the perfect Judge who will never condemn unjustly. That implies a strong doctrine of human freedom and responsible causality. Thus within the Muslim tradition there has always existed a tension between acceptance of the total unlimited sovereignty of God and the responsible freedom of human beings. It seems that, for a correct understanding of the Koran, both must be asserted. But theologians have found it very difficult to do this, without emphasizing one at the expense of the other.

Iqbal is in no doubt as to where he stands on this issue. He gives a very great degree of freedom to creatures. There can be no dispute, for a Muslim, that God is omniscient and omnipotent and perfectly wise, so it is natural that some theologians would think it both metaphysically and morally necessary that all things in creation must obey the divine will, down to the smallest detail. How can an omnipotent being do other than the best, and ensure that it comes about? Such a view is easily able to guarantee that all sentient beings will finally be fulfilled in relation to God, since God simply ensures that they will. It is more difficult on this view to explain why there is so much evil and suffering in the world. Most difficult of all is to give any real force to the Prophet's call to submit to God's will. One will submit if it is so decreed; otherwise, one will not. It is hard to retain a sense of personal responsibility and decision, and it is especially hard to accept that, if one rejects God, without having had any possibility of doing otherwise, and is sent to hell, that happens in accordance with a changeless and eternally just divine decree.

Iqbal does not base his strong affirmation of human freedom on the consideration that it may better explain the existence of suffering and of divine punishment, however. He bases it on a more general

---

[59] Koran 37: 38, 7: 39.   [60] Koran 82: 19.

metaphysical affirmation of the value of creative freedom as such, even or especially in the being of God. He sees temporal existence as an unfolding of potentialities, which is essentially open to the future and whose greatest value is that of creativity. God expresses the divine being in the existence of the universe. God chooses to create beings who can share in this creativity, realising their own potential within the growing organic unity which is the universe. The greatest good of creatures is a conscious and imaginative striving for realization in relationship. This good naturally has its exemplar and paradigm in the being of God itself.

For such a view, how would the omnipotence of the Supreme Ego be realized? It would not be realized in the conceiving and working out of one perfect plan, essentially completed in every detail even before creation. For Iqbal, what is wrong with this idea is that such a wholly predetermined universe would not in fact be the most perfect universe possible. Self-expressive creativity is not the same thing as either a necessary process of actualizing goods or a production of goods which is wholly arbitrary. If God necessarily creates this universe, as the best possible world, then God may indeed be free in the sense that the creation arises simply from an unconstrained will. But God will not be free to do otherwise, to realize the divine nature in any other way. Even God will be condemned simply to work out what is already predetermined within the immutable divine nature. Divine freedom will simply be the divine nature being what it is, unaffected by any other nature. But it is fixed and unalterable. God is constrained by fate, even though that fate is not an external power, but the internal necessity of the divine nature itself.

Many Muslim theologians have seen no alternative to this, and have in effect accepted that, in an ultimate sense, all things are necessarily what they are. Alternatively, they have rooted the nature of things in an inscrutable divine will, for which no reason can be assigned. If the universe is not necessary, then it must proceed by arbitrary divine command. It is hard to see great value in arbitrary decisions, but this may seem to be the only way to avoid complete necessity while preserving divine freedom and omnipotence. Iqbal strives, though in what is admittedly a suggestive rather than a completely worked-out way, to find a value for creativity which avoids this dilemma of positing either a God who is wholly necessary or a God who is wholly arbitrary.

The truly creative, he suggests, is genuinely new and unforeseeable in detail. It brings about forms of being which have never previously existed, and which could have been otherwise. Yet it is far from arbitrary, since it expresses the character and aims of the creative agent. If the creation of new forms of being and beauty is a very great good, not only because of the objects it brings about but also because the creative activity itself is of intrinsic value, then God will possess that good. Possessing it, God may intelligibly will that creatures should possess it, at least to some limited extent, and perhaps to the greatest extent that is compatible with the realization of a good divine purpose.

This may suggest a way in which the seemingly predeterministic verses of the Koran may be interpreted compatibly with genuine human responsibility. The promises of God, of delight for well-doers and pain for evil-doers, will certainly be kept. Nothing can stop that happening. That does not mean that humans are not free at all. On the contrary, it is precisely human freedom that will lead to delight or pain. It is the consequences of moral action that are eternally decreed, and from which there is no escape. God has decreed all that can happen, and what happens never escapes from divine control. But God does not directly desire us to suffer exactly as we do. God has decreed that we shall exist in a world in which such suffering may come upon us. But if it does, God will ensure that it is defeated by good, if only we turn to God in obedience.

This is not a form of complete determination, which leaves no creaturely (or divine) choices open. It is a sort of conditional determination—which decrees everything that can possibly happen, which decrees that certain acts shall be followed by specific consequences, which decrees that nothing can finally defeat the divine plan, and which decrees that the most evil creaturely choices will be brought within the scope of divine providence, and used to realize a unique sort of final good.

GOD AS ESSENTIALLY CREATIVE

Such conditional determination makes it more difficult for God to ensure that all beings will come to the delight of the divine presence in the long run. Might not some of them continue freely to choose selfish pleasure for ever? Iqbal thinks that the delight of the divine presence is so great, and the naturally created desire of the human soul for delight and for avoidance of pain is so strong, that it can be guaranteed in the end that every soul will be brought to repentance, to a turning away from a course of life which only brings self-destruction and pain in its wake. Those who think of hell as unending, as some Muslims do, believe that some souls may never repent, since repentance requires a true turning from self. The regret which follows from suffering painful retribution may itself be only a further form of selfishness—the selfish desire to avoid pain for oneself. Hell may therefore not bring repentance, but only increasing bitterness for the soul, and God will not be able to ensure that truly free souls will come to the delight of the divine presence.

A great many Muslims, including Iqbal, do not accept this argument. Hell, they argue, does result from commitment to selfish desire. But when that desire is seen to be self-defeating (and only hell makes it finally clear), the soul will at last discover the only thing which can satisfy its desires when they are rightly ordered. By a long and perhaps painful process of discipline, every soul will then return in conscious submission to its source. For 'Verily, to thy Lord is the return (of all).'[61] When God's plan is completed, nothing can exist which continues to contradict the divine will or frustrate God's desires. At that time, hell, a standing contradiction of the good purpose of God, must cease to be, and all will return to God, the one true self-existent reality. Iqbal thus proposes a way in which total divine sovereignty and responsible human freedom can co-exist. God wills that creatures shall be free to realize their creative natures in relationship to one another. Human freedom is such that it leads to frustration and destruction, until it learns to co-operate with the creativity of the divine will. God turns to creatures in mercy, to accomplish the fulfilment of the sovereign plan that in freely co-operative creativity, creatures may find their true fulfilment, and accomplish the divine plan without corruption or constraint. 'Behold (how) all affairs tend towards God!'[62]

Mohammed Iqbal's attempt at a reconstruction of religious thought in Islam has so far had few, if any, successors in the Muslim world. His rejection of the classical tradition and the attempt to replace it with a more temporalist, universe-including, and creative view of the Divine remains a fairly solitary effort. That is not, however, because it has been rejected, but just because Muslim thinking has not concerned itself much with such relatively

[61] Koran 96: 8.   [62] Koran 42: 53.

theoretical issues, preferring to leave the Koranic affirmations about God uninterpreted theologically. I do not think the theoretical issues can be neglected for long in a world in which the concept of God is so widely rejected and debated. More positively, the sort of reflective analysis Iqbal began to provide promises one way in which diverse religious traditions can begin to grow and to understand one another better.

It should at least be clear that there is not just one possible Muslim concept of God, which is distinct in unchangeable ways from a monolithic Christian concept. Iqbal provides something new to the Muslim tradition which yet claims to be a proper development of what has been implicit in it from the beginning. In moving away from classical traditions of immutable divine transcendence to a view of the Divine in terms of immanent creativity, Iqbal reflects a general movement of theological thought in the twentieth century, which can be discerned in a number of religious traditions. I have noted a similar movement in the thought of Abraham Heschel, who strongly emphasizes God's responsive creativity and attention to the finite. I have also noted the possibility of a Christian reconceptualization of God as self-expressive and unitive love, rather than as self-sufficient pure actuality. With such a reconceptualization comes the necessity of a reinterpretation of many doctrines which were formulated in terms of the classical viewpoint. In that reinterpretation, there are possibilities for comparative collaboration which may hold great promise for the development of a truly comparative theology.

4
The Upanishads

Jewish, Christian, and Muslim concepts of God share a common ancestry. They have all been strongly affected, in their classical forms, by Greek, particularly Aristotelian, philosophy. It is therefore not surprising that they show strong similarities. It may be thought that the Indian traditions, however, are very different. Their scriptural and philosophical backgrounds are certainly different. Nevertheless, an idea of the Supreme Being develops which deals with the same sort of reality as the Semitic faiths, though approached from a rather different perspective. I have had to be very selective in my treatment of the Indian traditions, if this volume was not to become totally unwieldy. I have consequently tried to deal with one of the central revealed texts of orthodox Hinduism, the Upanishads, and with one major twentieth-century commentator upon it, Aurobindo Ghose. This will provide a parallel to my treatment of the Semitic faiths, and will bring out the extent to which both traditions have been affected by the emphasis on temporality, creativity, and evolution, and the rejection of many classical forms of thought which has characterized philosophical thinking after the rise of the experimental sciences.

Though many non-theistic forms of religion exist in the Indian tradition, including most famously Sankhya and Buddhism, I have reluctantly decided to exclude them from consideration, and to concentrate on the more theistic forms. I thus side-step the issue of whether and to what extent Buddhists may adhere to a belief in something like a God, though I have to some extent dealt with that topic in *Images of Eternity*.[1] My concern here is solely with the articulation of concepts of God by some major twentieth-century theologians of various religious traditions. This will set the scene for my own development of a Christian concept within this wider framework and in the light of modern scientific thought.

---

[1] Keith Ward, *Images of Eternity* (Oxford: Oneworld Publications, 1993), ch. 3.

The central concept of the Upanishads is the concept of Brahman. Brahman may be translated as 'the Supreme', and a key Upanishadic doctrine is that 'This Self (*Atman*) is Brahman indeed.'[2] But what is this Self? 'Descry It in its Oneness, immeasurable, firm, transcending space, immaculate, unborn, abiding, great—this is the Self.'[3] The Self is not to be confused with the individual soul (*jiva*), with its personality, intellect, feelings, and will. It is 'one', beyond duality and diversity of all sorts. It is 'immeasurable', unlimited in existence, beyond space and time. It is 'immaculate', not attached to anything by desire or touched by suffering. It is 'unborn' and 'abiding', has no beginning, and it cannot be destroyed or hurt. It is 'wholly a mass of wisdom',[4] or understanding.[5]

The doctrine is of a transcendent infinity, boundless and unchanging, whose properties are understanding and bliss— 'Brahman is understanding, bliss.'[6] The religious quest is to realize union with the Self: 'An ocean, one, the seer becomes, without duality . . . this his highest bliss.'[7]. The quest is for a state of bliss and wisdom, and the way to it is through the practice of non-attachment: 'When all desires which shelter in the heart detach themselves, then does a mortal man become immortal: to Brahman he wins through.'[8]

It may sound as though Brahman transcends all finite things, as a wholly unlimited reality. Yet Brahman is not other than all things. Indeed, 'It consists of all things.'[9] This simple, infinite, impassible, immutable, eternal, and wise reality 'Is the life that shimmers through all contingent beings'.[10] He is the Self of all things: 'Those who see all beings in the Self, and the Self in all beings will never shrink from It.'[11] The Self is at once the Supreme Reality and that which is present, though hidden, in all things. The Self is 'the immortal hidden in the real';[12] it is in each finite thing 'as a razor fits into a razor-case'.[13] It is not a wholly distinct reality, though one may easily fail to see it, seeing only finite names and forms. To

---

[2] Brihadaranyaka Upanishad 4. 4, in R. C. Zaehner (trans.), *Hindu Scriptures* (London: Dent, 1966), 71.   [3] Ibid. 73.   [4] Ibid. 75.
[5] Ibid. 71.   [6] Brihadaranyaka Upanishad 3. 9, ibid. 60.
[7] Brihadaranyaka Upanishad 4. 3, ibid. 68.   [8] Ibid. 71.
[9] Ibid.   [10] Mundaka Upanishad, 3. 1, ibid. 190.
[11] Isa Upanishad 6, ibid. 165.
[12] Brihadaranyaka Upanishad 1. 6, ibid. 41.
[13] Brihadaranyaka Upanishad 1. 4, ibid. 36.

discern that Self becomes the goal of meditation. Because Brahman consists of all things, all things are one: 'That person yonder [the 'golden person in the sun'], I am he.'[14] The Self can be found within, since one is already part of it, and it can be found everywhere. It has become all things.

Although the Self is to be found within, in the 'cave of the heart', yet the Self always remains distinct from the individual soul or mind. It is 'He who, abiding in the mind, is other than the mind'. The Self is the true basis of mind, but is not to be identified with the mind. 'Whom the mind does not know, whose body is the mind, who controls the mind from within'[15]—it is the Self within you, the Inner Controller, the Immortal. Of this Self one can only say, 'No! No!'[16] It is impalpable, indestructible, free from attachment, and cannot be hurt. Being beyond duality, it cannot be grasped by dual concepts.

The general view is well expressed in what might at first seem a particularly enigmatic verse: 'Fulness beyond'—the boundless Self is beyond every finite form; 'Fulness here'—all things emanate from the Self, and are not separated from it; 'Fulness from fulness doth proceed'—the unformed Self gives rise to an infinity of forms; 'From fulness fulness take away; fulness yet remains'—the arising and destruction of innumerable worlds does not change the essential nature of the Self, beginningless and indestructible, free of all desire and change.[17]

THE TWO FORMS OF BRAHMAN

An obvious difficulty with this idea is that of understanding how such an unbounded and immutable reality can become, or consist of, all things. Clearly, it cannot literally 'become' anything it is not always. If it emanates a universe, it seems to contain limitations— indeed, to contain every finite form of existence. If it remains unbounded, however, then it cannot literally consist of all things. One clue to a resolution of this difficulty is provided by the fact that there is no idea in the Vedic tradition that the physical universe is created from nothing, not sharing the substance of the Self. Rather,

---

[14] Isa Upanishad 18, ibid. 167.
[15] Brihadaranyaka Upanishad 3. 7, ibid. 55.
[16] Brihadaranyaka Upanishad 3. 9, ibid. 59.
[17] Brihadaranyaka Upanishad 5. 1, ibid. 76.

one 'becomes' what one emits from oneself.[18] The coming-to-be of the universe is in one sense a change in the Self, as it takes on finite name and form. 'He knew that he was creation, for he had brought it all forth. Hence he became creation.'[19] In this becoming, however, the Self also remains changeless. That is, its essential nature is not changed, even though it is modified by diversifying into all finite things. Changeless Brahman infinitely transcends diversified Brahman, while containing it as a part of itself.

One is led to the view that there are two forms of Brahman, a higher, immutable and unlimited, and a lower, consisting of all things. 'There are two forms of Brahman, the formed and the unformed, the mortal and the immortal, the static and the moving, the actual and the beyond.'[20] The immortal, moving (i.e. that which causes change) beyond is the 'breath of life and the space within the self'; it is 'the Person in the sun'; it is 'the Real of the real'. The 'formed and the mortal' is the world of finite names and forms, the world in which souls are bound to desires and the law of karma.

Within each human person it may thus be said that there are two selves: 'one here on earth imbibes the law of his own deeds; the other, though hidden in the secret places of the heart, dwells in the uttermost beyond.'[21] Brahman which becomes all things becomes subject to desire and ignorance, and must return to pure knowledge of itself again, by the conquest of desire: 'When all desires that shelter in the heart of man are cast aside, then the mortal puts on immortality.'[22]

The two selves are in one passage compared to two birds: 'Two birds, close-linked companions, cling to the selfsame tree: of these the one eats of the sweet fruit, the other, eating nothing, looks on intent.'[23] The 'one who eats' is the self bound to ignorance and desire, to enjoyment and aversion. It may feel free, but in fact it is the prisoner of its own desires: 'The individual self is like a lame man

---

[18] The Indian tradition that the effect pre-exists in the cause, and thus is in one sense not different from the cause, clearly sets Indian theological thought in a different direction from Semitic theology. See Julius Lipner, *The Face of Truth* (London: Macmillan, 1986), 83 f.

[19] Brihadaranyaka Upanishad 1. 4, 1. 5, Zaehner (trans.), *Hindu Scriptures*, 1, 36.

[20] Brihadaranyaka Upanishad 2. 3, ibid. 44.

[21] Katha Upanishad 3. 1, ibid. 175.

[22] Katha Upanishad 6. 14, ibid. 182.

[23] Mundaka Upanishad 3. 1, ibid. 190.

weighed down by fetters made up of the fruits of good and evil deeds; like a prisoner, not his own master, bound.'[24] ' "This I am, this is mine," he thinks, and so of his own accord he binds himself as a bird entangled in a net. Hence the man who has the marks of will, conception and individual self-consciousness is bound: the man who is the opposite of this is free.'[25] If one can overcome the sense of individual self-separateness and discover one's inner unity with the Self of all, one will achieve liberation from suffering.

The Self is disguised from its own true nature in the forms of individual personality. In itself it is 'infinite, boundless, a mass of understanding'.[26] It is not a mere negativity or unconscious existence, but has the nature of wisdom or understanding. 'This Self is Brahman, all experiencing (*anubhu*)',[27] so it must be thought of as possessing knowledge and experience. Since it is also a being of bliss, it can be said to have an affective aspect. As the choice of the word 'Self' indicates, it is at least analogous to a personal reality. Yet it is not unambiguously personal in the sense of being a fully personal agent which creates the universe intentionally.

The Upanishads are concerned with the origin of all things, and offer various opinions about it. Sometimes it is said that all originates from Death or Hunger, a primal Nothingness which generates from itself all that is.[28] More typical, however, is the view that 'In the beginning this was the Self alone.'[29] The Chandogya Upanishad canvasses both views at 6. 2, but concludes that 'it was Being alone that was this in the beginning—one only, without a second.'[30] This Being thought, 'Would that I were many', and emitted the elements from itself. There is thus an ambivalence about whether the universe evolved from a primal Nothingness, or from some primeval, but unexplained, desire of a primal Self.

For the Brihadaranyaka Upanishad, the primal man brought forth the gods, who were his betters: 'though he was mortal, he brought forth immortals.'[31] No clear reason is assigned for the coming-to-be

[24] Maitri Upanishad 4. 2, ibid. 225.
[25] Maitri Upanishad 6. 30, ibid. 237.
[26] Brihadaranyaka Upanishad 2. 4, ibid. 47.
[27] Brihadaranyaka Upanishad 2. 5, ibid. 49.
[28] Brihadaranyaka Upanishad 1. 2, ibid. 33.
[29] Brihadaranyaka Upanishad 1. 4, ibid. 35.
[30] Chandogya Upanishad 6. 2, ibid. 105.
[31] Brihadaranyaka Upanishad 1. 4, ibid. 36.

of the world. It seems to arise simply from the nature of the Self, from its fear or hunger. The one Self is in the form of a man. He split in two to form husband and wife, and from that couple, all beings were generated.

Three further models are suggested in the Brihadaranyaka Upanishad. They are the web of a spider, the spokes of a wheel, and the sparks from a fire. 'As a spider emerges by threads, as small sparks rise up from a fire, so from this Self do . . . all contingent beings rise up.'[32] 'Just as the spokes of a wheel are together fixed onto the hub and felly, so are all contingent beings . . . fixed in this Self.'[33] These suggest a natural or even inevitable tendency to produce finite beings rather than some freely intended creation of the universe. The Mundaka Upanishad adds further models which are similarly naturalistic, the growing of plants on earth and the growth of hair on the head.[34] It may seem that, in failing to give a very clear or positive reason for the generation of the universe, parts of the Upanishads decrease the importance of individual, finite life and activity—an accusation which Aurobindo makes against some interpretations of the Scriptures. If finite reality has no purpose or goal, but is a sort of natural overflowing from the One, it may easily come to be seen as illusory, to be transcended entirely by the liberated soul.

On the other hand, the two main Upanishadic myths of creation speak of desire of some sort, of Brahman wanting companionship or duality. To the extent that the universe comes to be through some desire of the Self, it is positively willed, and the potential is there for the universe to be seen as having a positive function, perhaps of divine self-expression or 'sport' (*lila*), or the expression of some form of desire for relationship. The fully theistic view that the universe is caused by a Self which eternally possesses wisdom and bliss comes to clear expression in the Svetasvatara Upanishad: 'Maker of all is He, all-knowing, source of selves.'[35] Thus one can plausibly trace a development in the Upanishads from early notions of a more impersonal cosmic power or energy (*brahman*), which could be obtained and used in sacrificial rituals or by ascetic practice, to an

---

[32] Brihadaranyaka Upanishad 2. 1, ibid. 44.
[33] Brihadaranyaka Upanishad 2. 5, ibid. 49.
[34] Mundaka Upanishad 1. 1, ibid. 185.
[35] Svetasvatara Upanishad 6. 16, ibid. 216.

idea of a Self which knows itself and which chooses to emanate all worlds from itself, and which is in some extended sense a person; indeed, a 'radiant, immortal Person (*purusa*).'[36]

THE PRINCIPLE OF NON-DUALITY

When one reaches the developed view of the Self as 'eternal, everlasting and primeval',[37] there is obviously a difficulty in accounting for the existence of the 'lower Brahman'. If the higher Brahman really is self-sufficient, changeless, and wholly blissful, why should it give rise to anything other than itself? How can the existence of duality make any difference to or be added to what is wholly non-dual? How can the non-dual be related to anything at all, since relationship implies duality? Moreover, if the higher Self remains changelessly complete, how can I, as an individual, realize my oneness with it? Such realization on my part cannot cause any change in the Self. If I realize something that had not hitherto been realized, this realization cannot come to exist in the Self, so it seems that I must continue as a separate, albeit realized, self, and therefore not truly be one with the Self. Or if I am in some way wholly one with the non-dual self, I will no longer be an individual who is able to realize that fact. How is that different from my simply coming not to exist, and leaving the Self as it always has been? These ambiguities remain, and offer the possibility of the various developments within Vedanta as 'true interpretations' of the text.

One possible solution is to suppose that there always and necessarily remains a duality between higher, unchanging Brahman, and lower, diversified Brahman, of which I am part. Yet if that is so, the basic principle of non-duality is contravened, since there is a fundamental duality within Brahman itself. Perhaps non-duality is not an ultimate ontological principle, as if to say that there really is no ultimate duality, that all apparent duality is some sort of illusion (the interpretation of Sankara and strict Advaita).[38] Rather, the Upanishads are pointing to a form of non-dual experience, apprehended as wisdom and bliss, which is both the ultimate reality from

---

[36] Brihadaranyaka Upanishad 2. 5, ibid. 47.

[37] Katha Upanishad 2. 18. ibid. 174.

[38] 'In reality, the relation of ruler and ruled does not exist' (Sankara, *The Vedanta Sutras*, trans. George Thibaut, in *Sacred Books of the East*, ed. Max Müller (Oxford: Clarendon Press, 1990–)

which the universe of finite names and forms originates and which is accessible to human experience. The human experiences upon which the Vedic tradition is based are, after all, experiences of this sort, attained through ascetic and meditational practice.

Yet in so far as human persons can 'enter into', or participate in, this reality, it cannot in fact be wholly unbounded and non-dual. I am a finite subject of experience, and if, after having had a profound meditational experience, I remember experiencing oneness with Brahman, then I am the same individual who had such an experience. I cannot literally become the Infinite, without losing my identity altogether. Yet I may experience some form of unity with the Infinite, without either being merged wholly into it or being utterly distinct from it.

One might say that the higher Brahman is boundless in that it is not bounded or restricted by anything other than itself or what it wills. It is immutable in that it cannot be changed by anything other than itself or what it wills to be; and in its essential nature as perfect wisdom, understanding, and bliss it cannot change at all. It is beyond subject–object duality, in that it does not exist as a subject which apprehends objects external to its own being. The object of its awareness is itself, and what it knows is a nature of unlimited perfection. It is a self-subsistent, blissful self-knower.

This Brahman, however, wills to become manifold, to generate from its unchanging and essential nature a universe, or many universes, of finite names and forms. These forms are not other than Brahman, for they have no distinct, self-subsisting being. They are not the infinite being of Brahman. They are finite reflections of the unlimited perfections of Brahman; yet they never exist independently. In that sense, Brahman in its 'lower' or qualified form can consist of all things, while transcending all things in its own boundless existence. All things are parts of Brahman, parts of its willed self-expression. It is possible for finite souls to experience their true status as non-subsisting, as parts of one reality which is boundless; to apprehend in some way, though always from their own point of view, the self-knowing of Brahman itself. Ramanuja's image of the world as the body of Brahman seems an apt analogy, though it is no more than that.[39] Brahman spins the world out of itself, so that many refracted images of its own blissful wisdom may exist, living

[39] Ramanuja, *The Vedanta Sutras*, tr. George Thibaut, ibid. x/viii. 95.

by their share in the being of Brahman, finding their true identity in being part of the one unitary flow of the divine self-expression, perpetually renewed by its return to the non-dual source of its being.

THE IMMORTALITY OF THE SELF

In some way the perception of the unity of all things in the Self brings immortality: 'Whoso knows that he is Brahman, becomes this whole', and is thus imperishable. One attains immortality by losing one's sense of individual separateness, and realizing that one is part of the one imperishable Brahman. If one becomes this Self, and thereby attains immortality, it may seem that one is speaking of the total cessation of the soul in the One Infinite. But a more positive interpretation is possible, whereby the individual soul may realize the life of the Infinite in and through oneself, so that one becomes its vehicle and expression.

The Brihadaranyaka Upanishad states bluntly that 'after death there is no consciousness',[40] since there is no duality by which one could know the Self as another. The consciousness of the Self is a non-dual consciousness; it is not a self knowing something other than itself; its knowledge is its essential being; it is what it knows and its knowing—this parallels in an interesting way the similar doctrine in Aristotle's *Metaphysics*, book 12. Immortality, in the sense of individual persistence, is not a feature of such a view. Immortality consists in renouncing all attachment to self, and realizing the unity of Brahman, the Supreme Self, which is without beginning or end. 'This person, on being born and on being embodied, is conjoined with evil things.'[41] But there is also 'that form of his which is beyond desire, free from evil, free from fear'.[42] Consisting of wisdom (*prajna*), it knows 'nothing without, nothing within'. Then, 'An ocean, One, the seer becomes, without duality . . . this is his highest bliss.'[43] Thus the central teaching of the Brihadaranyaka Upanishad seems to be that to attain supreme bliss is to accept total non-duality. In that state, there is no suffering, no attachment, no desire unfulfilled. It is a transcendence of individuality, a returning to the Self 'without a second', from which all things emanate.

---

[40] Brihadaranyaka Upanishad 2. 4, Zaehner (tr.), *Hindu Scriptures*, 47.
[41] Brihadaranyaka Upanishad 4. 3, ibid. 65.　　　　[42] Ibid. 67.
[43] Ibid. 68.

Only such a very radical teaching of self-annihilation can interpret the otherwise wholly mysterious verse: 'Blind darkness enter they who reverence unwisdom; into darkness blinder yet who delight in wisdom.'[44] The point is that to delight in any finite existence at all is a form of blindness. 'Should a man understand the Self . . . what desire that he should to this body cleave?'[45] Once one sees that one is the Self, there is nothing at all to wish for. Seeing that the Self, in its non-duality, is worth more than all the dualities which are its finite names and forms, all attachment to such finite forms is quenched. 'Whoso knows this becomes immortal.'[46] Thinking of evil and good deeds one may have done, 'He shrugs them off.'[47] One becomes contented, recollected, and patient. For there is nothing desirable yet to be achieved, and nothing truly to be feared.

The Chandogya Upanishad also presents a view of liberation (*moksa*) as the ending of individuality. It describes Brahman thus: 'that from which all things are born, into which they dissolve and in which they breathe and move'.[48] 'It encompasses all this universe, does not speak and has no care. This my Self within the heart (smaller than a grain of rice) is that Brahman. When I depart from hence I shall merge into it.'[49] This may not be a conscious merging: 'all these creatures, once they have merged into Being do not know that they have merged into Being.'[50] Thus dreamless sleep, or a fourth state, beyond waking, dreaming, and dreamless sleep, becomes a depiction of release: 'When a man is sound asleep, when he is not conscious of dreaming, this is the Self.'[51]

But what, asks Indra, is the difference between this and simply being dead? Prajapati explains that the Self, immortal, incorporeal, when it confusedly identifies itself with a body, is held in the grip of pleasure and pain. But, freed from the body, pleasure and pain cannot touch it. So the Self 'plunges into the highest light revealing itself in its own form', as a glorified person (*uttara purusha*). Here one sees developing the idea of what might be called a glorified body, a body of bliss, which the Self will put on as it wishes, free from care and sorrow. The Taittariya Upanishad develops the idea of a self of

[44] Brihadaranyaka Upanishad 4. 4, ibid. 72.
[45] Ibid.
[46] Ibid.
[47] Ibid. 74.
[48] Chandogya Upanishad 3. 14, ibid. 88.
[49] Chandogya Upanishad 3. 14. 5, ibid.
[50] Chandogya Upanishad 6. 9, ibid. 109.
[51] Chandogya Upanishad 8. 11, ibid. 129.

understanding and bliss, which 'roams throughout these worlds, eating what he will, changing his form at will'.[52] In these brief passages, one finds a much more positive doctrine of continued individual existence, fully and consciously merged with the Self, in creative and joyful activity.

BRAHMAN AS ACTIVE AND INACTIVE

Along with the more positive idea of a continued liberated existence of individual souls, one finds a more positive idea of Brahman as an active, intending, sovereign power. The Chandogya Upanishad begins to develop a more recognizably theistic note than the Brihadaranyaka Upanishad. Brahman intentionally wills the universe to exist: 'It had this thought: would that I were many: fain would I create.'[53] The Self exists after death in a glorious body; it is a superhuman being (*uttara purusha*).[54] Yet the dominant note is still of a complete non-duality, and of the cessation of individual existence by 'merging' into the One Self. The Svetasvatara Upanishad goes further: 'He, the One, surveys, directs all causes',[55] which seems to give Brahman an active causal role, not only surveying but also directing. It is that from which all things emanate. Again, 'he wields the all-sovereign power.'[56] Parts of the Svetasvatara Upanishad sound very theistic: 'Higher and other is he than world tree, time and forms; from him the world evolves, fully diversified: righteousness he brings, evil repels, master of good fortune, immortal, self-subsistent, of all the home and ground.'[57] However, these active tendencies are checked elsewhere. Brahman is 'the self unbounded of universal form: it neither works nor acts'.[58] 'No parts has he, no part in action, tranquil, unblemished and unflecked.'[59] Once more one seems to require a Self which is inactive and untouched, and another Self which diversifies, wills good, and experiences all things. The relation of the individual soul to the Self, in either sense,

---

[52] Taittariya Upanishad 3. 10, ibid. 144.
[53] Chandogya Upanishad 6. 2. 3, ibid. 105.
[54] Chandogya Upanishad 8. 12. 2, ibid. 130.
[55] Svetasvatara Upanishad 1. 3, ibid. 203.
[56] Svetasvatara Upanishad 5. 3, ibid. 213.
[57] Svetasvatara Upanishad 6. 6, ibid. 215.
[58] Svetasvatara Upanishad 1. 9, ibid. 204.
[59] Svetasvatara Upanishad 6. 19, ibid. 217.

is ambiguous. If the Self is not me, it simply lives within me, as something other. If it is me, how can its individuality be accounted for, without incorporating duality into the Self? Either I will merge with the Self, when I overcome the illusion of self-consciousness, or I will achieve freedom and bliss, when I disentangle myself from egoistic attachments, and become fully aware of my grounding in the Supreme Self. The latter view often seems to be presupposed by the texts, even when it is being overtly denied: 'The man who has a teacher knows that he will remain in this world only so long as he is not released; then he will arrive home.'[60] But if *he* will arrive, and achieve release, it is apparently he, the very same person, who will continue to exist in Brahman. Moreover, 'only the Infinite is happiness';[61] but if that is not *my* happiness, it is of little relevance to my goals and purposes.

Thus there is an unresolved tension, within the Upanishads, about whether the Supreme Self is active or inactive, and about whether the released soul is dissolved into the Self or retains some form of individuality, while being one with the Self and released from sorrow. Perhaps this dialectic of thought is intentional. For, throughout the Upanishads, the utter ineffability of Brahman is insisted upon: 'That from which words recoil together with the mind, unable to attain it, that is the bliss of Brahman.'[62] 'Nowhere hath anyone caught hold of him: of him there is no likeness . . . his form cannot be glimpsed.'[63] 'Witness, observer, absolute, alone, devoid of attributes.'[64] 'Where knowledge is not of a dual nature, it transcends cause, effect and action; it is beyond speech, nothing can be likened to it, one cannot tell of it.'[65] The paradox is well captured in the Maitri Upanishad: 'Unthinkable, unformed, profound, concealed, faultless, compact, impenetrably deep, devoid of attributes and beyond the constituents of nature, pure, resplendent, the experiencer of nature's constituents, awe-inspiring, immutable, Yoga's Lord, omniscient, most generous, incommensurable, beginningless and endless, bountiful, unborn, wise, indescribable,

---

[60] Chandogya Upanishad 6. 14, ibid. 112.
[61] Chandogya Upanishad 7. 23, ibid. 121.
[62] Taittiriya Upanishad 2. 4, ibid. 139.
[63] Svetasvatara Upanishad 4. 19, 20, ibid. 212.
[64] Svetasvatara Upanishad 6. 11, ibid. 216.
[65] Maitri Upanishad 6. 7, ibid. 229.

all things emanating, the self of all, all things experiencing, Lord of all . . . endless in power, ordainer . . . at peace, soundless, without fear or sorrow, contented bliss.'[66] While indescribable, this being is omniscient, wise, and generous; it is perfect bliss and without sorrow. Such paradoxes may point to a realm of reality beyond the grasp of human thought, with all its abstractive and categorizing features. If so, it may not be surprising that one has to speak of the Supreme Reality and the final goal of human life in relation to it in paradoxical terms. One may need to speak of both action and inaction, both continuance and ending. In that way, we may be forced to admit that our forms of thought are not adequate to the Supreme Reality.

Nevertheless, a number of major problems stand unresolved, waiting for commentators to develop their own distinctive solutions. How can a being know everything and not know sorrow? How can it create everything and not act? How can it be a mere witness and yet be the sovereign Lord? How can it be indescribable and yet be so repeatedly described? How can I find bliss and freedom in the ending of my individual self?

Despite all these problems, the central doctrine of the Upanishads remains clear. There is one reality, which is understanding and bliss, unchanging and boundless. This reality emanates all things, including human souls, from itself. Those souls become attached to various finite objects and goals, and they fail to see the unity of all things in the Self. If they overcome attachment, they can experience a sharing in the bliss and wisdom of the Self, and they pass beyond individual consciousness to an awareness of their inward unity with the Self of all. That is release, and in it lies supreme bliss.

It is not necessary to have a clear solution to all theoretical problems in order to pursue the way to release. It is not necessary to decide whether one is seeking to lose one's individuality wholly in the Self or to fulfil oneself in a Brahma-world, ultimately, if one is to begin the way to overcoming egoistic delusion and ignorance, and become open to a deeper bliss and wisdom from a source beyond one's own conscious powers. Above all, it must not be forgotten that the Upanishads are understood within a context of sacrificial ritual and devotion to the gods of the Vedic pantheon, which places its complex and austere teachings within a set of practices which

---

[66] Maitri Upanishad 7. 1, ibid. 242.

suggest particular interpretations of the texts to various religious communities, each with their own line of authoritative teachers.

THE THOUGHT OF AUROBINDO

The Upanishads form the basis of Vedanta, one of the six main schools of Indian philosophy, and one which enshrines a definite set of spiritual practices and goals. Because of the polysemic nature of the texts, there are many schools of Vedanta. The three most important, historically, are those which follow the teachings of Sankara (*Advaita*), Ramanuja (*Visist-Advaita*) and Madhva (*Dvaita*). I have elsewhere discussed the work of Sankara and Ramanuja to some extent, comparing it with the writings of medieval philosophers in Europe, and finding many points of comparison as well as of contrast between them.[67] If one is looking for twentieth-century writers who belong to the Vedantic tradition, the two names which are likely to come first to mind are those of Radhakrishnan and Aurobindo Ghose (Sri Aurobindo). Their views are similar in broad outline, but I have chosen to concentrate on Aurobindo because his ideas are to some extent more systematically expounded. Radhakrishnan, for all his eminence, did not found a religious movement, but Aurobindo has a distinctive following, with head-quarters at the Aurobindo Ashram in Pondicherry, south of Madras. He has written a great many works, but *The Life Divine* is the major expression of his restatement of Vedanta for the modern world. A discussion of the doctrine of God, or of the Supreme Reality, to be found in that book will both present one modern religious interpretation of the Upanishads and also provide a counterpart from the Indian tradition to the Semitic views of God which have already been considered.

Aurobindo follows the central teaching of the Upanishads that the whole universe is a manifestation of a supreme reality beyond and underlying it. 'Matter is a form of veiled life, life a form of veiled consciousness.'[68] Consciousness is known in us as mind, an analytical, discursive, egoistic, and divided form of being; but it is transcended by a greater consciousness: 'Matter reveals itself as . . . Spirit in its self-formative extension.'[69] This Spirit is termed

---

[67] Ward, *Images of Eternity*, chs. 1 and 2.

[68] Aurobindo Ghose, *The Life Divine* (2 vols.; Calcutta: Arya Publishing House, 1939), i. 4.   [69] Ibid. 32.

'Supermind' by Aurobindo, since it is quite different from the limited and divided consciousness which we know in ourselves. Supermind is the cosmic consciousness, and is one omnipotent and omniscient form of being, corresponding to what is called 'God' in the Semitic faiths.

Supermind is not itself the ultimate reality, however. 'The universe appears as only a symbol or an appearance of an unknowable Reality . . . beyond defining thought.'[70] This is the 'Silent Self, inactive, pure, self-existent, self-enjoying'.[71] It is 'the Beyond', world-transcending,[72] inactive and non-dual. It is beyond all space and time,[73] a 'unitarian, indivisible consciousness'.[74] It may even be better to name it '*Asat*', non-being, in its freedom from all limiting conditions and concepts. Yet it is not simple non-existence; so it should also be termed '*Sat*', or pure Being, beyond all conditions. Aurobindo writes that '*Sat* and *Asat* are not opposites . . . but the last antinomy by which we look up to the Unknowable.'[75]

Some Advaitins teach that the whole universe is an illusion, and that non-dual *Sat* is the only real. But Aurobindo asserts that 'the pure Self of the Advaitins is . . . the great Refusal.'[76] To assert that it alone is real denigrates the material order, deprives it of purpose and moral importance, and leads to an other-worldly asceticism which is unhealthy and negative. ' "One without a second" has not been read sufficiently in the light of the other formula equally imperative, "All this is the Brahman." '[77]

At this point one of the distinctive features of Aurobindo's 'integral yoga' becomes clear. He wishes to dissociate himself from so-called 'world-denying' interpretations of the Upanishads, which stress the pointlessness and sheer unreality of the material order and of individual existence. He also wishes to deny the Sankhya doctrine that *Purusa* and *Prakriti*, soul and matter, are irreconcilably different forms of being. For him, the whole physical universe is an essential part of the being of Brahman itself, for it is the self-expression of Brahman. As such, it is real and it possesses intrinsic importance as a part of what the cosmic Self essentially is. 'The silent and the active Brahman are not different . . . they are one Brahman in two

[70] Ibid. 14. [71] Ibid. 33. [72] Ibid. 28.
[73] Ibid. 48. [74] Ibid. 150. [75] Ibid. 43.
[76] Ibid. 29. [77] Ibid. 30.

aspects . . . and each is necessary to the other. It is out of this
Silence that the Word which creates the worlds for ever proceeds . . .
an eternal passivity makes possible the perfect freedom and
omnipotence of an eternal divine activity . . . this infinite fecundity
of its own dynamic nature.'[78]

On the one hand, there is the Great Silence, the Unknowable,[79] a
simple unity beyond conception. But on the other hand, that same
reality is manifested as active Brahman, as Supermind, as the Word
or Idea or Truth-consciousness which dynamically creates an endless
series of universes out of itself. *Sat* is infinite potentiality. *Chit* is the
envisaged 'predetermined harmony which is always present to its
omniscient consciousness'.[80] *Ananda* is the 'eternal and immutable
delight of being moving out into infinite and variable delight of
becoming'; it is 'the root of the whole matter'.[81] The Supermind can
thus aptly be characterized by the Upanishadic phrase
'*Sachchidananda*', Being-Consciousness-Bliss. 'The Unknowable
knowing itself as *Sachchidananda* is the one supreme affirmation of
Vedanta.'[82]

One might therefore say that the Unknowable is *Sachchidananda*
in its purely non-dual aspect, whereas the creative, knowing, and
willing superconsciousness is the same *Sachchidananda* in its
dynamic aspect of power, of *Shakti*. 'The Real is behind all that
exists; it expresses itself intermediately in an Ideal which is a
harmonized truth of itself; the Ideal throws out a phenomenal
reality.'[83] In its Supermind aspect, 'Being, consciousness of knowledge and consciousness of will are not divided . . . they are a
trinity.'[84]

Aurobindo is insistent that the Supermind is not to be thought of
as a sort of passive contemplator of possibilities, to which a more
dynamic aspect may be added later. 'Causality . . . is an inevitable
self-development of the truth of the thing that is, as Idea, in the very
essence of what is developed.'[85] The Real comes to know itself in
consciousness of its Idea, which is the harmonized truth of the
infinite potentiality of its Unknowable ground. That Idea is itself

---

[78] Ghose, *The Life Divine*, 33.   [79] Ibid. 15.   [80] Ibid. 176.
[81] Ibid. 124.   [82] Ibid. 53.   [83] Ibid. 141.
[84] Ibid. 156.   [85] Ibid. 174.

essentially creative, passing over immediately into a dynamic self-expression. In fact, 'divine knowledge and divine will are one.'[86] 'The Movement is . . . an aspect of . . . a great timeless spaceless Stability . . . not acting though containing all this action.'[87] In this sense, one can speak of the universe as a freely willed creation: 'The energy that creates the world can be nothing other than a Will . . . consciousness applying itself to a work.'[88]

The idea of *Sachchidananda* as a Trinity is naturally enough suggested by the three Sanskrit terms which make up the word, and many Christians in India have come to use the term as a word for God. Aurobindo in fact has a number of notions at work, which do not all fall neatly into a threefold pattern. *Sat*, or pure being, is, as has been noted, often given a dual role with *Asat*, or that which is beyond being as we can conceive it. This Silent Self, however, can also be conceived as *Sachchidananda*, in its unitarian or non-manifest mode. As it moves into its mode of self-manifestation, it generates a Word or 'Real-Idea',[89] which is its consciousness of itself rendered conceptually specific. Sometimes, Aurobindo stresses the unity of this Consciousness and the creative power of *Shakti*, speaking of a Consciousness-Force, two aspects of the one omniscient, omnipotent being whose knowledge and will are the same. The Trinity is then completed by Bliss or delight: 'Existence manifests itself, because existence is in its nature Consciousness and Force: but the third term in which these, its two constituents, meet, become one and are ultimately fulfilled, is satisfied Delight of self-existence.'[90] At other times, Aurobindo makes the division in a slightly different way, speaking of Being, Consciousness, and Will as the three modes of the Trinitarian Supermind.[91]. And again he can speak of a 'fourfold principle' of Existence, Conscious-Force, Bliss, and Supermind,[92] which is presumably another way of formulating the distinction between *Sachchidananda* in its immanent being and in its relation to the world as dynamic creator.

THE EVOLUTIONARY PRINCIPLE

Aurobindo preserves the basic Vedantic doctrine that all reality is the manifestation of one ultimate Self. He is concerned, however, to

---

[86] Ibid. 166. [87] Ibid. 89. [88] Ibid. 17.
[89] Ibid. 33. [90] Ibid. 253. [91] Ibid. 156.
[92] Ibid. 265.

stress the reality, in its own sphere, of the triple world of matter, life, and mind, against views which may seem to deny or downgrade it. Most distinctively, he gives to history an importance which it rarely had in classical Indian thought. The universe is not a pointless overflowing from some already complete and wholly self-sufficient being. On the contrary, 'There must be some good and inherent reason in it [Brahman] for the manifestation . . . a secret and finally triumphant good.'[93] What is this good which history is meant to bring to triumphant realization?

'Life exists in Brahman in order to discover Brahman in itself . . . to fulfil God in life is man's manhood.'[94] The universe becomes important to Brahman as the arena in which Brahman ascends to self-knowledge. 'Through the individual it manifests in relation even as of itself it exists in identity.'[95] The universe, in other words, adds something real to Brahman, though not anything which does not spring solely from what Brahman is. In its cosmic manifestation, Brahman passes through an evolution from matter to life and mind, and beyond. 'Mind attains its self-fulfilment . . . when it consciously lends its energies to the perfect self-figuration of the Divine in ever-new forms and activities.'[96]

The story of the universe is the story of an involution of Spirit (*Purusha*) into its apparent opposite, Matter (*Prakriti*), and its subsequent evolution to historical self-consciousness. 'God having entirely become Nature, Nature seeks to become progressively God.'[97] To the unenlightened awareness, matter may seem to be the opposite of Spirit. Matter is inert, unconscious, purposeless, atomistic in character. Yet in fact 'Matter is Sachchidananda represented to His own mental experience as a formal basis of objective knowledge, action and delight of existence.'[98] Matter is the basis for an evolution towards perfect self-consciousness. Aurobindo asks, 'Is *Prakriti* really power of *Chit*, in its nature force of creative self-conscience?'[99] The question is rhetorical. Matter exists as the basis for the ascent to Life, and thence to Mind. 'Matter also is Brahman . . . the external body of the Divine Being.'[100]

Human life is the place where mind comes into existence; yet

[93] Ghose, *The Life Divine*, 38.   [94] Ibid. 45.   [95] Ibid. 53.
[96] Ibid. 32.   [97] Ibid. 55.   [98] Ibid. 289.
[99] Ibid. 95.   [100] Ibid. 7.

'Nature is seeking to evolve beyond Mind.'[101] Human existence has a purpose, and that purpose is to evolve beyond itself, to become Supermind. 'The conscious emergence of the full Sachchidananda in its creations by universality, by equality, by self-possession and conquest of Nature. This is the course and movement of the world.'[102] On the one hand, *Sachchidananda* is fully self-possessed, blissful and omniscient. As such, it is creator of all worlds. On the other hand, *Sachchidananda* emerges through a long evolutionary process, of which humans are a pivotal part.

'It is the Son of Man who is supremely capable of incarnating God.'[103] Aurobindo speaks of Incarnation as the goal of the historical process, although of course he has in mind a universal incarnation: 'The transformation of the limited ego into a conscious centre of the divine unity'.[104] The goal of human life is thus 'To know, possess and be the divine being . . . to build peace and a self-existent bliss . . . to establish an infinite freedom . . . to discover and realise the immortal life . . . this is offered to us as the manifestation of God in matter and the goal of Nature in her terrestrial evolution.'[105]

Aurobindo looks to a future in which this possession of the 'Life Divine', 'the transfiguration of the human soul into the divine',[106] will be fully realized. 'The ascent to the divine life is the human journey.'[107] Ignorance, suffering, and disharmony will be overcome. 'If we could grasp the essential cause . . . of error, suffering and death . . . we might hope even to eliminate them altogether.'[108] That essential cause is *Avidya*, the ignorance which 'proceeds by an exclusive concentration of consciousness'.[109] We think of ourselves as distinct, finite egos, and so we need to protect our own interests against those of others. This causes conflict, which in turn causes suffering, as we identify ourselves with the bundle of interests and desires which are in fact part of the one expression of the cosmic consciousness itself.

THE CAUSES OF SUFFERING

'The fundamental error of the Mind is this fall from self-knowledge by which the individual soul conceives of its individuality as a

---

[101] Ibid. 4. [102] Ibid. 132. [103] Ibid. 56.
[104] Ibid. 71. [105] Ibid. 2. [106] Ibid. 33.
[107] Ibid. 52. [108] Ibid. 69. [109] Ibid. 203.

separate fact.'[110] It is not the case that some purely extracosmic God creates pain and suffering for creatures, 'but Himself stands above and unaffected by them'.[111] Rather, it is the sole and infinite Existence-Consciousness-Bliss which has come to admit into itself that which is not bliss. Suffering and conflict and division are parts of the self-expression of *Sachchidananda* itself. 'There is an attraction in ignorance itself because it provides us with the joy of discovery . . . a great adventure of the soul . . . its result is a new affirmation of *Sachchidananda* in its apparent opposite.'[112]

This way of dealing with evil as a part of the manifestation of a wholly perfect being is in danger of trivializing it, or of seeing it as in some way good. It is very difficult to see how the 'sole absolute object' of the existence of the universe can be 'the joy of the dancing',[113] when so many creatures suffer. It is difficult to see how that individually experienced suffering can in reality be part, even an essential part, of 'one conscious being in many souls, one power of Consciousness in many minds, one joy of Force working in many lives, one reality of Delight fulfilling itself in many hearts and bodies'.[114] Aurobindo is often in danger of presenting suffering as part of the great adventure of the Absolute in its self-realizing evolution, so that 'In the passage to higher forms there intervenes the phenomenon of pain.'[115] At one point, he suggests that there are states of consciousness in which 'evil is a circling of the good around its own perfection'.[116] That is, I fear, a descent into unintelligibility, which does not take serious account of the way in which evil corrupts and destroys the good, and is not simply a step on the way to the expression of a higher form of good. This is perhaps the weakest link in the generally very attractive view that Aurobindo presents. Whereas Advaita relegates the whole realm of suffering to a form of non-reality, Aurobindo wishes to give the material world a positive function. Yet he fails in the end to give to suffering its own negative reality, consigning it to virtual unreality by insisting that it should be seen in the wider cosmic perspective as Delight.

This follows, however, from the basic view that 'An existence wholly self-aware . . . possesses the phenomenal being in which it is

[110] Ghose, *The Life Divine*, 207.   [111] Ibid. 113.   [112] Ibid. ii. 142.
[113] Ibid. i. 95.   [114] Ibid. 255.   [115] Ibid. 117.
[116] Ibid. 63.

involved, realises itself in form, unfolds itself in the individual.'[117] One can see why many traditional schools of Buddhism deny the existence of any permanent Self that could be seen as creator of the universe. How could an unchanging Self, which is a pure power of light, love, and joy, express its own being in a world of suffering? Are the sufferings of individuals simply subsumed under the bliss of the cosmic Self, so that they count for nothing, qua individual? The danger exists that individual selves will merely become means to the greater bliss of the One, 'The collective Will of mankind that works out with the individual as a means . . . a superconscious Might . . . the God in man, the Omniscient, the Omnipotent'.[118] So what is the importance of individual experience, as it is experienced by the individual?

The problem is that such experience is largely the result of *Avidya*: 'The nature of the ego is a self-limitation of consciousness by a willed ignorance . . . recovery can be effected by the right participation of the individual in the consciousness of the totality.'[119] However, since this ignorance must itself be a product of the creative power of *Sachchidananda*, it is hard to see how it can be a real error or corruption of any sort. It seems more a matter of a passing-over of the One into the many, in order that an ascent can take place which is then able to 'reconcile and unite opposites', which were always implicit in the One itself. 'The redemption comes by the recovery of the universal in the individual.'[120] But there was no real loss and there is no real recovery. The loss is a temporal forgetting, which is at the same time part of the journey of self-discovery by which the Absolute knows itself. The conclusion seems virtually inescapable that the whole temporal process is the gradual manifestation of what is timelessly true of the Supreme Reality.

If one considers the cosmic process from within it, one sees that 'The world is a movement that continually progresses and increases by the inclusion of all the successions of the past.'[121] There is a clear evolution of Self, with the past not forgotten, culminating (though perhaps not ending) in a conscious participation of the many selves in the reality of the One Self, acting as its vehicle of self-expression. At the same time, the One Self is beyond time and space, 'Holding eternally in itself that which it casts into movement and form'.[122]

---

[117] Ibid. 51. [118] Ibid. 18. [119] Ibid. 69.
[120] Ibid. 61. [121] Ibid. 93. [122] Ibid. 175.

Thus Aurobindo, when speaking of the Supermind, remarks that 'To a consciousness higher than Mind . . . time might well offer itself as an eternal present',[123] and might conceive and, in the very same act, issue all worlds from itself in 'a single indivisible act of knowledge'.[124]

Thus the Supermind does not really evolve in time, since it always is. However, 'Only the descent of the Supermind . . . can establish . . . the harmony of the Spirit . . . the Divine Ananda.'[125] Temporal evolution is necessary to Brahman being what it is. One must regard the evolving process as the temporal aspect which is necessary to the eternal reality of Brahman, as the unfolding of its always completed nature. It is hard to avoid the thought that one is, after all, a small part of some great world-process which is in some sense already completed. Aurobindo confirms this thought when he writes that Mind should 'serve passively as an instrumentation and phenomenon of *Sachchidananda*'.[126]

THE CLAIM TO A PERENNIAL PHILOSOPHY

A constant theme of Aurobindo's writing is that the human mind can only attain very partial views of Brahman. Thus Advaita, he claims, has a one-sided view which neglects the importance of matter and time. Any Vedantin school which stresses the oneness or the manifoldness of the self to the exclusion of the other aspect is imperfect. Thus he tries to hold as many diverse views as possible together, as partial aspects of a greater truth.

The difficulty, as with all such revisions of Vedanta which aim to present it as the 'perennial philosophy', is that it presents what is precisely a particular view of Brahman, which does exclude other views, if only on the grounds of their greater limitedness. This particular view is fairly clearly influenced both by Hegel and by Aurobindo's acquaintance with Christianity (he was educated at St Paul's School, London, and at Cambridge, where he took a First in Classics). The idea of an Absolute which objectifies itself in the universe and reconciles opposites so as to come to full self-consciousness through history, and particularly in human thought,

---

[123] Ghose, *The Life Divine*, 161.   [124] Ibid. 166.   [125] Ibid. 278.
[126] Ibid. 206.

is, after all, the basic Hegelian philosophy. Hegel insisted that Reason is competent to discern the nature of reality. In fact, he took the view that the whole of physical reality is a product of Absolute Reason or Spirit (*Geist*). His reaction to Kant was to abolish the noumenal realm, which was supposed to be beyond the grasp of theoretical knowledge, and hold that the temporal universe is the self-realization of Absolute Spirit, first objectifying itself in matter and then coming to know itself and thus being reconciled to itself in and through finite minds. Absolute Spirit is thus Trinitarian in form, moving from existence 'in itself', to an objectified and alienated existence 'for itself', and finally achieving a state in which it exists 'in and for itself'. 'There are', Hegel writes, 'three moments to be distinguished: Essential Being; explicit Self-existence, which is the express otherness of essential Being, and for which that Being is object; and Self-existence or Self-knowledge *in* that other.'[127] Time and history have an important part to play, and indeed are essential to the realization of Spirit. Time is 'the necessity compelling Spirit to . . . make manifest what is inherent'.[128] Hegel himself saw this as a deeply Christian philosophy, according to which Pure Spirit incarnates in time and then reconciles all time to itself in an eternal consummation. He saw the Christian dogmas of Incarnation, Atonement, and Trinity as pictorial expressions of deeper and more universal philosophical truths. Accepting Spinoza's interpretation of the infinite as all-inclusive, he included temporality and development in the divine being in a way impossible for Thomas Aquinas. Although Hegel's system is obscure and ambiguous, most interpreters see the process of history as completed in a timeless realized existence of Spirit, which therefore remains above, though inclusive of, all temporal processes. 'The essential Being is inherently and from the start reconciled with itself.'[129] God is not actually a developing reality. Rather, temporal development manifests what is timelessly true of Being's own self-knowing and realizing unity. This pattern of thought is reflected exactly in Aurobindo's system.

Such concepts as Word, Trinity, redemption, and incarnation are used quite naturally by Aurobindo, though in a sense transformed by their new context. To complicate the issue still further, Vedanta

---

[127] G. W. F. Hegel, *The Phenomonenology of Mind*, tr. Sir James Baillie (London: Oxford University Press, 1931; 1st pub. 1807), 767.   [128] Ibid. 800.
[129] Ibid. 780.

itself was a revised form of Vedic religion which had incorporated much material from the Buddhist tradition, so that it has been plausibly argued that 'Hinduism' itself is an offshoot of Buddhism, rather than the other way round. Far from being the original perennial philosophy, Vedanta is more likely to be a consequence of a successful re-writing of the Vedic tradition to fend off Buddhism by appropriating most of its key concepts. In the twentieth century, the tradition has again been rewritten to fend off Christian missions by appropriating their key concepts and adapting the apparatus of Hegelian philosophy.

Aurobindo's integral yoga thus represents a twentieth-century response from within an Indian religious tradition to a number of more recent religious and philosophical influences. It appropriates the idea of evolution and of the abiding importance of the material as the field in which the spiritual can find free self-expression. It appropriates Christian concepts of a creation through an eternal Word, of redemption through incarnation of the Supreme Spirit in material forms (though this is to come to all in future), and of a Trinitarian understanding of Brahman in terms of being, understanding, and will (one of Augustine's key analogies for the Trinity). It retains a form of ultimate non-dualism, the idea that all that exists is part of one Supreme Self. It retains the ideas of rebirth and karma, and in particular it retains a place for the idea of *Shakti*, the energy or power of material being, as a feminine aspect of the Divine. It is a new religious vision of some elegance and power, and it illustrates how one can use the scriptures of a tradition (in this case, the Upanishads), while taking insights from other traditions to illuminate and extend understanding.

THE SEARCH FOR COHERENCE

It seems that the passionate God of Abraham Heschel, who stands in a personal I–Thou relation to humanity and never offers humans actual unity with the Divine,[130] is far removed from this Unknowable, which manifests itself as one Mind in many minds, and calls the

---

[130] 'A thirst to become one with God . . . is alien to the biblical man. To him the term "union with God" would be a blasphemy' (Heschel, *The Prophets*, 356).

many to become instruments of the divine life. These are, quite simply, different and conflicting concepts of Ultimate Reality. If I had considered Buddhism, which I have excluded because it is non-theistic, another very different idea would have been apparent; namely, that there is no Ultimate Reality, no Absolute, at least of an enduring and substantial sort. Not even Aurobindo's admirable desire to see all views as partial aspects of one truth can manage to eliminate basic theoretical conflicts about Ultimate Reality (the final shipwreck of such a desire is that many people would strongly deny the claim that all views are partial aspects of one truth).

Nevertheless, it may be the case that each tradition can only be revealed in its full breadth and depth when it reflects the others from its own point of view. While one must decide for some views and against others, it may well be that the rejected views contain insights one has overlooked, and suggest modifications to one's own views that will enlarge and deepen them. If, from a Christian viewpoint, one looks sympathetically but critically at Aurobindo's integral philosophy, its main problems seem to be problems of coherence. Can one really think of *Sachchidananda* being eternally omniscient, even beyond time and space, enacting all things in one indivisible act, and at the same time as being an emergent reality in time, dynamically expressing itself in infinite fecundity? One might indeed say that ultimate questions about space, time, and infinity are so mysterious that anything might be possible. Nevertheless, the concepts we use do place some constraints on the things that we can intelligibly say. God may be beyond description by us; but we cannot be content simply to assert contradictory statements about God, with that intellectual shrug of the shoulders which says that all contradictions will be resolved in a higher realm.

If God is infinitely creative, without beginning or end, can one see this infinity as somehow completed in a timeless reality? For a temporal view of God, past and future are not symmetrical. The past is closed and unchangeable, but the future is open and can be changed. For a timeless reality, however, no object of its knowledge can be open or undetermined, unless it is eternally undetermined, since God cannot change from a state in which God knows that p is undetermined to a state in which God knows that p is determined. God can indeed know that p is undetermined at $t1$, and determined at $t2$. But if God eternally knows this, then it is eternally true that p is determined at $t2$. For someone at $t1$, it might be undetermined what p will be at $t2$. But in fact p is determined at $t2$ from God's viewpoint, eternally. That means that God cannot see the future as truly open.

One might attempt to split the being of God into one timeless consciousness and one temporal consciousness. For the temporal consciousness, the future is open, and God (among other beings) decides what it will be from moment to moment. The timeless consciousness either does not know temporal events at all, or God knows timelessly everything that God will decide (has decided/is deciding). Aurobindo excludes the former possibility, holding that God's timeless knowledge must include knowledge of temporal events. Since timeless knowing is strictly immutable, the timeless God cannot wait to see what the temporal God decides (which would entail a moment of waiting followed by a moment of knowing what had been decided). God's timeless knowledge cannot depend upon, cannot follow some temporal decision, since then it would be changed by some temporal event, which is *ex hypothesi* impossible. So God can only know what is decided in time by bringing it about. God's timeless knowledge must be causative of the temporal events that it timelessly knows. But that means that real causality belongs to the timeless God; the temporal God is not free to decide anything other than what is timelessly decided, from beginning to end. The temporal God cannot do otherwise than the timeless God decrees. The conclusion is that the temporal God is not significantly free, and cannot possess even a degree of free creativity and autonomy.

This clarifies the sense in which Aurobindo's system in fact deprives the individual of significant freedom and creativity, even as it attempts to preserve a sense of individual autonomy and purpose. We all play out our parts in the eternally decreed self-expression of the Absolute, and we are not free to depart from the script even for a moment.

In this scheme, do we have any individuality at all? The key point is that, of course, we are all really *Sachchidananda*, one Mind appearing as many minds. We are ignorant, suffering, and egoistic; so does it not follow that Mind itself is ignorant, suffering, and egoistic? It seems that, while Mind does all things, it suffers nothing. Who, then, suffers? Who suffers the sense of despair and futility, who perpetrates evil and destruction? The reason for positing centres of consciousness other than God is simply that God does not do evil and does not suffer, in the sense of feeling a sense of final despair. The universe may be an evolution from matter to Supermind and beyond; but if so, this cannot be conceived as the evolution of Supermind itself, which is unevolved and unchanging. It must rather be conceived as the generation by God of a reality of a wholly different sort, which can yet develop to a unity with God. In this unity, individuals can be aware of God as the one omnipresent reality, and thus as a reality which is within the self, which alone sustains them in being. They can become instruments of the power of God expressed in their world.

Aurobindo's thought seeks to give purpose and reality to individual and material existence, by making it the vehicle of the progressive self-manifestation of the Divine. It is difficult for him to do so as fully as he would like, however, because the material is, for him, nothing but the self-manifestation of the Divine, so that it has no independent reality. What could give fuller meaning to material individuality is the possibility of its own proper fulfilment by free relation to the Divine in a co-operative communion of being, by which both creature and divinity could obtain new modes of self-expression in mutual relationship. The meaning of historical existence is, as Aurobindo claims, the progressive realization of the divine life in and through individual personal lives. But that requires a real individuality and a real emergence, through growing response to the one unchangingly self-possessed source and goal of being, which itself manifests one part of its being in temporal and creative relationships.

THE PERFECTION OF THE DIVINE BEING

Like Iqbal, Barth, and Heschel, Aurobindo stresses the creative and temporal character of the Supreme (the Supermind) in a way that the classical traditions would not have done. Heschel particularly stressed the affectivity of God. Aurobindo's image of Brahman as including all finite feelings within its own being expresses a clear view that the Supreme is affected by all that creatures do and feel. Though Heschel opposed any idea of a union of divine and human, there is a common emphasis in both thinkers on the existence of passion or feeling in the Supreme Being, which contrasts strongly with classical theories.

Iqbal emphasized the creativity of God. Though Aurobindo may have difficulty with maintaining both the free creativity of individuals and the self-manifestation of Brahman in the universe, he too stresses the value and importance of time, creativity, and history for God.

Barth focused on the love of God, the will of God for fellowship, and the demand of God for justice. Aurobindo speaks of Brahman as willing to manifest the divine being in relation. Though for Aurobindo all finite minds are parts of the one Cosmic Mind, their destiny is to relate to one another in ways which properly bring joy and delight, equality and universality to all. The Brahman which is supreme consciousness and bliss is an all-including reality within which a communion of creative relationships exists.

Aurobindo's own stress, in keeping with the teaching of the Upanishads, is on the supreme wisdom and bliss of Brahman. Brahman is pure wisdom and in consciousness of it lies supreme bliss. Aurobindo's contribution to Vedanta has been to emphasize the importance of temporal emergence and finite individuality to the fulness of being which is Brahman, so that wisdom and bliss are to be manifested fully in time, and not only in a realm beyond change and causality.

From these four scriptural traditions a complex idea of God as the supremely perfect emerges. God is a being of affectivity, creativity, love, wisdom, and bliss. In the remaining parts of this volume I shall articulate a doctrine of God which, while constructed from a Christian viewpoint and on a Trinitarian basis, seeks to take into account and build upon this core idea of the Supreme. It is striking that such an idea arises within four different religious traditions, and that in each the concept of perfection is more relational and dynamic than was the case in classical theologies. The classical traditions are not, however, simply rejected. Aurobindo, for example, is careful to stress that *Sachchidananda* is in itself beyond all concepts and limitations that we can conceive. In this, too, he agrees with Iqbal and Heschel, who would also emphasize the essential mystery of God as far transcending any images we may have. Like thinkers in the classical traditions, Aurobindo articulates the mysterious infinity of God as a timeless and spaceless indivisible knowledge and power, remarking that none of our concepts are adequate to describe the Unknowable.

I have argued that the idea of a totally timeless creator God cannot escape contradicting the idea of a temporally creative God, since a 'single act' view of creation contradicts a 'creative and responsive succession' view. Yet there may be a 'higher', supratemporal aspect in God, as well as a 'lower', temporal and creative aspect. If the Supreme has a reality beyond time, in which time itself is grounded, that reality cannot be affected by temporal events, and thus cannot be said to know them—except on the supposition that its knowledge creates them, which contradicts the postulate that they have primary causal efficacy. The timeless—and therefore changeless—nature of God cannot change in knowledge. Thus it can be said only to know itself, in its infinite potentiality, and in a way beyond the possibility of our understanding. God knows the eternal nature perfectly and changelessly. In knowing that, God knows that in which all possibilities are grounded, though they may not exist as specific possibilities in the divine mind.[131] God in the temporal nature knows things successively and endlessly. It is the same God who is timeless and temporal, in different respects, who has eternal knowledge of the divine primordial nature and temporal knowledge of God's creative acts, their objects and responses to them.

If this is a coherent conception, Aurobindo may be right in speaking of a 'higher' and a 'lower' Brahman, one beyond being itself and the other the glorious Lord of creative power. He is right in seeing one as the temporal manifestation of the other, without which Brahman would be incomplete, since it would be lacking in creative efficacy. Strong analogies to a Christian doctrine of the Trinity can be found in this view. For a Christian view, as God turns towards the world, it is conceived in its archetypal possibility, thus generating the eternal Word or Truth-Consciousness. The Spirit stirs Creation towards embodying that archteypal image, which is given particular form in Jesus and final form in the consummation of all things. The Father delights in the completion of that creative activity, receiving into the divine consciousness the fruition of the Spirit's creative and co-operative work within and among creatures, building them up in the image of the eternal Christ and uniting them in one cosmic life. It is not hard to see here a statement, in different terms, of the view that Brahman manifests the divine being progressively in time so as to delight in the fruition of its self-expressive evolution. If the Christian view stresses more strongly the freedom and otherness of finite selves, it must be remembered that Aurobindo does want to affirm the reality of the triple realm of

[131] See Ch. 11, penultimate section ('Divine Imagination').

matter, life, and mind, and not collapse them into a mere illusion of reality. It could be that the non-dualism of Vedanta is more a statement of the sole self-existence of God, the total dependence of all things upon God, and the goal of finite existence as being the fulfilment of each self in the Self of All, than a denial of any distinction beween Creator and creature.

Of course, the Christian view of the Trinity is not that of Iqbal or Aurobindo, since it is founded primarily on taking Jesus as a foundational revelation of God. It stresses individuality, relationality, and community more than Aurobindo; it stresses the self-emptying of God and the historical goal of oneness with the Supreme more than Iqbal. But it is of interest to see how even in 'monistic' or 'unitarian' conceptions of God, there may be, and there may need to be, a recognition of some form of diversity in unity, which makes the Christian doctrine of the Trinity, while distinctive, not wholly at odds with concepts of the Supreme in other religious traditions.

PART II
On Speaking of God as Creator

5

The Objective Reality of God

In the four traditions that have been considered, there is agreement that the heart of religious belief is commitment to a being of supreme power and value, whether described as *Sachchidananda* or as God the sole creator of all things in space and time. Some of the most eminent twentieth-century theologians from those traditions all stress that God is involved with the universe, that there is a sort of divine pathos (Heschel), a divine will for fellowship (Barth), a divine emergent creativity (Iqbal), or a self-manifestation of the Divine in the forms of space and time (Aurobindo). In that respect, they all wish to modify their own classical traditions, which stressed the complete simplicity, eternity, and immutability of God. Yet they do not wish to reject the classical views. They all speak of God as infinite, as beyond human speech, as hidden 'in unapproachable light'.[1] They rather wish to complement the classical view by asserting that the same God who is infinite and incomprehensible, beyond all name and form, also manifests itself in real relation to the universe, in time, passion, and creativity.

All these views would claim to be based on revelation, on discernments of the nature of God which have come to prophets and sages in their own developing traditions of worship and prayer. Such revelations articulate the sense of an ultimate power on which humans feel themselves to depend and a supreme value which they can to some degree apprehend. But it is precisely belief in the existence of an ultimate power and supreme value which is held to be suspect or even irrational by many contemporary thinkers. There are many reasons for this, but a major one is a commitment either to a strong form of empiricism or to a strong form of materialism. Both these schools of philosophical thought are apt to think of themselves as committed to the supremacy of experimental science, They are so different, however, that they wholly contradict each other.

[1] I Tim. 6: 16.

Empiricism, in its strong form, maintains that all knowledge must be based on experience, that knowledge cannot go beyond what can be experienced, and that beliefs should never be stronger than the evidence compels.[2] Those who hold such a view could never be justified in believing in a supreme power and value, since the assertion of supremacy goes well beyond the fragmentary and fairly subjective experiences of God that are typical of human beings. It is often thought, on grounds of this sort, that one can never be justified in believing in God as the infinite source of all power and value.

Taken strictly, empiricism would make science itself impossible, since science has progressed precisely by making the sort of bold imaginative leaps of thought which enabled Newton to formulate the laws of mechanics and Einstein to frame the theory of relativity. What is most characteristic of modern science is its attempt to frame a unified and elegant mathematical model which will explain observed regularities in nature. Of course, as Karl Popper stressed, these hypotheses need to be checked, where possible, against careful observation.[3] But they go well beyond what observation alone would suggest, and are not derived from simple sense experience. Scientific hypotheses are typically intellectual constructions of great sophistication. They are refutable by observations; but even such refutations may be very hard to imagine—as with the general theory of relativity.

Theism also can be seen as an imaginative hypothesis, of theoretical unifying power and elegance, which is falsifiable by observation in principle, though decisive experiments are virtually impossible to conceive. In this respect, theism would compete with materialism, whose unifying hypothesis is that all that exists consists of material particles obeying a few ultimately simple laws, that no purpose or moral concern or benevolent design can be observed in nature, and that there are no acts of a supernatural being observable anywhere in nature.[4] The benefit claimed for the hypothesis of materialism is that it offers the best explanation of occurrences, by

[2] The classic statement of this view is David Hume, *A Treatise of Human Nature* (London: J. M. Dent, 1956; 1st pub. 1738).

[3] See Karl Popper, *The Logic of Scientific Discovery* (London: Hutchinson, 1956).

[4] It is hard to find thoroughgoing philosophical materialists, but a sophisticated account is Anthony Quinton, *The Nature of Things* (London: Routledge, 1973).

referring them to the operation of a few general laws, ultimately those of fundamental physics.

Considered as an hypothesis, materialism does not seem very strongly compelling. It does offer simplicity and elegance, claiming to explain everything with reference to just a few simple laws and entities, and thus appealing to a minimum number of kinds of things. But it is very counter-intuitive to suppose that everything that exists is a material particle or complex group of such particles. Consciousness is the most obvious counter-example to this. Thoughts, feelings, images, and dreams do not seem to have the properties of material particles, and very sophisticated theories, not simple ones, are needed to persuade one that they do. Moreover, it is far from certain that laws of physics wholly explain everything that happens, without exception, so that all other forms of explanation can be reduced to those of physics, and no events will occur that do not fall under such laws. Even if it is pragmatically useful always to seek to explain according to laws, one can never guarantee that the attempt will be successful. To think that all historical actions could be wholly explained in terms of physics, for example, is to leap so far beyond present possibilities of explanation that the hypothesis is about as bold and brash as anyone could imagine; it is certainly as bold as the theistic hypothesis.

Perhaps the chief iconoclastic strength of materialism is its denial of design, purpose, or benevolent concern to the processes of nature, and its denial of any evidence of non-human personal action in history. But these denials are not overwhelmingly convincing. The universe does seem to be amazingly ordered, which is at least suggestive of design. Its development from the Big Bang to a condition in which there are rational, moral beings, and its apparent push towards even more complex sentient forms of life, does smack of purpose.[5] The amount of suffering in nature naturally counts against there being a creator who is wholly opposed to any occurrence of suffering. But it is compatible with the creation of the universe by a being of supreme value and power, on condition that the universe is necessary for the existence of values which otherwise could not exist, which are highly desirable, and which will not leave suffering unredeemed. As for the question of providential actions in

[5] For a compelling account by a theoretical physicist, see Paul Davies, *The Mind of God* (New York: Simon and Schuster, 1992), esp. ch. 8.

history, the history of religions provides sufficient testimony to a form of moral ordering of history and to the efficacy of prayer to make any outright denial less than probative. The hypothesis of materialism is, in other words, rational but not very strongly or unequivocally supported by the apparent nature of things. In a contest of plausibility with theism, it would not be the obvious winner, in my view.

NON-COGNITIVE BELIEF IN GOD

But all this assumes that theism is a speculative hypothesis, a postulate that the universe is created by a perfect being. For a number of reasons, however, this is not a plausible assumption. Most obviously, theism is not primarily postulated in order to explain observed events. It is not adopted in a speculative, dispassionate spirit. It does not help one to predict anything in particular. Atoms were postulated because they help to explain why events happen as they do; and their postulation enables predictions to be made about what will happen in specifiable circumstances. God is not postulated to explain why things happen (although some accounts of religious belief by non-believers construe it as such). No precise predictions follow from the postulate of God. God is not a causal hypothesis.

At the beginning of this century, some philosophers and theologians, feeling the force of this point very strongly, held that to assert the existence of God is not to state a matter of fact at all. Factual statements, they felt, are primarily theoretical and dispassionate. They merely record that something is there, but imply no practical attitude towards it. They are asserted on grounds of evidence, and it will usually be proper to seek to assemble all available evidence against alleged facts, if they are very unusual or unlikely. Factual issues are in principle resolvable to everyone's satisfaction, usually by observation.[6]

In all these ways, belief in God is very unlike belief in the existence of some fact. If one asks how the concept of God is used, say in the context of a wedding or funeral service, it looks as if it is to give hope, inspire confidence and commitment, provide comfort, or

---

[6] The classic statement of this view in Britain is A. J. Ayer, *Language, Truth and Logic* (London: Gollancz, 1936), Ch. 6.

remind one of the fundamental conditions and limits of human life. Perhaps, then, one could think of the concept of God as being used primarily to express or evoke particular sorts of feelings and attitudes. Like poetry and drama, it would not directly make truth-claims, but would arouse emotions or help to motivate one to a moral way of life. Or the concept of God might be used in a prescriptive way, as recommending or prescribing a particular way of life, perhaps on grounds of its beneficial consequences to oneself or others. Neither of these views would involve the believer in factual assertions about unusual causal interventions in nature, like miracles, or improbable factual beliefs about a life after death. One of the simplest expressions of this view was propounded by the Cambridge philosopher R. B. Braithwaite. He maintained that the biblical stories are probably literally false, but act as psychological aids to living an 'agapeistic' or loving life.[7] When one says 'God is love', one is evoking a positive feeling of love in the mind and commending loving conduct. One is not saying that there is a supernatural being which acts in certain loving ways.

A number of twentieth-century philosophers have attempted to develop what is often called a 'non-realist' or 'non-cognitive' view of God. A classic discussion is to be found in an article by Antony Flew.[8] Flew argues that believers would allow no evidence to count against their belief that 'God is love.' Thus, according to strongly empiricist criteria, that belief is meaningless. R. M. Hare responds that theistic belief is not an assertion of fact. It is a *blik*, an expression of a fundamental set of attitudes which is not subject to empirical testing.[9] Such a view is developed in a number of works by D. Z. Phillips. Following some of Wittgenstein's remarks in the *Philosophical Investigations*,[10] he denies the Braithwaite view that a religious form of life is adopted in order to lead to some independently conceived way of life, like 'agapism'. Religious concepts, especially that of God, actually specify what the religious way of life is to be. They have a primarily practical function, to provide the conceptual framework for a distinctive form of life.

[7] R. B. Braithwaite, *An Empiricist's View of the Nature of Religious Belief* (Cambridge: Cambridge University Press, 1955).

[8] A. G. N. Flew, Theology and Falsification, in A. G. N. Flew and A. MacIntyre, *New Essays in Philosophical Theology* (London: SCM Press, 1955), 96–9.

[9] R. M. Hare, 'Theology and Falsification', ibid. 99–103.

[10] L. Wittgenstein, *Philosophical Investigations* (Oxford: Basil Blackwell, 1953).

'They form the framework within which those who live by them assess themselves and the events that befall them'.[11]

Such views form part of a more general philosophical position that our forms of language define what the world is for us. There is no way of 'checking' language against a non-conceptualized world, for we bring language into all our knowledge of the world. So there may be a 'religious language-game', organized perhaps around the concept of God, which enables us to see and act in the world in a specific way. On such a view, the meaning of the word 'God' is not what it refers to—some independently checkable fact—but how it is used, what attitudes it enables us to adopt, and how it brings us to react to our experiences. This might be called, in a broad sense, a functionalist analysis of the concept of God. Truth, in general, is not correspondence with independently ascertainable facts. It is something like agreement in forms of language which enables us to 'play the life-game' successfully.

Functionalism maintains that all language is rooted in practical activities of one sort or another, and none has privileged access to reality. Thus language about God can be interpreted as a particular 'grammar' which expresses its own distinctive way of seeing the world. However, this interpretation has a price. God-language becomes just one language-game among others, and its truth does not lie in any absolute correspondence to objective reality. If one asks why one should adopt it, there is no answer to be given, except that it appeals to one, that it just 'seems right', or that it exercises compelling power.

Such a view of God is at odds with most religious tradition, so it is not a good analysis of what religious believers have actually thought. It entails that God does not, for example, literally answer prayer, raise the dead, or judge the world. It prompts the question of why one should adopt a religious way of life, when so many alternatives are available. And it seems to eliminate any cognitive element in religion, thereby devaluing the mystical traditions of prayer in the church.

Ian Ramsey attempted a more cognitive analysis.[12] He roots religious language in experiences of a special character, 'disclosure situations' of cosmic discernment and total commitment. One

---

[11] D. Z. Phillips, *Faith and Philosophical Enquiry* (London: Routledge, 1970), 68.
[12] I. T. Ramsey, *Religious Language* (London: SCM Press, 1957).

discerns a 'depth' in things, when one sees the empirical and something more that cannot be described. This disclosure involves and calls forth a commitment to a responsive way of life. There is a sort of factual claim here, and so a cognitive element, though it is admittedly 'odd', in that the experience is indescribable. 'Miracle' marks such a moment of disclosure, though it does not contravene the laws of nature. The way of life to which one commits oneself is not arbitrarily chosen, but is a response to a discernment which cannot be guaranteed, but which may be evoked by the use of God-language. On such a view, the word 'God' is used to express and evoke a depth disclosure which reorients one's life. All talk of God is symbolic, taken from contexts in which disclosures occur and used to evoke them in others, not to describe some supernatural being.

Ramsey's view is similar in many ways to that of Paul Tillich, who insists that God is not 'a being', one individual to be set over against others.[13] Rather, God is 'Being-itself', beyond subject–object duality, the abyss and ground of all beings. This 'God beyond god' is the ultimate reality in which the world is rooted, but it is not an individual. It is known in 'ecstatic experience', when one perceives the depth and power of being in and through all beings. For Tillich, all talk of God is symbolic, except for the sentence, 'God is Being-itself', which is itself primarily apophatic. He holds that any 'literal' talk about divine omnipotence and omniscience (about a being who can do anything and knows everything) must be abandoned. One must speak instead of 'the power of being which resists non-being . . . and is manifest in the creative process',[14] and of the fact that 'nothing falls outside the *logos* structure of being.'[15]

I think it would be fair to regard both Ramsey and Tillich as holding that the concept 'God' does refer to facts, but not in the same way as ordinary empirical discourse. In this, of course, they agree with the classical tradition of philosophical theism, both in its Thomist and Hegelian forms. They differ from the tradition in denying, or at least seeming to deny, that God has particular causal effects in the world, that God ever acts in ways which transcend the normal operation of the laws of nature, and that God will ensure a literal life after death—'participation in eternity' is not 'life hereafter'.[16] They differ, in other words, about the empirical features of religious belief. The fundamental question is whether

---

[13] Paul Tillich, *Systematic Theology* (3 vols.; Welwyn: Nisbet, 1968).
[14] Ibid. i. 303.   [15] Ibid. 309.   [16] Ibid. iii. 437.

empirical and causal elements can be eliminated from the concept of God, whether the idea does not essentially embody metaphysical claims, and whether the idea of objective truth (of 'realism') is not more important than such accounts imply.

THE RELATION OF PRACTICE AND THEORY IN RELIGION

If one takes the statement that 'God is love' in anything like its normal sense, it does seem to entail some straightforward factual assertions. It entails, for example, that there is a being who sympathizes with suffering, who delights in joy, and who will do whatever is most appropriate to achieve the well-being of creatures. The first two of these claims are primarily claims about the mental state of some being. It was always a peculiarity of the empiricist view that the mental states of others were so hard to verify or falsify that the best one could hope for was an indirect appeal to behaviour or verbal expressions of a mental state. It seems perfectly intelligible to suppose that some being could be in such mental states without exhibiting any behaviour assessable by us, or uttering anything we could understand. The existence of such a being would make a difference to the way things are, precisely by adding to reality a certain amount of sympathy or delight and the necessarily accompanying knowledge. But it need not be verifiable by humans at all. This is one of the points at which a verification theory of meaning collapses.

If this being is supposed to do something to achieve the well-being of creatures, such actions will be verifiable, at least in a weak sense. That sense may be very weak indeed. A being may act and even cause quite spectacular things to occur without being correctly or clearly identified. God's actions may be such that many may dispute whether they are actions at all, since there is no visible agent. One has to assess the nature of a process, and decide whether it is likely to be intentional and aimed at realizing a valued state. This may well be disputed. Even if it is thought likely that certain processes are purposive, it may not be clear that the agent is one spiritual being, God; or it may not be clear that, even if it is God, God is in fact an omnipotent and omniscient being. Thus many things may be unclear and disputable, as far as verification goes, while God may indeed be aiming at the well-being of creatures.

It may be thought, and I myself think, that if the ultimate basis of the universe is redemptive love, this entails that there will at some time exist a state in which creatures attain the fulfilment for which, on the hypothesis, they were created. This would be a form of what John Hick has called 'eschatological verification', when many creatures have a clear sense of the presence of God and share the divine happiness, without suffering or ignorance.[17] That does not help verification now, but it does show that the assertion that God is love can have a clear meaning, even on quite a strict verificationist view. But the possession of such meaning does involve a factual question, however hard it is to assess, of whether the universe consists of processes of a well-ordered purposive tendency which will result in the conscious realization of great values in creatures. If it does, that increases the probability that there is a God who has so ordered it, and who shares its sufferings and joys. But perhaps one could only advance that view with confidence if one believed that God has revealed the divine purpose, action, and sharing in finite experience in some appropriate way. This is precisely the claim that religious traditions make.

When Flew points out that Christians will not allow anything to count against their belief that God is love, he is pointing to the fact that Christians commit themselves in trust to the authenticity of the disclosure of the divine love in Jesus. Nevertheless, this trust could be undermined by a demonstration that there are no purposes in nature, that the idea of divine action is incoherent, that no values will be realized in the cosmic process, or that Jesus was a deceitful magician. No such demonstration is at all likely to be forthcoming. At best, one is likely to have conflicting assessments of the plausibility of competing hypotheses. In that situation, a Christian is justified in continuing to put trust in the divine self-disclosure in Jesus as the one who tips the balance of plausibility, even while admitting the possibility that one could be mistaken. Theists do disagree with atheists about the facts. Theists think there are natural processes which can be correctly interpreted as divine actions, that there is a life beyond death, and that there is a personal creator of all things.

One problem some thinkers have with this idea is that it makes religion too much like a very badly evidenced science. It makes factual claims which to many seem implausible and which it seems

[17] John Hick, *An Interpretation of Religion* (London: Macmillan, 1989), 177–80.

impossible to establish to the satisfaction of all competent observers. Anyway, is faith a matter of accepting some extra facts, whether probable or not? Christian believers are not indulging in speculative cosmology, and may well not be in the slightest interested in such matters. They are more likely to be concerned with coping with problems of suffering, guilt, and meaninglessness in their daily lives, and with whether there is a power to give strength, affirmation, and meaning to their lives. Religion is a primarily practical affair, a matter of value-commitments and of a personal search for happiness and fulfilment. In stressing that point, theologians like Tillich are entirely right.

It is very questionable, however, to suggest that such practical commitments carry no theoretical commitments at all. In fact it seems clear that they must do. If I am wondering how to live, it is important for me to know if there is some objective plan or purpose to which I should be conforming, or if the universe is indifferent to my decisions, so that it is entirely up to me to decide how I should live. If I want to know how to think about my dead friends, it is important to know whether I can believe they are living in another form of being, or if I must come to terms with the fact that they are non-existent. If I am wondering how to pray, it is important to know whether I am to seek a relationship with a personal being or whether that would be a delusion.

The resolution of certain factual questions about the way the world is—and that is metaphysics, in its most down-to-earth form— is an essential precondition for coming to fundamental decisions about how to live and react to my experiences from day to day. That does not mean I must take a course in metaphysics before I can decide whether to pray. The factual beliefs in question will most likely just be taken for granted by me. Nevertheless, it is an important fact that some such beliefs are presupposed in my practical commitments. If I get time to reflect, it may be sensible to reflect on them, to see whether they are really justifiable or not.

Most so-called 'radical theologians' do take a set of factual beliefs (a basic metaphysics of materialism, usually) for granted. That is, they assume that the laws of nature are impersonal and non-purposive, that life after death is impossible, and that there is no objective personal reality—God—to relate to.[18] It would not be fair

---

[18] See Don Cupitt, *Taking Leave of God* (London: SCM Press, 1980).

to say that they are *basing* their religious views on a speculative, probabilistic, and theoretical world-view, though it is fair to say that their views presuppose a world-view which, however obvious it seems to them, is in fact highly disputed and very much less than certain. Traditional theists similarly do not *base* their religious views on abstract speculations about the nature of the universe. But their views presuppose that an objective personal God, a purposive universe, and a life after death are all features of the universe in which we live.

Religious beliefs presuppose metaphysical beliefs. Whereas radical theologians tend to argue that the metaphysical beliefs should be taken from the sciences, and theology must be worked out in the light of whatever the sciences say, more orthodox theologians tend to give a positive role to revelation in suggesting some metaphysical beliefs—for example, the existence of a purposive creator, whose purpose is discerned in the history of Israel and her religious leaders, or the existence of a final goal of creation, discerned in the resurrection of Jesus. However, they would not typically take revelation to be culturally untainted and immunized from development by relation to other forms of knowledge. Thus the early theologians used the philosophy of Plato to integrate revealed truth into a more general world-view. Aquinas used Aristotle to do the same thing. While revelation may suggest a certain way of interpreting scientific knowledge, that knowledge may itself prompt important revisions in theological understanding. It is not a one-way process, and one major limitation of radical theology is that it makes it impossible to relate revelation positively to science in order to achieve a new understanding. Scientific knowledge is so different from theological, according to radical theologians, that the two cannot interact.

THE METAPHYSICAL PRESUPPOSITIONS OF RELIGIOUS COMMITMENT

Radical theologians seem to me to retain the most fundamental point about religious belief, that it is a matter of a transformation of the self to realize a state of great value. D. Z. Phillips says, 'Before a man can see this world in the light of a reality which is beyond it, he must undergo a radical change.'[19] He must turn from the temporal

---

[19] D. Z. Phillips, 'From World to God?', in *Faith and Philosophical Enquiry*, 50.

to the eternal, which involves dying to desire and attachment to worldly expectations. 'The man who loves God cannot be touched by the world.'[20] Religion is not primarily a theoretical matter, but a matter of commitment to certain possibilities of living in and seeing the world. 'Seeing that there is a God in this context is synonymous with seeing the possibility of eternal love.'[21] 'Coming to see that there is a God is not like coming to see that an additional being exists'; it 'involves seeing a new meaning in one's life'.[22]

Is this just a matter of taking up a practical attitude, of trying to be self-renouncing or non-attached and creative? Or is it a matter of seeing and reacting to *the world* in a certain way—with reverence, gratitude, trust, and hope? One could adopt the former interpretation, and simply say that one ought not to be selfish, but should be non-attached and loving, whatever happens. If one asks why one should be loving, one might simply appeal to an 'absolute requirement', or to a moral sense, or, more probably, to a simple acknowledgement that it is right to be loving. This would be a form of pure moralism, with religion as a set of psychological aids to such a way of life. Such a possibility exists, but it is doubtful whether the use of a concept like 'God' would be very helpful in sustaining it.

The word 'God' refers to the way the world is, to the aspects of being which properly may evoke awe, trust, and hope. The radical move is to imply that the way the world is perceived to be, in the religious use of language, has little connection with the way it is perceived to be in the sciences, for example. Perhaps the sciences adopt an objective set of attitudes to the world, seeking to describe its observable features dispassionately and neutrally. Religious discourse may express a reactive response to the world, as emotionally responded to and affectively engaged with. But it is the same world to which these attitudes are being directed.

If one is affectively responding to the world, it is a proper question to ask whether one's responsive attitudes are appropriate or not. The adoption of some attitudes—of reverence before the spectacle of one man torturing another—would be wholly inappropriate. Phillips reiterates that the religious attitude operates, whatever the world is

---

[20] Phillips, 'From World to God?', 57.
[21] D. Z. Phillips, 'Faith, Scepticism and Religious Understanding', in *Faith and Philosophical Enquiry*, 21.
[22] Ibid. 17.

like. But that makes religious faith indistinguishable from the adoption of any arbitrarily accepted attitude.

More deeply, there is a Christian understanding of love which sees it as lying in a participation in a wider reality which operates in and through personal life, not as a personally adopted policy of life. The most fundamental Christian responsive attitudes—the theological virtues—are traditionally said to be 'infused'. That is, they are not generated from the self, but are participated in by a self which is open to them. In this way, faith is always a reactive, never a purely theoretical matter. But it entails the theoretical belief that there is an objective love, and therefore an objective source of love, a personal being in some sense, which stands over against one. Just as entering into a reactive relation with another person entails the belief that the person exists, so entering into a reactive relation with the world which involves such attitudes as reverence, love, and trust entails the belief that the reality one encounters in and through the world is personal in nature, in some way. The radicals are right in emphasizing the priority, in religion, of self-transformation, and the necessity of coming to apprehend God through the adoption of appropriate reactive attitudes. But they are, in my view, mistaken in thinking that self-transformation can be simply adopted as a personal policy, without participation in an empowering and transforming reality. And they are mistaken in thinking that one can adopt reactive attitudes of reverence, gratitude, trust, and hope without the theoretical belief that there is a personal reality underlying the world which makes such attitudes appropriate. Theistic faith is not a matter of establishing, on purely theoretical grounds, that a particularly large and strange object, God, exists. But it is a matter, for most theists, of entering into a reactive relationship with a personal reality which is encountered in and through the natural world. This entails theoretical belief that such a personal reality objectively exists. Metaphysics is needed to show the coherence of the idea of such a reality, and the way in which it has consequences for non-religious areas of human enquiry.

It is very easy to slip from the view that religious faith is a matter of self-transformation, made possible by the adoption of general reactive attitudes, to the view that it is not a matter of theoretical belief in the existence of God. In an earlier book, *The Concept of God*, I wrote, 'To say that there is one transcendent God is not to say that there is one individual (among possible others) which exists beyond the physical universe . . . God is not an additional entity.'[23] This statement is defensible, if it is taken in the restricted sense of denying that God is an individual among others of the same kind ('an additional entity'). But it could easily be read to be denying that there is a transcendent individual who is God at all. In that sense it would both be mistaken, and in conflict with my repeated assertions, in the same book, that God is 'a transcendent, mediately revealed reality',[24] which clearly speak of a singular reality not confined in its being to the physical universe. This shows how easy it is to deny one is making metaphysical assertions, while all the time they are clearly present.

In a similar way, I wrote, 'Concepts of God cannot describe, even analogically. They should specify attitudes . . .'; and again, 'There is no question of the images referring to anything, in a straightforward sense.'[25] What I wished to deny was any natural mode of access to the inner being of God, and that would simply be an assertion of divine ineffability. But the words could reasonably be taken as an assertion of non-realism about God, as if to say that the concept of God does not refer at all, but has some other, purely attitude-specifying, humanly oriented or regulative use. The shadow of Kant looms over the words and deprives them, I would now say, of clarity. If concepts of God specify attitudes, one is committed to saying something about the object which properly specifies such attitudes; and indeed, I do speak of God as supreme value, cause of human liberation, as a unitary reality, and so on. We do not discover God as an object in the world. But we do discover God as a reality which is mediated through experience, precisely through our adoption of attitudes which make God's presence apprehensible. To say that the function of God-language is to specify attitudes is not to deny it objective reference, since to speak of how it is appropriate to react to God is precisely to say what God is truly like, at least in relation to us. A reaction against superficial and over-literal caricatures of theism has led to incautious statements which fail to capture the important element of metaphysical commitment which is involved in any reflective faith-commitment.

Gordon Kaufman does something similar in his book, *In Face of Mystery*. Professor Kaufman expounds and practices an attractive

---

[23] Keith Ward, *The Concept of God* (Oxford: Basil Blackwell, 1974), 117.
[24] Ibid. 205.   [25] Ibid.

view of theology as 'imaginative construction'. All theological concepts are, he says, human constructs. All pictures of God are limited and culture-relative, and one must never hold that one has finally grasped the mystery which is God. This leads him to reject the idea of God as a cosmic agent: 'The idea of a God who is "outside" the universe is scarcely thinkable today.'[26] 'It is not held that the ideal [to which one should be devoted] actually exists.'[27] And he is embarrassed about using words like 'purpose' with regard to the universe.[28] Yet he says that 'God stands for something objectively there.'[29] That 'something' is described, albeit hesitantly, as a 'serendipitous creativity working in and through' the cosmic process, an extra-human activity which produces humans, which draws them towards fulfilment, and which even 'claims our full loyalty and devotion.'[30] Whatever Kaufman says, these words carry clear logical entailments. 'Creativity', used as a singular noun, reifies the multifarious processes of cosmic history as a Power which works in and through them; it is, logically, an individual being. This being 'produces', 'draws', and 'sustains'; and these words entail some sort of agency not improperly describable as personal. Moreover, it is this being, not a non-existent construction, which is an object of unqualified devotion, which entails that it instantiates the highest values conceivable. Why should the reification of the cosmic process in this way be more intelligible than the reification of an existent cosmic agent? Why, indeed, should anyone wish to 'live and act in harmony with the basic . . . historical trajectories,'[31] much less be totally devoted to them?

It seems to me that Kaufman is not advocating a form of non-realism or constructivism in theology at all. Rather, he thinks of God as essentially involved in the cosmic process, as that which engenders it and draws it towards humanization; that is, as a fundamental unitary causal power of being. Moreover, this power is identified by him with the norm of humanization found in the Christ-event. God is both the creative energy and the ideal lure of the cosmos. But this is not a denial of a 'literally existing being', as he sometimes asserts; it is a reconception of just such a being. Metaphysics is there, in full force, exercising perhaps its most

[26] Gordon Kaufman, *In Face of Mystery* (Cambridge, Mass.: Harvard University Press, 1993), 271. [27] Ibid. 327. [28] Ibid. 304. [29] Ibid. 320. [30] Ibid. 9. [31] Ibid. 336.

important function of deconstructing anthropomorphic imagery, to expose its underlying truth-claims.

THE SENSE OF THE INFINITE

Metaphysics is therefore essential to religious faith. If one is to pursue a way of self-transcendence in relation to supreme value, then one must have some underlying idea of what that supreme value is, what sort of relation is possible with it, and what goal is reasonable for human striving. A religious metaphysical scheme is not adopted as a speculative theory, in order to explain or predict observable events. It is founded upon the teachings of prophets and teachers in a particular tradition of worship and prayer. Whereas the scientists' question is, 'Why do events occur as they do?', the religious question is, 'Is there any meaning or significance in my existence?' The scientist is looking for general principles which will account for complex reactions. The religious believer is looking for something, however vaguely conceived, which can give meaning and value to human life.

The believer is not looking for a theoretical explanation, but rather for some experience which will actually give meaning, which will endue life with significance. It must therefore be a transformative experience. It will not predict what is going to happen; it will rather empower one to face whatever happens with patience, courage, and hope. It will be an empowering experience of a reality which gives meaning to all one's experiences. That is the basic theistic goal, and the search for God may be defined as the search for a reality which can provide such an experience.

Religious prophets and teachers speak authoritatively from that experience. They speak as those who recognize a basic disease in the human condition, a sense of rebellion, estrangement, or ignorance of truth, and as those who have overcome it, or who have seen the way to its overcoming. Various images have been used to characterize the proper human relationship to the empowering reality, which prophets and mystics have experienced to some degree. One may speak of submission, reconciliation, or knowledge, of living relation or unity, of fulness of life or extinction of desire. All such concepts seek to evoke a sense of the authentic human response to a reality which can give supreme happiness in fulness of life.

Sometimes the existence of God has been treated as though it was a matter of inferring the existence of a supra-cosmic being by abstract argument. The 'Five Ways' of Thomas[32] have been treated in this way, and found wanting. It is better to regard such arguments as pointing to features of existence which may be capable of disclosing a supreme empowering value to one who seeks. Thus the infamously boring First Cause Argument does not provide a watertight deductive proof of anything. It asks one to contemplate the dependence of all finite things, their impermanence and lack of inherent power to exist. It asks one, by contrast, to frame the idea of a being which is self-existent, incapable of coming into being or passing away, a fulness of being which is unrestrictedly actual. Finally, it asks one to see all finite beings as generated from and interpenetrated by the unlimited self-existent, so that they become finite images of its infinite actuality. The conclusion of the argument is not a theoretical assent to the proposition that there must be some uncaused cause to start the universe going. It is an experiential realization that all finite beings are limited expressions of an infinite self-existent power which has the character of pure intelligence and bliss, and which can be known in and through all finite things. As E. L. Mascall puts it, 'syllogistic statement was primarily a device for persuading our minds to apprehend finite beings in their radical finitude.'[33]

In a similar fashion, the other 'ways for demonstrating the existence of God' state that God is of supreme value, is necessarily what it is, and sets goals of participated value for every created universe. They do not simply *state* that; they seek to bring one to sense that reality, by seeing finite things in the appropriate way, *sub specie aeternitatis*. These are not demonstrations, in the sense of deductive syllogisms, comprehensible by any rational agent. They 'demonstrate', or make clear, the nature of God as the Infinite mediated in and through finite beings, and apprehensible as such by those who are open, through self-renunciation, to the sense of transcendent being.

Friedrich Schleiermacher was bringing this point out when he spoke of religion as 'the sense of absolute dependence',[34] and as 'the

---

[32] Thomas Aquinas, *Summa Theologiae* Ia 8. 2 a. 3 (Blackfriars edn.; London: Eyre and Spottiswoode, 1963–81).

[33] E. L. Mascall, *He Who Is* (London: Darton, Longman and Todd, 1966), 192.

[34] Friedrich Schleiermacher, *The Christian Faith*, ch. 1, para. 4 (Edinburgh: T. & T. Clark, 1989 1st pub. 1830), 8. 12.

sensibility and taste for the infinite'.[35] What has misled many about his characterization of religion is the thought that religion is merely a matter of the occurrence of certain feelings or states of mind, without objective reference. This is clearly not what Schleiermacher meant. For him, the sense of dependence was an 'intuition' (*Anschauung*) with epistemic content. Feeling is the proper mode of apprehending the objective reality of the self-existent, not a purely internal mental state.

The disadvantage of this way of putting the point is that it seems to make religious experience almost wholly aesthetic, without essential connection to intellectual belief or practical action. Again, however, Schleiermacher's aim was to stress that religious belief is not founded on a process of speculative inference or, as Kant had argued, as a back-up for moral commitment. It is based on the sense for the Infinite; but that sense immediately entails the beliefs that there is a self-existent reality, that all finite realities are not self-existent, and that consciousness of the Infinite (which is equivalent, in its fullest sense, to identity with God) is the highest form of human consciousness. It also immediately implies a revaluation of all finite aims and concerns, as they are placed in the context of this 'God-consciousness', and so it has practical implications, though it is not itself a moral principle.

THE NECESSITY OF THEOLOGICAL REALISM

Once one has the idea of a self-existent supreme value, it is natural to go on to explore the general relation of this value to the physical universe, and the forms of conscious relation to it which are possible for human beings. Within the Semitic tradition, the supreme value was apprehended by the prophets primarily as a moral demand for justice and the promise of a society of peace. The supreme value was to become embodied in a society of persons. In contrast with this future ideal, present society was seen to fall under judgement, as unjust and violent. The prophets proclaimed judgement on the present, the necessity of repentance, and the promise of a future fulfilment through the power of the Ideal. Within this complex of ideas, God was construed as the Holy Will, whose nature is manifest

---

[35] Friedrich Schleiermacher, *On Religion*, 2nd Speech, tr. Richard Crouter (Cambridge: Cambridge University Press, 1988), 103.

in the beauty of the natural world, who shapes history as the arena of its demands and promises, who is the Just Judge and Liberating Saviour.

Within the Indian tradition, the supreme value was apprehended by the teachers of wisdom as Pure Mind, as unlimited intelligence and bliss, perfect and complete in itself. The supreme value is the one ultimate reality, and it can be known by an overcoming of desire and escape from the wheel of suffering. The present world emanates from the Real, but is itself relatively unreal, bound by desire. The teachers proclaimed that suffering results from attachment and selfish desire, and taught the way to overcome ignorance of the Real. Within this complex of ideas, God is conceived as the Self of All, manifest in the universe and yet concealed by finite desires, knowable as the non-dual consciousness which is hidden in the heart of all dualities.

There are many varieties of interpretation possible within these very general traditions. God may be interpreted as Pure Will, issuing commands which are simply to be obeyed, and determining everything that happens in every last detail. The Supreme Self may be interpreted as a wholly non-dual Absolute, inactive and without qualities, knowledge of which requires detachment from all likes and dislikes. Others may interpret God as one whose inherent value attracts beings to itself in love, and who leaves beings free to create their own futures. The Supreme Self may also be interpreted as supreme wisdom, compassion, and bliss, which is manifested in all finite things, in so far as they overcome purely selfish passion.

The theologians, from both Semitic and Indian traditions, whom I have considered, though they were chosen simply on the grounds that they would probably be selected within their own traditions as among the outstanding theologians of the twentieth century, all interpret the Supreme in the latter, more persuasive and responsive set of ways. In doing so, they are seeking to elucidate the nature of the reality which is apprehended in worship and prayer, as that which is knowable in and through the universe, in the light of knowledge of the universe which has increased greatly since the seventeenth century.

The hypothesis of God is not a scientific one, but it does affect the way the universe is. Consequently, growing knowledge of the nature of the universe will modify, or may confirm or undermine, the theistic hypothesis. Specifically, if theism is true, all finite things must be refracted images of a greater, self-existent fulness of being, which gives purpose and value to the universe. The articulation of this purpose and value is the task of theology, working both from the revelatory basis of religions and from general knowledge of the nature of the universe. Conceptions of the self-existent will change, as different perceptions of purpose and value within the universe become plausible. Yet the primary perception of a self-existent foundation of all beings will also guide one's general perception of the character of the basic laws and principles of the physical universe.

One may with justification be very hesitant about one's ability to achieve any finally formulated truths in this process. But to avoid the issue by isolating religion in a privileged realm beyond criticism is also to deprive it of its proper function, which is to relate human life to a perception of things as they most truly are. Non-realist views of God fail to see the essential connection between the appropriate adoption of specific reactive attitudes to experienced reality and metaphysical beliefs about the character of that reality. The theistic view is that the whole physical universe depends upon and mediates a reality of supreme power and value, which can be apprehended in the empowering experience of salvation, liberation, or release. The theological task is to fashion forms of speech which will communicate an authentic sense of the object of such experience. The theological attempt to speak of God will not easily claim finality, and the theologians considered in Part I illustrate how new views may emerge in old traditions, in response to new perceptions of the context of human existence. Yet theists are committed to the metaphysical hypothesis of one self-existent and supremely valuable source of all beings. To abandon it is to abandon any grip that religious thought has on reality.

6

Metaphor and Analogy

APOPHATIC THEOLOGY

Theologians are committed to articulating a coherent concept of God
as a self-existent supreme power and value. Yet is it possible to speak
of such a reality in language which, after all, is primarily suited to
refer to more mundane finite things? It may seem not, and it has
become widespread in modern theology to say that all talk of God is
metaphorical. This view, I suggest, stems from a failure to analyse
the notion of metaphor in sufficient detail. A metaphor is a figure of
speech which describes one thing in terms which primarily describe
another.[1] One has to understand the primary use before one can
understand the metaphorical use; and one has to realize that a
straightforward, or literal, description is not being attempted. It is
essential to the function of metaphor that there must be a literal
description, which in this case is negated. Metaphor is parasitic upon
literal description.

Could there be something—perhaps God?—which is such that
every statement about it is metaphorical? If so, one would be saying
that no literal statement can be made about God. Paul Tillich holds
that there is one, and only one, literal statement about God, that God
is Being-itself: 'God is being-itself or the absolute. However, after
this has been said, nothing else can be said about God as God which
is not symbolic.'[2] Could one go even further, and deny all literal
statements about God? Some of the remarks of apophatic theologians
in many religious traditions suggest that one could. The statement of
the Upanishads, '*neti, neti*', 'not this, not this', is often quoted.[3]

---

[1] A good account of metaphor and its religious usage is given by Janet Martin
Soskice, *Metaphor and Religious Language* (Oxford: Clarendon Press, 1985).
[2] Paul Tillich, *Systematic Theology* (Welwyn: Nisbet, 1968), i. 265.
[3] *Brihadaranyaka Upanishad*, 4. 5. 15, in R. C. Zaehner (trans.), *Hindu Scriptures*
(London: Dent, 1966), 75.

Sankara asserts that of Brahman itself nothing can be said.[4] The *Tao Te Ching* begins with the statement, 'The Tao that can be expressed is not the eternal Tao.'[5]

There is a strong tradition in Christianity, too, of the ineffability of God, the utter transcendence of the divine nature over any human thought. Basil the Great writes, 'It is from his activities (*energeia*) that we come to know our God, while we do not claim to come anywhere near his actual essence (*ousia*).'[6] So it may seem that it is a common teaching of many religious traditions that the Supreme is wholly ineffable, and cannot be described at all. But such an appearance is deceptive.

It is difficult to know exactly what the Cappadocian Fathers had in mind when they distinguished the nature from the operations of God. But since a question about the *ousia* of something is often a request to be told the sort of thing it is, one may take the divine essence to be that which is definitive of God as God really is, that which makes this entity God and not something else. When one asks about the operations of God, however, one is asking about the things God does, or about how God relates to the world, about the actions in the world of a being of a certain nature.

Obviously, the actions of a being express its nature to some extent. Some philosophers would hold that it is my actions which define my nature, what I am. But it is quite conceivable that a being might conceal its nature or act in ways which reveal, at best, only a small part of what it is. Suppose, for example, we meet a being from another galaxy which appears to us only as a blob of light. It causes systematic changes in its environment, which we conceive as actions, since they seem to exhibit purpose and design. Yet we may have no idea of what is going on in its 'mind', whether it has thoughts and feelings like ours, or how much about it there is that is invisible to us and that we cannot understand. All we see are the apparently purposive changes in the world around it. We might say that these changes do show how that being wishes to relate to us. In one sense,

---

[4] 'Brahman is being devoid of form' (Sankara, *The Vedanta Sutras*, trans. George Thibaut, in *Sacred Books of the East*, ed. Max Müller (Oxford: Clarendon Press, 1900), xxxiv. 307.

[5] *Tao Te Ching*, trans. Ch'u Ta-Kao (London: Mandala Books, 1982), 17.

[6] Basil, Letter 234, in M. Wiles and M. Santer, (eds. and trs.), *Documents in Early Christian Thought* (Cambridge: Cambridge University Press, 1975), 11.

then, they do show something of the nature of the being; they show that the being can and wishes to relate to us in these ways. But they may not show what that being is like 'from the inside', or when it is not relating to us. Its inner processes may remain quite mysterious to us.

It does not seem to be an absurd supposition that there may be something which human concepts simply cannot describe at all, if it is so different from anything we know that we are at a loss to know how to describe it. However, even in saying, if we do, that it is a 'thing' and that it is different from all other things, we are saying something about it. Basil was not supposing that the essence of God was unknowable, in the sense that it might be blind energy or a malevolent committee of demons for all we know. If God is indescribable by us, it is because God is a reality of greater, not lesser, intelligibility, beauty, and bliss than any we can imagine.

Theists get to the notion of divine ineffability by starting with the power and wisdom of a personal creator, as seen in the world; or by starting with personal experience of a presence which seems to be both awe-inspiring and mysterious. Only when one qualifies these initial concepts by successively denying all limitations on the Creator and denying the adequacy of all specific descriptive terms to characterize the object of experience does one come to say that God is ineffable. In other words, the idea of 'the ineffable God' is not simply the idea of something unknowable. Since it is necessarily true that whatever is unknowable is unknown, this would entail that such a God was quite unknown. But it is essential to theism to claim that one *knows* the ineffable God; one is acquainted with what is beyond understanding. One can put this by stressing that the idea of the ineffable is not just of some ineffable thing or other; it is the idea of an ineffable *God*, that is, of a creator truly known to us in experience, yet whose essential nature transcends our understanding. Certain statements, for Basil, and for all orthodox Christians, are unequivocally true of God—that God is more perfect than human beings, that God is one, and that God is Trinitarian in being. It is just that one cannot comprehend what such a being is really like, in the fullness of its reality. It is misleading therefore, even though they said it themselves, to say that, according to Basil the Great or the apophatic theologians, we have a purely negative knowledge of God.

Immanuel Kant perhaps came closest to having such a doctrine of negative knowledge in the *Critique of Pure Reason*, when he argued that, because of the Antinomies of Reason, we can know that the real world is not as we suppose it to be, though we can be certain that there is a real world.[7] The 'proof', repeated in various forms by many later Idealist philosophers, shows that this world is contradictory (that we can prove contradictory propositions to be true of it), and therefore we can know it is not real. In Kant's case, one can resolve the antinomies of space and time by positing that they are not objective realities, but forms of sensory experience, from which it follows that reality must be positively unlike them—but, of course, we cannot know in what way.

It is rather unsatisfactory to say merely that reality is completely indescribable, since it seems to get one no further towards knowing what reality is. At that point, the antinomies of freedom and necessity, and of contingency and necessity, suggested to Kant that, though one could *know* nothing of the real world, one was forced to think of it in a specific way, as a necessary demand of Reason. One had to postulate God, freedom, and immortality for practical purposes to do with the regulative employment of the Understanding in respect of the phenomenal world.[8] So Reason compels one to think the unknowable in a specific manner. One has no knowledge of it, theoretically speaking; but one has a thought of it, which one must adopt for practical purposes. The justification for thinking of the unknowable in a specific way is that Reason compels us to do so, as a condition of the possibility of scientific investigation into and of moral action in the world.

For this argument to succeed, one must show both that phenomenal reality, as ordinarily conceived, is contradictory, and that some urgently practical and totally unavoidable necessity compels one to think of reality in a specific way. It has to be said that few have been convinced that Kant succeeded in either of these tasks; and it seems likely that his concept of a noumenal or intelligible world, as the very name implies, is a hangover from the pre-Critical philosophy which permitted real and indeed certain knowledge of the intelligible realm, which was in no doubt that reality was 'intelligible' or noumenal, and saw the phenomenal world as a sort of confused appearance of what only pure Reason could

---

[7] Immanuel Kant, *Critique of Pure Reason* trans. N. Kemp Smith, (London: Macmillan, 1952; 1st pub. 1781), Transcendental Dialectic, bk. ii, ch. 2.

[8] Ibid. Appendix to the Transcendental Dialectic.

truly discern.[9] Divorced from that full-blooded metaphysic, Kant's demythologizing of the noumenal is likely to seem rather like the Cheshire Cat's smile—no longer fully appealing once the cat itself has gone.

I therefore doubt whether a Kantian philosophy can provide an adequate construal of divine ineffability, in its idea of a wholly unknowable reality which one is nevertheless compelled to speak of in a particular way. If reality is completely unknowable, no cognitive claims can be made about it at all, not even that it exists, or that it is unitary rather than plural, or that it is good rather than bad, or that it is the cause of phenomenal experience. The concept of noumenal reality seems itself to be incoherent. Further, the reasons Kant gave for thinking that the regulative idea of God was practically necessary are generally judged to be almost wholly unconvincing. He thought we needed to postulate a God in order to view the world as an ordered systematic whole; but physicists can apparently dispense with God without too much regret. He thought we needed to postulate God in order to reinforce our moral commitment; but moralists tend to think of such an appeal to God as an abandonment of morality for the sake of long-term prudence. We do not need to postulate God to back up any of our independent practical commitments. We do not even need God in order for us to be happy, altruistic, and psychologically well-balanced, as any Freudian analyst will testify. The Kantian system attempts to provide a pragmatic justification for a realist ontology, but it only succeeds in emptying the real of content—since nothing true can be said of it— and reducing justification to a matter of personal preference—since, once pure Reason is deprived of its apodictic force, we can apparently say anything as long as it 'works for us'.

SPEAKING LITERALLY ABOUT GOD

John Hick uses the Kantian distinction of noumenal and phenomenal to support his claim that the Divine Reality is unknowable, though it appears in various forms in various cultures.[10] Like Kant, however, his words show that he does not really believe this. He does claim to know some things about the Real—that it is a supremely valuable

---

[9] See Keith Ward, *The Development of Kant's View of Ethics* (Oxford: Basil Blackwell, 1972), ch. 1.

[10] John Hick, *An Interpretation of Religion* (London: Macmillan, 1989), 4.

reality;[11] that it makes possible, and is thus causally effective in bringing about an 'unlimitedly good end-state';[12] that it manifests itself to human experience in a number of ways which are not wholly misleading.[13] He also wishes to rule out some alleged experiences of the Real as inadequate—experiences of the Real as malevolent, as having no causal effects on the future, or as entailing no ontological claims about how the world is. So he does work with a criterion of adequacy, embodying ideas of moral demand and promise for the future, and with a concept of the Real as one supreme cause. He is a theist who is concerned to show how God may be experienced in many traditions, which partially show aspects of the divine being. Some of these ways are more adequate than others, though one might be unwise to claim that one was wholly adequate and all the others quite inadequate by comparison. It is, however, quite clear that Professor Hick believes there is one supremely valuable reality which can bring us into conscious relationship with itself, a relationship which will realize human hopes for a fulfilled and happy existence. His complete rejection of non-realism in favour of some form of 'cosmic optimism'[14] shows his commitment to ontological realism, and against the view that we can know nothing of what is truly real.

Since Professor Hick is a religious realist, he does not really believe in a noumenal reality at all as something of which one can say absolutely nothing. He rather believes that there is a reality of supreme value, love, and power (for it can and will bring us all to final happiness by knowing and loving it). This is a definite claim to knowledge of the Real. It is quite consistent to go on to say that our knowledge of the Real is very inadequate and may well be mistaken in many details. It will be affected by our culture, our background knowledge, and temperament. Now we see in a glass darkly, though we hope to see face to face; but at least we claim to know there is a face, however dimly discerned, to be seen.

Kant's complex doctrine of a regulative use of concepts, in accordance with which we think of a reality which is theoretically completely unknown to us, does not at all solve the problem of how one can speak coherently of God. Nor does it preserve the mystery of the divine being, since it reduces that being to a mere peg on which

---

[11] 'An ultimate unity of reality and value' (ibid. 33).
[12] Ibid. 180.   [13] Ibid. 247.   [14] Ibid. 208.

to hang a few useful devices for helping us achieve our chosen goals. The mystery of God is, after all, best preserved by the orthodox claim that God's essence is ineffable, meaning not that one knows nothing at all about it, but that one admits that in its perfection, its value, and its power it transcends our understanding. The divine being in its essential constitution as self-existent is wholly beyond our comprehension; but it is truly known to us in the relationships which it establishes with the created order.

The incoherence of a doctrine of the total ineffability of God can easily be shown. If I say, 'There exists something of which I can say nothing', I have contradicted myself. If I say, 'X exists', I am saying something about X. So, if I say, 'There exists an X, of which I can say nothing', that entails, 'I am saying something about that of which I can say nothing'; and that is a straightforward contradiction. Even overlooking that fact, if I say 'X exists', but know nothing else about X, then I have communicated nothing significant. X might be a colour, a number, a person, a wavelength, even a dream. If I have no idea at all of what X is, there is no point in saying it exists.

If one speaks of the ineffability of God, one is using the word 'God', and the inescapable fact is that the word has a meaning already. I am not free to make it mean whatever I want, like Humpty Dumpty. One thing that it means, according to the *OED*, is 'an adored or worshipped object'. To adore is to attribute value or to acknowledge that some object is of supreme value. Thus in saying that God exists, one is saying that some object of supreme value exists. Is that a literal truth? In saying that X has supreme value one is saying at least that X is the proper object of attention, delight, and satisfaction. That is the literal meaning of 'is of supreme value'. Does one wish to deny that literal meaning of God, in any sense? Presumably not, since that is precisely what one does wish to say of God, that God is a proper, indeed the only proper, object of worship.

Thus if one uses the word 'God' in its proper sense, one is committed to at least one literally true statement about God, namely, that God is an object of supreme value. But this entails many other literally true statements. For example, if one thinks that anything is a value, then God cannot be of less value than that. God cannot, for example, be less powerful than any other being or less knowing that any other being. That God is more powerful and knowing than any other being is a literally true statement, entailed by one of the simplest definitions of God.

GOD AS BEING-ITSELF

Tillich's attempts to evade this point are unconvincing. It is instructive to consider what Tillich says about God. He accepts that there is one literal ('completely non-symbolic') truth about God, that God is Being-itself. But he is prepared to accept a number of synonyms for 'Being-itself', including 'the absolute',[15] 'the ground of being', 'the power of being',[16], 'the ground of being and meaning'.[17] Common to all these expressions is the term 'being', the present participle of the verb 'to be', which can be used as a noun, meaning 'something which exists'. However, Tillich writes that 'It is as atheistic to affirm the existence of God as it is to deny it.'[18] He wishes to deny that God is '*a* being', alongside others or above others. God is not a finite being of the same category as others, even of the best of them. What is required is 'a level qualitatively different', so that one can speak of 'infinite or unconditional power and meaning'.[19]

It seems clear that Tillich does not wish to use 'Being-itself' to refer to an object which exists. He wishes to speak of 'the power of being in everything and above everything'. Indeed the term 'Being-itself' requires so many other statements to unpack its meaning that it is misleading to say there is only one non-symbolic statement about God. It requires, for example, the assertion that there is a power which is in everything, giving everything existence; the assertion that there is a power above everything, 'beyond potentiality and actuality'; and the assertion that this is one and the same power. The picture is that every finite thing receives its existence as something that is not essential to it. 'Existence' is viewed as a power which gives being to everything, but which is more than (is 'above') all finite things. This is an essentially Platonic idea of 'being' as the most fundamental abstract property, which enables potential things actually to exist. It is very like Aquinas's term '*Actus Purus*', the pure actuality without potentiality, except that for Tillich 'being' is presumably in everything that is, as well as unrestrictedly itself. Tillich modifies Aquinas's picture of unrestricted being, which excludes everything finite, by making being include everything

---

[15] Tillich, *Systematic Theology*, i. 265.   [16] Ibid. 261.
[17] Ibid. 262.   [18] Ibid. 263.   [19] Ibid. 261.

finite. But the sense in which this inclusion is to be understood remains very unclear.

Tillich is proposing a strictly ungrammatical use of language to try to break through the normal subject–object pattern of language and perception. He seeks to generate a vision of all things as participating in, and mediating, a 'power' which is beyond yet in them, and which is self-existent. It may seem odd to call this a straightforward 'literal' truth, since the term 'being' is used in a distinctive way, and it has no normal usage to which this is similar. It is a predicate (as in 'X exists, or has being') used as a noun. This could be seen as simply vacuous; but it might be seen as a way of evoking a vision of the finite in the light of the Infinite. The use of 'infinite' in this way is another example of the reification of a property without one precise meaning, but with connotations of 'endlessness' or 'uncountability', to evoke a sense of that which is unconditioned by anything other than itself. It is used in this sense by both Schleiermacher and Tillich. Such terms are not being used metaphorically, since it is not false that God is a power giving existence to everything and being self-existent. So it is not incorrect to call this use literal, since it reifies verbs or adjectives to refer to 'that which is self-existent, or unconditioned'. But this is a special and unique use of language to sponsor a certain unusual way of seeing the world. Its terms are being used, one might say, analogically, their meaning being intensified and broadened to refer to a reality which is at the limits of human comprehension. It is not being said that God is a being very like others, which possesses a property (of 'existing') which is like that property (if it is a property) possessed by other beings. It is being said that there is a unique form of unrestricted, necessary existence. We can frame such a concept, but it lies at the limits of intelligibility (some would say beyond them). Perhaps one could call terms like 'Being', and similar terms like 'the Infinite', 'the Eternal', or 'Absolute Spirit', iconic analogies. They push linguistic expressions out of their normal grammatical usage altogether, to point to a new way of seeing and interpreting experience. They are 'iconic', because they aim to bring one to see finite beings as icons, or images, participating in self-existent Being.

To give it some content, the term 'being' needs to be complemented by other terms, and Tillich, as I have noted, does this. He uses the terms 'power', 'meaning', 'absolute', 'ground', 'infinite', and 'unconditional', too. These qualify the term 'being'. Thus to speak of 'power' is to speak of that which is able to act, of that which has strength or force. A common root of these connotations is that of causal efficacy. The power of being is that which is causally efficacious in bringing things into existence, which, as Tillich puts it, 'resists non-being'. By using this term, he reifies the predicate of 'existence' and attributes to it active causal efficacy. It is what makes everything to be what it is, what is not in the power of anything else.

God is an ultimate or unconditional power. That is, nothing external limits God in any way; 'God is his own fate';[20] God is the only cause of what happens to God, and causes everything else to be as it is. This looks like a fairly traditional statement that God is the prime uncaused cause of all things; 'God is being-itself', it seems, entails 'God is omnipotent cause of all.' Why, then, is Tillich uneasy with such a statement? It is because he thinks that the ascription of any property to God renders God unacceptably finite. 'As the power of being, God transcends every being.'[21] But what does 'transcend' mean here? It has a double meaning; that which is beyond, in a factual sense, and that which is higher, in an evaluative sense. If one thing transcends another, it is being said to be of greater value than that other. Thus God is not merely different in kind from any finite thing; God is greater, perhaps infinitely greater, in value than any finite thing. God is 'the creative and abysmal ground of being'; God infinitely transcends all finite beings, while they all participate in God's power.

At this point, Tillich calls the phrase 'creative and abysmal ground of being' a symbolic statement.[22] Yet it is merely a spelling-out of what is involved in Tillich's use of the phrase, 'God is being-itself.' It merely asserts that God is the power which gives being to all things and that God is not conditioned by any other thing. It is therefore a non-symbolic statement. When Tillich calls a statement symbolic, he means, in part, that 'its proper meaning is negated by that to which it points.'[23] But what is the proper meaning of 'God is the creative ground of being'? It has no proper, usual, meaning. It is a term of art, invented precisely to point to a unitary self-existent cause of all finite beings.

[20] Tillich, *Systematic Theology*, i. 265.
[21] Ibid. 263.
[22] Ibid. 264.
[23] Ibid. 265.

DIALECTICAL THEISM

From what Tillich denies, it is apparent that he thinks God is a being whose existence fulfils all essential divine potentialities. Being beyond the finite, there is no possibility in God. The divine nature is 'above existence'. It is 'beyond finitude and infinity', beyond potentiality and actuality, and is not conditioned by anything other than itself. He accepts that the categories of substance and cause are used of God. But, he says, 'the category of causality is being denied while it is being used',[24] since God does not belong to the series of causes and effects. This again seems to be false. 'God is a cause' is not false as such. It is only false that God is a member of a series of finite causes and effects. The category is not being denied; it is being extended, to speak of a cause which is not itself caused.

Tillich says that God 'has the power of determining the structure of everything that has being'.[25] God is not subject to this structure; so God is that power which determines the nature and existence of everything. That is one definition of omnipotence: God determines the nature of everything other than God, and nothing determines the nature of God. God's nature may have limits, for all we know; but if so, they are internal to God. God is the only source of all beings.

Why, then, does Tillich reject 'a highest being who is able to do whatever he wants'?[26] Because it *makes God a finite being*, who stands before many possibilities and asks which God should actualize. Placing potentiality in God, it makes God *less than pure being*. Rather, God is 'the power of being', transcendent over the creative process, but manifest in it. Now is there a real difference between 'the ultimate power of being', and 'a highest being who is able to do what he wants'? The former expression abstracts and reifies the concept of existence; it gives to 'Existence' a power which is unconditioned, that is, a sole determination of all finite beings. What is the difference between this and 'a highest being'? None at all, unless the highest being is construed as a finite object alongside others, with contingent desires and a power of arbitrary decision. But that is simply an inadequate idea of a highest being. The highest being, properly construed, is the sole source of all other being, and its desires and decisions are not arbitrary, but rooted in its essential nature. What Tillich is doing is to distinguish between a very

[24] Ibid. 264. [25] Ibid. 265. [26] Ibid. 303.

inadequate idea of God as omnipotent, and a more abstract formulation of the same idea. It is misleading to construe this by saying that every statement about God is symbolic.

There is a substantive issue of interpretation, however. It is whether the idea of God has room for potentiality; whether, in any sense, God falls under a subject–object scheme.[27] Tillich wants to say that God transcends all categories; but, of course, he cannot consistently do that, if he means that every categorical term must be denied of God. That would make God wholly ineffable.

Does God transcend the category of being? In one sense, yes. God does not exist in the same way that tables or people exist. But in another sense, God not only exists, but is the only true self-existent. If one said, 'God does not exist', and meant, 'There is no God', that would be false. If one meant, 'God does not exist as we do', that is true. Therefore 'God exists' will be true, though it will not apply to a property familiar to us in other cases. The proper term for such a use of language is 'analogical'. Some terms apply properly to God, though we cannot imagine or understand what the reality to which they apply is really like. Some terms will be literally true of any being to which analogy applies. It is literally true that 'it is false that the greatest power in the created universe is the greatest power there is.' It is literally true that 'the whole universe depends for its existence on something other than itself.'

We can say of a beetle, 'It has experiences', even while having no idea at all of what its experiences are like. It is just that we believe the environment produces some affective state in beetles. So we can say, 'God knows all things', while having no idea of what it is like to know all things. We just believe that nothing is unknown to God. Is it literally true that God knows all things? I think one should say that it is, without asserting that the divine knowledge is like ours or even comprehensible to us. God does not *transcend* the category of knowledge, though knowledge in God is very different than it is in us.

What Tillich is really doing is to stress the difference between the divine being and any finite being, and to warn us against thinking of God as a very great member of the class of finite beings. But he is led to make statements about God which are not in fact licensed by his arguments. This comes out clearly in his discussion of eternity.[28]

---

[27] Tillich, *Systematic Theology*, i. 309.   [28] Ibid. 304 ff.

Eternity is, he says, 'neither timelessness nor the endlessness of time'. It is 'the transcendent unity of the dissected moments of existential time'. God includes temporality, but an endless 'dissected time' would be condemnation for those who had to endure it. One can use the symbol of an eternal present, 'moving from past to future but without ceasing to be present'. The future must be open; yet God must be able to anticipate every possible future. Time must be taken up into a unity which transfigures it, without depriving it of creative openness. It sounds as if this is really a doctrine of a temporal God, without the defects of finite temporality.

But Tillich elsewhere denies this. 'To speak of a becoming God . . . subjects God to a process which has the character of a fate or which is completely open to the future and has the character of an absolute accident.'[29] God must then unite both pure being and becoming in a form of being beyond both. The problem now is that apophatic theology has led to contradiction. The divine life is 'beyond the distinction between potentiality and actuality'.[30] Whereas Thomism allocated God to the realm of pure actuality, without any potentiality, Tillich wishes to place both actuality and potentiality in God, in an unresolved dialectic which points— 'symbolically'—not to a highest being, but to the power of Being-itself.

In the introduction to the second volume of *Systematic Theology*, Tillich asserts that he wishes to commend a form of theism which is 'ecstatic', beyond naturalism and supranaturalism. The supra-naturalist view sees God as 'a being, the highest being . . . alongside and above' all other beings.[31] This view, he holds, brings God under the categories of finitude, placing the 'divine world' alongside the natural, determining a beginning and end to divine creativity, making God a cause alongside others, and attributing individual substance to God.

The question is whether Tillich in fact manages to avoid, whether he can possibly manage to avoid, a supranaturalist view himself. He asserts that there is an 'infinite distance between the whole of finite things and their infinite ground',[32] that the created is 'substantially independent of the divine ground',[33] yet that it remains 'in substantial unity with it'. Ironically, he uses the spatial metaphor of

[29] Ibid. 274.   [30] Ibid. 311.   [31] Ibid. ii. 6.
[32] Ibid. 7.   [33] Ibid. 9.

distance and the concept of independent substance to assert his own view; presumably, behind the metaphor lies the literal truth that the ground of being is different in kind from created things, and the concept of substantial independence is exactly what underlies the metaphor of a being 'alongside the world'. If one speaks of a highest being alongside the world, the spatial imagery expresses that there is an unconditioned reality which is substantially independent of created reality. Tillich just is a supranaturalist, and is trying to draw a distinction which does not exist.

TILLICH AND SUPRANATURALISM

Does this make God finite, or limit God? In one sense, yes. As Tillich sees, 'the theologian cannot escape making God an object in the logical sense of the word.'[34] If one is to speak of God at all, one must treat God as an object of reference, as something that can be referred to. But he thinks that God nevertheless must transcend the basic subject–object structure of being. How could one speak of such a reality? Tillich's answer is—symbolically. Unfortunately his doctrine of symbolic speech remains sketchy at best. In the second volume he says that a symbol uses an ordinary meaning, which is 'both affirmed and denied'.[35] This makes a symbol sound like a metaphor. Its literal meaning is denied. But it represents 'the power and meaning of what is symbolised through participation'. In his most extended discussion of the topic in *Systematic Theology*,[36] he says that a symbol 'points to something beyond itself', and participates in the power of the Divine. Such participation results from the occurrence of some 'revelatory situation', in which a person is grasped by ultimate concern. In a revelatory disclosure, some term drawn from ordinary discourse is given a new, transformed meaning, and can then be used to express or evoke a similar disclosure for others. The symbol is thus not descriptive, but evocative; as such, symbols can grow or die, not through speculative analysis, but through types of experience which they evoke or fail to evoke. To turn symbols into descriptions of a supranatural realm is to miss their meaning, to misuse them and sever them with their roots in religious experience.

---

[34] Tillich, *Systematic Theology*, i. 191.   [35] Ibid. ii. 10.   [36] Ibid. i. 264 ff.

Tillich is right to make the point that religion is not just a form of speculative metaphysics, but lives in human experiences which liberate from self and anxiety and give a courage to be, by participation in a reality of ultimate power and value. As I argued in the previous chapter, metaphysical questions cannot be avoided as to what this power and value is, and what its relation is to the physical universe. Tillich does not avoid such questions. On the contrary, he places his view of religious language within a rather complex analysis of the basic ontological structure of being (the subject–object structure) and its polar elements.

The critical question is how one can distinguish symbols which truly point to the Divine from inadequate or misleading religious symbols, of which there must be many. Tillich is quite sure that any symbol which points to a merely finite being is inadequate, and he is concerned that symbols should be referred to the unconditioned power of being. But this means that they do point to a supranatural reality, in that they do not point to any finite or natural reality.

What is the relation between the negated meaning of the symbol and its affirmed meaning? Why should some symbols be chosen rather than others? Is it just a contingent, accidental fact that some terms happen to have evoked transformative experiences? Or are some terms more objectively appropriate than others? If so, what can make them appropriate, except that they do manage somehow to depict the nature of that to which they refer? Indeed, it is not possible to refer intentionally unless one can provide some description of the referent, however inadequate. So if symbols refer at all, some description of the referent must be forthcoming. It is not enough to say that the literal meaning of e.g. 'good' is negated, while it is affirmed in some other, evocative, sense. That evocative sense has nothing to do with the word 'good' unless something about goodness is appropriate to the referent. This now becomes a standard doctrine of analogical discourse, according to which a term is used of God in an analogical sense, in an extended meaning, but it still literally applies to God.

One can say that God is a being, but a unique being. God does not participate in being, as received from another. God is self-existent being, the only being who possesses existence necessarily. There is nothing incoherent in calling God an individual who necessarily exists, who is of supreme value and a cause of everything, without being caused by anything. God is the self-existent supreme power and value. I think this is what Tillich means by saying that 'God is Being-itself'. But, not seeing that this in itself entails a number of literal truths about God, Tillich falls into the trap of thinking that all other positive statements must be denied of God in a literal sense. That, in turn, misleads him into distinguishing his position from that of supranaturalism, which regards God as a highest being, cause, and substance, and which he then sees as a literalization of what can only be said symbolically.

TIME AND PROVIDENCE IN TILLICH

God does fall outside the subject–object structure, since there is nothing over against God by which God is constituted as a self, no wider reality to which God belongs. However, in so far as God is Creator, and is thus causally related to the universe, God does constitute the divine being as a subject in relation to other subjects, but also as one who participates inwardly in all things; as a power of creativity which realizes itself in particular forms; as a freedom which is also a self-realization.

At least some basic categories do apply to God, and Tillich is mistaken in thinking that these categories can only apply to created reality ('the categories are forms of finitude'[37]). For example, God is the cause of finite reality, with its polarities. Being self-existent, God is the only truly substantial reality. God is not spatial, in being confined to some space; but is present in every space, as well as existing non-spatially. As for time, God is present at every time, and it remains to be determined whether there is a temporal (i.e. changing) aspect in the life of God itself.

Tillich's view presses him to a temporalist view of God, but he is prevented from accepting it because of his doctrine of symbolic language. He wants 'a dynamic element in the structure of being'.[38] 'It is impossible', he says, 'to speak of being without also speaking of becoming.'[39] This insight is undermined, however, because he takes all the elements of ontology to apply only to finite being, so that God, as Being-itself, must exclude all non-being and all finitude, and so any real becoming. All one can say is that God is 'beyond potentiality and actuality'. God is also 'beyond essence and existence',[40] so that 'to argue that God exists is to deny him'. This is

---

[37] Tillich, *Systematic Theology*, i. 214.
[38] Ibid. 199.
[39] Ibid. 200.
[40] Ibid. 227.

the *reductio ad absurdum* of Tillich's theory, though one might trace the same sort of claim to pseudo-Dionysius, and it goes back to Plato's assertion that 'God is beyond being.'[41] The negative way, however, in its classic form, needs to be complemented by the way of eminentation, so that one must say that God is beyond existence as we see it in finite things, yet truly exists more fully than any of them.

Following up this clue, one would expect Tillich to say that God is potential, insofar as God is creative, but without the negative features of loss and anxiety that characterize finite temporality. And so with all the polarities that Tillich outlines.

'As being-itself God is beyond the contrast of essential and existential being.'[42] That is true, in that God is the source of all Forms or essences and also the source of all finite beings. Nevertheless, God has a nature (an essence) and God exists. Both God's basic nature and existence are necessary, and thus not subject to any power of fate or accident. It is not wrong, as Tillich asserts, to say that God exists.

God 'is the eternal process in which separation is posited and is overcome by reunion.'[43] Here, Tillich amends the Thomist idea of God as *Actus Purus* by including in it an element of process from potential to actual. But he undermines his own case by saying that this process must be simultaneous, for 'in God as God there is no distinction between potentiality and actuality.'[44] Here, the vagueness of symbolic language enables Tillich both to affirm and deny that God is 'living'—becoming as well as being; but it also means that he simply contradicts himself. A clearer doctrine of analogy would enable him to put the point more helpfully by saying that God does contain potentiality as well as actuality, in such a way that the creative process is always and necessarily governed by an immutable nature.

Tillich simply cannot avoid ontological statements. He affirms, for example, that 'the divine life is essentially creative.'[45] While asserting that 'it is meaningless to ask whether creation is a necessary or a contingent act of God',[46] he obviously believes it is necessary. He denies this only in the sense that there is some necessity above

---

[41] Plato, *Republic* 509; trans. Desmond Lee (Harmondsworth: Penguin, 1974), 309.   [42] Tillich, *Systematic Theology*, i. 262.
[43] Ibid. 268.   [44] Ibid.   [45] Ibid. 293.
[46] Ibid. 280.

God which constrains God. He believes that nothing is given to God which influences the divine being,[47] and that essences are created by God.[48] These are all ontological statements, and it is misleading to suggest that, as purely symbolic, they contrast with a more literalist 'supranaturalism'.

The same falsely drawn dichotomy surfaces in Tillich's discussion of providence. Providence, he says, is 'not an additional factor',[49] a supranatural factor. It is 'the quality of inner directedness', such that 'no situation whatsoever can frustrate the fulfilment of his ultimate destiny.' He is saying that there is a fulfilment of creaturely existence, beyond this natural universe, and that 'God is asked to direct the given situation toward fulfilment.'[50] But if God really directs each situation towards fulfilment, this is nothing other than a supranatural additional factor, not perceptible to empirical observation or testing. Again, Tillich misstates what he is rejecting (which is abrupt interference in nature), and this leads to a vacuous doctrine of God and of human destiny. Fulfilment must refer to a future state, even if beyond this physical universe; it cannot refer to a state 'beyond potentiality and actuality'. Such vacillations lead Tillich to reject miraculous acts of God, a literal life after death, and God as a highest metaphysical being, while all the time the words he uses commit him to affirming them, in however qualified a sense. We cannot make words mean whatever we like; if we use them, we are committed to their entailments. I have tried to show how a resort to 'symbolism' cannot evade the fact that theists are committed to some literal, if analogical, statements about God. It is only by failing to recognize the meanings of the words one is using that one might deny this.

METAPHOR

Metaphorical usage is very important in religion. When Jesus is said to be the Word of God, no one supposes that he is literally spoken by God; the falsity of that is just too obvious (unfortunately the same seems not to be true of 'Son of God', which is logically similar). The term 'Word' is taken as a technical term, referring partly to the historical person, Jesus, and partly to the Form of the divine being

---

[47] Tillich, *Systematic Theology*, i. 281.   [48] Ibid. 283.
[49] Ibid. 296.   [50] Ibid. 297.

which was present in (incarnate in) that person. The introduction of this technical term, stating that in God there is Father, Word, and Spirit, nonetheless trades on the other, normal meanings of 'word'. There is felt to be something appropriate about it, though it is extremely hard to say just what that is. One might think of a word as that which expresses a thought, or as that which commands or communicates, or as that which embodies meaning. Because of the many contexts in which 'word' is used, and because of the history of the term in the Hebrew religious tradition, it calls up an indefinitely large and unbounded series of associations and ideas. Precisely because of its indefiniteness and its associative power, it can provoke the imagination to make new connections, to perceive similarities and to gain insights which would otherwise be unobtainable.

Lying behind the metaphor, there are some literal truths which are conditions of its applicability. For example, Jesus must have been the sort of person who could appropriately be taken to express the divine purpose; there must be a goal of the existence of the universe, some reason for its existence; God must be rational or wise; and there must be some distinction in God which is expressed, however crudely and inadequately, by the idea of a 'speaker' and an 'expressed thought'.

It would thus be false to say that all statements about God, or about incarnation, are metaphorical. It is also false, however, to say that metaphors can simply be translated, without loss or change of meaning, into literal statements. 'Jesus is the Word of God' carries an evocative and associative power, an openness to new interpretations, and a lack of specificity which enables it to express and evoke feelings and thoughts in new and subtle ways. There is a sense in which 'Jesus is a word' is obviously false; yet, as the religious context becomes primary, a new primary meaning emerges, which is more like analogy. It is more like saying, 'Jesus is like a word in certain ways, though not in others.' Especially when 'Word' is capitalized and used with a definite article, it may be felt to be no longer a metaphor. The sense of inappropriateness diminishes, and one may feel that Jesus is literally the Word of God; it becomes a title. Yet the sense of strangeness is always able to be reawakened, as one recalls other uses of the term, so that one is always prompted to make new connections with other areas of thought and seek more adequate descriptions of the God who was believed to be fully present in Jesus.

Other titles are used alongside it: Jesus is the Good Shepherd, the Vine, the Son. This increases the associative interplay of terms, and helps to prevent the belief that one has provided an exhaustive or adequate description of Jesus in relation to God. Some literal things are true of Jesus, if these expressions are appropriate at all; but the use of multiple metaphors emphasizes the inadequacy of human thought to comprehend God. It also encourages reactive attitudes which relate one positively to God. The terms do claim an objective reference; but they do so in a way which expresses and evokes distinctive affective states in those who use them. They say, 'This reality which you can never adequately apprehend is such that one appropriate, though partial, attitude to it is like the attitude you might have to a shepherd . . . ' The attitudinal aspects of faith discussed in the previous chapter are of crucial importance to religious life. What non-realists ignore is the fact that, if attitudes are appropriate, there must be something in the facts which makes them so. The use of metaphors affirms this, while reminding one that our means of expressing the truth are woefully inadequate.

In a helpful discussion of metaphor and religious language, Janet Martin Soskice says, 'one can refer to someone or something without providing an exhaustive or unrevisable definition.'[51] She is led, however, on three or four occasions, to state a view which contradicts that to which she is in general committed. This occurs when she says, for example, 'We do not claim to describe God but to point through his effects . . . to him.'[52] While exhaustive and unrevisable descriptions are questionable, some descriptions of God, however vague and inadequate, are presupposed in any reference to God at all. She quotes an example from Saul Kripke, that one might successfully refer to Columbus without knowing any truths about him. But one's reference could not possibly succeed if it were not true that Columbus was a human being who lived in the past, or that he is a person who has been widely referred to by others as the discoverer of America, so that there is something he did which explains such an attribution, however false. Vague descriptions are presupposed by successful reference. Those who use metaphors of God are committed to the view that some descriptions can be given of God as a condition of referring to God at all, even though they

---

[51] Soskice, *Metaphor and Religious Language*, 128.   [52] Ibid. 140.

would be unwise to seek to translate all metaphors into literal statements.

When discussing Anselm's formula, that God is that than which no greater can be conceived, Janet Martin Soskice says that 'the definition does not describe but rather gives a designation.'[53] But in saying 'that', the definition speaks of a unitary individual (not many non-substantial elements); and in saying 'greater', it speaks of a maximally valuable state, which that individual possesses. Moreover, Anselm clearly thinks that the idea of such a maximally valuable state entails the idea of 'being the cause of all', being omniscient, and so on. Thus the formula *does* describe. While Soskice is right to emphasize the referential power of metaphor, its untranslatability, and religious function, she is wrong to suggest, as she sometimes does, that literal statements about God are not possible.[54] Elsewhere she takes the point fully, saying that 'not all our talk of God is metaphorical',[55] and that, I think, is her considered view.

METAPHOR, ANALOGY, AND LITERAL SPEECH

A similarly helpful treatment of the indispensable role of metaphor in religion is given by Sallie McFague,[56] with a similar lapse into a denial of any literal truths about God. McFague says that 'no words or phrases refer directly to God'[57], thereby ignoring the word 'God' itself. 'No authority . . . can decree that some types of language or some images refer literally to God while others do not. None do.'[58] 'Predicates such as omniscience, infinity, omnipotence and omnipresence do not properly apply to God.'[59] McFague, however, also describes herself as a 'critical realist',[60] and is committed thereby to saying that, in referring to God, one does refer to something. This 'something' can only be identified by description, however vague and inadequate, and that description will refer literally to, and properly apply to, God. She gives such a description herself, in saying that 'there is a personal, gracious power who is on the side of life and its fulfilment, a power whom the paradigmatic figure Jesus

[53] Ibid. 138.
[54] 'The Christian . . . will not or cannot transpose his concept of God into supposedly imageless speech.' (ibid.).   [55] Ibid. 66.
[56] Sallie McFague, *Models of God*, (London: SCM Press, 1987).
[57] Ibid. 34.   [58] Ibid. 35.   [59] Ibid. 39.
[60] Ibid. 193.

of Nazareth expresses and illuminates.'[61] That description ascribes personal being, grace (or love), power, causality, and existence to God. Such attributes are not metaphorical, since they are necessary to define the object to which all theistic metaphors are intended to apply.

The reason for hesitation about saying that one can describe God is the immense difference one feels there must be between the creator of all space and time and any finite object in space-time. While it is literally true that God is the only creator of everything other than God, this literal truth places God in a unique category. How could any term which properly applies to finite objects apply to God in the same sense? Richard Swinburne argues that much theological language 'uses words in the same sense as they are used outside theology'.[62] He gives, as examples, 'God is good, wise, and existent',[63] and holds that, though having these properties amounts to something very different in God than it does in creatures, yet the term univocally denotes the same property.[64] That means, he says, that God 'resembles the standard objects [to which the term 'good' applies] in the respect in which they resemble each other to the extent to which they resemble each other'.[65]

While I think Swinburne is right to argue for a literal use of theistic concepts, this seems to push matters too far. There is a marked obscurity about what it is for a term to be used 'in the same sense' which makes this position difficult to assess. Do wise things all possess the property of wisdom to the same extent? That cannot be so, since there are many degrees of wisdom, and Swinburne agrees that God's wisdom will be much greater in degree than that of any creature. Perhaps it comes down to saying that 'wisdom' is recognizably the same thing in many instances. But Swinburne defines 'analogy' as resemblance to a standard property-possessing object which is greater than resemblance to an object not possessing the property in question. Thus 'X is wise' is analogous attribution if X is more like standardly wise objects, in the property in which they resemble each other, than it is like non-wise objects. Since 'resemblance' is a matter of degree, there can be no sharp line between univocal and analogical language for Swinburne's view. All will depend on whether there are significant differences between the

---

[61] McFague, *Models of God*, 192.
[62] Richard Swinburne, *The Coherence of Theism* (Oxford: Clarendon Press, 1977), 84.   [63] Ibid. 72.   [64] Ibid. 79.   [65] Ibid. 58.

sort of (e.g.) wisdom God possesses and the sort of wisdom creatures possess. But there are very significant differences, which is enough reason to call all literal attributions to God analogical.

The concepts of 'existence' and 'goodness', as applied to God, have been considered in discussing Tillich. In the case of 'wisdom', persons may be called wise if they can discern connections, perceive creative solutions to problems, see logical compatibilities, see what is troubling people, understand difficult issues and analyse them clearly. Wisdom is an intellectual skill, of a rather complex sort. One can see when someone is not wise—when they never see a point, jump to impractical solutions, and make logical errors. One can think of a perfect wisdom, which understands things perfectly and knows the best resolution of every difficulty. Wisdom is analytically connected to knowledge, understanding and judgement. Thus anything with these intellectual skills, to whatever degree, can properly be called wise.

God knows all things, understands all things, and knows the best thing to do in all situations. So, one might say, God is univocally wise. God will never be stupid, and will always be perfectly wise. But if one asks of Swinburne whether this is univocal or analogical attribution, one will be required to ask whether God has wisdom 'to the extent that wise people have wisdom', or whether God is more like wise people than like not-wise (or stupid) people.

Of course, God has wisdom to a greater extent than any wise person. But in God, wisdom is also a different sort of property. God is necessarily wise; God cannot fail to be wise. In God wisdom is not a skill, which needs to be learned, can be practised or increased, and which constitutes a praiseworthy virtue. Wisdom follows from, is part of, the perfection of the divine nature. So it sounds very odd to say that divine wisdom is possessed to the same extent or even in the same way as creaturely wisdom. It is possessed in an entirely different way, as a necessary and maximal property which is inseparable from the divine existence.

Moreover, if one proceeds to ask how divine wisdom is exercised, it soon becomes clear that it will not be, as in the case of human wisdom, by a laborious accumulation of experience, by difficult inferences and by trial and error, or by hunch and intuition. It is infallible, effortless, and complete. It is wholly unimaginable by us, since we do not know what it would be like to possess complete understanding of everything, or even whether such a state is possible. We can verbally state its possibility, but cannot be sure that it is really possible, and certainly cannot have any experience that would let us guess what such a state would be like.

So is divine wisdom like human wisdom? It is a hypothesized extrapolation of human wisdom to its highest conceivable degree. It is thereby taken out of every context of learning, action, and effort in which we see it function, and placed in a context (of the divine nature) which we cannot even imagine. It seems reasonable to say that wisdom is ascribed analogically to God.

There is reason in Swinburne's own account to say that this is so. Wisdom is essentially a property of persons. It is persons, or intellectual beings, who may possess wisdom. If wisdom is taken univocally, then God is seen as straightforwardly a person. But is 'God is a person' univocal or analogical? Swinburne says that it is analogical.[66] So divine wisdom is a property of a being which is only analogically like creatures, which is 'more like' persons than it is 'like' not-persons, but which is not exactly like persons. If a property is predicated of a being which is only analogically like another being, which in fact belongs to a different genus, this is good reason for calling the predication itself analogical. Moreover, wisdom pre-supposes knowledge, and knowledge is, according to Swinburne, attributed to God analogically. Since knowledge is part of the sense of 'wisdom', since knowledge is analogically predicated, and since if part of the meaning of X differs in two cases then the whole meaning of X must differ, it follows that 'wisdom' is analogically predicated, after all.

THE CLASSICAL DOCTRINE OF ANALOGY

The belief that linguistic terms are predicated of God literally and analogically is most closely linked with the name of Thomas Aquinas. His statements on the issue are much less systematically formalized than in the writings of the later scholastics, and broadly in keeping with the account given here. Question 13 of the first part of Aquinas' *Summa Theologiae* is devoted to the question of language about God. Thomas says bluntly, 'It is impossible to predicate

---

[66] Swinburne, *The Coherence of Theism*, 71.

anything univocally of God and creatures.'[67] He gives two main reasons for this. First, 'wisdom' is a quality in creatures but not in God, since God is perfectly simple, and has no qualities. Thus 'wisdom' must apply to the essence of God in a way we cannot conceive. Second, God is different in genus from creatures, so nothing can be said of God which is the same as what can be said of creatures.

The first of these reasons must be modified if the doctrine of divine simplicity is given up, or interpreted more weakly to signify the indivisibility of properties in the divine nature. Clearly, if divine simplicity is affirmed in its strongest sense (as it apparently is by Thomas), no words could apply to God univocally at all, since all of them abstract from a specific aspect of beings. In a weaker sense of 'simplicity', if the divine properties are indivisible and that indivisibility affects the manner in which each exists (if divine wisdom is partly what it is because it is indivisible from divine power and goodness), univocal predication will still be ruled out.

The important features of the doctrine of analogy are that certain things can be truly said of God—as that God is wise, knowing, powerful, good, and existent. Indeed, God is perfect wisdom, and in that sense the term primarily applies to God. Nevertheless, if we want to know what 'wisdom' or 'goodness', 'knowledge' or 'existence' mean when applied to God, we cannot assume that they mean just what they do when applied to finite creatures. In God, they are necessary and indivisible, and are predicated of a being who is the perfect and self-existent cause of all, whose reality stands at the limits of human conceivability. God will act in ways which are supremely wise, but God's perfect and necessary wisdom flows from a form of being which is beyond imagining. Wisdom properly applies to God, but in virtue of a form of being which, in its unique perfection, is itself beyond our conception. The way in which the property is present is quite different.

Aquinas puts it elegantly when he says that 'so far as the perfections signified are concerned the words are used . . . more appropriately than they are used of creatures . . . But so far as the way of signifying (*modus significandi*) is concerned the words are used inappropriately, for they have a way of signifying that is appropriate

---

[67] Thomas Aquinas, *Summa Theologiae*, Ia q. 2 a. 3 (Blackfriars edn.; London: Eyre and Spottiswoode, 1963–81).

to creatures.'[68] Words like 'wise' do not have a wholly different meaning when they are applied to God. God is such that all things in Creation are ordered in the best way to achieve the ends which God desires. But it should not therefore be thought that God is the same sort of thing as a wise person, or that in assembling a set of such attributes we thereby know just what God is. Thomas says, 'Such words do say what God is . . . but fail to represent adequately what he is.'[69] The nature of the being who orders things rightly to their ends remains beyond all our conceptions, though they are correct, so far as they go.

If one would speak appropriately of God, one must say that God is a reality of supreme value, wisdom, and power, and that in the Divine Life these perfections are possessed in an indivisible and self-existent manner that wholly transcends human understanding. The articulation of the doctrine of God consists in spelling out more precisely what this implies. Heschel, Barth, Iqbal, and Aurobindo all engage in this process, from within their own religious traditions, and using both analogical and metaphorical images from their scriptures. Heschel regards God as unknowable in essence, yet positively related to the finite in passionate attention. Barth holds that God is 'totally other', and yet can be appropriately known by a gracious self-condescension in which God enters into loving fellowship with creatures. Iqbal speaks of 'the Infinite', using this reified adjective to point to the unconditioned reality of God. He sees God as both the self of the world and the creative co-worker with creatures. These analogies complement and limit each other, so as to loosen some of the implications one might otherwise draw from them. Similarly, Aurobindo articulates the idea of Brahman as that of infinite being, a Supermind of wisdom, power, and bliss, which is manifested in emergent creativity.

Many metaphors can be used to help the mind to create images of God which will inspire devotion and practical response. But it is not the case that all talk of God must be metaphorical or symbolic. Even though the divine being in itself must remain beyond the grasp of the human mind, there are still many literal statements which are true of it in its relation to the created universe, however inadequately they represent that to which they refer. If the theist is committed to

---

[67] Aquinas, *Summa Theologiae*, Ia q. 13 a. 3.   [69] Ibid. Ia q. 13 a. 2.

speaking of God, as a reality of supreme power and value, the theist is also committed to providing some literal, if analogical, description of the reality of God. What theologians like Tillich fear is that the concept of God provided by speculation will be so inadequate to its object, so anthropomorphic, that it will be positively misleading. The theologian's task is to avoid that danger, while providing a characterization of God that is rooted in scriptural tradition and coherent with the best available knowledge of the natural universe. In Part 3, I shall seek to develop a Trinitarian notion of God, from within a Christian perspective, which takes account of the core idea of God as supremely creative, passionate, loving, wise and blissful which has emerged from analysis of some main scriptural traditions in Part 1. If I claim thereby to produce a literal description of an objective supranatural reality, it must not be forgotten how tentative, analogical, and exploratory such a description must be. When all has been said, the human mind must silently bow before the mystery of self-existent perfection.

PART III
The Nature of the Creator God

7

Divine Power and Creativity

The concept of God has been considered in four religious traditions, through the work of twentieth-century theologians in those traditions. Some would consider the unitarian concepts of Judaism and Islam and the panentheist account of Vedanta to be quite distinct from the Trinitarian theism of Christianity. I have suggested that the issue is rather more complex, and that such simple distinctions, while not entirely false, conceal more than they reveal. All the traditions considered posit a certain complexity in God, as well as a total dependence of all finite things upon the uniquely self-existent being of God. In one aspect, God is said to be ineffable, infinite, and transcendent of space-time. But in another aspect, these theologians consider God to be really related to space-time, to be passionately concerned with it (Heschel), to take it into a fellowship of love with God (Barth), to be related to it in co-operative and creative freedom (Iqbal), and to be involved in a temporal and progressive process whose goal is the manifestation of the divine life in time (Aurobindo). They all reject the classical, philosophically determined doctrines of their own traditions, in favour of a greater stress on the importance of temporality, creativity, and individuality. In the formulation of these ideas of God, the scriptural traditions function importantly as a revelatory basis, but the replacement of Greek and Sanskrit philosophical traditions by post-Hegelian thought, and the impact of scientific cosmology, has prompted similar revisions in each tradition. Scriptural traditions can no longer function in isolation, simply repeating the standard formulations of the past. Contemporary approaches to the idea of God must take into account the place of one revelatory tradition within the wider range of such traditions, and the ways in which it needs to respond, whether by modification or reaction, to changes in reflective and scientific thought.

Revelation has been characterized as the communication of truths beyond normal human cognitive capacity.[1] The idea of a creator God

---

[1] Keith Ward, *Religion and Revelation* (Oxford: Clarendon Press, 1994), 343.

is a natural human hypothesis. By that I mean that it springs from natural human feelings and propensities to believe. These feelings may be misleading or ignoble in some way, as David Hume thought they were.[2] To say that a belief is natural is not to say that it is reasonable without more ado. The course of philosophical discussion over the last few centuries suggests that it is certainly beyond normal human cognitive capacity to *know* that there is only one Creator. The basic truths of revelation, I have argued, are those which describe the nature of a supremely valuable reality held to underlie sense experience, which set out a final human goal in relation to that reality, and which show the way to liberation from self and the attainment of the true human goal. Those truths are, in a given religious tradition, received on authority from prophets or sages who are believed to have experienced the Supreme Reality in an exceptional manner, to have achieved the goal of liberation from evil or sin, or at least to have exhibited supranormal powers which confirm their empowerment by the Divine, and to have been inspired by extraordinary wisdom and insight into the nature of the human condition and of the reality of which human life is part. Religions trace their origin to individuals, known or unknown, who are possessed of outstanding wisdom, depth and intensity of experience, and sanctity. In developing these human qualities to a great degree, they are believed to become people who can express the Supreme Reality in word or deed, and who are able to mediate its power to others.

Revelation does not occur as a sort of supernatural interruption into the otherwise ordinary course of human affairs. It is best seen as a manifestation of a continuous, but often unremarked, interaction between the spiritual reality in which the cosmos is embedded—so religious believers think—and human minds which are by nature inclined to respond to it in varying degrees of awareness and obedience. Some minds, partly because of their historical context and partly because of their psychological make-up, become acutely responsive to what one might see as the attractive power of the spiritual Ideal. They may become vehicles of revelation, their thoughts inspired to new insights, their feelings inflamed by the closeness of their awareness of the Supreme Spirit, their wills

---

[2] David Hume, *The Natural History of Religion* (Oxford: Clarendon Press, 1976; 1st pub. 1755).

reoriented towards that which they see as supremely good and irresistibly attractive.

What such prophetic figures communicate is not immune from limitations of culture and ordinary human knowledge. But that is not by any means to deprive them of spiritual authority. While their teachings have a cultural history and are enriched by human imagination and reflection, those factors are themselves seen as responses to the guiding providence of God, in bringing truths about the divine being and purpose to human awareness. The revelatory traditions of Judaism, Christianity, Islam, and Hinduism are different, but each of them embodies a claim to insight into the divine being through inspiration, experience, and divine empowerment. In each of them, from an earlier basis of ideas of tribal gods or spirits there develops one controlling idea, which is that of God as the greatest conceivable being, a being than which nothing more valuable can be imagined or conceived. It is this controlling idea which is then reflectively articulated in the light of general human knowledge and against a particular philosophical background.

GOD AS THE GREATEST CONCEIVABLE BEING

In the biblical tradition, the great prophets, who are close to God through prayer and trusting obedience, become the recipients of visions and of divine locutions, which build upon their basic culturally grounded belief in a morally demanding presence, seen as exercising a judging and yet liberating power for justice in the experience of their nation. In the Hebrew tradition, a pattern of experiences is sustained and developed which reinforces certain fundamental attitudes of faith. A sense of reverence before the complex order and beauty of the world suggests the idea of an underlying power and wisdom. Historical experiences of catastrophe and liberation suggest the idea of an uncompromising demand for justice and a promise of future fulfilment. The sense of a strengthening presence in times of despair and of a creative power in times of happiness suggests the existence of a personal reality underlying the realm of sense experience. Over generations, the concept of one just and loving power behind the events of history becomes a dominant focal point for sustaining such attitudes and commitments. It is the God who is characterized in that way who speaks through the prophets, so that the idea of God is not seen as simply a reflective hypothesis integrating a number of human experiences. It is rather seen as expressing an active self-manifestation of the divine nature, focused in the lives of prophets whose historical situation and personal commitment enable them, with all their limitations of outlook, to become vehicles of a continuing divine self-disclosure in that tradition.

In the Bible, one can see in the development of the Patriarchal and prophetic tradition a growing apprehension that the God of Abraham, Isaac, and Jacob is a transcendent being of supreme power and value. If God makes all things, then only God is uncreated. God is the one source of all power, and nothing can limit God in any way that God does not will. In a sense which remains yet to be clarified more fully, the biblical God is omnipotent: 'I know that thou canst do all things and that no purpose of thine can be thwarted.'[3] If God is holy and worthy of unlimited devotion, then only God is of supreme intrinsic value, the most desirable of beings: 'Great is the Lord, and greatly to be praised, and his greatness is unsearchable.'[4] In other traditions there is a similar reflective development of the idea of God or Brahman, the ultimate reality, as possessing supreme power and value. The Koran unequivocally asserts God's omnipotence: 'God is all-knowing and all-powerful.'[5] It equally clearly affirms God's unparalleled greatness: 'To God applies the highest similitude; for He is the exalted in power, full of wisdom.'[6] In the Upanishads, Brahman is said to be of supreme power: 'The Lord of Self so great sends out rulers, though he [alone] wields the all-sovereign power.'[7] Brahman, being absolute intelligence and bliss, is also the best of all possible beings: 'Depend on This, the best; depend on This, the ultimate.'[8] On grounds of scriptural testimony, the ultimate reality is asserted to be of unsurpassable power and greatness or value.

Further reflection on the ideas of supreme power and value shows that they are more intimately connected than one might at first suppose. One might think that supreme power may be without value. Karl Barth even supposed, at one time, that supreme power

---

[3] Job 42: 2.   [4] Ps. 145: 3.   [5] Koran 16: 70.
[6] Koran 16: 60.
[7] *Svetasvatara Upanishad* 5. 3, in R. C. Zaehner (trans.), *Hindu Scriptures* (London: Dent, 1966), 213.
[8] Katha Upanishad 2. 17, ibid. 174.

was not of value—'Power itself is evil.'[9] 'To possess the power to do everything without distinction would be a limitation.'[10] But he is here thinking of power without any reason for doing anything in particular, without any wishes or desires. A blind power, without any other properties, would not be a supreme power at all. The highest power is not a purposeless energy; it is the power to act, to bring states about through intention. This introduces the idea of value immediately. The Supreme Power would choose for itself the most desirable life, so it would will itself to be a being of supreme value, of supreme desirability, that is, of supreme goodness. The creator cannot choose its own nature, since that nature must exist prior to any actual choice being made. Even so, it would be a limitation of power to have a nature one did not desire, that one would not have chosen, if one could. In that sense, a supreme power will have a nature that it would have chosen. Only such a nature will not be a limitation on God, since otherwise divine power will be limited by a divine nature which God would rather not possess. However, if divine power is only limited by a nature which God would choose, that is no real limitation. It follows that a supreme power will necessarily be of supreme value.

Similarly, one might think that supreme value might be powerless. One might think of a Supreme Good without any causal efficacy at all, as Iris Murdoch has suggested.[11] But again, one would be thinking of a Good which is not in fact supreme. For Anselm was surely right in thinking that it is clearly more valuable to exist indestructibly and to be able to accomplish whatever one wills than to be a non-actual Form or Idea. Therefore the Supreme Value will necessarily be an existent being of supreme power.

There may be no Supreme Power or no Supreme Value. But if there is, then they will be one and the same being. It is such a being which is the source of all causal powers and finite values in whatever created universes there are. Anselm construed this being in a particularly elegant way when he defined God as '*Aliquid quo maius nihil cogitari possit*'—that than which no greater can be conceived.[12]

[9] Karl Barth, *Church Dogmatics*, ed. G. W. Bromiley and T. F. Torrance (Edinburgh: T. & T. Clark, 1936–77), ii/1: 534.   [10] Ibid. 533.

[11] Iris Murdoch, *The Sovereignty of Good* (London: Routledge, 1970), see 71.

[12] Anselm, *Proslogion* ch. 2, trans. M. J. Charlesworth (London: Notre Dame University Press, 1979), 116.

This concept, even though it is the product of a very sophisticated process of reflection, is implicit in biblical revelation, and it is a basic idea which seems to possess no cultural limitations or defects which would lead one to qualify it further. It is an idea which is common to the Jewish, Christian, and Muslim faiths, which all share a common prophetic ancestry. But it is present in the Hindu tradition, too, as similar processes of reflection led the Vedic sages to centre all the divine powers and virtues in one Brahman of unrestricted being, consciousness, and bliss, Sachchidananda. The Hindu way stresses the inner experience of union with such a non-dual ultimate reality, but reflection on its ultimacy leads to the idea of unique self-existence and unlimited perfection, thus connecting it at the deepest level with the idea of God as the greatest conceivable being.

Nevertheless, the idea of God as the one and only Creator, possessing supreme value and power, is undetermined in many respects. There are many ways of spelling out exactly what is involved in having supreme power or in being of supreme value. When one considers specifically Christian revelation, it holds some surprises for many ideas of power and value. Some notions of supreme power think of it as an all-determining will, which does exactly what it wants and leaves humans wholly at its mercy. The Christian revelation in the person of Jesus, however, suggests a paradoxical idea of power as revealed in weakness, working through love in the passion and apparent defeat of the Cross.[13] Some notions of supreme value think of it as wholly self-contained, untouched by suffering or by relationship to what is other than itself. Christian revelation, however, sees redemptive love as the supreme value, which relates to others and shares in their suffering.[14]

These ideas, which derive not so much from reflection as from acceptance of the Incarnation and the Cross as revelatory of the divine nature, are so surprising that even the greatest Christian theologians have found it hard to make them central in their thought. It is, surprisingly, only in the twentieth century that some theologians have tried to make them the fundamental basis of a Christian idea of God. There are very good reasons why this should have been so, and it is important to see what those reasons are. It is also important to assess their strength, and to ask whether making

---

[13] See Jürgen Moltmann, *The Crucified God* (London: SCM Press, 1974).
[14] See John Taylor, *The Christlike God* (London: SCM Press, 1992).

the revelation of the divine nature in Jesus Christ central in one's thinking would support or weaken those reasons.

THE DIVINE NATURE: POWER

In thinking about God, one way to start is by examining in more detail the idea of a greatest conceivable being, and to spell it out by specific reference to some of the data of revelation. The idea itself may seem to be utterly abstract and vague, to be without content.[15] After all, may people not have totally different ideas of what a 'great being' is, and conceive of very different beings as the greatest they can think of?

It is likely, however, that there would be agreement on at least some of the properties which are 'great-making', which it is better to possess than not to possess. An obvious example would be power, in the sense of capacity to do what one wants. Would any rational person hold that it is better not to be able to do what one wants than to have such ability?

It may be said that some people would rather do what they are told, so that they would not have to make their own decisions. But if they are oppressed and enslaved, tortured and manipulated, they could not desire their situation. One can only rationally wish to be obedient to a being which is fundamentally benevolent, and which has the power to express its benevolence. Those who wish to obey, like soldiers in an army, are assuming that they will be led by people who do not simply wish to abuse and enslave them. They must believe that those who command are basically honourable or benevolent or in some other way worthy of respect, and that the commanders have the power to put their wishes into effect. In other words, they are committed to holding that it is better for those who command to have power than that they should not.

Those who prefer to obey may do so because they prefer order to the possible anarchy of all deciding for themselves, or they may wish to give honour to one who represents what they value and respect. In that sense, many people do not wish to possess supreme power themselves. They may actually prefer not to be able to do everything that they want, but to be under the control of another, who will take

---

[15] John Hick calls it a 'purely formal concept', in *An Interpretation of Religion* (London: Macmillan, 1989), 246.

responsibility for ordering their lives. Discipline may be preferred to personal freedom.

The question of whether people want to be powerful themselves is a different question from that of whether the possession of power would be universally agreed by rational agents to be a good thing, to be a property possessed by the most estimable of beings. Those who prefer to obey will rationally wish that the one they obey should have sufficient power to ensure the obedience of others, to protect his or her values and decisions, and to order their lives in a reasonably efficient way. It would be absurd to obey a powerless leader. It is precisely because many people feel very keenly their own in-adequacies that they prefer to follow others. If one examines what qualities a good leader would have, wisdom, benevolence (at least to the followers), and power are essentially desirable. That being is better which possesses power, at least when allied with wisdom and benevolence. One may indeed feel, with Thomas Hobbes, 'Better a bad king than a state of perpetual war.' But it is hardly disputable that 'Better a good king than a bad king', and a good king will need to possess sufficient power to carry out his wise and benevolent policies.

The best being to obey would be one with knowledge, power, and benevolence, so that obedience will not bring great suffering, but will bring many things one wants. Even if one does not want power or autonomous freedom of decision oneself, one must think that it would be good if some being with great knowledge, wisdom, benevolence, and power existed, which could plan one's life for one. Even timid, other-directed, and subservient people, when they think it through, will have to admit that it is better for some otherwise good being to possess power to do what it wants than not.

Another possible objection, however, is that, as Lord Acton said, power corrupts and absolute power corrupts absolutely. Might it not be better, then, if no absolute power existed? This objection is answered by reiterating that the property in question is not brute power, which may go along with selfish passion or ignorance, but 'knowledge-wisdom-benevolence-power'. Such a power is incorrupt-ible, since it would only be exercised in bringing about states which are known to be good and which are willed for the sake of their goodness. So there is at least one complex property, including benevolence and power, which all reflective thinkers would accept as necessarily belonging to a greatest conceivable being. As I have already suggested, the idea of supreme power implicitly contains the more complex property of supreme value, of perfect being. That point will be argued more fully,[16] but all one needs for the moment is that some definite complex property is entailed by the very idea of a greatest conceivable being.[17] The idea of a greatest conceivable being is not vacuous or wildly different from one person to another. It embodies a claim about value that may be called universal, in that all rational agents would accept it on reflection, and objective, in that it is true for all actual and possible rational agents whatsoever, and does not depend upon the particular constitution of human beings.

THE IDEA OF MAXIMAL POWER

If power is a perfection—a property it is better for a perfect being to have than not to have—then it seems clear that the more power such a being has the better. Can there be a maximally powerful being? Such a being would be so powerful that no other being could possibly surpass it in power. It must be indestructible by any other possible power. That means that it must exist of necessity, since only necessary beings are wholly indestructible. It must also be the source of every other being. Otherwise a being might come to exist which was more powerful than it, or which in some way could restrict its power. The greatest possible power cannot be limited in any way by anything other than itself, unless it wills to be, and such limitation will always be under its control. Clearly, there can only be one such being, since the wholly independent existence of another would limit its power, if only by existing whether or not its existence was desired. An omnipotent being will thus be a creator of everything other than itself. It will have total power over all actual and possible created things.

Proposals have recently been made that there could be two or three (or even more) omnipotent beings, on condition that they necessarily act in harmony with one another.[18] Such necessary harmony, however, needs to be ensured in some way, and the most obvious way of ensuring it is to make all omnipotent beings derive

---

[16] See Ch. 9.
[17] Swinburne in an analogous way suggests the derivation of all divine properties from one property of pure limitless intentional power. See *The Christian God* (Oxford: Clarendon Press, 1994), 150–8. [18] Ibid. 173 ff.

from the (necessary) causal agency of one primal omnipotent being. I discuss this possibility in Chapter 13. But with the addition of this proviso, it becomes apparent that it is this uniquely unoriginated cause which has supreme power, since the power of the other beings, however great and however necessary, is wholly dependent upon its nature and causal activity. There can only be one underivatively necessary being, even if it necessarily generates other beings of immense power.

Some views of God deny that omnipotence, construed in this sense, is possible. Some process theologians claim that no being, not even God, can be the source of all power. For, they argue, to have actual existence is to have the twofold power of self-determination and causal efficacy, and if anything exists other than God, it must have a power other than God's. Thus David Griffin holds that many natural powers exist which are not capable of being wholly determined by God, though God may have various sorts of influence upon them.[19] Griffin picks out what he calls the 'omnipotence fallacy' as one which has misled many philosophers and theologians. This is the fallacy of moving from the assertion that a state of affairs, S, is logically possible, to the assertion that God can create S. He is surely correct in taking this move to be fallacious. It is logically possible for a world of irredeemable evil to exist, but God cannot create it. For Griffin, this is a metaphysical limitation. But omnipotence theists, too, would rule out the creation of such a world. This is because God is necessarily good, so that such a world, though conceivable in itself, is not conceivable as creatable by a perfectly good being.

One might put this by saying that any creatable world must be compatible with the nature of the Creator. Any creatable world must also be compatible with the purposes of the Creator in creating it. Thus if God wills to create a world of free, partly self-determining moral agents, then even God cannot wholly determine their actions. Divine power is limited—though not in any bad or avoidable way—by the divine nature and the divine purposes. Griffin wants to make the point rather more strongly than this, however. He holds that it is a metaphysically necessary truth that all actual beings must be self-determining to some extent. If that is true, then God cannot wholly

[19] David Griffin, *God, Power and Evil* (Philadelphia: Westminster Press, 1975), 264 ff.

determine any creatable universe. He gives four main reasons to support this metaphysical limitation on God. (1) It gives a better account of the existence of suffering and conflict in the universe. (2) It reflects the fact that we do not experience any powerless actualities. (3) It avers that omnipotence, to have content, must be exercised over other existent powers. And (4) it suggests that to be actual is to receive into oneself causal influences from others, so that even the divine actuality must be causally influenced by others.

The question is whether these reasons successfully undermine the prima-facie coherent claim that omnipotence, the possession of maximal possible power, must be the power wholly to determine all other realities—whether or not that power is ever fully exercised. I am not convinced that they do. Process thought does provide a persuasive theodicy, but that theodicy can be shared by an omnipotence view that gives good reason for God's freely limiting the exercise of divine power. And the attribution of omnipotence provides a clearer guarantee that evil will eventually be eliminated from creation, so that the divine purpose is assured of final fulfilment, and is not doomed to be always obstructed by others.

As for the second reason, it is not so much that we see powerless individuals existing, as that we do seem to see actual individuals whose powers are wholly determined by something other than themselves. Those forms of animal or insect life which seem to be wholly instinct-driven provide prima-facie good examples of this. Such beings possess powers, but they are wholly dependent upon the powers of others. As Griffin points out, theologians like Augustine and Aquinas held that even free human acts are in fact wholly determined by God to be what they are, since they hold that freedom and determination are compatible.[20] Such a view is a logically possible one, on a particular interpretation of freedom, even if one rejects it. So, while I accept Griffin's point that God cannot wholly determine what God wills to be self-determining, I am unconvinced by his wider assertion that all beings are necessarily self-determining to some degree simply by being actual.

The third and fourth reasons depend upon a definition of 'actuality' which is, at best, highly contestable. Omnipotence can be exercised upon actualities which exist in space-time, without their

---

[20] 'The very act of freewill goes back to God as its cause' (Thomas Aquinas, *Summa Theologiae* Ia q. 22 a. 2 (Blackfriars edn.; London: Eyre and Spottiswoode, 1963–81).

having any independent power. And there can be actualities, perhaps only God, which do not causally depend upon any prior causes. In saying this, it may seem that I am merely asserting the opposite of what Griffin says, without supporting argumentation. That is, in a sense, true. But it must be borne in mind that one is seeking to understand what maximal power could be. I am suggesting that the traditional theistic notion of omnipotence seems coherent, and that process arguments against it are themselves too contestable to be overwhelming. Nevertheless, process thought does provide valuable insights into the ways in which divine power might best be exercised.

It is coherent to hold that God is capable of determining all beings, though God may not wish to do so. Further, all powers can derive from God, even though they may then, by divine will, have a limited power of self-determination. God must uphold that power and permit its exercise, and is thus omnipotent in the sense that God could determine everything, and if God does not do so, it is by divine decision. As Creator, it is within God's power of free decision to create a universe containing partly self-determining beings or not. For Griffin, on the other hand, the existence of a realm of finite actualities is necessary, and one of God's primary roles is to order those actualities, which is what 'creation', in his view, consists in. God must create some universe of self-determining beings, and then cannot wholly determine what shall happen to them, since that is ultimately up to them. I can see no compelling reason, however, to posit these beliefs as necessary truths.

Griffin's hypothesis does, nevertheless, provide some rationale for there being a created universe at all. He argues that there must be such a universe of finite actualities, that even God has no choice in the matter, but that God freely creates certain forms of order among such actualities.[21] God is not the creator of the universe *ex nihilo*, since it exists as a process without beginning or end, and God is primarily not the creator out of nothing, but the one who seeks to order and lure it towards greater perfection. For the religious traditions I have considered, God does create out of nothing. God freely brings to be things other than God. But why should such a being bring anything to be? The suggestion that there is no reason

---

[21] Griffin, *God, Power, and Evil*, 276–81.

would reduce the universe to just the sort of arbitrariness that atheists posit. But what sort of reason could there be for creating anything, either in the classical *ex nihilo* sense or in the process sense of free persuasion? The simplest answer to this question, in the case of any finite mind, is that one will act for the sake of good, that is, for the sake of bringing about a state which realizes some desire, or which at least is rationally desirable. Desires or beliefs about the states that are rationally desirable are not within conscious control. The fact that one has certain desires or that one finds certain states desirable is just a given fact of one's nature, which one does not choose—even if one can choose whether or not to pursue a given desire. Is it the same for God? Is the universe the product of divine desire, which God does not choose to have? If God brings about certain states because God considers them to be desirable, the universe might have a sort of necessity, as resulting from desires which God necessarily has, and which naturally express themselves in creation.

THE GIVEN NATURE OF GOD

God must have a given nature, which is not chosen, but which God possesses of necessity. It does not make sense to suppose that God chooses the divine nature completely, since there must already be a choosing nature in existence to make such a choice. For any choice to be made, there must already be knowledge of what could be chosen, power to choose, and some rational criteria of choice. There must therefore already exist a being with knowledge, power, and standards of choice. The divine nature cannot be caused by any other being, since then the Creator would not be the creator of everything other than itself. It cannot come into being out of nothing, since that would make it purely arbitrary and random. And it cannot cause itself, since a thing would have to exist in order to bring itself into existence, which is absurd. The divine nature is not capable of coming into being or passing away. In that sense it is immutable. Thus it seems that there is a given, immutable, uncreatable divine nature, which conceives possible states of affairs, has the ability to bring a universe into being, and has certain desires, or conceptions of and inclinations to produce states which are pleasurable or in some other way worthy of rational choice. God is essentially knowing, powerful, and wise, and cannot either create or destroy or change these basic properties, which constitute the divine nature.

To some theologians and philosophers, it is a restriction on God's power to possess a nature which God is unable to change. They accordingly think of God's creativity as including the capability of creating the divine nature itself. Thomas Morris proposes that God might be thought of as the cause of the divine properties—'It just seems to me that there is nothing logically or metaphysically objectionable about God's creating his own nature', he says.[22] What is wrong with the idea of divine self-creation is that, for X to be a creator, X must have thoughts, intentions, and the power to realize them. These are logically necessary conditions of X's creating anything. They are thus logically necessary conditions of X's creating its own properties. Such properties, at least, cannot be created, since they are presupposed by all acts of creation. Creation is causing to be what would otherwise not exist. Even if creation is thought of as a possibly timeless activity, what is created depends causally upon the act of the Creator. Thus, if anything is created, there must exist, in a causally prior way, an intending powerful being. It follows that God cannot create those very intentions and powers which are causally prior to the act of creation.

Morris holds that God's nature causally depends upon God; but what is this God without a nature? In speaking of causal dependence, one is ascribing power to it; but such power is part of a nature, and so it, at least, cannot causally depend upon God. The divine nature is uncreated, even by God, since it is presupposed by all creation. Morris offers an admittedly weak analogy, but it is too weak to do any work at all. He supposes a materialization machine which materializes itself as it ceases to exist; so in the end, it can be described as self-created. The inescapable truth, however, is that some original version of the machine must have existed to get the process started. Somewhere, there is an uncreated nature, and that must be regarded as inescapably given.

DIVINE NECESSITY AND EVIL

Karl Barth suggests that the divine freedom is such that God must be conceived as choosing the divine being itself. 'God's being is . . . his

---

[22] Thomas Morris, 'Absolute Creation', in *Anselmian Explorations* (Notre Dame, Ind.: University of Notre Dame Press, 1987), 172.

willed decision', he writes.[23] And again, 'There is no moment in the ways of God which is over and above this act and decision.'[24] But it is a logical truth that the making of a decision presupposes the existence of a being which has the power to decide. Such a being must have knowledge of what it might decide and the power to decide. It cannot decide to have such knowledge and power, as though it was a blank nothingness which could decide to become wise and powerful. The divine knowledge and power are presupposed by any decisions God might make; and this is a moment in the being of God which is over and above a free decision.

It is possible that Barth may be misusing language slightly in a rhetorical way, and that what he means is that God *freely assents to* the nature which God has and affirms it. That is a rather different matter, and there is every reason to think it is true. God's nature is just as God desires it, and God chooses its continuance just as it is. Nevertheless, the existence of that nature cannot properly be spoken of as chosen. It necessarily is what it is. Perhaps Barth is concerned to affirm that nothing compels God to be as God is, that God owes existence to no other being. That also is true. God's necessity is *a se*; it derives from no other and is constrained by no other. If one thinks of freedom as affirmation of one's nature—'Freedom means to . . . be determined and moved by oneself'[25]—then God is indeed supremely free. Such freedom is quite compatible with divine necessity, but it does not involve any possibility of alternative choice in God.

A further consideration which makes it implausible to think of God as wholly deciding the divine being itself is to be found in the existence of evil and suffering in creation. If God necessarily has knowledge of what is logically possible, and if these possibilities are rooted in the divine nature itself, then God does not choose what is possible. God can decide what is to become actual, but possibilities are antecedent to any decision. It may be thought that God should be able to choose possibilities, but reflection shows that this cannot be unrestrictedly true. For a start, God's own 'given' existence entails that God's existence is possible, and so at least the set of possibilities entailed by God's existence and nature are not chosen by God.

---

[23] Barth, *Church Dogmatics*, ed. G. W. Bromiley and T. F. Torrance (4 vols.; Edinburgh: T. & T. Clark, 1936–77), ii/1: 271.   [24] Ibid. 272.
[25] Ibid. 301.

Nevertheless, are those possibilities not such that they *could have been* chosen by God, so that they set no constraint or limitation on God's power and freedom? This may sound plausible, except that it is odd to speak of even a hypothetical choice of possibilities. The trouble is that possible states of affairs, unlike actual ones, are governed by relations of logical necessity which even an omnipotent being is not free to change. There may be states which exist by logical necessity—I believe that the existence of God is such a state. In such cases, their negation is not possible, though it may seem so to an imperfect understanding. Most states, however, and perhaps all particular states of a contingent space-time universe, do not exist by logical necessity. They are logically contingent. It is logically necessary that the negation of any possible contingent state is logically possible. If it is possible for X to be hot, it is necessarily possible for X to be not hot. If it is logically possible for X not to suffer, then it is necessarily possible that X suffers. Moreover, if it is possible for one state to be greater or lesser in intensive quality than another, and no maximal term is assignable to such a series of states, as seems to be the case with both happiness and suffering, then X may always suffer more than X does suffer. Thus it will be impossible even for God to put any limit on the degree and amount of suffering (or of happiness) that is possible. Because of this, many possible contingent states, including states of great suffering and happiness, are not even hypothetically choosable or variable by God. They must, in so far as they are logical possibilities, be what they are. They are contingent as to their actuality, but necessary with respect to their possibility.

God is still free with respect to possible states in two important senses, however. First, God is very largely, though not perhaps entirely, free in the choice of actual states. Some limits to freedom may exist because God's choice of some states may entail an inability to choose others. If God chooses to create free beings, for instance, God cannot make them aways do good.[26] Yet God may intelligibly be said to choose such limits hypothetically, in that God assents to them as conditions of being perfect in love. God will certainly be able to assent unconditionally to the actually perfect divine nature, and may

[26] See the discussion by Alvin Plantinga, 'The Free Will Defence', reprinted in Baruch Brody, *Readings in the Philosophy of Religion* (Englewood Cliffs, NJ: Prentice-Hall, 1974), 186.

also assent to the existence of a created universe containing much possible and some actual evil, if that possibility is a necessary condition or consequence of very great goods.

Second, God may possess an unsurpassably great degree of creative freedom in generating new forms of particular possibility out of the necessary array of relatively indeterminate possibilities in the divine understanding. There may be no completely specified set of possibilities in the divine understanding, but rather a set of archetypal values and forms of being which will be extended and specified more particularly by what may be termed the divine creative imagination, either prior to or perhaps in responsive relation with the existence of some created actual states. In this way, the total set of possible states is not immutably fixed, though a great range of possible states, setting parameters for creative specification, must be regarded as immutable and a 'given' part of the divine nature.[27]

It seems, therefore, that the possibility of great suffering will necessarily exist in the divine understanding, and that even though God assents to the actual divine nature and to the actual existence of any created universe, God cannot eliminate the possibility of pain and suffering. If suffering exists, it must derive from God—there is nowhere else for it to derive from, if God is the one and only Creator. Its actual existence does require explanation, but one can see that its possibility is not a matter of divine choice, as though it need not even have been a possibility. It is hard to see how a God who could decide even on what was to be possible could rationally decide to make extreme suffering possible, if God could exclude that possibility. In that case, a universe without even the possibility of suffering would seem to be preferable to a universe in which suffering is necessarily possible. However, if suffering is a possibility which exists by necessity, then even God cannot exclude it as a possibility, though God could exclude it as an actuality that God wills. As Leibniz put it, 'Evil springs . . . from the ideas that God has not produced by an act of his will . . . in the ideal region of the possible, that is, in the divine understanding.'[28]

One might pursue the Leibnizian picture further by supposing that possibilities do not exist as isolated atomic propositional units.

---

[27] See the penultimate section of Chapter 11 ('Divine Imagination').
[28] G. Leibniz, *Philosophische Schriften*, ed. C. K. Gerhardt (Berlin: Weidmann, 1875–90), vi. 313.

They are interconnected, in such a way that each possible state is a member of a total integrated set of states which constitutes a possible universe. One cannot simply take a possible state out of one set and insert it into another without changing its character. One can say that specific possibilities are integral to a complex cosmic whole. If this is the case, not even a being with the greatest possible power of intending and deciding, not even God, could exclude the possibility of suffering from a universe which contains certain specific goods that God might will. God cannot will suffering, as such and for itself. But, in willing a universe that contains distinctive and great goods, God might necessarily not be able to exclude the possibility of suffering. God will not intend the suffering either as an end in itself or as a *means* to good; but God may not be able to intend a particular form of good without permitting the possibility of suffering.

So far as the divine being is concerned, God can choose to actualize only what is good, so as to be the greatest conceivable being. But many possible universes which, as containing new and distinctive sorts of good, are creatable by such a God, will nevertheless contain possibilities of suffering which may be actualized, even though not directly intended by God. It would be very difficult to maintain belief in a perfect God who simply *intends* extreme suffering to exist, as it does in our universe. If one makes the whole divine being, including the possibilities within it, subject to divine decision, it will be hard to avoid that belief. Suppose, however, that the divine nature is necessarily what it is, at least in certain basic respects, which include the array of possibilities in the divine understanding. Then one may see how God could not exclude the possibility of extreme suffering in a universe like ours, if God wills this universe (that is, if God wills us, as integral members of it) to exist at all. In this way, the positing of a necessary, given divine nature provides a more coherent explanation of the existence of suffering in a universe created by a greatest conceivable being. This is a strong reason for denying the Barthian doctrine that 'there is no moment in the ways of God which is over and above this act and decision.' Only if there is such a moment can one maintain that a God who is the most perfect possible being can intentionally bring into being a universe which necessarily contains the possibility (and therefore which can contain the actuality) of extreme suffering.

THE NECESSITY OF CREATION

The British theologian Paul Fiddes also stresses an element of choice in the divine nature. He writes in a context of struggling with the idea that 'the world is in some way necessary for the being of God.'[29] He wishes to hold that God chooses to suffer for the sake of love, and this leads him to hold that creation is 'necessary in some sense to him', since it enables God to express and even fulfil the divine being in love. Wishing to affirm this, and yet to mitigate the sense of placing God under any sort of necessity, Fiddes proposes that 'God is free to be what he chooses to be.'[30] God can thus choose 'whether to be conditioned or not', and can 'choose that the world should be necessary to him'.[31]

This notion of God choosing that something should be necessary to the divine being is incoherent in the same way as the notion of God choosing to be whatever God is. God may choose to limit the divine being by creating beings who have some degree of autonomy. But even God cannot *choose* that the divine being should be such that it *must* create. Fiddes finds it unsatisfactory to suppose that God needs the world 'in the sense that there is some intrinsic necessity in his nature, binding his free choice'.[32] Thus he objects to the view of many process theologians that creativity is a necessary property of God, on the ground that it 'subordinates God to a principle of creativity which is beyond his decision'.[33] Why does he object to necessity in God? It can only be because he finds this to be some sort of constraint on God. However, I have already argued that the notion of a wholly self-decided God is incoherent. God must have a nature. Nothing other than God determines what this nature is. There is no independent principle of creativity which forces God to conform to it, even though Whitehead at least once misleadingly spoke of God as 'the primordial creature' and of creativity itself as 'the ultimate'.[34] In saying that God is necessarily omnipotent, one is not saying that there is a principle of omnipotence that God must conform to. It is simply better to be omnipotent than not. And it is better to be necessarily omnipotent than to be contingently

---

[29] Paul Fiddes, *The Creative Suffering of God* (Oxford: Clarendon Press, 1988), 57.
[30] Ibid. 67. [31] Ibid. 68. [32] Ibid. 74.
[33] Ibid. 135.
[34] A. N. Whitehead, *Process and Reality* (New York: Free Press, 1978), 31.

omnipotent. For contingency implies the possibility of failing to be omnipotent and of perhaps never having been omnipotent. If omnipotence is good, it is better to be unable to gain or lose it. Process philosophers argue that it is in a similar way better to be creative than not. If this is so, then it is perhaps better to be necessarily creative than to be contingently creative.

In any case, it does not make sense to speak of God as constrained by the divine perfection. Would it be better for God to be able to be imperfect, evil, malevolent, weak, or ignorant? Surely not. Perhaps what worries Fiddes is that, if God is necessarily good, it would make no sense to praise God for being good. After all, God has no alternative, and one does not praise someone for what they cannot help. On further reflection, however, there is surely something odd about praising God for being good, realizing that God might decide not to be good—why should God be constrained by immutability?—so that we may find ourselves one day blaming God for badness. To praise God is to revere and admire divine perfection, not to congratulate God on making good decisions.

Thus the reply to Fiddes's unease about divine freedom is that necessary goodness is no constraint upon God, but a property necessarily possessed by any perfect being. Karl Barth held that, while God is necessarily good, God's actualization of this goodness in the form of loving relationship to created beings—as Barth puts it, God's decision for fellowship—is a genuine decision, which God was free not to make.[35] Fiddes objects to the idea, espoused by Barth and standard in Christian tradition, that God might have chosen not to create. While it is God's free decision to create, God 'chooses to be completed through the world',[36] so the creation is part of God's decision to be God. Without creation, God would not be complete, would not be the reality God has chosen to be.

All this does is to involve creation in the incoherence of the idea of divine self-determination. Fiddes wishes, at the same time, to make creation more necessary to God than Barth did (since it is necessary to fulfilling the divine nature), and to make the divine nature as such not strictly necessary (since it is a result of divine choice). Yet he is using a Pickwickian notion of choice here, since he also says that

---

[35] Barth, *Church Dogmatics* ii/1: 311: 'God is self-sufficient and independent . . . he would be no different even if the [creatures] all did not exist.'
[36] Fiddes, *The Creative Suffering of God*, 68.

'there can be no meaning in the phrase, "he need not have done so" '.[37] The divine choice is such that it is necessarily what it is. Barth holds that God necessarily chooses to constitute the divine self as loving, in the Trinitarian relation; but God chooses to create, when God need not have done so. Fiddes extends the idea of God's necessary choice to include creation, since 'a desire for relationship and fellowship is certainly essential to love',[38] and God essentially constitutes the divine self as loving. 'There can be no question of God's not longing for our love', for God 'has freely chosen to be in need'.[39] What force remains to the idea of choice, however, when it makes no sense to say that it could have been otherwise? There may be an important distinction to be made between divine necessity and divine freedom, but it is not helpful to deny necessity altogether to God, on behalf of an argument for total divine freedom.

NECESSITY AND FREEDOM

John Zizioulas in a similar way makes a contrast between what he terms ancient Greek thought and Christian thought. The Greeks, he holds, saw being as constrained by necessity, and human person-hood as harmonizing with this rational necessity. The person, however, is a 'free, unique and unrepeatable entity'.[40] Christians, he holds, found the being of the Trinity itself in the person of the Father. The Father is the ultimate cause of the Trinity, and in this sense the person is the cause and the constitutive element[41] of the substance or nature, not the other way around. Persons are not bound by 'ontological necessity', but act in freedom. Thus 'the Father out of love—that is, freely—begets the Son and brings forth the Spirit.'[42] Zizioulas concludes that 'that which makes a thing to exist is not the substance or nature but the person or *hypostasis*.'[43]

This claim expresses the same sort of incoherence as those of Barth and Fiddes. For if the person is a cause, then it must have properties in virtue of which it is a cause. Indeed, Zizioulas stresses that it is a free cause, one which acts out of love. Presumably this entails that it acts out of knowledge and by intention. So the person

---

[37] Ibid. 74 f. [38] Ibid. 72. [39] Ibid. 74.
[40] John Zizioulas, *Being as Communion* (London: Darton, Longman, and Todd, 1985), 33.
[43] Ibid. 42 n. [41] Ibid. 39. [42] Ibid. 41.

must have a nature, which it does not freely choose. It would be hard for an orthodox Christian to maintain that the Father might not generate the Trinity; so it looks as if the sense of 'freedom' that is being used here is entirely compatible with necessity, after all. The alleged contrast of ancient Greek and Christian thought is far from apparent.

I think the clue to what is going on here is a distinction which Anselm makes between 'necessity' and 'will'. In *Cur Deus Homo*, Anselm argues that 'necessity is always either compulsion or restraint.'[44] In this sense, no necessity precedes or compels the will of God. If necessity is conceived as a blind force of compulsion, then God is not necessary. But it is still a fact that not everything about the nature of God can be chosen, and that the divine nature cannot be either arbitrary or wholly contingent (i.e. existing for no good reason). God consents to the divine nature, in the sense that it is what any perfectly rational and good being would choose. God's being is of supreme and unsurpassable value. There is no actual constraint or compulsion in it that God does not freely choose. If this is so, the point all these theologians are making is that God is not some sort of impersonal substance from which the universe arises by a natural and inevitable and unwilled emanation—the Neo-Platonic emanation of the many from the primal One. God is a personal being of love and freedom, who affirms the divine existence as of supreme value and in that sense wills it to be. Moreover, in a distinctively Christian insight, the supreme value is ecstatic love, an overflowing of being to share value.

In this insight that supreme value is ecstatic love lies the foundation of Fiddes's claim that God chooses the necessity of creating others. Zizioulas, like Barth, would hold that love can exist between the hypostases of the divine being itself, and so draw back from the wider claim that God necessarily creates a universe. In any case, in a carefully expressed sense, for which necessity is clearly distinguished from constraint and compulsion, it is no restriction on God to say that there are necessities in the divine nature. These necessities will include, for Christians, the generation of the Son and the Spirit from the Father. They are necessities, not of constraint, but of love. It is hard to say whether they will also include the

---

[44] Anselm, *Cur Deus Homo*, trans. S. N. Deane (La Salle, Ill.: Open Court, 1982), 288.

creation of some universe. Norman Kretzmann argues that 'the Dionysian principle' suggests that good necessarily overflows, since it is diffusive of itself by nature.[45] As Thomas Aquinas says, 'The sharing of being and goodness proceeds from goodness.'[46] Not only that, but 'this divine love, I say, did not permit him [God] to remain in himself, without offspring—that is, without the production of creatures' (Thomas, quoting Dionysius).[47] Kretzmann argues that this suggests that God necessarily creates some universe, though not any particular one. The Thomist belief that God's will is identical with God's essence, so that everything God wills is part of what God necessarily is, makes it hard to evade this conclusion—though it has to be said that Thomas explicitly denies it when the issue is explicitly posed.

The appeal to love as the supreme divine value is characteristically Christian. But similar considerations exist in other traditions. As has been noted, Heschel argues that, in so far as God is personal, God will transcend the divine being in itself in attention to the non-self.[48] Iqbal holds that God necessarily has some character, and the world is the character of God. Aurobindo sees *Sachchidananda* as expressing its nature in time, and thereby coming to true realization of itself. Barth wishes to preserve a very strong sense of divine freedom. Nevertheless, he holds that God constitutes the divine self in relation to the world in an eternal decision behind which we cannot go. In all these views, from very different traditions, the Divine is seen to have a positive relation to a created universe, which connects that universe essentially to the nature of the outflowing goodness of the Divine. For all of them, not only does the nature of God issue in created being; created being makes a real difference to God, as it enables God to express the divine self in a distinctively relational or personal way. There is a decisive break here with classical views which typically hold that God would be complete without any universe, and that no universe makes any difference to God. This is in part due to a clearer awareness of the sense in which finite goods

[45] Norman Kretzmann, 'Goodness, Knowledge, and Indeterminacy in the Philosophy of Thomas Aquinas', *Journal of Philosophy* 80 (1983), 631–49.

[46] Thomas Aquinas, *Summa Contra Gentiles* I. 37. 5, in Aquinas *Opera*, ed. R. Busa (8 vols.; Stuttgart, Gunther Holzjor, 1974–80), vol. ii, my translation.

[47] Aquinas, *In Librum Beati Dionysi: De Divinibus Nominibus* IV. ix. 409 (Rome: Marietti, 1950), p. 135, my translation.

[48] Abraham Heschel, *The Prophets* (New York: Harper, 1962), 486.

have a distinctive reality, which cannot exist within the divine being itself, and which therefore add some goods to reality which cannot exist in God alone. It seems to be characteristic of twentieth-century religious reflection to give to finite being, to time and history, a value which is integral to the divine being itself.

THE DIVINE PERFECTIONS

The realization that finite goods cannot, as such, exist in God leads inevitably to the blunt assertion that even the greatest conceivable being cannot contain in itself all possible goods. It thus leads to a decisive break with the classical view that God contains all possible perfections.[49] To gain a better idea of what goods the divine being can or cannot contain, the idea of a greatest conceivable being must be analysed further. So far the idea of maximal power has been defended as a coherent perfection, and it has been suggested that a complex property of 'knowledge-power-benevolence-wisdom' will necessarily characterize God. Since God will affirm and assent to all necessary divine properties, one can say that the necessary properties of God must be those that would be chosen as of supreme value by any being of sufficient power and knowledge to do so. But can one say with confidence what properties any omnipotent and omniscient being would choose?

I think that to some extent one can, and one can begin by emphasizing the conceptual connection between goodness and desire which has already been noted. An omnipotent, omniscient being will certainly be rational, since it will know what goals are possible and what the most effective way to obtain them is. What any rational being desires is, as such, good. Aristotle even defined goodness in terms of rational endeavour.[50] It is a plausible view that the existence of any good depends upon the existence of some consciousness which values it as good. It is not very plausible to think that one state of the universe would be better than another if no being was conscious of the difference. It is hard to see what 'betterness' would come to in such a case. The philosopher G. E. Moore once held that

---

[49] Aquinas, *Summa Theologiae*, Ia. q. 4 a. 2: '*In Deo sunt perfectiones omnium rerum*'
[50] Aristotle, *Nicomachean Ethics*, bk. 1, in *The Philosophy of Aristotle*, ed. Renford Bambrough (New York: New American Library, 1963), 286.

a beautiful universe, unseen by anyone, was better than an ugly universe.[51] But it seems to me that without being appreciated or disliked, no state of the universe would really be of greater value than any other. If that is so, value must consist in appreciation by some consciousness.

What is good is what is valued, approved of or desired by some mind. Some goods can be better than others, in the sense that some mind can prefer them. Moreover, it will be reasonable to prefer some goods to others. For example, it is rational to prefer a good which is longer-lasting, more intense, and which holds more potential for interest and so is fairly complex. It is clear, however, that different minds will prefer different goods, and that there will be a huge number of different sorts of valued states, not all of them being directly comparable to one another. How, for example, could one compare the good of hearing a Beethoven symphony with the good of an exhilarating country walk? Both are good and desirable. Yet not everyone may desire them, and there is no obvious common scale of values on which they could be placed. Much will depend on the context of such experiences, and perhaps one would choose to have both, without trying to rank them in comparative value.

If God is thought of as a being of supreme value, will God include all possible values in the divine being, to the highest degree where that is applicable? John Yates writes, 'A perfect being . . . must possess the sum total of all logically compossible attributes which could be reasonably conceived as bestowing value on their bearer.'[52] He makes it clear that he means that such attributes must be purely actual states, without any element of potentiality in them. That is almost certainly an incoherent idea, since many goods are incompatible with one another, and there is not one set of compossible goods which is greater than all others. For example, many people would find good, would prefer and choose, a state of trying to attain some object with difficulty but with some hope of success, even though there is a risk of failure. The risk increases the value of the process for many people. But such a value, of disciplined and

[51] G. E. Moore, *Principia Ethica* (Cambridge: Cambridge University Press, 1951; 1st pub. 1903), 83 f.
[52] John Yates, *The Timelessness of God* (London: University Press of America, 1990), 281.

difficult effort, is incompatible with the good of instant attainment, of pleasure without effort, which others would prefer. One can have both these goods one after the other, restful pleasure after disciplined effort perhaps. But one cannot have a state in which both exist at the same time, in one state of consciousness. Indeed, many sorts of rest are valued precisely because they are the result of striving and anticipation, and would lose their value without such a preceding state. In that sense, many goods are essentially temporal. They would lose their distinctive character if one tried to unite them in one conscious state.

Consider a piece of music. At any moment during its performance, it lacks many things, including the conclusion of the piece. But would one call the first movement of a Mozart symphony imperfect because it does not include the last movement? It would rather be imperfect if it did include the last movement, since that would destroy the dramatic tension and progression of the piece. What goes wrong is taking one temporal slice through the music, and insisting that the perfection of the piece must be found there. But it is not. It is not found at any point during the performance, not even at the playing of the final chord. It is only in the whole temporal development that this sort of good can exist at all, and its temporality is essential to the sort of goodness it is.

A certain model of perfection can hold one captive. It is the model of perfection as a visual space which can be contemplated all at once. But why should this be? One might find perfection in the unfolding of a theme through many variations to a resolution; it would be the temporally extended whole which would be perfect. Is a process imperfect because any temporal slice of it is incomplete? Why can one not speak of a continuing, permanently uncompleted, but supremely creative activity as perfect, that is, as the best possible example of its type of goodness? The obvious answer is that it lacks something; at any given moment it lacks all the properties still to exist in future. But some lack is unavoidable in any concept of perfection. After all, the *tota simul* will necessarily lack all temporal properties; it cannot possess any property which is essentially temporal. Is this then an imperfection? God, all are agreed, must be whatever it is better to be than not. A timeless God could not possess any essentially temporal good. Would it not be greater to possess some such goods, in addition to even an infinite non-temporal good? It seems to me a plausible supposition that it would.

DIVINE DESIRES

Bearing this in mind, one can see how the present absence, together with the future anticipation, of good is essentially involved in certain good states. The anticipation, the envisaging and deliberation, the planning and gradual execution, are often in themselves pleasurable states. If one is engaged in a creative process, it is essential that there should be some good yet to be realized. The encounter with various problems in the way of realization and their creative resolution is a very great good, for most creative people. Such a good may also involve frustration, the possibility of at least relative failure, and many periods of unproductive torpor. Yet without them, the creative process would be too easy, not so valuable, and not so valued when it gets going.

If one is speaking of God, one cannot speak of such things as failure and torpor. But one may wish to speak of the imaginative and creative realization of goods as itself a great good, and one that involves something analogous to desire, desire for the existence of such goods, in God. It is often said that the existence of a desire entails some lack in God. A desire is for the existence of some good, so its present lack of being is a privation of good. For this reason, theologians have been reluctant to ascribe desire to God, if such ascription means that God must lack some good, and thus be less good than God might be. If God is primarily known as the Creator, however, then it may be that divine desire is a good, the good of creative activity itself, in which the creator realises new and imaginative forms of beauty and intellectual complexity. If such creative activity is good, then it entails some unrealized desire in God; namely, particular aims which God realizes in the creative process, but which cannot be instantaneously and effortlessly wholly realized without destroying the good of the process itself.

The existence of such desires in God does not mean that God is perpetually frustrated, in not having what God wants. It is not that God wants something which God does not have, and frets because God has not got it. On the contrary, God wants to have the desires God has, desires for future goods. God does not fret or feel frustrated or incomplete in not having them already realized. It is a good thing that there are many goods which may be realized if God wishes, and it would be contradictory to wish to have them already realized without creative action. What is required here is a clear distinction between 'desire' in the sense of a frustrated wish, and 'desire' in the sense of a calm and creative realizing of new forms of goodness. To have desire in the former sense is an imperfection; but to have desire in the latter sense is a perfection, for it is a condition of creative action, which is itself good.

It may well be, even though it seems paradoxical at first sight, that the most perfect possible being is one that does not possess every good property, nor even an unchanging state consisting of a large set of compossible properties. For the possession of the great good of creativity entails the non-possession of many goods yet to be creatively realized, and the existence of desire for their realization. So one arrives at the idea of God as desiring to realize creatively many sorts of good.

This is the idea which Mohammed Iqbal stressed, in seeing God as essentially creative.[53] Divine power may not be the total determination of everything in one timeless act. It may rather be an endless imaginative creation of new realities and valuable states. Such an interpretation of power as creativity prompts a non-determinist picture of the universe as open to new initiatives. It suggests the possibility of a truly responsive relationship of God to creatures which may have their own limited creativity. It gives to created reality an importance and value for God that it cannot have when God is considered to have the fulness of value in the divine being from all eternity.

IMMUTABLE AND CONTINGENT DIVINE PROPERTIES

It looks, in any case, as if one cannot assert that God actually possesses all possible goods. For if all the goods God possesses are actualized in one state, then the being of God must exclude all temporal goods, all the goods of creativity and imagination. God, so conceived, will lack an indeterminately large number of goods altogether. On the other hand, if God is to possess such temporal goods, then God cannot actually possess them all at once, which would contradict their nature. One will have to think of something like an infinite realization of an endless series of goods. God will be unexhaustibly creative of good, but will not actually possess all possible goods immutably and timelessly.

[53] See Ch. 3.

This does not mean that God is in a condition of total changeability and that one cannot therefore be sure of what God will be in future. A condition of such everlasting creativity in God is that God should immutably and indeed necessarily possess precisely those properties which are necessary conditions of being an inexhaustible creator of good. God will necessarily possess the property of being the source of all creativity. God will necessarily possess knowledge of all the good things that might be created, and of the best way in which they might be realized. God will necessarily possess unlimited power, which can continually produce new goods. God will necessarily find supreme happiness in the contemplation of the good things thus produced. God will necessarily be incapable of being brought into being or of being destroyed. Thus God will necessarily possess the sort of properties which Anselm himself specified: 'Truly are You perceptive, omnipotent, merciful and impassible, just as You are living, wise, good, blessed, eternal, and whatever it is better to be rather than not to be.'[54] I have, however, given a different interpretation of the attributes of impassibility and eternity than Anselm, taking them to signify, respectively, 'power of indestructibility' and 'everlastingness'. God must possess these properties necessarily, since it is better to possess them necessarily than to possess them contingently (so that they could be lost, changed, or impaired). God will never change in the possession of these properties, and there is accordingly no possibility that God will change unpredictably.

These properties are essential to the divine nature; and though God would freely choose them, in fact they can neither come into being nor pass away nor be changed in any way, either by God or by anything else whatever. God therefore possesses a number of essential or necessary properties. But God also possesses a number of contingent properties. Broadly speaking, the set of essential properties which exist in relation to a created universe consists of what may be called dispositional properties.

God's beatitude consists in the actual enjoyment of the divine goodness. But it also consists in the disposition to take delight in the things that God does and knows. The dispositional property of having the inclination to delight in all values is the necessarily possessed property. The occurrent property of actually enjoying some set of existing values is contingently possessed. For if there is an endless creation of values from the being of God, then the set of existing values will continually change. Thus the occurrent state of God's delighting in such a set of values will also continually change.

God's wisdom is the disposition to order all things to their proper fulfilment. This is a dispositional property, and it is necessarily possessed. But there is also an occurrent state of divine wisdom, by which God sees all possible and all actually existent things in their proper order and relationship. This occurrent property is contingently possessed, since it will change in correlation with changes in the actual existence of beings.

God's power is the disposition to bring states into being for the sake of their goodness. This capacity is necessarily possessed. God can never lack such power, nor suffer any constraint upon it, unless such a constraint is self-imposed. But the actual exercise of divine power on any given occasion is contingent, since it is exercised in specific ways which could be other than they are, or indeed need not exist at all.

God's omniscience is the capacity to know everything that becomes actual, whenever it does so. This capacity is necessarily possessed. But God's actual knowledge will be of all possibles and all actuals, and it will change as the set of actual existents changes. The occurrent state of divine knowledge is accordingly contingently possessed. It changes and it could have been otherwise in any given case, if God had created different actual existents.

The set of contingent properties consists of all those particular states of the divine being which form the particular content of the divine knowledge and beatitude, and the particular exercises of the divine power and wisdom. The dispositional properties are immutable; the occurrent properties are in continual change, as the divine awareness lives in a process of everlastingly self-expressive dynamic creativity.

The thesis that God is in a state of perpetual change requires a modification of the classical hypothesis that if God is perfect, change in God is impossible, since change requires either an increase or a decrease in perfection. That classical hypothesis does not, in any case, seem compelling. There are properties which a perfect God must possess, like happiness and power, which have no maximal term, so that no being can, as a matter of logic, exhibit them maximally. One could always be happier than one is, however happy one is. It is good for God to be happy, and to be happier than any other actual being. But whatever state God is in, it is always logically possible to be happier. If this is so, even in a perfect being not all change would necessarily be for the worse (as Aristotle held it would be[55]). It would always be possible to increase in non-maximizable perfections, or to vary their precise quality, even if their intensity is lessened to some degree. It may be preferable to have a great variety of differing goods, even of lesser intensity, than one unvarying good. Yet this would not render the previous state of the divine being less than perfect, since it would still be the greatest actual degree of happiness at that time, and there simply is no maximum possible degree. This logical point is made elegantly by Charles Hartshorne, who developed the 'principle of dual transcendence' for construing divine perfection most plausibly. God's happiness, or similar intensive properties, may be unsurpassed and unsurpassable by any other actual being at a given time, but surpassable by itself at some future time.[56] This seems an intelligible construal of a notion of perfection for any property which does not have a maximal degree, and it helps to undermine one argument for the strict and total immutability of God.

The same is true of the property of power. It is easy to construct a verbal maximum of power, just by saying that God is omnipotent. But it is much harder to spell out just what is involved in this notion. If power is construed as capacity, does it make sense to say that there is a number of capacities such that no number could be greater? If there is an infinite number of possible capacities, to say that God possesses all possible capacities is to say that God possesses no definite assignable number. That may well be true, and indeed I think it is implied by the biblical notion of supreme divine power. God may have numberless capacities; God may be wholly unrestricted in power. But is that to say that God is actually in an unchanging state of exercising maximal power? Or is it not rather to say that there is literally no end to the number of ways in which God may exercise power?

What happened in the classical doctrine was a capitulation to a basic metaphysical temptation to turn dispositions into states, to

[55] Aristotle, *Metaphysics* 1074^b.
[56] Charles Hartshorne, *Creative Synthesis and Philosophic Method* (London: SCM Press, 1970), 227 ff.

deny time, potentiality, and change by somehow subsuming them under changeless actuality. This might be called the temptation to hypostatize potentiality, to think that powers and capacities can be explained by translating them into wholly actual states. The truth may in fact be precisely the reverse, namely that one can only explain the nature of many actual states by knowing the sorts of development, relationship, and behaviour of which they are a particular expression. One can say that God has maximal power; but one is not thereby saying that some actual state that God is in constitutes the complete actualization of such power. One is saying that God has inexhaustible capacities, that there is no end to the number of things God can do, and that all other powers depend upon God's. To possess perfect power is not to be in some state such that all possible powers are exercised at the same time by the same being—a dubiously coherent idea. It is to be able to exercise an innumerable set of powers limitlessly, without restriction or limitation. Maximal power is, after all, maximal potency, not maximal actuality. It is more like a potency for infinite realization than the possession of some occurrent property of 'being powerful'.

Thus an omnipotent, omniscient, and perfectly wise being will be necessarily good, in the sense that it will maximize in its own being a great number of compossible intrinsically desirable states.[57] God will be good as the supreme object of rational desire, whose being is fulfilled in the contemplation of its own supreme goodness. God will necessarily possess omnipotence, omniscience, wisdom, and goodness, but will contingently possess the specific states which are the actual exercises of that power, knowledge, and goodness.

Some theologians have found difficulty with the idea that God may be both necessary and contingent. H. P. Owen, for example, bluntly says that the idea is self-contradictory.[58] The appearance of contradiction disappears entirely if one simply says that God possesses both necessary and contingent properties. There is no contradiction at all in that claim, since one is not saying that God is both necessary and contingent at the same time and in the same respect. One is saying that God necessarily possesses certain

[57] Richard Swinburne gives an argument for this conclusion in *The Christian God*, 65–71.

[58] H. P. Owen, *The Christian Knowledge of God* (London: Athlone Press, 1969), 105 ff.

dispositional properties—and, of course, many occurrent properties, too, such as God's knowledge of the eternal divine nature itself—and contingently possesses many occurrent properties—namely, those which are related to the temporal and contingent processes of the created universe, which God continually and creatively brings about.

This should not be a very surprising notion of a God who is, after all, seen in the major scriptural traditions primarily as Creator. But even in the realization of supreme value in the divine being itself, one cannot coherently think of all possible values somehow summarized into one timeless actual state. One must think of God as bringing into being, within the divine life, an endless series of goods or desirable states. Perfection is not the actual possession of every possible sort of goodness, which is a logical impossibility. It is the possession of an infinite power which by nature creatively manifests itself in endless forms of particular goodness.

Neither Indian nor Semitic traditions have, however, been happy to accept the idea of temporality and change in the divine being itself, or the associated idea of potentiality in God which the notion of everlasting temporal creativity entails. At this point the Semitic faiths have been most influenced by their common Greek philosophical background. In examining that background, it will be possible to understand the attraction of an attribution of pure timelessness and actuality to the Divine. My suggestion will be that such an attribution arises from a misleading application of the insight that God must be greater than any human thought can comprehend.[59] The infinity of the divine being must be asserted; but that is compatible with the view, central to all revealed religions, that the Infinite makes itself truly known in creative self-manifesting activity in relation to finite beings. The classical traditions in theology have, I will argue, failed to reconcile these two aspects of the divine being in a fully coherent way.

[59] Anselm, *Proslogion*, ch. 15: 137: 'You are also something greater than can be thought.'

8

Divine Wisdom and the Intelligibility of the Universe

GREEK IDEAS OF PERFECTION

What has governed the classical idea of divine perfection in the Semitic traditions is the Platonic view that the world of space and time is a half-real image of the real world of intelligible Forms. Such Forms are beyond time and change, and temporal things are real only in so far as they participate in the timeless. The Forms are arranged in a hierarchy, the highest being the Form of the Good, which in some way gives rise to all the others. All good things are good by participation in the form of goodness itself. Plato speaks of all beds participating in the Form of perfect Bedness, which the soul can perceive in intellectual cognition.[1] In the same way, the Form of Goodness itself can be intuited by the soul which has trained itself in gymnastics and pure mathematics. For such a view, any supreme being (though Plato has no clear doctrine of such a being) would have to be beyond time and potency. It would have to have more the character of a subsistent Form or essence than of a particular individual.

It should be said that it is not at all clear that Plato held this view consistently, or as a systematically worked out view. But it is present in his works, and it fundamentally influenced thinkers for over two thousand years, to enshrine in their minds an idea of the timeless as the truly real. Later thinkers, who regarded themselves as followers of Plato, began to speak of the vision of Goodness as the aim of a spiritual quest of mystical perfection. Plato himself had a much more prosaic account. A course of tough physical exercise and geometry was what was needed to give a vision of the Good. Plato may not have been the mystic some have thought him to be, but a rather austere intellectual with decidedly authoritarian and elitist views.[2]

---

[1] Plato, *Republic* 597ᵃ. (Harmondsworth: Penguin, 1974).
[2] See Karl Popper, *The Open Society and Its Enemies* (London: Routledge, 1945).

Nonetheless, through the influence of Philo and the Neo-Platonists, Western theists worked with an assumption that God, as supreme reality, must somehow be a timeless subsistent Form. Though Aristotle came to be an even more important influence in medieval times, the basic Platonic idea of the Good remained dominant.

Aristotle repudiated the existence of a separate world of Forms in general, but when he came to think about the notion of a perfect being, he resorted to the basically Platonic notion. His view can be found expressed in the *Physics*, book 7, and *Metaphysics*, book 12. Aristotle argues that 'Everything that changes is something and is changed by something and into something.'[3] Everything that changes is changed by another. There cannot be an infinite regress of such changes, or there would be no explanation for the existence of the whole series. So there must exist an unchanged thing, which accounts for all changes. Aristotle does not hold, however, that there must be some temporally first unchanged cause of change. On the contrary, he holds that 'it is impossible that movement should either have come into being or cease to be.'[4] Time has no beginning or end. Time is measured by change or motion, therefore movement must be continuous, without beginning or end.

At this point Aristotle's thought takes what must seem to us a curious turn, for he holds that only circular motion is continuous. The clearest cases of continuous circular motion are the heavenly spheres, whose movements account for all other changes in the universe in some way. Each heavenly sphere has its own mover— there are either forty-seven or fifty-five of them—but all the other heavenly spheres take their motion from the outermost sphere, the sphere of the fixed stars. It has existed without beginning. Since its motion needs to be explained, it must be moved by 'something which moves without being moved, being eternal, substance and actuality'. This ultimate mover is absolutely unmoved. Its 'very essence must be actuality',[5] otherwise it might cease to exist, and so it could not cause ceaseless movement. It must be simple, without parts or magnitude. For 'it produces movement through infinite time.' Yet it cannot have infinite magnitude, since there is no such thing. And it cannot have finite magnitude, or it could not produce movement through infinite time. So it has no magnitude, and is not

---

[3] Aristotle, *Metaphysics* 1070ᵃ ed. and tr. W. D. Ross (Oxford: Clarendon Press, 1928).   [4] Ibid. 1071ᵇ.   [5] Ibid.

in space. Since space is what individuates by allowing extensive magnitude to exist, the First Mover is without divisible parts.[6] Since it is not in space, it cannot move. And since movement is the first sort of change, upon which all others depend, it cannot change in any way.

Thus Aristotle arrives at the idea of a substance which is non-spatial, simple, immutable, purely actual, and eternal. It 'can in no way be otherwise than as it is',[7] and so one has the notion of an absolute explanation of change. All change requires an explanation of why it changes as it does. An explanation will be *absolute* if it shows that the ultimate reason lies in a reality which cannot be other than it is, and which causes change while being logically unchangeable. This is an absolute explanation, since if it can be shown that a substance cannot be otherwise, and that it necessarily does what it does, explanation has come to an end.[8] If it can be shown that the substance necessarily and continuously causes change in the universe, then one sees, as fully as one possibly could, why things are as they are.

ABSOLUTE EXPLANATION

The basic argument is mixed up with many details and physical assumptions which must seem to anyone today either odd or mistaken, or both—assumptions about the perfection of circular motion, the heavenly spheres and their eternity, and so on. Yet there remains an attraction about the idea that explanation terminates in necessity, an attraction felt strongly by contemporary cosmologists.[9] If we could only get an absolute explanation of the universe which is somehow necessarily true, then at last our quest for explanation would be satisfied. It must be admitted that the Aristotelian explanation remains purely hypothetical. It cannot be shown that some substance cannot be otherwise than it is, or even that such an

---

[6] Aristotle, *Metaphysics* 1073^a.

[7] Ibid. 1072^b.

[8] The idea of an absolute explanation is defined by Richard Swinburne, in *The Existence of God* (Oxford: Clarendon Press, 1979), 76. He does not believe there can be an absolute explanation of contingent occurrences.

[9] See the comment of Steven Weinberg: 'We would prefer a greater sense of logical inevitability in the theory' *The First Three Minutes* (London: André Deutsch, 1977), 17.

idea has any content. It cannot be shown that all changes in the universe necessarily follow from the existence of such a substance. Aristotle's supposition of one ultimate prime mover of the outer heavenly sphere, and fifty-five (or forty-seven) subsidiary but equally unmoved movers for the other heavenly spheres, carries no conviction. How, in any case, could its existence necessarily give rise to and account for all the changes we see in the universe? Presumably the connection between the First Mover and its effects is not deductive, since deductive relations hold only between propositions. There are no purely deductive relations between real existents. The appeal must again be to some sort of factually, not logically, necessary connection. But, while such a notion may not be incoherent, it is hard to see just what sort of 'explanation' this is, which remains basically incomprehensible to us.

The biblical writers never raised the question of why God is as God is or why God does what God does. They encountered God in their history as a providential, glorious, loving, and holy being, who came to be seen as the creator of heaven and earth. The universe could be accounted for by tracing it to the will of God, though the prophets never claimed to understand that will in more than the tiny part of it which touched their own destiny. The question of what could account for God was never raised. It remained an ultimate mystery.[10] It is clear, however, that nothing other than God can account for God. Either God cannot be accounted for—which makes the divine existence and nature something which just happens to be the case—or the divine nature accounts for its own existence. To 'account for' is to give a reason; thus the reason for God's existence must lie in that existence itself. To that extent, a reflective theism does seem to point to an idea of a self-explanatory being, which is what Aristotle was seeking to articulate.

Aristotle sees that the best reason for the existence of anything is its goodness: 'the real good is the primary object of rational wish.'[11] If I ask, 'Why should X exist?', a good reason is that it is intrinsically valuable that it should exist. The good is that which can be reasonably desired; and it is good in itself that there should exist a state which consists in the contemplation of supreme beauty and goodness. This is the best of reasons for the existence of a being of supreme goodness, namely, that its existence is supremely desirable,

[10] See Job 42: 1–6   [11] Aristotle, *Metaphysics* 1072ᵃ.

not least to itself.[12] Of course, that something is desirable does not entail its existence. It is rather that the best reason that something *should* exist is its intrinsic value. But if there is something which, as Aristotle has suggested, cannot exist otherwise than as it does, the best reason for its existence would lie in its supreme goodness. One might conceive of a necessary being which was not good. Then one could think of no reason for its existence, and it would be rationally inexplicable, even though necessary, just as much as any merely contingent brute fact. To be rationally explicable, it has to contain the reason for its existence in itself. So a rationally explicable being is a necessary being which is supremely good. Hypothetically, a supremely good being might not exist; and a necessarily existent being might not be good. But a supremely good necessary being is ultimately explanatory, in that it necessarily desires its own existence as that which is most worthy of existence, and does not derive it from any other being.

None of this establishes that a necessary being exists, or even that the idea of a necessary being is non-vacuous. I think we just cannot see how any being could exist of necessity.[13] But I do not think we can rule out the notion as incoherent. It is incomprehensible to us, as one might expect of a supreme being. But one can suppose that there might be a necessary being which, if it is supremely good, would be an ultimate explanation for its own existence at least.

If one enquires into the conditions of the possibility of a necessarily existent being, one may begin by reflecting that, as Kant said, it will be a being whose non-existence is impossible. Thus it will exist in every possible world. No possible world can exist without its being present. Kant suggested that every particular thing can be thought away, in some possible world.[14] But it is a plausible supposition that, if something is ever possible (exists in one possible world), then it is always possible (it is a possibility in every world). So the complete array of possibles cannot be thought away in any world.

---

[12] See John Leslie, *Universes* (London: Routledge, 1989).

[13] Immanuel Kant, *Critique of Pure Reason*, tr. N. Kemp Smith (London: Macmillan, 952; 1st pub. 1781), A592–4.

[14] Ibid. A595. Nevertheless, Kant never lost his attachment to an argument to a necessary being which he gave in the *Nova Dilucidatio* of 1755 (Berlin: German Academy of Sciences, 1902), i. 395 ff, a version of which I present in the next paragraph of the text.

One might simply say, in objection, that possibles do not exist. But the Platonic reminiscence continues to haunt us, that the possibility of things is not a mere non-being. It is a potentiality to be. It has some form of existence. If so, it must have some form of actuality, an actuality which Plato called the intelligible realm, and which Augustine called the mind of God. In this realm, all potentialities for being exist, not as actual, and yet not as simple nullities. Beneath the actual existence of things around us, there hovers a vast world of possible reality, a realm which may be called the 'depth of being', or, in Boethius' phrase, the 'infinite ocean of being'.

The depth of being is the actual foundation of all possibilities for being. If it did not exist, then no possibilities would exist. It exists, as one and the same unbounded reality, in every possible world, since all possibles exist, as possible, in every actual world. The depth of being is beyond all finite actual beings. It is the root and source of every possibility for being. In the Vedantic tradition, as expounded by Aurobindo, it is *Sat*, the unlimited reality which is the foundation, the 'storehouse', of every possible actuality. In the thought of such an unbounded reality which sustains all possibilities, which gives form and intelligibility to every possible world, which cannot be thought away without destroying the possibility of every world, lies the hint of what necessary being may be. It cannot be thought, and it cannot be thought away. Beyond every finite actuality, it is the actual foundation of every possibility. Theists assent to it, not merely as the result of an abstract argument, whose success is always in doubt. They assent to it as the 'cloud of unknowing' of contemplative prayer, arising out of a feeling for the deep yet mysterious intelligibility of being, and a sense of the complete aseity of God, as unrestricted being.

If God is the depth of being, God is also the power of being. A reality which cannot fail to exist is a reality which carries the power of existing in itself. No finite thing has the power to exist of itself. Things may come into existence or pass away, but the power which gives them existence is from beyond them. Only in the case of God is the power to exist fully possessed and inalienable. God is the self-existent, 'one without a second'.[15] Having the power to sustain being

---

[15] *Chandogya Upanishad* 6. 2. 1, in R. C. Zaehner (trans.), *Hindu Scriptures* (London: Dent, 1966), 105.

in itself, only God has the power to give the gift of being, to bring potentiality into actuality. The creative power of being is what makes potencies truly capable of being. They will exist only by that power. In the Vedantic tradition, the power of being is *Chit*, construed by Aurobindo as creative consciousness. It not only passively contemplates possible beings. It actively holds them in being, and gives to them real possibility, the power-to-be. As it necessarily actualizes its own possibility, so it has the power to actualize other possibilities, from the unbounded store of potentiality inherent in its own nature. It is an active and creative consciousness, an intelligence whose object is its own unbounded nature.

The divine power of actualization operates primarily upon itself. If one asks which potentialities will be actualized, then one may consider that potentialities are not simply neutral in being. Some have intrinsic value and some intrinsic disvalue. There is good reason to actualize possible states of intrinsic value and to suppress possible states of disvalue. In actualizing those parts of the divine nature which are capable of actualization, God will actualize a set of supreme values out of all the possible states which God could instantiate. Such an actualized set constitutes the manifestation of being, primarily the supreme beauty, the supreme value, of the Divine Self. This manifestation of being is *Ananda*, the divine joy or bliss, arising from the contemplation of supreme value, actualized from the infinite depth of being by the creative power of being. Aurobindo's characterisation of the Divine as *Sachchidananda*, the infinite depth, creative power, and blissful beauty of being, offers a way of understanding God as necessary self-existent supreme value.

In this way, one may catch some glimpse, however fleeting and fragmentary, of how one might think of God as necessarily existent and supremely good. The question of the creation of beings other than God remains open on this account so far, though clearly God may freely actualize possible worlds if there is good reason to do so. What this account suggests is that God, as necessarily existent, who is both the self-existent power of being and the all-conceiving depth of being, will actualize in the divine nature a supremely valuable set of states which, manifesting a pure wisdom and beauty, will express the glory of being.

THE VALUE OF CREATIVITY

It is some argument like this that Aristotle may have had in mind, when he moved from the assertion that the First Mover cannot be other than it is, to the assertion that it must be in itself supremely good or desirable. Aristotle holds that if God is supremely desirable, then God might move other things by desire: 'the final cause, then, produces motion as being loved (*hos eromenon*).'[16] This, he thinks, explains how something can move without being itself moved. It can move as an object of thought or desire moves, by being an object of desire. We are to think of the outermost heavenly sphere as turning in a circle out of love for the necessarily existent supreme goodness. The Supreme Being loves itself; for, as perfect, it 'thinks of that which is most divine and precious, and it does not change; for change would be change for the worse.'[17] It is itself the most precious object of thought, so 'it must be of itself that the divine thought thinks'; the divine thought and its object are the same. God is the contemplation of the divine being, in one self-reflexive and changeless act.

Aristotle's explanation of change seems to require that the heavenly spheres are inhabited by souls which are capable of desire, and which desire their supremely good movers. The ultimate unmoved mover turns the outermost sphere by its goodness; in that sense, God is 'the love that moves the sun and other stars'.[18] Most commentators accept that the First Mover, for Aristotle, will have no knowledge of the physical world, being absorbed in changeless self-contemplation. God does not create matter out of nothing, since matter always exists. The physical world takes form by desire for the divine perfection, but God remains unmoved by whatever happens beneath the starry spheres.

The Aristotelian idea of God clearly depends upon many assumptions which would not be widely shared in modern physics. To be blunt, his physics was mostly mistaken, and his deliberations about the perfection of circular movements in nature are of no scientific interest. It is even rather odd that his idea should have been used to construct an idea of God, since it specifically excludes the idea of creation. Aristotle's God does not create the physical

---

[16] Aristotle, *Metaphysics* 1072[b].   [17] Ibid. 1074[b].
[18] Dante, *Il Paradiso*, canto 33.

universe, which always exists; it does not actively affect the physical universe, or even show awareness of it. It simply gives rise to circular movements among the heavenly spheres by its own intrinsic perfection, which arouses their desire to move in circular ways.

What attracts some people to an Aristotelian view is that it seems to offer the prospect of an absolute explanation for the existence of the universe. If all change stands in need of explanation, then the best possible explanation will be one which appeals to an unchanging reality which gives rise to change in other things, an unmoved mover. But one still has to ask, why does that unchanging reality exist, and why does it cause change in other things? The only possible answer to the first question is that it exists necessarily, because there is no alternative to its existence. But what can answer the question of why it brings about other things? The most obvious possibility is that change necessarily arises from the unmoved mover. This universe emanates from it either as the only possible world (Schleiermacher),[19] or as one of the totality of all possible worlds, all of which are existent (Spinoza),[20] or as the best possible world (Leibniz).[21]

Theists have not usually taken any of these options, however, as they have usually thought that this is not the only, or the best, possible world. The appeal must simply be to the will of God; and then, unfortunately, one has introduced a huge element of the inexplicable, of sheer mystery, at the critical point. The whole point of a completely explanatory being was to leave no change unaccounted for. But appeal to a creator who could have done otherwise leaves the very basis of all physical changes unaccounted for, except by reference to the inscrutable will of God. The case is made worse by the consideration that it is hard to see how a God who is wholly necessary can have a contingent will. Not only is the necessary being incomprehensible. It is incomprehensible why it wills as it does. It seems incomprehensible how it can be both necessary in nature and

---

[19] F. Schleiermacher, *The Christian Faith* pt. 1, sect. 2, para. 54 (Edinburgh: T. & T. Clark, 1989; 1st pub. 1830), p. 211: 'Everything for which there is a causality in God happens and becomes real.'

[20] Spinoza, *Ethics*, prop. 16, tr. A. Boyle and G. H. R. Parkinson (London:). M. Dent, 1993; 1st pub 1677), p. 16.

[21] Leibniz, *Monadology*, para. 55, in Leibniz, *Philosophical Writings*, ed. G. H. R. Parkinson, tr. Mary Morris and G. H. R. Parkinson (London: J. M. Dent, 1973; 1st pub. 1714), p. 187.

contingent in will (which is part of its nature) at the same time. This is a strange sort of 'explanation' indeed!

Something can, nevertheless, be done to show how such an ultimate incomprehensibility is supremely intelligible, and the basis of the intelligibility of the created universe. What, after all, could explain God's choice to create this, rather than some other, universe? Nothing except the will to create certain values rather than others, or not to do so. Is appeal to such a will a real explanation? It may well seem that if one's ultimate appeal is to the mystery of the divine will, one has given up any attempt at ultimate explanation. There is a sense in which appeal to divine choice has greater explanatory power than appeal to blind chance. One will be able to explain the existence and nature of the universe by supposing that it is conceived and rationally chosen for the sake of the goods it produces.[22] That is very different from saying that there is no explanation for it at all.

But can one account for the actual set of values which are chosen for actualization? Appealing again to the idea of supreme value, one may argue that there is a value in creative choice, in freedom to act in undetermined, truly original ways. If there is such value, it may be better for a supremely perfect being to be creative in some respect, as part of divine perfection. God will be essentially creative, though precisely what God creates will be subject to pure divine creative decision. In this way, one might argue that a perfect being is essentially a creator, with freedom and potency in many respects, not a purely actual being whose creation of the world remains without satisfactory explanation. The explanation of contingent creation is in terms of the value of creative freedom, and it may be entailed by the existence of that value that not every specific occurrence can be 'explained', in the sense of deductively derived from some set of premises. For such quasi-deductive explanation would eliminate precisely the creative freedom which is part of the supreme goodness of the First Mover.

What one needs to examine is the model of explanation which is being appealed to in all such metaphysical speculations. The model which has attracted philosophers has often been that of deductive inference, where events are explained by showing that they inevitably follow from their causes. But if one's dominant model of

---

[22] Richard Swinburne rightly holds that this is better than no explanation at all (*The Existence of God* (Oxford: Clarendon Press, 1979), ch. 4).

explanation is rather that of intended value, then events will be explained by showing that they contribute to the existence of some rationally desirable state. Instead of saying that God explains by necessarily producing a specific universe, one may suppose that God explains by exercising the value of creative choice—which requires that no purely deductive explanation will be adequate. Aristotle does appeal to an 'intended value' model, in regarding God as the final cause of the universe, that for the sake of which the universe exists. But he is unable to regard God as the efficient cause, since matter is uncreated, and God does not play an active part in making things what they are. Rather, things just pattern themselves on the divine perfection, so that they imperfectly mirror values which exist fully in God.

The problem for theologians was to make God the efficient cause of all things, without compromising the simplicity and unchangeability which are characteristics of the Aristotelian picture of God. The account classically developed was an heroic failure. It was heroic in showing how matter could be produced by God without change in God, in imitation of the divine perfection. It was nevertheless a failure, since it could not account for the contingency of the universe. That which is wholly necessary can only produce that which is necessary. A contingent universe can only be accounted for if one makes free creativity a characteristic of the First Mover, which entails placing change and contingency within the First Mover itself—a forbidden move, for any Platonist or Aristotelian.

The 'best possible explanation' requires a reference both to necessity and to the choice of goodness. For Aristotle, God is both the necessarily existing being and the supremely good being; but God is unable actively to bring other things about, nor would God wish to do so. However, one can conceive a God who is able to bring other things into being for the sake of their goodness, a sort of goodness that cannot exist in the necessary being itself. A good reason for the existence of the universe is that it instantiates forms of goodness that could not otherwise exist. A universe is brought into being for this reason, by a being which exists necessarily, as supremely good and possessed of unlimited potency for other forms of goodness. The existence of this sort of reason entails that this is not a necessitarian universe, so that there cannot be a sufficient, all-determining first cause. But it also rules out arbitrariness, for it is not arbitrary to bring something about because of its goodness. This revision of Aristotle gives a more plausible sense to seeing God as 'the love which moves the stars'. For love can now be seen as active creativity, freely realizing endless finite goods, in a way impossible for Aristotle's utterly changeless self-contemplating Prime Mover.

We can perhaps begin to discern how the very necessity of the divine existence, which, as supremely valuable, includes the value of free creativity, will entail the existence of a creative, and therefore contingently acting, will in God. We can see how such a will must be unpredictable, even though it always wills for the sake of good. Such a God can be both incomprehensible and an absolute explanation. One can in principle explain the universe as fully as possible by showing how it is necessary for the actualization of specific forms of goodness, and how a being which actualizes such goodness is the self-existent ground of all possible being. But one can see that what accounts for the specific choices of such a being, and what it is that makes divine existence necessary, are matters beyond the possibility of human comprehension. One can see that there is, or may be, an absolute explanation, and that if there is, and perhaps precisely because there is, we would be unable to grasp it fully, since it ultimately lies in the mystery of the divine essence and freely creative will. It lies in the mystery of the divine wisdom, which is the unfathomable reality underlying the intelligibility of the universe.

THE IDEA OF DIVINE NECESSITY

The very possibility of God as a necessary being could, of course, be denied. One clear form of denial is given by Richard Gale.[23] He argues that if God is supposed to be a perfectly good being which exists necessarily, that excludes the possibility of a world without a God, or of a world with unjustifiable evil in it, or of a world which is evil overall. For a necessary being is a being which exists in every possible world, by definition. Yet these other conceivable states, says Gale, are intuitively logically possible; therefore God cannot be a necessary being—there are possible worlds in which God does not exist. Indeed, Gale holds that 'if God is so conceived [as having necessary existence], it follows that he does not and cannot exist.'[24] This is certainly false and a careless slip on Gale's part. If God is

[23] Richard Gale, *On the Nature and Existence of God* (Cambridge: Cambridge University Press, 1991) 224–37.
[24] Ibid. 202.

conceived as existent in every possible world, what follows is merely that no world is possible without God. Now to this Gale simply retorts that he can imagine a world without God, therefore at least one world is possible without God, therefore God cannot be a necessary being. But this is only so if it follows from the fact that Gale can imagine x that x is possible, and I see no reason to accept that. One can imagine an infinite number of worlds without God; all one has to do is think of all possible worlds and subtract God from them, leaving them otherwise the same. This is a prima-facie argument for the possible existence of such worlds. But does it *follow* from this that such imagined worlds are existentially possible? This would require the axiom: 'Whatever I can imagine is possible'. Far from being true, this seems false in many cases. Mathematicians imagined squaring the circle for centuries; but it has been proved not to be possible. I can imagine that there is an even number which is not the sum of two primes; but such a thing is probably not possible. The plain fact is that what one can imagine is not a reliable guide to logical possibility in complex cases. And if logical possibility means lack of contradiction, it is almost certainly untrue that any state at all which is not self-contradictory might actually exist. We simply have no idea of the conditions of the possibility of real existence. The Humean Ontological Argument, that what one can conceive is actually possible, is no better than the Anselmian Ontological Argument, that since we can conceive a necessary being, it must exist. If a perfectly good necessary being exists, then unjustifiable evil is not existentially possible in any world; and we would see this if and only if we could clearly conceive the conditions of real existence and possibility. So Gale should have said that, if God is conceived as having necessary existence, it follows that many things we think we can imagine are in fact so sketchily, incompletely, or confusedly conceived that they cannot even possibly exist. Is that very surprising? I should have thought it was a fairly familiar philosophical experience, as anyone should agree who has met a range of Absolute Idealists, sense-datum theorists, central-state materialists, and phenomenologists. At least some of them are talking about things that are not even possible—Gale even thinks theists are, or might be, such people. I conclude that, for all we know, there is a possible being which, if it is possible, is actual. The argument to it mentioned here is not an argument from concepts alone, an ontological argument, but from the postulate of the absolute intelligibility of the cosmos, the completion of that search for understanding which is such a natural and valued trait of the human mind. That requires, if taken to its fullest conclusion, the grounding of all actual states in a reality which necessarily exists and thus uniquely and fully answers the question, 'Why is there anything at all?'

As necessarily existent, and having both necessary and contingent properties, the general nature and existence of the contingent properties being necessarily rooted in the necessary properties, and their specific actualization being subject to the necessary property of being freely creative, God is not an arbitrary or random brute fact. As the foundation of value, God can provide a reason for actualizing a set of possibilities as expressive of some set of ultimate values. And as free and creative in particular actions, God can avoid both the morally dubious determinism of sufficient reason and the rationally dubious randomness of brute factuality.

THE FIRST CAUSE ARGUMENT

Muslim philosophers and the Jewish theologian Maimonides all adapted Aristotle's thought to develop their notion of God. The inheritor of their arguments, and the philosophical theologian who articulated the classical concept of God most elegantly and fully, was Thomas Aquinas. Aristotle's argument resurfaces, without explicit reference to its cosmological background, in Thomas Aquinas's first of the Five Ways for demonstrating God's existence: 'Of necessity, anything moved is moved by something else . . . now we must stop somewhere.'[25] The key principle Thomas appeals to is the principle, which I am inclined to accept, that the actual is prior to the potential. Mere potentialities do not exist; they must be founded on prior actualities. When something comes into existence (all change is a bringing into being of what was previously only able to be), it must be brought about by something already actual. The hard question is what sort of actuality this might be, and how possibilities might be 'in' it. Aquinas's answer to this question rests on a Platonic and Aristotelian framework which most philosophers feel lacks plausibility.

[25] Thomas Aquinas, *Summa Theologiae* Ia q. 2 a. 3. (Blackfriars ed.; London: Eyre and Spottiswoode, 1963–81).

First of all, Aquinas characterizes change (*motus*) as a movement from potentiality to actuality (in the example he gives, from being potentially hot to being actually hot). He argues that a thing cannot change itself (cannot make itself hot), because it 'cannot at the same time be both actually X and potentially X'. It is apparent from his example that the cause of change must actually possess the very property it is to bring about in its effect. 'Fire, which is actually hot, causes wood, which is able to be hot, to become actually hot.'

From this argument, it would follow that all causes would actually possess all the properties of their effects—an axiom Aquinas accepts: 'any perfection found in an effect must be found also in the cause.'[26] Since there cannot be an infinite regress of causes, there must be one first cause which possesses actually all possible existent properties, at least '*eminentiori modo*'. Since it will be wholly unchanged, it is purely actual, possessing all possible properties in a higher manner.

Thomas Gilby, in his notes on this part of the *Summa*, remarks that 'for us it has become congested with traffic-blocks';[27] and it does indeed seem to many philosophers a peculiarly difficult, obscure, and unconvincing argument upon which Thomas will later hang so much. It is very hard to see exactly why all change should have to be brought about by something which actually possesses the property that is to be brought into being. The example of fire is not convincing at all, since we know perfectly well that heat can be caused e.g. by rubbing sticks vigorously together. Heat is the accelerated motion of molecules, and that can be caused by all sorts of processes which do not involve the application of an already existing heat.

In general, it looks wildly counter-intuitive to hold that all new properties must be replicas or shadowy images of already existing properties. The whole development of the cosmos seems, on the contrary, to show an emergence of new properties over time which had never previously existed. The hypothesis that all perfections in effects must be found in their causes looks purely a priori, rather like Aristotle's hypothesis that all the spheres must move in perfect circles. Is there really any reason to accept it?

One may think that the genesis of new properties must be caused by something with the *power* to originate them, with a knowledge of

---

[26] Aquinas, *Summa Theologiae* Ia q. 4 a. 2.   [27] Ibid. edn. notes p. 192.

what properties may be produced, and with a reason for producing them. As Thomas says, 'It is necessary that there be a form in the divine mind, a form in the likeness of which the world was made.'[28] God can actualize such forms for the sake of the goodness of their actuality. But power or capacity in God entails change in God as such a power is exercised, which Thomas cannot accept. He must accordingly construe such a power simply as the possession of the property that is to be brought about, in a higher manner. How could the unchanging possession of a property explain its coming to be in another? If I paint a picture, the picture does not somehow exist 'spiritually' in my mind before I paint it. I have the power to bring it into being; but that means I have imaginative skills and capacities. A capacity is not just the set of actions in which it results. Nor is it the actual, though shadowy, possession of what is yet to be brought about. It is more like the possession, in an actual substance, of a disposition to act in a certain way. Reference to a manner of temporal unfolding is essential to understanding causality. It seems impossible to understand change by reference to something wholly changeless or non-temporal. The changeless cannot account for change, because it lacks precisely that dynamic element which is the basic principle of change. The Aristotelian programme of trying to account for process by appeal to substance has proved to be fruitless in natural science, and it is equally fruitless in metaphysics.

The whole of physical science rests on the assumption that changes need to be explained, as a presupposition of understanding the world. Science assumes that the universe is intelligible. But how does one actually explain changes? The Aristotelian model, of looking for some changeless property or Form which would do so, is just what modern science has rejected as vastly unprofitable. What has taken its place is some variety of 'covering law explanation'.[29] One cites a law such that, whenever X happens, then Y happens. Such laws, ideally stating mathematically quantifiable regularities of behaviour, form the basis of modern science. Instead of Aristotle's four elements, air, earth, fire, and water, one has a list of elementary

---

[28] Ibid. Ia q. 15 a. 1.
[29] C. G. Hempel and P. Oppenheim, 'Studies in the Logic of Explanation', *Philosophy of Science* (1948) 135–75. Though hardly a final account, this sets out the basic form of lawlike explanation in the sciences.

particles and laws governing the way they interact over time, in various conditions.

The positing of an actual property (of heat) does not in fact explain other things' becoming hot at all. Why should a hot thing bring about heat in other things? Perhaps one may hold that it just naturally does so; its nature is to radiate heat, by contagion. But why does it radiate heat in just the way it does, to the things it does, when it does? Why should the bringing about of heat in Y be *explained* by asserting the presence of heat in X? Indeed, if X already possesses heat in perfection, why should it produce what is likely to be an inferior degree of heat in anything else? This only has the verbal appearance of explanation. It does not actually explain anything, and it is not surprising that no scientist ever uses the principle to explain changes in the world. No purely actual state can satisfactorily explain a temporal process.

One may, of course, ask why the fundamental laws of nature are as they are. If one does so, one is not looking for some more general law under which they fall. One is asking for a *reason why* they exist. That reason can, so far as I can see, only take one of two forms: either there is no alternative to them (they are necessary), or it is good that they exist (they are of intrinsic value). If so, perhaps the best possible form of explanation would combine both sorts of reason, and lie in the existence of a being which exists necessarily and which intentionally creates things for the sake of their intrinsic value. The necessarily existing being would have the essential property of creativity, and this would entail that not every created state would be necessary, in the sense of being sufficiently determined by some cause. Even God would not be a sufficiently determining cause, since the same God could have created different states.

Aquinas's argument rests on the claim that all changes need to be explained; so, if there is to be any final explanation, anything which stands in no need of further explanation, it cannot itself include change. Any change in God would need explanation in terms of something other than God, so God would not be the Supreme Being and final explanation of all things. However, even if one agrees that all changes need to be explained, it seems more plausible to think that such explanation must lie in the elucidation of fundamental laws, or principles of change, which are either necessary in themselves or which are conducive to the realization of value. Consequently, there may be changes in God, the ultimately explanatory being, as long as they are either necessary or conducive to the free realization of values. Changes in God will occur in order to implement the specific contingent occurrent states which provide content for the essential divine dispositional properties of power, knowledge, wisdom, and benevolence to a maximal extent, i.e. inexhaustibly.[30] Far from God being a totally changeless being, the requirement of an absolute explanation for change leads to the idea of a reality of supreme value which includes in its own being changes which proceed, not randomly, but in accordance with intelligible patterns of value realization.

The ultimate explanation of change is not in fact given by referring to the unchanging possession of some property which will come to exist, in an inferior mode, in its effects. It is given by reference to dispositions and valued states which make change intelligible. One does not end up with a being which already possesses all the properties it can ever produce—which threatens to make the production of any properties superfluous, and which makes the production of any genuinely new properties impossible. One ends with a being which is of supreme value, and which produces genuinely new values out of the imaginative creativity which is its essential nature.

GOD AS OMNIPOTENTIAL

The idea of God as maximal potency rather than pure actuality would probably seem, to a Thomist, to reduce God to virtual non-existence, since the merely potential is not, as such, real. But this thought may be due to a refusal to accept that dispositional properties are irreducible to occurrent properties. Divine potency is not a lack of any perfection. It is precisely the possession of creative freedom. And, of course, it is not to be conceived as a mere potentiality, a sort of pregnant non-existence. It is founded upon a primordial actuality. Of that actuality, one can perhaps say nothing, since it is beyond all the distinctions which language inevitably makes. It is an actuality of infinite fulness, a plenitude of being greater than all the finite forms of perfection conceivable by us. Yet this is an actuality which in a certain sense must include potency in itself, whose being is infinitely capable of further expression. The

---

[30] See the argument in the previous chapter for the coherence of this possibility.

being of God is never complete, in the sense of having come to an end and being incapable of further activity. But it is always complete, in that it contains in itself all the resources necessary to realize infinite forms of goodness and to be at every time unsurpassably great.

It is in fact incoherent to think that a God who is free to create any universe or not—as the traditional Christian view maintains—contains no potentiality at all. Suppose that the omnipotent God had not created any universe. Then, since God could have done so, God would have the unrealized potential to create. In fact, God would have the potential to create any one of a huge, perhaps limitless, number of universes. Far from being purely actual, God will be infinitely potential—though of course God will be actual as instantiating a sort of value which may be unmixed with evil and supreme of its class. The paradox of the classical view is that, if God is timeless, and cannot exist in successive states, the divine potential can never in fact be realized. Not having created any universe, God will not now be able to create any universe. So God will be both infinitely potential and yet incapable of realizing any of that potential. Such a God will be relatively disadvantaged in power compared to a God who can create many universes (one after the other), thus both having potential and being able to realize it. In this respect omnipotence seems to require temporality in God.

It is unfortunate that classical theologians did not pursue the logical point that an omnipotent being is a being potent for anything, and thus supremely potential. The very biblical statement often quoted for support—'I am that I am'—turns out to be rendered by most Hebrew scholars, 'I will be whatever I will be.'[31] Here one finds encapsulated the change from seeing God as purely, but immutably, actual to seeing God as unlimitedly but creatively potential.

These points are reinforced if one considers just what is great-making about omnipotence. It seems that the simple possession of a capacity, perhaps forever unrealized, is not itself of value. Omnipotence is more like an instrumental value, a condition of realizing an unlimited number of valuable states, without the possibility of being frustrated or restricted in any way. It is desirable to have unlimited capacities, but only because that enables one to do many

---

[31] Exod. 3: 14.

things that one wants to do. In this way, it seems that divine omnipotence strongly implies the actualization of divine power in an unlimited number of ways. That in turn seems to require that the perfect God is unlimitedly potential, and thus that the divine being generates of itself the time in which that potential can be endlessly realized. Time is not an alien power which restricts the being of God. It is that form of the divine being itself which enables God to be unlimitedly creative.

THE DOCTRINE OF PURE ACTUALITY

Although this account would not have been acceptable to Aquinas, much of what Aquinas wanted to defend remains in it. God is the primary cause of all things, and is not changed by anything prior in existence. God is able to bring all things into existence, and the divine existence provides a maximal explanation for their existence. God's general nature and existence is necessarily what it is, even though I have argued that the divine being will also include many contingent properties. Some of Aquinas's views, however, which I would judge to be results of relatively unfruitful and obscurantist parts of Aristotelian metaphysics, are in marked tension with important elements of Christian revelation, and need to be reformulated in the light of subsequent philosophical criticisms.

The main view is the doctrine of the pure actuality of God, which entails complete lack of potentiality and thus of temporality in the Creator.[32] This may seem an absolutely central plank in Aquinas's theology, and of course its removal would occasion reformulations of his theological views at many points. However, he was himself a notable reformulator of Christian doctrine in the light of what were then (in the thirteenth century) new and radical Aristotelian thoughts. And I think that virtually all he wanted to preserve, theologically, can be preserved and even illuminated more clearly by such reformulation.

Thomas stressed that, though we can say many literally true things about God, those things do not apply to God as we understand them.[33] While saying that the perfections of all things exist in God,

---

[32] 'In the first existent thing everything must be actual; there can be no potentiality whatsoever' (Aquinas, *Summa Theologiae* Ia q. 3 a. 1)
[33] Ibid. Ia q. 13 a. 2.

he also said, 'A creature is not like God as it is like to another member of its species . . . but resembles him as an effect may in some way resemble a transcendent cause.'[34] With regard to objects that are corporeal, he says, 'Any name that expresses perfections of that [corporeal] sort together with a mode [of being] that is proper to creatures can be said of God only on the basis of simile and metaphor.'[35] Thus it turns out that, when Aquinas says that God contains actually all that can be in creatures, he does not mean that God contains these properties in the same way as they will be in creatures. On the contrary, all the properties God contains in fact comprise one incomprehensible property, which is identical with the divine nature itself, and 'what pre-exists in God in a simple and unified way is divided amongst creatures as many and varied perfections.'[36]

Moreover, the basic picture Aquinas is working with is that of a divine intellect, which contains in itself the ideas (or essential natures) of all things. 'The divine essence comprehends within itself the excellences of all things . . . for instance, in having intellective cognition of its own essence as imitable by way of life without cognition, it takes up the form proper to plant.'[37] God, in knowing the divine essence, knows all creatable things; and since, in knowing, the mind, according to Aristotle, takes on the form of its objects, it is in this way that the form proper to plants, and presumably the forms of each individual plant, are existent in the divine intellect.

It seems to me that these points qualify what Aquinas may seem to have said about the pure actuality of God. He began by arguing, in a standard Aristotelian way, that all changes need to be accounted for, and that they are accounted for by reference to a being which possesses in act what it is going to bring about. It now turns out that God does not actually possess any finite properties at all. All one can really say is that the ideas (Forms) of all things are in the divine intellect, that the cause of changes must have the *power* to cause them, that 'what a thing does reflects what its active self is.'[38] Since

---

[34] Aquinas, *Summa Contra Gentiles* I. 33. 6, in Aquinas, *Opera*, ed. R. Busa (8 vols.; Stuttgart: Gunther Holzlor, 1974–80), vol. ii.   [35] Ibid. I. 30.

[36] Aquinas, *Summa Theologiae* Ia, q. 13 a. 4.

[37] Aquinas, *Summa Contra Gentiles* I. liv.

[38] Aquinas, *Summa Theologiae* Ia q. 4 a. 3.

the divine intellect is identical with the divine essence, and is, as such, wholly inconceivable by us, the way the forms exist in God must be quite unlike the way they are supposed to exist in human minds—namely, as discrete and particular. That is, after all, little more than to say that God is the ineffable source of all changes, bringing them about in a wholly intelligible way, ordered to good.

If, with this qualified doctrine, one asks whether there can be changes in the divine being itself, one may arrive at a rather different answer than is contained in the official Thomist doctrine. One must first of all say that, since the Divine is ineffable, one cannot confidently deny change in God. If God is not temporal in quite the way we can imagine it, God is not timeless as we imagine it either. Secondly, since there are manifest changes in the universe, and God is the source of them, there must, on the official view itself, be something in God which manifests change 'in a higher manner', no doubt, just as 'all perfections must be in God.' Thirdly, if God accounts for change by intelligible, good, and active power, then that power, which is in itself unchanging, can quite naturally engender change within the divine being as well as in things other than God. There can always be potency in God, which is 'accounted for', in a logical sense, by the actuality of the essential nature of goodness, wisdom, and creativity. Indeed, the essential and immutable nature requires concrete and contingent content, and therefore requires an element of change, and thus of temporality and potency, in the divine being itself.

The idea of God as the actual sum of all possible perfections is a philosophical idea derived from Plato and from some remaining Platonic elements in Aristotle and then in Aquinas. If the metaphysical underpinning of a world of Forms is renounced, one can reformulate the idea of perfect being in terms of a God who is unsurpassably desirable and the necessarily existing creative source of infinite goodness. This more dynamic concept seems more adequate to the biblical tradition, to the basic idea of God as Creator and to the Trinitarian doctrine that the nature of God contains real distinctions and real causal relations.

In the Indian tradition, too, the classical tradition of Sanskrit philosophy held that the supreme being, Brahman, was a wholly perfect and unchanging reality. In that tradition, however, there was always the complication that Brahman unfolds itself into the many forms of the finite world, so that in some sense it is also creative and complex. Sometimes, as in Advaita Vedanta, this complex creativity seemed to be downplayed by assigning it to the realm of *avidya*, interpreted as illusion. Aurobindo countered this negative tendency by stressing the importance of time and emergence to the self-manifestation of Brahman. In Aurobindo's work, *Sachchidananda* is seen as a dynamic power, necessarily manifesting itself in the joyful wisdom of creation.

If there is a necessarily existent, dynamically creative God, then an absolute explanation of the universe will exist. One will be able to explain why the universe must be as it is in its general features, and how its particular features are accounted for by the freely creative activity of the Supreme Being, which is itself a necessary part of divine perfection. To say that there is such an absolute explanation is not to imply that humans could have access to it, since both the essential divine essence and the creative divine will are beyond human comprehension. It is to say, however, that the universe is intrinsically intelligible, not chaotic or inelegant, and that it is a product of perfect intelligence and wisdom. The universe seems to show total intelligibility in its elegantly lawlike ordering, as well as a finely tuned suitability for the production of sentient and rational life forms, which can realize creative activity themselves. This suggests that the universe may well be founded in a cosmic wisdom fundamentally concerned with the actualization of many complex forms of value, through co-operation with created subjects of awareness and action. In both Indian and Christian thought, one finds the idea of a threefold divine being which is the ineffable and incomprehensible source of all goodness, the creative cause of infinite good, and the completed and perfect possession of every actualized good, fully realized in the divine being itself. It is in this sense that God provides an absolute explanation for the existence of the universe, an explanation which turns out to be identical with a specific interpretation of the idea of the greatest conceivable being. As such, God is the proper object of unlimited devotion, the one and only reality worthy of true worship.

9

Divine Love and the Goodness of Created Being

THE ESSENTIAL GOODNESS OF CREATION

God, as that than which no greater being can be conceived, possesses an essential nature. God necessarily exists, as omnipotent, omniscient, wise, and perfectly benevolent. God is supremely happy, since any being which does not possess the maximal degree of happiness that is logically possible will be less than perfectly great. Since happiness consists in the satisfaction of rational desire, God will be of unsurpassable goodness (rational desirability). I have argued that this means God will create new realizations of value, which will be included in one ever-extending and perfectly appreciated experience of actualized value. There is accordingly at least an analogue of time in God, though the divine time transcends the elements of separation, loss, and anxiety which are parts of a human experience of time. Divine time is qualitatively different from creaturely time. It is an unlimited possession of creative life, not a desperate clinging to an always vanishing present. Such a God will be truly a living, active God, everlastingly creative and inexhaustible in apprehended value, the source and final realization of infinite forms of goodness. It is an idea of God closely resembling this that Heschel, Iqbal, Aurobindo, and many contemporary Christian theologians would espouse.

It would be irrational for such a God to create something because it is undesirable. The only intelligible reason for creation by an omnipotent being is that creation will actualize forms of goodness, of desirable existence, which otherwise would not exist. Those who suppose that an omnipotent being may do evil[1] are thinking of divine power as if it was sheer brute force, operating without any constraints of intelligence and intention at all. But a rational being

---

[1] For instance, Thomas Morris, in *Anselmian Explorations* (Notre Dame: University of Notre Dame Press, 1987), 57.

with perfect knowledge can only bring about states which are themselves intrinsically desirable, or which are necessary conditions or consequences of such states.[2]

What has been primarily considered so far is simply the creation of new states of value within the being of God. It is an important fact, which the classical tradition has not fully appreciated, that there is such an essential creativity in God. But when one speaks of God as Creator, one usually has in mind the creation of subjects of experience and agency which are other than God. God is different from such created subjects, and does not, perhaps, experience their conscious states. So it seems theoretically possible that God may intentionally cause suffering to occur in such creatures just because God wants to, and in that sense an omnipotent being may do evil. The omnipotent God will, however, do nothing without a reason, and will always act for the sake of some envisaged end. Why should such a being cause suffering in creatures?

In knowing what is good for oneself, and being prepared to choose it, one also knows what is good for any being like oneself in the relevant respects; that is, most generally, any sentient being. One is, on grounds of reason, committed to the belief that it is irrational to choose X as good for oneself and deny that it is a good for others, when they have the same reason for choosing X. Kant was, I think, correct in arguing that a purely rational being would be unselfish, in the sense of not preferring itself above others.[3] At the same time, a being which experiences only its own pleasure and pain will be rational, in a prudential sense, to choose its own pleasure over that of others, if there is a conflict between personal good and the good of others. Such a conflict may arise because the means of well-being are in short supply, or because helping others involves the sacrifice of personal happiness. The creativity of creatures will therefore experience a tension between the abstract rationality of justice and the desire-driven rationality of prudence. Free creatures may, and often do, choose prudence over justice. In doing so, they are choosing what they see as good for them, not what is good in general and as such. In God, however, such a distinction cannot exist.

---

[2] See Richard Swinburne, *The Christian God* (Oxford: Clarendon Press, 1994), 65–71.

[3] Immanuel Kant, *Fundamental Principles of the Metaphysic of Ethics*, trans. T. K. Abbott (London: Longmans, 1959; 1st pub. 1785), 49.

If God is rational, then God, in knowing that X (say, pleasure) is good for the divine Self, also knows that it is good for sentient creatures. God experiences pleasure in the contemplation of the beauty of the divine nature, and in the creative activity which endlessly realizes new values in the divine being. This pleasure does not have to be obtained at the expense of others, since there simply are no others, unless God creates them. God never competes with others for scarce resources, since God can create whatever resources God wishes, and give them to whom God wishes. Helping others can never decrease God's happiness, since God's power is unlimited. Since God is supremely wise, if God creates others, there must be a good reason for creation. That reason must lie either in the intrinsic value of what is created or in the new and distinctive pleasure such creation gives to God. It is unintelligible to suppose that a perfectly wise creative being of unlimited power, a being of supreme understanding and bliss, might create something because it has no value or because it is positively undesirable and bad. It may at first seem possible, however, that a perfect God might create things which, though they are bad in themselves, give a great and distinctive pleasure to God.

One is thinking here of a being of enormous power, which might just decide to exercise that power in destructive action, or which might just find pleasure in the causation of pain in others. God is not, however, just a being of enormous and undirected power. God is that being which possesses every property which it is better to possess than not. Power is one such property, but it is far from being the only one. Others include supreme happiness and wisdom. If happiness arises from the contemplation of perfect beauty, then the destruction of such beauty will decrease happiness. God may create new forms of actual finite beauty, and thereby new forms of divine happiness. But God could not exercise the divine power in ways destructive of beauty and being without decreasing the divine happiness, which is impossible. God will therefore create only for the sake of the beauty or intrinsic desirability of beings.

Nor can God be conceived as finding pleasure in the pain of others. For it is positively undesirable to any being that it should suffer. The more beings there are who are happy, the more happiness there is in existence. The more beings there are who are unhappy, the more unhappiness there is in existence. There is no reason why a perfectly happy and powerful being should cause unhappiness to exist, when it could increase the amount of good by causing happiness to exist instead.

It is true that God cannot decide what gives God pleasure. So one might think that God may just find pleasure in the pain of others. However, God can ask whether it is better to feel pleasure in others' pain, or to feel pleasure in others' happiness. There is no doubt that the latter is better, since it allows for a greater total amount of good in existence. A malevolent God will therefore know that it would be better to find pleasure in the pleasure of others, i.e. would know that it would be better to be other than God is, in certain respects. So God will not be the best conceivable being, which contradicts the very idea of God, and shows that a perfect God cannot take pleasure in the suffering of others.

In any case, it is unintelligible to think that a perfectly knowing being can take pleasure in the suffering of others. God is perfectly knowing; and perfect knowledge involves understanding and appreciation.[4] It is inconceivable that God could *appreciate* suffering, as though contemplation of it could increase divine happiness. Any being's happiness would be decreased by the knowledge of another's suffering, if such knowledge was inward and direct. God will know creaturely pain as it truly is, as painful and undesirable for the creature. It is impossible to see how a truly empathetic knowledge of creaturely pain could be pleasant. In the case of humans, such perverse pleasure can only exist because the pain is not felt as painful by the torturer. The torturer does not truly enter into the victim's experience, but regards it from outside, as a consequence of his own power. God must be thought of as having direct and inward experience of creatures. In that case, God cannot find pleasure in it. The only way God can increase the divine happiness is by creating, and participating in, the happiness of creatures.

An even more telling consideration is that one of the greatest forms of happiness lies in positive relationship to other subjects of creative action and appreciative experience, in a sharing of action and experience which is mutually enhancing. As Aquinas saw, goodness is essentially diffusive. 'It befits the Divine goodness that others also should partake of it.'[5] Would a being of supreme

---

[4] This point will be argued for in Ch. 10.
[5] Thomas Aquinas, *Summa Theologiae*, Ia q. 19 a. 2. (Blackfriars edn.; London: Eyre and Spottiswoode, 1963–81).

perfection be content to remain alone in contemplation of its own essential beauty? Or, given unlimited creative power, would it not bring into existence other beings who could share in such contemplation? It is good to diffuse goodness, to multiply it, so that the perfection of being is essentially relational rather than monadically self-enclosed. Karl Barth goes to the heart of the Christian perception of God when he sees the divine perfection, not as residing in self-sufficient goodness, but in an eternal decree for fellowship, for a self-giving and sharing love.[6] Such relational sharing of creativity and experience does seem to be a great good, which it is better to possess than not, and so will essentially belong to God.

God, it might be said, might still make some creatures such that they derive pleasure from the pain of others. But, since God is omnipotent, God does not have to make them this way. Since God creates for the sake of good, God will maximize good by making happiness increase by knowledge of the happiness of others, and thus make creaturely malevolence irrational. The idea of a malevolent omnipotent creator proves to be incoherent, on reflection. The omnipotent God is necessarily good, not only in the sense that God will choose for the divine self the most desirable states, but also in a second sense, that, if God creates, God will do so for the sake of the goodness of creatures, in order that new forms of intrinsic goodness may come to exist. That is what divine benevolence is.

THE EXISTENCE OF EVIL

This argument may, however, seem to succeed in logical coherence only at the expense of empirical plausibility. It seems to suggest that God will only create a universe in which every being is made happy by the happiness of every other being, a paradisal state without suffering, frustration, destruction, or death. The actual universe is only too clearly not like that, so something has gone wrong, or some vital fact has been omitted. The argument has proceeded on an assumption which has been common in traditional theological thinking, that the universe is exactly, in every detail, as God intends it to be. I think the argument draws correct inferences from the

---

[6] Karl Barth, *Church Dogmatics* ed. G. W. Bromiley and T. F. Torrance (Edinburgh: T. & T. Clark, 1936–77 ii/1: 369. 'God's very being is mercy . . . his readiness to share the distress of another.'

perfection of God to the sort of universe God could intend to create. Since this universe is not at all like that, one is forced to conclude that the universe is not just as God intends it. But how can this be, if God is its creator?

The Creator is not malevolent, in that God does not intend evil. However, it was pointed out in Chapter 7 that the divine nature, being necessarily what it is, may not be intended in every respect. It includes the array of possible universes and states, and these necessarily include the possibility of suffering (necessarily, because suffering actually exists, and whatever is actual is necessarily possible). God may assent to the inclusion of such a possibility among the array of possible states because it is a necessary condition of the whole array, with all its internal logical relations, existing at all. Yet God will not intend that the possibility of suffering should be actualized simply for its own sake. Nevertheless, if God intends to produce goods which can only exist in a specific integral universe, then the possibility of suffering may necessarily exist in that universe, even though God does not intend such suffering to be actualized.

In that case, one might suggest, God should not intend that universe. God should intend a better one, or none at all. It may be, however, that all possible universes involve at least the possibility of suffering. Theists are precluded from saying that the universe is, as such, undesirable. It can rationally be desired, though not everything in it can be desired. One has to say that God desires the good things in the universe, and therefore desires the universe in which alone they can exist. God does not desire the suffering in the universe, but cannot prevent its possibility. The crucial question arises: is the good that can result from this universe worth the suffering that may come to exist in it? Obviously, an enormous good is worth just a little suffering, and a tiny good is not worth enormous suffering. If this is so, at least one is accepting the principle that goodness can outweigh suffering; it is a question of the amounts involved. In general, God will be justified in creating any universe in which the good vastly outweighs the suffering, or perhaps at least in which it has the possibility of doing so for every sentient being, as long as the possibility of suffering is necessary to the existence of that universe.

I have spoken only of the *possibility* of suffering. But where suffering is possible, it may become actual, given the requisite conditions. It may be that some actual suffering is unavoidable, in certain universes. This will be the case in any universe in which there is an emergence of new properties through some sort of evolutionary process. For in any such universe, there will have to be death and the distress it causes. There will almost certainly be competition for survival, which entails conflict. There will be suffering caused by failure to achieve new goals and by experimentation to find new modes of life. If evolutionary emergence is a condition for specific goods, some actual suffering will necessarily occur. In this sense, though God does not intend every instance of suffering, God does intend a universe in which some such suffering will inevitably occur. God is the source of that suffering, and bears responsibility for it. But it makes a profound difference to the situation if God does not desire it for its own sake, but rather intends that it should be diminished and abolished wherever that is possible, whether by divine or by creaturely action.

There is much suffering, in any universe of rational and moral persons, which will probably be avoidable, and will only be realized because of some failure of creatures to act in accordance with the will of the Creator. Much of the sorrow produced by death, for example, is due to the sense of utter loss which is caused by a lack of knowledge of the presence and purposes of God, which is in turn caused by a failure to conform one's will to the divine will. Huge amounts of human suffering are caused by hatred, lust, and selfishness. Though God creates persons so that their true happiness is increased by the happiness of others, it is possible for persons to become malevolent because of their desire to win power over others at any price. God's intention is a community of creative love. But in the very idea of such a community lies the possibility of its destruction through lack of love. When this is actualized, it is not through the divine intention, but through human desire and perversity. One fails to love others through attention to the pleasures of the self. But self-indulgence inevitably results in suffering, both for others and for oneself. As the Buddhist teaching makes clear, self-regarding desire is the cause of the greatest human sorrow.[7] Self-regard is necessarily possible in any world of sentient wills. Only if it can be destroyed at its root can the purpose of creation, the existence

---

[7] 'When his cravings overcome him, his sorrows increase . . . but whoever in this world overcomes his selfish cravings, his sorrows fall away from him' (*Dhammapada* 24, tr. Juan Mascaro (Harmondsworth: Penguin, 1973), 83).

of a community of love, be realized. Different religious traditions seek to offer ways of destroying self-regard and achieving fulfilment by relation to the Supreme Good. Religions arise precisely because the world is perceived to be 'fallen from', or out of harmony with, its true good.

There are thus two major qualifications to be made to the view that a perfect God should create a paradisal universe, or should create a universe every detail of which is intended to be just as it is. The first is that God may intend to create an emergent universe, containing probabilistic processes which will lay the basis for subsequent free and creative creaturely actions. In that case, many particular states will not themselves be intended, and God wills their abolition whenever, in the course of the emergent process, that becomes possible. The second is that creatures may impede the divine intention, turning their part of the universe into an arena of destructive conflict and alienation from the source of their being. These qualifications restore plausibility to the idea of creation by a perfectly good God. The greatest conceivable being cannot be malevolent, in that it cannot intend suffering to exist for its own sake, or simply for the sake of greater pleasure. God will be necessarily good, not only in being of supreme intrinsic value, but also in creating for the sake of actualizing distinctive forms of goodness. Such creation, however, may entail the possibility of much suffering, and the actuality of some. What the reaction of the greatest conceivable being will be to that fact will be the subject of the next chapter.

THE CREATION OF FREE CREATORS

It has been suggested that all creatable universes may contain the possibility of suffering. May it not, then, be better if no universe is created at all? In considering this question, one may begin with the thought that it is clearly a good thing if there are other subjects of experience besides God who can experience desirable values and perhaps even share in creating them. God experiences infinite forms of goodness, throughout endless time. In a sense, there cannot be any greater goodness than that; such perfection is unsurpassable. Yet if goodness consists in the apprehension of some desirable state, the sum of goodness in existence is increased by the existence of many conscious agents. The existence of many agents also makes possible the realization of new forms of goodness, in the shared creation of new values and the shared experience of realized goodness. Thus the existence of a community of agents would significantly increase the quantity and variety of the forms of goodness. This gives an intelligible reason why God should create a universe which makes possible a community of rational agents—for the sake of forms of goodness which otherwise would not exist. The nature of a particular universe will govern the forms of goodness which exist, and so there are many, perhaps infinitely many, universes which are creatable by God. Each of them will express in its own way something of the unlimited potency of God for actualizing value. Each will be empowered in a unique way by the co-operative creativity of God, as the unsurpassable value and sole originative power. Each will contribute to the being of God the realization of distinctive values which would otherwise have no actuality. Of course, each will also carry a potential for suffering, for disvalue. The nature and extent of these disvalues, and the possible ways of mitigating or removing them, must figure largely in any consideration of the goodness of creation. Yet it seems plausible to suppose that the goods may so far outweigh the evils, and many of the evils themselves may be able so to contribute in some way to the forms of goodness, that a universe oriented to the emergence of a community of rational agents may be greatly desirable.

Such a picture seems to give apt expression to the basic Christian affirmation that 'God is Love.'[8] This is a God who does not remain alone in the contemplation of beauties that God alone has produced. This God brings finite persons into existence in order to realize unique forms of goodness in them. God gives them a share in divine strength and the knowledge of the divine presence, to urge them on to their own proper fulfilment. God receives into the divine being the values which they have brought about. God has compassion for their sufferings and ensures that they can issue in an overwhelmingly greater good. God establishes fellowship with them in unshakeable concern for their well-being, while yet assuring them of their own proper, if necessarily limited, responsibility for determining their own forms of existence. This relationship, established wholly by God, is supremely one of love and, indeed, helps to articulate what true love is.

[8] 1 John 4: 16.

This seems to commit one to the belief that God must create a universe of finite persons, as a condition of realizing the divine nature as love. As has been seen, Heschel argues that God is personal only in attending to others. Iqbal argues that divine freedom is realized in relation to the creative community of creatures. Aurobindo sees the universe of finite selves as a necessary manifestation of the relational being of *Sachchidananda*. Barth suggests that the disclosure of the divine nature in Jesus Christ specifies the nature of divine goodness, not as the (Aristotelian) timeless contemplation of supreme perfection, but as ecstatic, self-giving love. If this is indeed the highest form of goodness, it would be odd for God to lack it. In that sense, the creation of some universe may be necessary to God.

It is important to distinguish this point, which is firmly based on revelation, though not confined to one tradition, from the argument that God is obligated to create a universe by some form of Utilitarian, or highest-possible-good, consideration. God cannot be obligated to create the greatest possible number of goods, since the number of creatable universes is infinite, and there is no greatest possible number. It is implausible to suppose there is any particular number of universes God is obligated to create, since God could always create a greater number than any given number. So, though it is good if God creates a universe, God cannot be said to be under any obligation to do so. Creation is not morally necessary for God.

The complex idea of 'necessity' needs some disentangling. If necessity is thought to imply constraint, then there is no constraint on God to create a universe. God does not have to do so whether or not God wants to. If necessity is taken to be strict logical necessity, so that it would be self-contradictory to say that God exists and no universe exists, then creation is not logically necessary. If necessity is taken as a notion of moral obligation, so that God would fail in some duty if God failed to create, then creation is not necessary. In these three senses, the creation of a universe is not necessary to God.

Yet if the supreme value is self-giving love, and if God is essentially of supreme value, it will be of the nature of God to create some universe of persons within which love can be realized. Divine creation will be free, in the sense that no particular universe follows from the nature of God. Creation will not arise from any lack or limitation on God's part. It will be a natural expression of the being of God. As Aquinas put it, 'The understood good is, as such, willed',[9] and 'the good is diffusive of itself and being.'[10] God, in willing the divine being itself as the supreme good, also wills those beings which are 'diffused' from it, not by constraint or lack, but by joyful willing. In this carefully qualified sense, some creation is necessary to God, since it follows from what God necessarily is. The willing of a fellowship of love with free persons is a natural expression of the supreme goodness of God. This particular universe is in no sense necessary to God, since an infinite number of other universes might have been created. So one can preserve the important theological points that this universe is created out of goodness, not out of blind necessity, and that none of us is strictly necessary to the being of God, so that our existence is a free gift of grace.

CREATION AND NECESSITY

It is part of the traditional notion of creation that God need not have created any universe at all. The traditional view, rather surprisingly, in fact leaves rather less real freedom to God than has been suggested here, and threatens to make this particular universe necessary to God, even though that is far from its intention. It is ironic that the traditional (Thomist) account actually leaves less freedom to God than a view which permits God to choose a universe from among a whole set of real alternative possibilities, to express the divine goodness and love in a unique way. Contrary to expectation, belief in creativity as a necessary property of God enables one to maintain the gratuitousness of our particular existence in a way which the traditional view cannot do. This is because the traditional notion holds that the creation of a universe, or of any number of universes, can make no difference at all to God.[11] God, being strictly immutable, cannot change, whether or not God creates any universe.

I have already queried the idea of strict immutability. Aristotle said that in a being which actualizes supreme perfection, any 'change would be change for the worse'.[12] However, it seems reasonable to

---

[9] Thomas Aquinas, *Summa Contra Gentiles* 1. 72, in Aquinas, *Opera*, ed. R. Busa (8 vols.; Stuttgart: Gunther Holzlor, 1974–80), vol. ii.   [10] Ibid. 1. 37. 5.

[11] Karl Barth, surprisingly, expresses this view: 'God is distinct from everything . . . he would be no different even if they all did not exist' (*Church Dogmatics* ii/1: 311.   [12] Aristotle, *Metaphysics* 1074[b].

think that immutability is only a perfection under certain conditions. If the state of any being is as good as it can possibly be, then it is better for it to be immutable than to be subject to decay or destruction. And one may think that God must be as good as can possibly be. In Chapter 7, however, I argued that it is possible to agree with Aristotle, and with theists generally, that God cannot change for the worse. But God can change by increasing non-maximizable perfections, by varying incompossible sets of perfections, and by realizing new perfections of creative activity. The idea of God changing some perfections of the divine being in at least these ways seems a coherent one. If so, one can readily make the prima-facie plausible claim that the creation of a particular universe must cause some change in God. It is not that, if God creates, God must first of all be in a state of not having created, and then change to enter into a state of creating. I do not find anything incoherent about a changeless or non-temporal creation. It is rather that, if God wills a particular world—say, possible world 23—to exist, God will be in a different state than God would have been in if God had willed world 21 to exist or had willed no universe to exist.

On the traditional theological view, God would have remained the same, whether or not any universe existed, and whether world 21 or world 23 exists. It accordingly follows that there cannot be an item of divine willing which consists in willing that world 23 exists, or an item of divine knowledge which consists in knowing that world 23 exists, since, if this world had not existed, God would have lacked that item of will and of knowledge. Indeed, God would have possessed an item of knowledge which contradicted it, namely, that world 23 does not exist. Since the existence of world 23 or its non-existence makes a difference to divine knowledge, God would not have remained the same whether or not it existed. It follows that, either (1) there is something God does not know—that some world actually exists (or that the world necessarily exists—which guarantees that God could not have been different, but conflicts with the initial hypothesis)—or (2) some divine knowledge is contingent on the divine decision to create this universe. If God could not have been otherwise, then all other possible worlds are not in fact possible. Their existence is ruled out by the necessary being of God. They are possible only in being conceivable without contradiction, in being thought or imagined by God.

Thus when God brings a universe into existence, God knows

something additional to knowing all possible worlds; God knows that at least one of them is actual (and that God has actualized it). Of course, the existence of a universe introduces a very large number of facts into the divine knowledge—not only that a universe exists, but that every state of affairs in it is actual. If the created universe is contingent, then there will be a huge amount of contingent knowledge in God. For any knowledge that X contingently exists must itself be contingent. God might necessarily know, of any contingent universe, that it exists or not. But God cannot have necessary knowledge that a particular universe exists which is contingent. God will, it seems, have many contingent properties: all those properties entailed by the knowledge that a contingent universe actually exists, and by the creation of such a contingent universe.

Indeed, it seems that the idea of omnipotence entails that any omnipotent being must necessarily possess contingent properties. For if an omnipotent being cannot create any contingent world, then there are a great number of things it cannot do, and it is not omnipotent. But if it is possible to create some contingent worlds, then the creation of any such world must itself be contingent (i.e. some other contingent world could have been created). So any being which can create contingent worlds must logically be capable of contingent acts. It must necessarily be contingent in some respects. Far from necessity and contingency contradicting one another in God, it appears that certain necessary properties entail certain contingent ones—as the necessarily possessed divine property of being able to create any contingent world compossible with God entails the necessary possession of contingent properties by God. Thus only a God who is necessary in the possession of some properties (including existence, omnipotence, goodness, and omniscience) and contingent in the possession of others (a particular exercise of the capacity freely to create some of many possible universes) can be truly omnipotent. Only such a God can freely create a truly contingent universe.

THE CLASSICAL ACCOUNT OF CREATION

One might argue that, according to the classical account, God could have created a different universe if God had wanted to. But in fact God could not have wanted to, and so it is impossible that God could

have done so. This is the view taken by Aquinas, that the creation of
the universe is not absolutely necessary. It does not follow from any
self-evident logical truth. But it is necessary *ex suppositione*, on the
premiss that God has decided to create it. And it is hard to see how
God could have decided otherwise, without being other than God is.

Thomas distinguishes 'absolute necessity' from 'hypothetical (*ex
suppositione*) necessity'.[13] He defines absolute necessity as that which
is 'such from the implication of the terms, as when a predicate is
entailed in the definition of a subject'. It is clear that he means strict
logical necessity, for which something follows by definition. Now
the universe does not follow by definition from God; it is not a
strictly logical deduction from the being of God. As far as logic goes,
since God is infinite, infinitely many worlds could flow from God.
Thus Thomas can say that the universe is a product of the divine
will, not of some necessity of the divine nature, something that
follows, whether it is willed or not.

The universe, says Thomas, is hypothetically necessary. On the
supposition that God has willed it, it cannot be other than it is.
However, this is not the end of the matter. Thomas sees and states
the lurking objection very clearly. 'Whatever God knows he knows
necessarily. Now as his knowing is his being so also is his willing.
Therefore whatever he wills he wills necessarily.'[14] The divine will is
identical with the divine nature, which is necessarily what it is. It
follows, then, that the divine will is necessarily what it is. How can
Thomas evade this conclusion? He cannot. He admits that the divine
willing is essentially necessary (*in se est necessarium*). Yet, he says, the
divine knowing is 'of things as they exist in the knower', whereas the
divine willing is of things as they exist. All things have a necessity as
existing in God, but not as existing in themselves. This is a fudge. If
God wills universe X to exist, then God knows that God wills X, and
knows that X is actual, not merely possible, or an unactualized entity
in the divine mind. Since God is omniscient, part of the divine
knowledge must be what God in fact wills to exist. In knowing the
divine self, God knows the divine willing of X. Now Thomas says,
'Since, therefore, God has no potentiality but is pure actuality, in
him intellect and what is known must be identical in every way.'[15]
What is known is not different from the substance of the divine

---

[13] Aquinas, *Summa Theologiae*, Ia q. 19 a. 3.   [14] Ibid. Ia q. 19 a. 4.
[15] Ibid. Ia q. 14 a. 2.

intellect itself. The divine intellect, however, is not different from that essential being which is the divine substance, since 'in God to be and to know are the same.'[16]

The Thomist doctrine is that God knows the Divine Self, and all its acts of willing, in simply being, in that uniquely unrestricted way which constitutes God as '*esse suum subsistens*'. It follows that God's knowledge of things in the world cannot be causally dependent upon the existence of those things. On the contrary, 'his knowledge must be the cause of things when regarded in connection with his will.'[17] 'Things other than himself he sees not in themselves but in himself, because his essence contains the likeness of things other than himself.'[18] God knows everything that is, was, and will be in simply knowing the divine essence; indeed, God's knowing is strictly identical with that essence.

The essence of God, however, is such that it cannot be otherwise. It is not contingent; it contains no potentiality whatsoever: 'In the first existent thing everything must be actual; there can be no potentiality whatsoever.'[19] Total lack of potentiality entails the impossibility of being otherwise, since, if one could be other than one is, that is a potential, however much it may be forever unrealized. It is not enough to say that God, being timeless and therefore immutable, having such and such a nature, cannot now have any other nature (this is necessity *ex suppositione*). For if one says that God could have had a different nature in some respects, this 'could have' is a potentiality for possibly having been different. At least that is so, unless the 'could have' is simply a narrowly logical 'could have'.

This is the only way to render Thomas's doctrine consistent—to say that, as far as we can see (which is not very far), God could have done other things than God did, and so could have been otherwise. Thomas is clear that 'God can do what he does not do'.[20] But how can he avoid the implication that there is potentiality in God? Only by holding that this 'can' is a narrowly logical 'can'. That is, it is possible to set out a list of propositions which describe a universe which is creatable by God, but which does not exist, since God has not willed to create it. Since such a universe may be internally

---

[16] Ibid. Ia q. 14 a. 4.
[18] Ibid. Ia q. 14 a. 5.
[20] Ibid. Ia q. 25 a. 5.

[17] Ibid. Ia q. 14 a. 8.
[19] Ibid. Ia q. 3 a. 1.

logically consistent, and logically consistent with the existence of God, one can say that it is a creatable universe; God, in that sense, could have created it.

This narrow logical sense is a purely conceptual one, however, and so it need not involve real potentiality in God. To say that it is logically possible for me to turn into a turnip does not entail that I actually could turn into a turnip, that species-changing is one of my potentialities. Narrow logical possibility is quite compatible with factual impossibility (something's being impossible because of what is already the case). So with God, to say that it is logically possible for God to create other universes does not entail the factual possibility that God could do so or that God could ever have done so, that it is one of God's potentialities. In fact, being pure actuality, God could not have been other than God is. So it is not factually possible for God ever to have created a different universe than the one God wills to create; that is, this one. This factual impossibility is caused by the being of God itself, which renders impossible anything that is incompatible with it, such as its being different than it is.

THE CLASSICAL ACCOUNT OF DIVINE KNOWLEDGE OF CREATION

This account is corroborated by Thomas's exposition of what it is for God to know the universe God has created. God's knowledge of the divine self is essentially necessary, and is indeed identical with God's essential nature. But so is God's willing of X. 'As the divine existing is essentially necessary so also is the divine knowing and the divine willing.'[21] But the divine knowing, he claims, is of things as they exist in God, so that 'whatever God knows he knows of necessity.' This is because God's knowing is identical with God's being; God's being is necessary; therefore God's knowing of that being is necessary, too.

Thomas distinguishes, however, *scientia visionis*, God's knowledge of things that at some time actually exist, from knowledge '*simplicis intelligentiae*', knowledge of simple understanding, of things God does not create, but which are abstractly possible.

What is the distinction between these forms of divine knowing? It is founded on the fact that God wills the objects of the former to exist

---

[21] Aquinas, *Summa Theologiae*, Ia q. 19 a. 4.

outside God, as well as in God. Within God, therefore, there are two forms of knowledge, distinguished by the divine willing. The divine willing, says Thomas, is related to things as they exist in themselves. As such, they have no absolute necessity. Apart from God, they would not exist at all, much less necessarily. Therefore, Thomas concludes, God's will is not necessary, since it relates to things the existence of which is not necessary.

This argument is fatally equivocal. The relation of God's will to anything which does not exist of necessity cannot be a necessary relation. But if God necessarily wills something to exist, then, even though its existence is not necessary in itself, it is dependently necessary. As has been seen, the divine willing is identical with the divine knowing, which is necessary. So it must be necessary, and this establishes the necessity of the universe's existence. While this universe cannot be deduced from the being of God, it is necessarily caused by the divine nature, which is absolutely necessary. Thomas's view creates a major problem. If the universe does not flow deductively from God, yet it does flow necessarily from God, what sort of necessity can this be? It is a necessity to which there are logical alternatives, yet which could not in fact be other than it is.

I think Thomas is right in his general claim that God wills the divine goodness, and does so necessarily.[22] Moreover, he says, 'A thing has a natural tendency . . . to spread its own good to others.' The creation of good is a natural tendency of a perfectly good being. So Thomas says, 'he wills them [created things] in willing his own goodness.' This, of course, most naturally argues for the necessity of creation. God's own goodness is complete without other things, says Thomas. But would it be complete without the tendency to spread itself to others? Certainly, it would be different if it did not will others in willing itself, for then, its willing of itself would naturally be different than it is; it would not include the willing of others. Perhaps it would still be goodness; but it would be a different specific sort of goodness.

Now how do things proceed from God? Not from necessity of nature, says Thomas—by which he means, not by an inevitable, unintelligent process. They proceed 'by the resolution of his intelligence and will'.[23] Nothing accounts for why this universe exists except that God intelligently and knowingly wills it. Again,

---

[22] Ibid. Ia q. 19 a. 3.   [23] Ibid. Ia q. 19 a. 4.

one must recall that, for Thomas, 'intelligence, will, and power are identical in God.'[24] In one and the same act, God conceives every possible state of affairs, and wills to produce some of them. 'By one act God understands everything in his essence, and similarly by one act he wills everything in his goodness.'[25] And those acts are the very same single act. If Thomas means to say that the same act by which God understands the divine self, by which God is, is the act by which God wills the world, then this world is, in all its detail, part of God's being what it is. If this world is contingent, then God must be contingent in some respect. It is not enough to say that God creates some contingent causes (which sometimes fail of their effects) and some necessary causes (which never do).[26] For it remains true that all those causes are caused by the one single act which is identical with the necessity of the divine being.

What Thomas depicts is a God whose own perfection is infinite and unlimited; whose nature naturally overflows into the creation of others who can share in that goodness; and whose creation is a free and intelligent creativity, which can never exhaust the limitless resources of the divine being. Because of the Platonic influence on his thinking, he never found the logical key to resolve his dilemma of how God could be necessarily existent and how creation could be truly free and contingent. That key, once formulated, is supremely simple: that which is necessarily omnipotent necessarily expresses its nature in endless contingent actualizations of its unlimited power. There is no necessity, factual or logical, about this particular universe. What is necessary is that God should generate, through intelligence and will, many good states of many different sorts; and among them, contingently and gratuitously, is a universe like this.

CREATION AND FREEDOM

If Thomas's philosophical framework generates unnecessary paradoxes about divine actuality and potentiality (that God contains no potential, but could create other worlds than God does), and about divine necessity and contingency (that God could not be otherwise, but creates a world that could), it also generates a paradox of divine sovereignty and human freedom. While accepting that finite agents

---

[24] Aquinas, *Summa Theologiae*, Ia q. 19 a. 5.   [25] Ibid.
[26] Ibid. Ia q. 19 a. 8.

'abandon the divine will by sinning', Thomas also insists that 'from [God's] plan no effect can stray in any way at all.'[27] It follows from this that it is by divine will that finite agents abandon the divine will, and that they are punished for doing so. In one way, this view resolves the problem of evil completely. If the world in some sense necessarily follows from the changeless existence of God, God cannot be held blameworthy for anything. One will just have to accept that things are necessarily what they are. But in another way, Thomas forces himself into an insoluble dilemma. He holds that God creates the world because it is good. Yet he not only sees how much suffering there is in the world; he compounds it by believing that God is the ultimate and invincible cause of human wrongdoing, who nevertheless punishes wrongdoers with eternal torments. Even if things are necessarily as they are, how can such torment be just if human freedom is such as to be compatible with total divine determination of every event?

Augustine had already considered this problem at some length, and he replied: 'Punishment falls justly upon those acts which are wills and not necessities.'[28] Distinguishing between the *natures* of angels and men, which are created and remain good, and their *wills*, he holds that the will can perversely prefer a lesser to a greater good. There is no cause for this outside the will itself; 'Seek the cause of this evil will, and you shall find just none.'[29] He does not mean that the wills are arbitrary or wholly random causeless phenomena. He means that there is no cause in the universe outside the will which determines it to decide as it does. It is itself the only cause of its decision for good or evil. So it bears sole responsibility for the consequences of its choice.[30] Such evil wills deserve punishment, for

---

[27] Ibid. Ia q. 19 a. 7.

[28] Augustine, *City of God*, bk. xii, ch. 6, ed. R. V. G. Tasker, tr. J. Healey (London: J. M. Dent, 1945), 351.   [29] Ibid. bk xii, ch. 6: 349.

[30] This strand of Augustine's thought leads to the 'libertarian' or contra-causal view of freedom, which stands opposed to the 'compatibilist' view held by Augustine most of the time, by most traditional theologians, and by many philosophers, perhaps most famously Kant. I have assessed Kant's view negatively in *Kant's View of Ethics* (Oxford: Basil Blackwell, 1972), summarized at 168 f. There is a large modern literature on this debate. A good sample is in T. Tracy (ed.), *The God Who Acts* (State College, Pa.: Pennsylvania State University Press, 1994). My view is the libertarian view of William Hasker in that book, and of Alvin Plantinga in *God and Other Minds* (New York: Cornell University Press, 1967) and Richard Swinburne in *The Existence of God* (Oxford: Clarendon Press, 1979).

turning away from God to their own selfish good. God knows their turning and their end; but knows also that God will bring good out of their choice, for the universe as a whole. The world is good, then, because in it many will be brought to supreme joy; because even out of evil much good will be brought; and because evil wills are justly punished.

Augustine's argument, besides its commitment to a morally questionable doctrine of endless torment, focuses attention on the idea of a will, not a necessity, which may be justly punished for its choice. Can Augustine legitimately make such a distinction, given his belief that the world flows from the immutable and necessary being of God?

The argument that he cannot may be set out as follows:

(a) God is perfect actuality, and as such could not have been other than God is. A complete account of what God is must include a statement of what acts God performs. So if God could not have been otherwise, God could not in fact have done other than God does.

(b) All temporal events are caused by God.

(c) [from a and b] Therefore no temporal event could have been other than it is.

(d) Creaturely acts of willing are temporal events, even though not causally determined by any other temporal event.

(e) [from c and d] Therefore no creaturely acts of will could have been other than they are.[31]

Of course one can distinguish between events which are causally determined by other events, and events not so determined, or which are determined by desires of the agents, and call the latter 'free'. It is clear, however, that free events are causally determined by God, even if they are in accordance with the desires of the agent. Why should an act of will be justly punished, if it is determined by God? The point of Augustine's argument is surely that one should only be punished for what one is solely responsible for. That is why acts of will can have no external physical cause, which would pass on at least

---

[31] This argument is not a form of the well-known modal fallacy, 'Necessarily, if God wills E, then necessarily E'. For the premiss is precisely that 'God necessarily wills E, since God is both simple and necessary.' See Kathryn Tanner, *God and Creation in Christian Theology* (Oxford: Basil Blackwell, 1988), 73–6.

part of the responsibility. But it turns out that they all have a cause external to the will itself, namely, the eternal decision of God.

Augustine cannot say that God can create a will so that it is free to choose either X or Y in a way not determined by God. For if the choice is made of X, many events will follow which will be quite different from those which would follow from the choice of Y. God has to bring all those subsequent events into being. So if God left the choice truly undetermined, God would have to let the subsequent creation depend to an indeterminate extent upon some creaturely act. That God cannot do, since God is unaffected by creatures in any way, being wholly immutable.

Neither can Augustine say that God can leave a will indeterminate, and yet foreknow how it will choose, and act accordingly. Such foreknowledge would still be a knowledge caused by some creaturely act. Augustine says, 'The creatures also do they [the angels] know better in the wisdom of God, the workman's draft, than in the things produced.'[32] God does not wait until things actually exist in order to know them; but God causes them to exist as a result of changeless divine knowledge: 'He saw that what He had made was good, because He foresaw that He should make it good.'[33] There is no escaping the conclusion that God wills to bring into existence finite wills, angelic and human, which God necessitates to choose evil by their non-finitely caused acts. Many would recoil from this hypothesis that God determines a will to make a choice which is then punished eternally. God cannot help it, being necessarily what God is. But few will call such a God 'just' as readily as Augustine did.

The simplest way to mitigate the difficulty is to take the course that Origen and Gregory of Nyssa took, and guarantee final salvation and unending bliss to all.[34] The combination of divine necessity, the possession of full, perfect, and supremely desirable reality by God, and a guarantee of final universal bliss may convince even Ivan Karamazov that his ticket is non-returnable, that moral outrage is misdirected, and that the journey of every created life will eventually

---

[32] Augustine, *City of God*, bk. xi, ch. 29: 338.

[33] Ibid. bk. xi, ch. 21: 330.

[34] Gregory of Nyssa, 'Sermon on I Corinthians 15', in M. Wiles and M. Santer eds. and trans., *Documents in Early Christian Thought* (Cambridge: Cambridge University Press, 1975), 257 f.

lead out of despair.[35] There we might happily leave the matter, if it were not for a nagging suspicion that Augustine has touched on something of fundamental importance in his distinction between 'will' and 'nature', between choice and necessity, however unsatisfactory his treatment of it may be. Is there not, after all, more to be said about human malice and evil than that it is inevitable? Is there not more to be said about divine judgement and mercy than that they are necessary attributes of a being which cannot be other than it is? Are there no deeper senses of divine grace and human freedom than this?

DIVINE FOREKNOWLEDGE AND TEMPORALITY

As has been seen, contemporary theologians in many traditions tend to place a greater emphasis on divine and human freedom than Augustine and Aquinas did. Suppose, then, that one posits finite choices which are not determined by God, which God leaves truly indeterminate; what might follow for an account of creation? Most obviously, each choice will open a set of alternative futures. These alternatives are open, in that God, at the moment of creating the first choosing agent, cannot have determined what choice it will make. God may know what all the alternative possibilities are. But God cannot know, in advance of finite choices being made, which alternatives will be made actual. It may be said that God can *foreknow* which will be actual. But, if the choices are truly undetermined by God, that foreknowledge will depend upon what the creatures decide. God will be passible, in that divine knowledge will be partly determined—as to which possibles are actual in this universe—by the acts of creatures.

Since God cannot decide what further events to create until God knows which possible alternative has been actualized, God cannot be said to create the whole universe in a single non-temporal act. God will first have to create a choosing will, then see what it chooses; and only then can the next segment of the world be created. God's creative action will be continually responsive to creatures. It must therefore have an internal successiveness, in which God does one thing after another.

[35] F. Dostoevsky, *The Brothers Karamazov*, tr. D. Magarshack (Harmondsworth: Penguin, 1958), 287.

God can only foreknow X if X will actually be the case, and this is determined by the choice of P, where P is some finite will. God can predetermine a response to X, as foreknown by God; so one might suppose that God could still foreknow and decide upon the whole state of the universe before it is brought into being. But what God cannot do is to envisage a possible, but non-actual, universe in which P chooses X, and decide to create *that* universe in view of the choices which God foresees being made in it. For in any universe which God actually creates, P may decide in a number of unpredictable ways, thereby modifying the universe which God is in process of actualizing into a different possible universe.

One may argue that God can create any possible universe. There is a possible universe in which P chooses X. Therefore God can create that universe. This argument is used by Anthony Flew to support his view that God could, and should, create a universe in which all free agents always make good choices.[36] But it does not work. The fuller description of the universe in question is that in it, P freely (i.e. not determined by God) chooses X. That is a possible universe; but it is not a possible universe that God can wholly determine. Then one would have the contradiction that God determines wholly a universe in which some things are not determined by God; i.e. there is some event which God both does and does not determine. The underlying fallacy here is the fallacy of hypostatizing the possible. Just because a universe is logically possible, it does not follow that it can be actualized by divine fiat. There are many apparently possible universes that God cannot create, since creating them would be self-contradictory. God cannot wholly determine any universe in which some events are free (i.e. not wholly determined). God can, of course, create any universe in which there are free agents. But God cannot know, before they choose, which of the alternatives God places before them they will choose. God can thus only foreknow such a universe as about to be actual if it will actually exist. And that cannot be wholly within God's power of choice.

The most plausible response to this situation is to renounce the idea of foreknowledge of free creaturely acts; indeed, to see such foreknowledge as an imperfection, not a perfection of the divine

---

[36] A. G. N. Flew, 'Divine Omnipotence and Human Freedom', in *New Essays in Philosophical Theology*, ed. A. Flew and A. MacIntyre (London: SCM Press, 1955), 149–55.

nature. In Augustine's scheme, God's foreknowledge did not depend on any creaturely act, and could not be changed by any such act. The price to be paid is that creatures have no genuine contra-causal freedom. But on this revised scheme, God's knowledge depends logically upon free creaturely choices having occurred. Further, God's creation of succeeding states of that universe depends upon dependent knowledge; so God's knowledge of what even God is going to do is dependent upon creaturely acts. God must now logically be conceived as having successive states of knowledge and action in the divine being. There will be a primal state of causally independent knowledge and a successive series of states, each of which causally depends upon the others.

It follows that there is some state of God in which God cannot know as actual something that will be actual—namely, the primal state which is wholly independent, and therefore cannot include any causally dependent knowledge resulting from creaturely acts and God's responses to them. Divine knowledge increases co-temporally with the sequence of created temporal states. If one admits an element of temporality in God, then one can accept that God foreknows whatever is causally implicated in the present state of the universe, and whatever God decrees will happen. But one can also accept that the divine knowledge will increase, because God knows more facts as actual when more of them are actual. This is not an increase in the perfection of knowledge, which consists in knowing everything actual at every time. Nor does it attribute imperfection to earlier states of God, when God knew fewer facts as actual, because fewer were actual. Richard Swinburne has argued that divine omniscience can and should, for a temporal God, be coherently interpreted to mean 'knowledge at each time of all propositions that it is logically possible that he entertain then'.[37] If creation is not a single timeless divine act, but a continuous process of generating and sustaining a complex interplay of many creative and created freedoms, then omniscience must include the responsive and ever-extending knowledge of all the new states that such freedoms actualize.

---

[37] Swinburne, *The Christian God*, 133. The literature on divine foreknowledge is extensive; one good source is Baruch Brody, *Readings in the Philosophy of Religion* (Englewood Cliffs, NJ: Prentice-Hall, 1974), selections 3.6–13. With a relatively small qualification, I accept Swinburne's account.

THE RELATIONAL NATURE OF DIVINE LOVE

If real temporality is accepted in the divine being, and if real contingency (not merely logical) is introduced into the world, one can allow for the possibility of a free choice against the divine will. In that case, creatures could do things which God did not plan, but which God permits for the sake of the goods of freedom and the co-operative and communal love which freedom makes possible. God would be related to creatures in a series of changing acts which partly depend on the free actions of creatures. The divine acts will be such as to persuade creatures, if possible, to turn from self-regard to share in the divine love. Divine sovereignty can bring into being genuinely, undeterminedly free creaturely agents, and interact with them in judgement on their self-regarding choices and in a love which seeks to persuade them to love goodness for itself, and to love God for the intrinsic perfection of the divine being. One might say, with Barth, that divine judgement on the evil acts which destroy the beauty of creation, though it is real and fearful, is never God's sole or final word.[38] The universality of the divine love and the immutability of the divine decree for fellowship with creatures will never foreclose the possibility of fulfilment for any created being. The divine perfection is most fully expressed in an interactive, responsive, and creative love, whose purpose is to draw all creatures from the self-imposed isolation of their fallen self-regard to a sharing in the communal reality of divine love.

For the classical view, God cannot have a history, cannot change in any way, and cannot be affected at all by whatever happens in history. Among religious views, it is above all the Christian doctrine of incarnation which seems most at odds with this view. On one plausible, and orthodox, reading of the Incarnation, a human, temporal life is taken into such an intimate union with God that it is said to form one 'person', one reality, with God. Moreover, this is seen as a foreshadowing of the destiny which awaits much, and perhaps the whole of, creation, as it is incorporated into the life of Christ. Though, as creator of physical time, God must be beyond physical time, the revelation of the divine purpose as *theosis*, in Christ, suggests that time itself is to find its fulfilment in God, that

---

[38] 'His wrath is not separate from but in his love' (Karl Barth, *Church Dogmatics*, ii/1: 363).

the things which God creates are somehow to be brought to participate in the being of God itself, as Jesus is united to the Divine in the Incarnation. One might then see the creation as the causing to be of things that are other than God, though patterned in some way on the divine nature; and the bringing of those things to participate in the divine nature, resulting in a finally realized state of supreme joy. The history of humanity will be a part, perhaps a small part, of this process, by which finite things are first projected out from the being of God, and then return to it, introducing to the divine being itself forms of interior relationship, of plurality and goodness, which could not exist in the divine nature considered simply as uncreated and immutable.

This suggests a certain triadic distinction in the divine nature. One may speak, as John Macquarrie does, of the primordial, the expressive, and the unitive being of God.[39] Professor Macquarrie associates this distinction with the three persons of the Trinity. While that is a suggestive association, I believe that a rather more complex account of the Trinity is needed, and that this threefold distinction has a different role, not confined to the Christian tradition, which I hope to bring out in the final chapter. One can speak of a primordial divine nature, the divine as it exists immutably, an ineffable reality which in some way contains the possibility of all forms of being, object of its own contemplation and love. This nature will not be changed by anything that happens in time, and will not be added to by the bringing of finite beings into union with itself. There is also the expressive divine nature, the creativity which gives rise to finite forms of value in time. Such creativity actualizes a certain sort of potentiality in God for bringing about finite realities. It introduces an element of potency in God, as source of all actual powers, which may be endlessly realized in new temporal forms. Professor Macquarrie seems to me entirely right to stress that the creative activity of God consists in letting-be, as much as in bringing to be, so that a limited, but real, autonomy of creatures may exist. Thirdly, there is a unitive aspect of the Divine which takes finite things into union with itself, being affected by all the finite processes in which it has played a creative part. In this

---

[39] John Macquarrie, *Principles of Christian Theology* (London: SCM Press, 1966), 181–5.

aspect, God is continually being changed, such change in turn forming the basis for new creative acts.

For such a view, which results from a fairly natural exploration of the Christian ideas of creation, incarnation and redemption, God has a history. The physical universe makes a difference to God, and indeed is a natural extension of the divine being, which brings it to a new form of self-realization. This is a very natural implication of any view which makes incarnation a central model for its doctrine of God. If the uncreated divine nature 'becomes flesh', and if that flesh is united to God indissolubly, though unconfusedly, for ever; and if all humanity is to be included in that assumed humanity, so as to exist 'in Christ'; then the relation of God and the universe is one of mutual relationship, change, and realization through interaction. Time has an importance and a purpose which is lacking in the Greek tradition that was so influential in shaping the classical forms of Semitic theism.

10
Divine Awareness and Bliss

EXPERIENTIAL KNOWLEDGE

In the previous chapter, it was seen that the classical account of divine knowledge holds that the divine knowing is identical with the divine essence. God creates the whole universe in a single timeless act, and God is eternal and wholly immutable. On such a view of creation, 'what is temporal cannot be the cause of anything eternal.'[1] God creates the whole of the universe, from beginning to end, in one act, an act which is identical with the simple essence of God. In God, one thing does not happen after another; so there cannot be two states, one consisting in God's creating of the universe, and another consisting in God's being affected by that creation. It follows that God cannot be affected by creation in any way, and that, in particular, divine knowledge is not caused by the occurrence of temporal events. On the contrary, 'the divine intellect through its knowledge is the cause of things.'[2] God knows the universe God desires to create in knowing the divine being; and that knowledge is the cause of things coming to be, exactly as God knows them.

It also follows that God cannot do anything as a result of things that happen in time, except in the sense that God may (e.g.) timelessly cause someone to pray and, in the same creative act, may cause a later temporal event which 'answers' the prayer to exist. It is essential to see that, on this account, God creates the response in the very same act as the request, and does not wait for the request before deciding whether to answer it. God's one creative act is not modified in any way by anything that happens in time. God cannot wait to see what Abraham will do before God decides whether or not to make a Covenant with Abraham's descendants. God must decree Abraham's acts and the Covenant and its fruition in the history of Israel, in one and the same act. This makes prophecy and providence easy to

---

[1] Thomas Aquinas, *De Veritate*, q. 2 a. 14, in Aquinas, *Opera*, ed. R. Busa (8 vols.; Stuttgart: Gunther Holzfor, 1974–80), vol iii, my translation.
[2] Aquinas, *Summa Contra Gentiles*, 1. 61. 7, in Aquinas, *Opera*, vol. ii.

understand, since God decrees everything to happen, and thus may cause people earlier in time to know infallibly what God has decreed to happen later. God will, in one act, arrange all things so that they inevitably fall out according to the divine plan. It also means that God knows exactly what will happen in the whole of history, at the origin of the universe, so there is no problem with divine foreknowledge. There are distinct advantages in the idea of single-act creation.

There are distinct disadvantages, too. Perhaps the greatest is that such a God cannot really enter into loving relationship with created persons. There can be a sort of impersonal concern for the well-being of creatures. But, since there can be no response to creatures, there can be no reactive attitudes to their successes and failures. As Abraham Heschel emphasizes, the Bible speaks frequently of divine anger, divine grief, and divine joy, and pictures God as a bridegroom passionately caring for his bride. But a timeless God would be unable to react in such ways, since God would be unable to react at all. God determines creatures to act as they do. If I make you do something, it is inappropriate for me to be angry when you do it. It is equally inappropriate for God to rejoice when sinners repent, since God has caused them to do so from all eternity. Just to reinforce this point, on the classical view God would have been no different if God had not created sinners; so God cannot feel anger at them, when God would not have felt anger if they had never existed. All talk of God having feelings must be purely metaphorical. It can refer only to changes in creatures, not to any change, or any reaction, in God. A being which is incapable of change is also incapable of having a real relationship with creatures. As Aquinas says, 'Being related to creatures is not a reality in God.'[3]

This raises a concern for the sense in which God is omniscient. Omniscience has often been construed as the knowledge by God, of every possible proposition, that it is either true or false.[4] There is no problem with a single-act creator's being omniscient in this sense, since God determines of every possible proposition that it is either true or false. But knowledge of the truth-value of propositions is a

---

[3] Aquinas, *Summa Theologiae*, Ia q. 13 a. 7 (Blackfriars edn.; London: Eyre and Spottiswoode, 1963–81).

[4] See Anthony Kenny, *The God of the Philosophers* (Oxford: Clarendon Press, 1979), 10.

very thin sort of knowledge. What is of greater value and importance to conscious beings is the awareness of facts in all their particularity. To know that it is true that a sunset exists is a different thing from being aware of, appreciating, and savouring the actuality of a sunset. One might contrast conceptual knowledge, which does not involve or change the knower except by apprehension of a true proposition, with experiential knowledge, which both involves and changes the knower by modifying conscious states and sensibilities. God could have absolute conceptual knowledge, whether or not any universe exists. God would know, of all possible propositions, that they are either true or false. Of course, as I have pointed out, contrary to the classical view, if no universe existed, there would be a difference in God, but it would be a small one. Some propositions which might have had the truth-value 'true' would have the truth-value 'false' instead—a small enough difference, to be sure. But what would be entirely lacking to a knowing agent, if no universe existed, would be experiential knowledge. If nothing exists, then nothing can be experienced. Would it not be a major lack in the greatest conceivable being that it had no experiential knowledge at all? And does such knowledge not entail that the objects of experience actually exist, so that God is changed in knowledge by their existence?

DIVINE HAPPINESS

It is agreed that one important perfection is happiness. But happiness is not a distinct, identifiable state, a contentless feeling. Happiness is an affective state, a state of enjoyment, and there must be something which is enjoyed, some content to the affective state. If any being is to be supremely happy, it must be conceived as experiencing objects of beauty and complexity which give the richest as well as the most intense forms of happiness.

Classical theists usually accept that God is supremely happy. But for them the content of the divine consciousness must be simply its own purely actual perfection. It is not denied that there is a content, only that it is conceivable by humans. God has experiential knowledge, but only of the divine self. Of course, in having such knowledge, God knows the perfections of all possible things, in a higher and uniquely simple manner. The coherence of this conception largely depends on the coherence of the notion of perfection as pure actuality, and one collapses with the other. One might, unkindly, see the classical move as a double application of what Whitehead called the 'fallacy of misplaced concreteness'—the mistake of taking the abstract to be the real.[5] Both applications are standardly Platonic. First of all, the abstract concepts of things, their natures or Forms (*eide*), are taken to be more real than their empirical instantiations. God knows only such intelligible Forms, since God lacks sensory knowledge altogether. But, in doing so, God knows the world in a more real manner than God would do by apprehending its sensory particularity. As Anselm put it, 'Every created substance exists more truly in . . . the intelligence of the Creator, than it does in itself.'[6] Then, by a second abstraction, all abstract Forms are said to exist in the one simple essence of God, in an undivided and ineffable manner. In knowledge of this essence— and the knowledge is itself the essence—all particular realities are known in a truer way.

God, however, not only knows the actual world; God knows all possibilities. If things as known in God are more real than things as they exist in the universe, then it seems that the possible worlds which God knows in the divine self are more real than the actual world we experience. That a given possible world becomes actual can make no difference to God's knowledge; so what is the difference between actual and merely possible worlds? The most important difference, perhaps, is that in actual worlds there are other subjects of experience than God, whereas in possible worlds, God is the only subject; all others are imaginary. In actual worlds, then, there are valuable states of consciousness which are not God's, though God will know that they are actual. Are such finite consciousnesses more real in God than they are in spatio-temporal reality? This seems an implausible view.

Normally one would think that actual states are more valuable than merely possible states. It is better for me to be actually happy than for me to be merely possibly happy, given that I exist at all. But God can derive as much enjoyment from the contemplation of merely possible states—since they are actual as envisaged in the divine mind—as from actual states, which do not affect divine

---

[5] A.N. Whitehead, *Science and the Modern World* (Cambridge: Cambridge University Press, 1927), 64.

[6] Anselm, *Monologion*, ch. 36, in Basic Writings, S. N. Deane (tr.), (La Salle, Ill.: Open Court, 1962), 146.

knowledge in any case. If so, there is no reason for creating any actual states, except to bring into existence other subjects of enjoyment.

Suppose God knows that, in some possible but unactual worlds, John is extremely happy. God will also know that, in other possible but unactual worlds, John suffers every possible sort of pain; and every sort of pleasure, too. God will know all these things in the same manner. But God will also know that John does not exist in the actual world; so no one really suffers any of these pains or pleasures. God will be imagining people suffering every possible sort of pleasure and pain, in many possible but unactual worlds, though no one really enjoys or suffers at all. In what sense can God enjoy such knowledge? Imaginary people are not suitable objects of sympathy; neither are they suitable subjects of rejoicing and love. But the point of beginning to speak of divine knowledge was partly to maximize divine perfection and happiness. The thought was that conceiving all sorts of beautiful worlds would make God maximally happy. Now it turns out that God will also have to conceive every possible sort of pain and tragedy. If the divine conceiving of beauty is real enough to give God happiness, must the divine conceiving of pain be real enough to give God sadness?

We seem compelled to say that, if conceived pain does not cause sadness, then conceived beauty cannot cause happiness after all. On the Platonic view, this difficulty could be side-stepped, since God has purely intellectual knowledge, not knowledge of actual feelings. Even so, God is granted beatitude, which is a sort of feeling. The classical view admits that the appreciation of beauty, the unmixed beauty of the divine being, is a good and the cause of pure happiness in God.[7] Given a commitment to the reality of particulars, it is at once apparent that finite beauty is of a sort which cannot exist in the same sense within the nature of God. Thus appreciation of any actual beauty is a good which is additional to the good of contemplating the divine nature. God can appropriately rejoice in the particular beauties of the world; indeed, as the greatest conceivable being, it would be a lack if God did not rejoice in any such beauty that exists. Classical theists complain that a temporal God is limited in knowledge by being ignorant of many future facts. But they restrict divine knowledge even more severely, by denying God any

[7] Thomas Aquinas, *Summa Theologiae*, Ia q. 26 a. 1.

knowledge by acquaintance of the most important aspects of past and present reality, namely, the finite goods of the world and the feelings of finite sentient creatures.

PARTICULARITY AND SUFFERING

A Leibnizian picture of God as knowing all possible worlds gives God knowledge of things in all their particularity, and is thus a great extension of divine knowledge over the Platonic view, which, despite Aquinas' disclaimers, gives God only a knowledge of general natures (unless there is a Form for every particular). The trouble is that all these Leibnizian particulars are merely possible, and so not appropriate objects of real joy or sadness. Perhaps one can revert to Aristotle's point that the highest happiness is produced by contemplation of the highest good, the most desirable of states.[8] This cannot be contemplation of all possible worlds, which include the least desirable of states as well as the most desirable. One will have to think of God as contemplating a state of great beauty, wisdom, intelligibility, and magnificence, without any suffering, ugliness, decay, or chaos. This state must now be sharply distinguished from the conception of actual or possible worlds. The price of supreme bliss is ignorance of the possible and actual pain, transience, and frustration of finite things. Aristotle was right; the supremely blissful knows only its own pure being, untouched by the world and even by the possibility of the world. If God is really omniscient, however, and if one accepts that knowledge of spatio-temporal facts in their particularity is something over and above knowledge of essential natures, one will have to give God knowledge of the actual world. Spatio-temporal instantiation gives a form of actuality which is necessarily lacking to intelligible natures, which exist eternally as possibilities, whether or not they are instantiated.

If God lacks knowledge of spatio-temporal facts, then God lacks an important form of experiential knowledge. The knowledge of possibilities is different from the knowledge of instantiated (i.e. actualized) possibilities. The question is, how is this difference to be marked in the divine experience? On the classical view, the fact that a given possible world becomes actual can make no difference to God. Divine happiness results simply from knowledge of intelligible

8 Aristotle, *Metaphysics*, bk. 12.

Forms—a consequence of the axiom that God could have created a different actual universe, but would not have been changed in any way by that fact.

Suppose one thinks of God as eternally willing the actualization of a specific universe. One cannot think of God as first deciding to create the universe, and subsequently enjoying the beauty of creation. The creating and enjoying would be simultaneous, so that God enjoys the act of creating and its object in one changeless act. Even this entails a small amendment to the classical view, since the precise character of God's experiential knowledge will be different than it would have been if God had not created. But God can appreciate the complex beauty of creation in a timeless way.

This seemingly small amendment, however, entails a much greater departure from the classical position. If one thinks of God as actually appreciating particular facts, being happy in the experiential knowledge of their beauty and order, does it not follow that God must also be experientially aware of the suffering, ugliness, and disorder which exist in the actual universe? This seriously compromises the unmixed happiness of God, since it is hardly possible that experiential knowledge of suffering will enrich one's happiness. In thinking of the beauty of the world, experiential knowledge differs from merely conceptual knowledge by involving sensitivity and appreciation, a quality of delight or enjoyment which is an appropriate response of consciousness to apprehended beauty. But what is the appropriate response to suffering? It will certainly not be one of appreciation, enjoyment, or delight. The appropriate affective response to the suffering of another is compassion, coupled with a determination not to remain in contemplation of that state, but to change it as effectively as possible. It is grossly insensitive serenely to contemplate another's pain. But does that mean one can, or should, have no experiential knowledge of it?

Some views of divine perfection require that God should be unaware of suffering in any experiential sense. For such awareness would lessen the quality or intensity of the divine bliss, and make the divine existence less than wholly desirable. However, this seems to represent the triumph of a wholly a priori theology at the expense of both revelation and common sense. If an omniscient being is experientially aware of good, how could it fail to be experientially aware of evil, in the form of suffering?

One might as well argue that a perfect being could not possibly create evil, and therefore that evil does not exist—a position to which philosophers like Boethius come dangerously near.[9] Theology, however, must take account of the facts as they are. Suffering does exist; and if the Creator is a perfect being and the only source of all being, then one must accept that the perfect being does create evil. I have suggested that suffering is rooted in the eternal possibilities of being, and its real possibility, and perhaps some degree of its actualization, is necessary to the emergence of any final complex good such as we can experience. God is perfect, in that God actualizes in the divine being an infinity of unsurpassable values, and so is the supremely desirable ideal and object of worship. In creating, God wills to realize a fellowship of love, a community of co-operating subjects of experience and action. The possibility, and some actualization, of suffering is necessary in such creation. If that is so, a God of love will creatively co-operate to overcome suffering wherever possible, and will guarantee a consummation in which all created beings that consent to redemption will be transfigured into the divine life.

Such a perspective modifies the initial concept of perfection as pure and unmixed beatitude. It posits that some great goods are such that they cannot be achieved without at least the possibility of suffering. Either the divine being must exclude such goods, and thereby possess a restricted set of perfections; or it will include such goods, at the cost of including suffering, too. If perfection is not a monadic concept, referring only to one individual and its self-contemplative state, but a relational concept, implying an ecstatic self-giving, a mutual co-operation, and a freely accepting receptivity, then perfection might include suffering, though only as a moment in its movement to relational fulfilment.

THE DIVINE EXPERIENCE

If the perfect in some manner produces suffering in the universe it creates, then to lack experiential awareness of that suffering would be to turn away from its own creation, as something unbearable to contemplate or experience. If God can experience the goods of creation, then God must also experience its sorrows. They must

[9] Boethius, *The Consolation of Philosophy*, bk. iii, ch. 12: tr. V. E. Watts (Harmondsworth: Penguin, 1969), 112.

enter into God's experiential knowledge of created being. If one can properly speak of divine joy in the beauty of the universe, one must also speak of divine grief or pity at the sorrows of the universe. Heschel makes it clear that this is the prophetic idea of God which is enshrined in the Hebrew Bible. Thus it is an idea close to the heart of the Semitic revelation, and not a dispensable metaphor.

Strictly speaking, this passibility of God may seem not to entail divine temporality, since it could be realized in the timeless decision by which God creates this universe as a whole, a decision which would at the same time determine God's own affective attitudes to that universe. Thus Barth can say, 'He is not impassible';[10] yet 'God cannot be moved from outside, but from inside His own being He shares it in sympathetic communion.'[11] One is to think of God as determing the nature of the universe and the divine affective attitude to it in one timeless act. Yet it is hard to think of God determining the divine nature as X if God is wholly changeless. For immutability entails that God cannot determine the divine self to be other than it already is. The idea of such self-determination suffers from the self-referential incoherence that was articulated in Chapter 7.

If one asks how God feels joy or grief, it should not be supposed that humans are somehow able to imagine what it is like to experience as God does. We can say that God must feel joy, since joy is a perfection. But God will not feel happiness as we do after a good pint of beer on a Saturday night. Will God know what it is like to enjoy a pint? It is plausible to suppose that perfect knowledge must involve knowing *what it is like* to have all the experiences that conscious beings have. To know what it is like to have a sort of experience, one must arguably have actually had such an experience. Maybe perfect 'knowledge of what it is like' to have a toothache of a certain sort would require having the toothache. How can even God do that? Does it even make sense to suppose that God has toothaches, as well as experiences of murdering, raping, and pillaging, presumably?

Suppose someone enjoys torturing a baby. God cannot have an experience correctly describable as, 'I am now enjoying torturing this baby.' God forbids torture; God must feel grief at the suffering of the baby, and revulsion at the behaviour of the torturer. God

[10] Karl Barth, *Church Dogmatics*, ed. G. W. Bromiley and T. F. Torrance (4 vols.; Edinburgh: T. & T. Clark, 1936–77), ii/1: 370.   [11] Ibid. 371.

could not torture anyone, and so could not experience doing such an action, let alone enjoy it. Nevertheless, God might know the feelings of the torturer in a way that we never could; does God not know the secrets of the heart, the interior mental states of all creatures?[12] God could experience the feelings of the torturer, not as God's own feelings, but precisely as the feelings of another. Such an experience would be set in a context of revulsion, grief, and condemnation, so it would not be the experience as the torturer has it. Yet God would have an inward and affective knowledge of the torturer's total mental state. In a way wholly unparalleled in human knowledge, and thus totally non-anthropomorphic, God has direct access to the inner feelings of creatures. God will not experience the hatred and despair a torturer experiences. But God will have experiential knowledge of those feelings, and will affectively respond to them in the most appropriate way—perhaps by a mixture, impossible for us, of anger and compassionate love.

Whitehead spoke of all finite experiences being 'included in' God.[13] This is perhaps a less restricted idea of omniscience than that which excludes all finite experiences completely from the being of God. Yet it may misleadingly suggest that the finite feelings of creatures are actually God's own feelings, and also undermine the real autonomy of creaturely existence. So it is probably better to say simply that God inwardly apprehends such feelings, experientially knowing exactly what it is like to have them. As God delights in appreciating beauty, so God will find joy in contemplating the joy of creatures. God will feel compassion and sorrow at their pain, and will feel revulsion and anger at their malice and greed. What it is like for God to know human passions inwardly and to feel joy, compassion, and anger, we do not know. But it would restrict divine knowledge unacceptably to deny either such inward knowledge or such affective joy, compassion, and anger in God.

Some people feel that the passionate God portrayed in the Bible is too anthropomorphic, too much like a rather irascible person who likes the smell of a good sacrifice and tends to get annoyed if people get their rituals mixed up. It should be clear that the sense in which God is being regarded as passionate here is not anthropomorphic in

[12] Ps. 139: 1–6.
[13] A. N. Whitehead, *Modes of Thought* (Cambridge: Cambridge University Press, 1938), 350.

that way. God knows, in a way not open to any human person, from 'inside', as it were, the experiences of every creature. God will know what an experience feels like to the experient. But God will also know the background awareness, motives, and tacit penumbra of cognition and feeling which surround that conscious experience, though it may not be consciously recognized by the experient. God will know the experiences of all those affected by the experient's acts. And God will set all that in the context of an infinite divine beauty and bliss, giving possibilities of transformation and healing quite unrecognized by finite experients. This is not a human form of awareness. It is endlessly rich, wholly conscious, wholly inward without excluding the inwardness of others, universal in scope, and understood and ordered by supreme wisdom and love. It contains no element of overwhelming passion, disordered egoism, or ignorance; no helpless submission to the vagaries of circumstance; and no feeling which is not under the complete control of a supremely rational love. This being which intuits in its own awareness the subjectivity of every other being, and which responds to all of them with infinitely creative power, is far removed from some humanlike consciousness, tossed about by its largely arbitrary, wilful, and ignorant responses to events which threaten it and which it cannot control. It is a vital, living, absolute awareness, and precisely as such it infinitely transcends any and all created beings in dignity and power. Such uniquely direct and inward knowledge is very far from any sort of human experience. It is not inferential and abstractive, as the classical, Platonically influenced view is. But it is just as remote from the experience of human persons.

It hardly needs saying that the divine experience is not merely made up of all creaturely experiences, as though God was just the experiential dustbin of the universe—a picture which Whitehead's idea of God as all-inclusive may suggest. God directly knows all experiences, but also reacts to them in a way appropriate to an all-perfect creator. As God knows each experience, God will react with an appropriate affective response, whether it be of joy, grief, or revulsion (what the Bible calls 'anger'). It is such a response to suffering that constitutes the divine compassion. Where suffering exists, it is a greater mark of perfection that a supreme Creator should respond to it with compassion than that the Creator should merely note its presence by assigning an appropriate truth-value to one of the set of propositions eternally in the divine mind.

It is not enough, of course, that God should merely feel compassion. Although the presence of such negative feelings (negative in that they are responses to disvalues, not to values) in God must be admitted, and considerably modifies the Aristotelian notion of perfection, they cannot have the last, or even a preponderant, word. If creation is for the sake of goodness, beauty, and joy, God must be able to ensure that such positive values will vastly outweigh those disvalues whose possibility has been necessary to the existence of this universe. This is why Heschel distinguishes sharply between a God who is helplessly subject to passion, and a God who wills to be passionately involved with the world, but has the power to ensure the triumph of the divine purpose. The God of supreme compassion will also be a God of transforming power, who will seek to eliminate evil from creation, and will finally ensure that its elimination will be complete.

THE GOD WHO SUFFERS

My main argument has been that it is better to have experiential knowledge than to have purely conceptual knowledge, that knowledge of particulars cannot be given by knowledge of abstract Forms in the divine being, and that, if suffering exists, it is better to feel compassion for it than to be unmoved by it. So it is a reasonable requirement of omniscience that God should have experiential knowledge of both the suffering and the joy of creatures, though that experience will in God be transformed by knowledge of the ineffable perfection of the divine being itself. This an argument for pathos in God which strongly supports Heschel's interpretation of the biblical revelation.

From a Christian viewpoint, Paul Fiddes has adduced three further considerations which, in my view, are persuasive.[14] The most important is the central place of the Cross in Christian thought. Christian tradition has not hesitated to say that God suffers in the passion of Jesus Christ. At the same time, the classical tradition has sought to exempt the divine nature from suffering, ascribing it truly only to the human nature of Jesus. Many theologians now feel this way of making a division between the divine and human natures of

[14] Paul Fiddes, *The Creative Suffering of God* (Oxford: Clarendon Press, 1988), ch. 6.

Jesus to be an unacceptable one.[15] On the view I have outlined, it would not be true that God only knows what creaturely suffering is in the life of Jesus. God would be directly aware of all creaturely sufferings, and respond to them both in compassion and in active concern. The Cross is not the only place where God suffers. It is nevertheless the place which manifests the true nature of God as passionately affected by all the sufferings of creation.

Secondly, Fiddes suggests that the sort of divine love manifest in the life of Jesus is not just a serene beneficence, which leaves the lover untouched. It involves a sharing of experience, a suffering-with, a preparedness to be wounded to make others whole.[16] Eberhard Jungel puts it well when he writes, 'The theology of the Crucified One is speaking, then, of a heightening, an expansion, even an overflowing of the divine being, when it considers God as the total surrender of himself for all men in the death of Jesus.'[17] That 'total surrender' of the divine being is not, however, a tragic gesture of hopeless self-abandonment. While the resurrection of Jesus does not detract from the gravity of suffering and death, it nevertheless expresses the belief that God is able to heal the destructive consequences of suffering, and redirect them to the creation of a distinctive good. The self-giving of God is the way to the relating of all things to the self of God, and thus the deepest form of divine self-affirmation.

Thirdly, it may be thought that a God who creates a world in which many creatures suffer, but who does not experience suffering at all, is in an important sense indifferent to suffering. God creates suffering for others, but is unmoved by it. Even if such suffering is in the cause of ultimate good, it may be a less than truly loving creator who causes suffering to others, but does not share in pain. This is one argument used by Aurobindo to argue that God is not an 'extra-cosmic being', but one who 'enters into all things'.[18] The Christian view would be able to accept this, and yet stress the real individuality of finite centres of consciousness, whose suffering God

[15] See Jürgen Moltmann, *The Crucified God* (London: SCM Press, 1974).

[16] Isaiah 53: 5: 'With his stripes we are healed.'

[17] Eberhard Jungel, *God as the Mystery of the World* (Edinburgh: T. & T. Clark, 1983), 368.

[18] Aurobindo, *The Life Divine*, (2 vols.; Calcutta: Arya Publishing House, 1939), vol. i, p. 113.

is directly aware of, but without it being strictly the suffering of God. God cannot suffer in the sense of being seriously subject to injury. But it may be proper to speak of God knowing what it is like to suffer, and being subject to a degree of frustration of the divine desires and purposes. If one can properly speak of divine beatitude, maybe one may also speak of divine suffering, as a voluntarily accepted solidarity with the suffering in creation.

Thus one may think of God, *qua* perfect being, as supremely happy in the contemplation of the divine perfection, inconceivable by us. Then, God will delight in the beauty of the actual world, have compassion and anger towards its suffering and evil, and show mercy to those who repent. God's being will be affected by the nature of the world, so that if the world is contingent, then in at least these respects God's being will be contingent, such that it could have been otherwise. God will be supremely affected by the world. Yet it remains importantly true that the world never passes beyond divine control. If God is affected by creation, it is because God so wills it. God cannot be changed in essential nature by what happens in the world, and the changes God does undergo cannot ever destroy the divine being. If it is God's will to create what is truly other, then God cannot wholly determine what that other shall be. Yet God sets the limits of its being, and they can never be passed. If God is love, and love is related to what is other, then God's love will issue in a universe which is not wholly determined by God in every respect, but which can never pass beyond the presence and influence of the divine being. The limits of divine power and the limits of creaturely freedom are the limits set by divine love. Such a love may suffer and may have to endure much with patience; but it cannot be defeated, and its ultimate triumph is assured. It is that insight into the nature of divine love, as the foundation of the universe, that the experience of the Cross and Resurrection of Jesus evoked in the first disciples. It is an insight which remains as startling and as illuminating today as it was then.

11

God and Time

Heschel emphasizes that God relates in personal ways to creatures. Iqbal writes that God limits the divine freedom in order to co-operate with the free acts of creatures. Aurobindo expounds a view of Brahman as realizing itself relationally in the existence of many selves. Barth holds that the central Christian insight into the divine nature is that God is love, and love is expressed in relationship. For all these theologians, real relation is an important element of the divine being, even though there exists nothing other than God which has wholly independent existence. God brings into being that which has a certain degree of autonomy. If God really relates to those who are created as distinct beings, God must show some of the qualities which mark the most valued forms of relationship between autonomous persons. In the case of human persons, these will include respect for the autonomy of the other, delight in the being of the other, compassion for the sufferings of the other, a giving and receiving of experience, insight, and feeling, a co-operation in realizing states and activities of value. This is how a perfectly wise and loving relationship is understood at its best in human communities, and it is that sort of perfection which will be realized at its fullest in God, who is the most perfect conceivable being.

Yet the manner in which such love can be realized in the divine being, considered purely in itself, is not easy to conceive. The sort of love that has just been described seems properly to belong only to suffering, limited, developing persons who exist in community. Only then will compassion be appropriate; only then can co-operation be required to achieve new goals; only then can persons learn from others; and only then can persons share their essentially finite experiences. God, as the perfect Creator, will not be able to realize all these properties. However, if God truly relates to created persons, then God can realize compassion for their sufferings as well as delight in their enjoyments, can help them to achieve their freely chosen goals and can share their experiences. In this way, many forms of love, as we understand it at its highest, will be realized in God only as God relates in freedom to finite persons.

It may seem, however, that if God is the Creator, God cannot truly relate in freedom to creatures, since all that they are, in every aspect of their being, derives from God. There can be no possibilities for them which are not determined by God. There can be no surprises for God, since God knows, and determines, all the possibilities that creatures have. It is conceivable, however, that God may create a person who has the power of deciding between various possibilities. What is possible is determined by God, but what becomes actual may be determined by creatures.

One might think, in a preliminary way, to be modified later,[1] of God as having in the divine mind every possible combination of musical notes. Every sonata that could ever exist will be there, as well as millions of utterly horrible combinations of notes and chords. One can think of Mozart as picking out one of these possibilities, one of the better ones, of course, and making it actual. As far as Mozart is concerned, he is exercising creative autonomy, though he can never succeed in creating something that is not already in the mind of God. If it is the case that actual existence makes a difference to divine knowledge, then Mozart will cause God to know something that God would otherwise not have known, the actuality of a particular combination of notes. Perhaps one may reasonably suppose that God will appreciate and enjoy Mozart's sonata, in a way in which God will not enjoy all the merely possible sonatas which exist in the divine mind. In this way, creatures may not be able to do anything which has not been envisaged by God; yet they may extend God's knowledge and appreciation by their independent power of choice. In a real sense, then, creatures may share their experiences with God and modify God's experience, just as God may modify their experience by causing them to discern new possibilities for choice.

Creatures can be responsible for the exercise of their talents. They can choose for themselves which possible path of life will become actual; and in their consequential experiences of joy and sorrow, they will give God opportunities for sympathetic joy and compassion. God and creatures can co-operate in realizing values, since God can make values possible and provide a causal impetus to the efforts creatures make to actualize creative possibilities. In so far as God

[1] See the penultimate section of this chapter ('Divine Imagination').

creates beings which are limited, developing, and communal by nature, God can actualize the divine being as love in a pre-eminent way, sharing the experiences of all creatures as fully as possible and working for their well-being in ways which do not impede their autonomy.

The existence of such autonomy opens up the possibility that creatures will not make the creative and co-operative choices that God desires them to make. Where communities can be built up through co-operation and altruism, they can also be destroyed through conflict and egoism. God will necessarily condemn such choices and the appropriate reactive attitude to them will be one of disapproval. At this point the Christian insight into the character of divine love is that God shares in the destructive consequences of egoism, in order that creatures should be reunited to God through the implanting of the divine love within them. God is not only the one who relates to the community of finite persons as another person. God is also the one who is inwardly aware of all experiences, and who therefore suffers with the suffering and seeks to transform such experiences into a sacrament of the divine being. And God is the one who acts inwardly in creatures to bring them to the perfection God wills for them, by uniting them to the divine life. This is formulated in the Trinitarian idea of God as the Father who loves what he brings forth from himself, as the Son who is the image of the Father's glory, receiving and returning the Father's love without resistance, and as the Spirit who implants the divine love in the hearts of creatures. The Trinitarian God, who is the source of love, who is the completed inclusive object and true image of love, and who is the creativity of love, is a spelling-out of what it means for God to be Love, as this is illumined by divine self-manifestation in Jesus Christ. God as Trinity realizes the fulness of the divine being as love, as God creates a universe of finite persons and 'enters into it' to unite it to the divine self. The Trinitarian God essentially has a history, which is the history of the genesis, the suffering and the fruition of relational love in a community of persons, united in and through the divine life as its source and goal.

DIVINE KENOSIS

Although this seems a very natural way to conceive of God as embodying the perfection of love, it has never been unreservedly accepted by classical theologians. There are many reasons for this, but one main reason is that it seems to them to limit the power and knowledge of God. It limits God's power, because it places some acts of creatures outside divine determination, and it makes God dependent in some respects upon the acts of beings other than God. It limits God's knowledge, because it implies that God cannot know what is going to happen until creatures have decided. God cannot know the future with certainty, and so prophecy and the providential arrangement of events become very risky enterprises.

The worry about divine power seems to me to be capable of a fully satisfactory resolution. God has the power to determine everything if God so wills. But if God wills to give some beings a limited degree of autonomy, then God can do so. God's dependence will never be such that the essential divine perfection is threatened; and if it is a requirement of love that one should be to some extent vulnerable and reactive, then such dependence is a perfection, not a limitation, in God. Those who take the life of Jesus to be a revelation of the character of God may well be disposed to think that a vulnerable love is the best exercise of a power which works through love and not through compulsion.

The worry about the future being unknown is also susceptible of ready alleviation. If anything at all might happen, then God would indeed not be in control. If one envisaged creaturely choices as forming a sort of 'branching tree' of possible acts, then one might very soon have a huge range, exponentially expanding, of possible futures, and at any one point of time God would not be able to foresee very much of what will be actual even in a few centuries. Contrary to this picture, however, all possibilities are wholly determined by God, or are rooted in the essential divine being. They do not have to form a branching tree, for which the future becomes more and more uncertain as more and more possible paths branch off, until it becomes wholly unpredictable. One may think, instead, of possibilities as forming an interwoven lattice, such that there are many possible paths, yet all lead to a limited range of determinate outcomes. One very simple picture of this sort is of a journey from the North Pole. A number of people are told that they may choose their manner and direction of travelling, as long as they continue to move gradually further and further from the starting point—that is the 'branching tree' model. It may seem that their paths will diverge to infinity. But that is far from being the case. There are many ways of travelling; but, given only that one has to keep travelling in a generally southerly direction, everyone will end up at exactly the same place, namely, the South Pole.

So it may be with the array of possible free actions; all will depend on what may be called the temporal topography of the universe. At any one moment the array of real possibilities available to any creature can be either more or less limited. Sometimes there may be not more than one real possibility—that is, a possibility under the voluntary control of the creature. At other times, there may be quite a large number of choices. Possible tracks of different creatures will cross and overlap, so that some tracks may progressively close off the number of possibilities, while others may open up new directions. Even where there is much choice for any individual, the general direction of change will be highly predictable. The laws of probability in quantum physics give an illuminating model of how particular possibilities can be open, while the future of a system consisting of such open futures can be highly predictable.[2]

To give another simple example, God can leave it open to many individual physicists to take a route which will lead to the discovery of the laws of mechanics, but might make it certain that some physicist, within some finite period of time, will discover them. Even if all physicists turn out to be so lazy and selfish that none of them discover the laws, God can inspire the mind of one of them to make the discovery. Just because God does not determine everything, it does not follow that God cannot determine anything. Many particular determinations will not undermine the reality of human freedom, in all the areas that remain. It would be implausible to hold that, just because God will determine many human actions, God is thereby destroying all significant human freedom. All that the strongest desirable human freedom requires is that each person will have a choice in determining their own lives for good or evil. God can easily set up real possibilities so that such an element of choice remains for everyone. Yet even precise events far in the future can be predicted with certainty, while huge swaths of history are unknowable in detail until creatures have decided them.

There is a temptation to think that either God determines

---

[2] 'Chance is the means for the exploration and realization of inherent possibility, through continually changing circumstances' (John Polkinghorne, *Science and Providence* (London: SPCK, 1989), 38).

everything or cannot tell what is going to happen at all. A more plausible picture is that God can foresee that the divine purpose will be fulfilled, and can foresee some details of its fulfilment, since God determines these things to be. But the particular way in which it is fulfilled is left to creatures to decide, within fairly definite limits. In this picture, providence is the ordering of things to good, and the guarantee that they will result in good. God always directs the process of creaturely choice. God does so by setting the real possibilities on each occasion, by the influence of the divine character, which is present to and in principle knowable by creatures on each occasion, and by causally determining those outcomes which are necessary to the fulfilment of the divine purpose.

PROVIDENCE AND FREEDOM

It has been objected that 'a temporal deity is logically incapable of executing a universal plan.'[3] This claim is false, since a temporal deity could determine everything in advance if it chose. The question is not one of temporality as such, but of whether creatures can act with a degree of autonomy. If they can, then by definition God cannot unilaterally decide everything that is going to happen. But if God has a universal plan, is it not true that 'the logical possibility of frustrating his plan at any, and so every, point, cannot be denied'?[4] It does not follow that if God's plan can be frustrated at any point, then it can be frustrated at every point. It may logically be frustratable at any point, but at not more than one point, or at a rather small number of points overall. Neither does it follow from the fact that creatures are significantly free (free at some points which enable them to determine their own destinies for good or ill) that they are free at every point. A more careful statement of the position a believer in created autonomy might hold is that God's plan (what God desires) can be frustrated at many points. For example, God desires everyone to do good, but free agents may often do evil. God can so order things that these deviations from the divine plan will be taken account of by a number of back-up plans, and will form part of a broader plan which cannot be frustrated. Even if everyone, on every occasion of free choice, frustrates God's plan, God will at

[3] John Yates, *The Timelessness of God* (London: University of America Press, 1990), 275.   [4] Ibid. 274.

the least have succeeded in the plan of creating free agents who can decide their own destinies. But more than this can be said.

The autonomist is often faced with the alternatives of either accepting that all actions are determined by God, whose will is irresistible, or that they are totally free, in the sense of being equally, and perhaps arbitrarily, balanced between possible outcomes, so that not even God can have the slightest idea what will happen. Such dichotomies are usually ill-formed and misleading, and there is almost always an overlooked possibility not captured by either alternative. So in this case, an autonomist may hold that humans are responsible for making their own decisions, but that decisions are not simply arbitrary. They are based on carefully or carelessly thought out principles for obtaining good, whether for oneself or for beings in general. People vary enormously in what they think is good, on how carefully they consider the question, and on how far they take the good of others into account. They often think very little, opt for self-destructive pleasures, and act out of self-regard. Yet Christians believe that all people are created by a God of supreme love, so that they might find their fulfilment in unity with divine love. They are created with an inherent longing for love, for relationship with God, in which true happiness lies. This means that the way of destructive self-regard is a form of pathology, an ignorance of what true fulfilment and happiness are and of the presence of God as Creator. Choosing one's own good in preference to the objectively good as a means to happiness is always self-defeating. It renders impossible the higher goods of one's own being which one was created to realize. It imprisons one in self-regarding desire, and in the end makes one unable to give or accept love. The basic choice, in short, is between one's own good and the intrinsic good. It is always intelligible for created selves to choose the former, even though such a choice will end in self-destructive isolation and self-exclusion from a community of love in which alone true fulfilment can be found.

God wills that all should be saved, should enter the community of love. On the classical view, very few are in fact saved, and yet God alone determines this, prior to any actual human choices.[5] If the classical theorist holds that God's plan is not frustratable, the logical

---

[5] John Calvin, *Institutes of the Christian Religion*, bk. iii, ch. 21, tr. H. Beveridge (Grand Rapids: Eerdmans, 1989), 202 f.

consequence is that God does not will that all should be saved. God must will the damnation of many; but while that is a consistent belief, it is a morally intolerable one. If God's will is that all should be saved,[6] is this will frustratable? The autonomist has accepted that the divine will is frustratable, at least on occasions of free choice. So it looks as though the will for universal salvation is frustratable. However, what is partly frustratable is not necessarily wholly frustratable. It is logically possible that God's will that I always do good is frustrated, and yet God's will that I find fulfilment in God is not frustratable, since I have been created to seek such fulfilment. I will eventually return to the proper orientation of created being, when I find through repeated experience of suffering that other paths lead only to destruction and the diminishing of being.

Gregory of Nyssa defended this position,[7] basing his argument on such texts as Ephesians 1: 10: 'He has made known to us . . . the mystery of his will, according to his purpose which he set forth in Christ as a plan for the fullness of time, to unite all things in him, things in heaven and things on earth.' If it is God's plan to unite everything in heaven and earth in Christ, then this plan is not ultimately frustratable. Rational creatures, however, are to achieve this destiny only through the exercise of their own freedom, which may lead them into selfish desire, ignorance, and suffering, until they learn obedience to love through the suffering they endure.

There are, it may seem, two ways in which salvation can be obtained. It can be obtained by grace, by divine action alone; or it can be obtained by merit, by human striving. On the former view, no reason can be given why God chooses some for salvation and not others; this is put down to the mystery of the divine will. It seems to me that a God of supreme love will not simply choose to damn anyone; so, in so far as salvation is by grace, it will be for all. That is a requirement of the logic of divine love. On the latter view, it is easier to explain why some may be damned—because they do not strive for goodness, because they are evil or unfaithful. It is conceivable that someone may turn away from the objectively good

---

[6] 1 Tim. 2: 4.
[7] Gregory of Nyssa, 'Sermon on I Corinthians', in M. Wiles and M. Santer (eds. and trs.), *Documents in Early Christian Thought* (Cambridge: Cambridge University Press, 1975), 257 ff.

and thus from their own fulfilment, thereby suffering the self-torture of destructive passion and frustration. That would be describable as hell, and it has seemed possible to many, perhaps most, theologians, that creatures may remain in that state for ever.[8] If the only reason they have for turning from hell is itself a self-interested one—fear of suffering, not love of the good—then it is possible that they will be trapped by self for ever. The only requirement on a God of love would be to continue to hold out the possibility of repentance and forgiveness, even if it was never responded to. There might come a point at which it was no longer practically possible for creatures to repent, though God would never cease to be a God of forgiving love.

But even if some creatures could end thus, could *all* creatures end in such a sorry state? There is a limit to what a God of love could do to accomplish human salvation, if in the end it depends on human effort. But perhaps there is a third way. Between irresistible grace and heroic human endeavour, there is the possibility of an efficacious divine power which requires only human recognition and acceptance to take effect. God can embrace the suffering which is the result of evil, in the hope of turning the perpetrators of evil to penitence. God can strengthen feeble efforts toward goodness by co-operating love. God can infuse a knowledge of the divine beauty and perfection in those who are prepared to receive it. In these ways, the appropriate human disposition is one of surrender and acceptance—of faith—rather than of continual moral striving. Even though God will not compel free creatures to love, it might seem unnatural for anyone truly to experience the destructive effects of self-regard and then to encounter such self-giving, empowering, fulfilling love and reject it. One might reject it in a moment of rebellion, seeking an unrestricted freedom or the exploration of desire or a sense of power. But when such a choice has been seen to be ultimately self-defeating, the realization must surely come that one exists only by divine power and that the only lasting happiness is in self-abandonment to the divine presence.

It may seem to be conceivable that some creatures should permanently reject the divine love which is the only foundation of their own existence; and, as long as it remains possible for them to

---

[8] Augustine, *City of God*, bk. xxi, ch. 17, ed. R. V. G. Tasker, tr. J. Healey (London: J. M. Dent, 1957), 339.

repent if they would, it may seem that they may continue in being, consistently with the love of God. One cannot positively guarantee that this will not happen, and Jesus' teaching holds it out as a possibility—especially, one should note, for the pious religious leaders of his day. On the other hand, God creates for the sake of the goods that creatures can co-operatively realize. So God creates beings that have a natural inclination to good and to co-operation. The creation of such a universe, I have suggested, inevitably carries the possibility of destructive evil, but the evil (as the classical tradition has always held) is parasitic on the good, and can never outweigh it. For that reason, the possibility must be excluded that *all* free creatures should choose evil and bring suffering on their world for ever. One obvious way of excluding that possibility is to ensure that rational freedom will tend to the true good, even if after long periods of freely chosen illusion. Only in that way can hope truly outweigh the terror of suffering. Self-destruction, one may think, cannot be an ultimate choice. When human passion at last exhausts itself, the divine beauty, unique and unsurpassable, can begin to be recognized for what it truly is. Then it will begin to exert its intrinsic attraction and power to make each finite self an image of its own unlimited perfection. If God is omnipotent love, therefore, the divine purpose can be frustrated in many particulars, since divine love will not compel. But it cannot be frustrated in its final outcome, since God's power in its ultimately irresistible attraction, will not suffer love to be defeated. One cannot positively guarantee that this will happen. Yet it is an outcome one can rightly hope for and pray for, if God's universal love indeed wills the salvation of all created beings.

For either of these understandings of the divine purpose, providence is not the planning, in every detail, of the future of the universe. It is the irresistible ordering of the universe to final goodness, the ability of God to respond to every free act of creatures in such a way as to bring it finally to good, or to eliminate its negativity from the fully realized goodness of creation. This is an understanding of providence which gives creatures genuine freedom and yet does not subject God to the possibility that the divine purpose in creation might finally be defeated.

THE TIMELESSNESS OF GOD

All this, however, entails a form of temporality in God, and that is a notion that has been anathema to classical traditions in theology. For classical theologians, to make God temporal would be to subject God to a power which limits the divine being and makes it less than perfect, even less than fully real. The key move is made by Plato early in the *Timaeus*, and throughout most of his dialogues. 'We must begin', he says, 'by distinguishing that which always is and never becomes from that which is always becoming but never is. The one is apprehensible by intelligence . . . being eternally the same, the other is the object of opinion and irrational sensation, coming to be and ceasing to be, but never fully real.'[9]

The world of ideas, of possible states of affairs, is immutable in the sense that, if something is ever possible, then it is always possible. For most modern philosophers this is true precisely because the merely possible is not fully actual. If possibilities have any sort of existence at all, it is as conceived or as conceivable by some mind. They are abstractions, and to say that the possible exists is a grammatical mistake, rather like saying that the hypothetical is actual. For most modern philosophers, only the temporal and particular is real. Plato saw things very differently. Influenced by Parmenidean thought, he held that only the changeless is fully real. As Anselm puts it, 'What began from non-existence, and can be thought not to exist, and returns to non-existence unless it subsists through some other . . . such a thing does not exist in a strict and absolute sense.'[10]

The thesis of the relative unreality of the temporal is an axiom of much Greek thought. It is directly reflected in Augustine's *De Trinitate*. 'There would be no changeable good things unless there were an unchangeable good. So when you hear a good this and a good that which can at other times also be called not good, if without these things, that are good by participation in the good, you can perceive good itself by participating in which these other things are good . . . if then you can put them aside and perceive good itself, you will perceive God. And if you cling to him in love, you will straightaway enter into bliss.'[11]

Not only is this absolute Beauty and Good the highest object of the mind's contemplation, it is the highest object of its own contemplation. As Aristotle puts it, 'It must be of itself that the divine thought thinks (since it is the most excellent of things), and its thinking is a thinking on thinking.'[12] Thus arises the idea of the divine mind as absorbed in contemplation of its own perfection, and finding the highest possible happiness therein. Here also is one Augustinian model of the Trinity—as the source of the thought of its own perfection; the thought itself, as object of the divine mind; and the enjoyment of that thought as supremely beautiful—all of which, thinker, thought, and contemplative enjoyment of it, belong inextricably together in one unity of being.[13] God is love, in the sense that God contemplates and finds delight in the perfection of the divine being. This might be called a view of the immanent Trinity, of that threefoldness in the divine being which is the source and pattern for the unfolding of the Divine as love in the created universe. But the sense of 'love' which is being used here lacks precisely that relationality and reciprocity which characterizes the greatest value of love, as we normally understand it. It is, indeed, an analogy of love which can exist in the Divine itself, without relation to any universe. It is the immanent form which the 'economic Trinity' unfolds in created time, as the manifestation in relationship of the greatest conceivable perfection. But it is in itself beyond relationship and duality.

I do not think one can ignore the testimony of some of the greatest sages of many religious traditions to the existence of a pleroma of beauty and goodness which is changeless, unsurpassable, and complete in the divine being. That testimony is found in Aurobindo's conception of *Sachchidananda* as Being, Truth-consciousness, and Enjoyment as well as in Augustine's exposition of the immanent Trinity as a beatific state of self-contemplating perfection. While the Bible does not indulge in metaphysical speculation, the idea of the glory and and majesty of God is the idea of a beauty, power and

---

[11] Augustine, *De Trinitate*, bk. viii, ch. 2, tr. Edmund Hill (New York: New City Press, 1991), 244.

[12] Aristotle, *Metaphysics*, 1074[b].

[13] Augustine, *De Trinitate*, bk, xiv, ch. 3: pp. 378 ff.

wisdom which is complete and wholly unlike the scattered fragments of it that are visible in the temporal realm. There is a haunting echo of truth in Plato's expressive phrase, 'Time is the moving image of eternity',[14] presenting refracted images of an actual whole which is beyond conceptual cognition entirely. If one thinks of God as the ground of all possibilities, one may think of those possibilities being gathered up, maximized, and united in one simple and inexpressible reality which may be called unrestricted actuality. Thus one arrives at an idea of God as *Actus Purus*, the *esse suum subsistens* of Aquinas and the classical tradition. The twentieth-century theologians I have considered do not wholly reject this view. Indeed, they stress that God, as infinite reality, possesses a fullness of being which is unchanged by any temporal flow. The mistake they see in the classical tradition has not been to have said this. It has been to suppose that this is all that can be truly said of God.

THE TEMPORALITY OF GOD

But what is the nature of the relation between that timeless perfection and the temporal world of changing images? It is clear that the timeless cannot be affected by the temporal in any way. There can be no question of the temporal making the timeless to be, even in part, what it is, or entering into it when it has not always been there. But the same being who is timelessly actual may also be temporally potential. That is, it may manifest its being temporally, without in any way changing in itself. This would, of course, be incompatible with a radical simplicity in God. But the doctrine of the Trinity, with its talk of the Father begetting the Son, and the Spirit proceeding from one or both, seems very hard to square with a doctrine of radical simplicity in any case.

Paradoxically, there is something incomplete about the concept of a perfect being which is wholly complete, in the sense of being wholly actual, without any potentiality. For what such a being would lack is precisely potentiality. One may claim this is no lack; but this will only be so if potentiality is, as such, an imperfection. Potentiality need not be thought of as mere non-actuality. It is better thought of in terms of capacity, the capacity for creative action and

---

[14] Plato, *Timaeus* 37.

for relationship. Is it not better to possess such a capacity than not to possess it? It seems so; but the price is a necessary incompleteness in the divine being. This incompleteness would hold, however, only of its temporal aspect, where it is a necessary condition of temporality as such. In its eternal aspect, the divine being would be complete and *a se*, from, in, and for itself.

The objection that the Divine cannot possess both an eternal and a temporal aspect is not open to Christians, who hold to a belief in the Incarnation, where humanity and divinity are both held together in one subsistence or *hypostasis*. Here, eternal and temporal are bound together in an inseparable unity of being. For an Incarnational view, there is nothing odd, indeed it would be entirely natural, for an eternal God to be able to manifest itself in temporal forms, so that its essential being and its temporal manifestation would be held in an inseparable unity. If two natures, a divine and a human, can exist together in one person, then there can be no objection in principle to saying that two 'natures', a timeless and a temporal, can exist together in one unitary divine reality.

If one can find some support for a doctrine of divine temporality in the doctrine of the Incarnation, there is also support in the doctrine of creation, a doctrine which was not usually accepted by the Greeks. That doctrine suggests that the temporal, as created by God, is both real and good. Naturally, the Creator must be beyond created time, but does seem to relate to temporal events in a positive way. To say that time is created is not to say that it is unreal. It is to say that it is dependent for its reality on God. It can as easily be argued that the nature of the effects suggests something positive about the being of the cause, as that the cause must be quite different from its effects. The natural suggestion is that there is something in God which is the natural ground of temporality, so that the Creator will not be the wholly timeless, as we understand it. If time is real, and is even a perfection or the necessary condition of some perfections, then God will have to be temporal at least in some analogous way.

If God is present at every time, the clearest thing to say is that, in creating space-time, God creates temporal relations in the divine being itself. That is, by the same act by which God creates events in spatio-temporal relations, so God thereby creates the relation of being co-present with many times. Thus one is able correctly to say, at each time, 'God *now* exists'—which, strangely, is not true on the classical view, since for that view God, properly speaking, has no temporal properties.[15]

To assert the reality of the temporal is to say that the passage of time, its continuous flow from a fixed past to a relatively open future, is a fundamental feature of created reality. To turn that dynamic flow into a spatialized representation, like a four-dimensional space-time grid for which everything is fixed, is to misrepresent its basic character, to turn it into something other than it is. There is no harm in using such a grid as a mathematical device for discovering laws of nature, which are usually treated as time-invariant. But confusion is caused if the fundamental experience of temporal flow is then said to be somehow illusory or 'merely subjective'.

THE REALITY OF TIME

There is clearly an important metaphysical question about the reality of time.[16] As I have stressed, much classical Christian theology has been written in terms of the Greek preference for the reality of the timelessly intelligible over the flow of experience and creative agency. It is illuminating to ask how things might look if that preference is reversed—as it is by the vast majority of post-seventeenth-century philosophers.

For Platonists, only the changeless is fully real; and at once it is clear that for such philosophers, God must be conceived as fully changeless, since God must be conceived as fully real. Anything in time is such that at some time it does not exist. If it exists now, then it does not yet exist in the future, and it has ceased to exist in the past. Thus it is in many respects non-existent. Even its present existence is fleeting and transitory, since the present is a constantly moving point with no stability. Moreover, all temporal things depend solely for their existence on God, so they do not exist in the fullest sense of being self-existent, being through their own power

---

[15] There is much discussion on this topic in the literature, beginning with J. M. McTaggart, *The Nature of Existence* (2 vols.; Cambridge: Cambridge University Press, 1927), vol. 2. My sympathies are with Richard Swinburne, *The Christian God* (Oxford: Clarendon Press, 1994), 90 ff., and with the general argument of Nelson Pike, *God and Timelessness* (London: Routledge, 1970).

[16] For a philosophical treatment which supports the view taken here, see John Lucas, *A Treatise on Time and Space* (London: Methuen, 1973).

alone. Whatever exists through its own power alone cannot be brought into being or destroyed, and so it is immutable. But immutability only belongs to that which is beyond the possibility of change; that is, to the timeless, which is logically incapable of change.

It can be further argued that the fully actual cannot be capable of becoming more or less actual. It must have the greatest degree and perfection of existence possible. This again seems to preclude the possibility of change, which would either add to or diminish the perfection of the divine being. To reinforce these arguments, the very notion of creation, which entails that the whole of space and time are brought into being by something beyond them, suggests that God is beyond time, and thus timeless. It is not surprising that the Platonic doctrine of the full reality of the timeless and the biblical doctrine of the creation of heaven and earth seemed to be mutually reinforcing, and to lead to the idea of a wholly timeless, immutable, self-existent divine being.

Once one has developed that idea, it also clarifies those elements in Christian writing which emphasise the total foreknowledge and foreordination of God. A timeless God will create the whole universe, from its first to its last moment, in one single act. There is thus no difficulty in such a God knowing everything that will ever exist in time, or in determining what will be in the future, since what is to us future is created and known by God in one single act. Nothing is future to God and nothing is past to God. Thus the knowledge of God seems to achieve a maximum perfection, and divine omnipotence is seen as God's complete determining, in one act, of everything that will ever be. The knowledge and sovereignty of God is thereby magnified to the fullest extent possible. Once in the system, the idea of a timelessly eternal God becomes almost irresistible.

But is it true that the temporal is not fully real, that it does not strictly exist? Time is seen as a deeply unsatisfying mode of existence by a whole range of poets and philosophers, and one cannot dismiss their feelings with a mere counter-intuition. What is unsatisfactory about time? One element of this feeling is the sense of loss which time seems inevitably to carry with it. The present moment cannot be halted, so that one can stay and contemplate it at leisure. It constantly moves on, leaving the past as something no longer experienced. So the good things of life are lost too soon, and as time moves on it carries us inexorably towards future evils, or to goods which will themselves pass away before we sufficiently enjoy them.

Human consciousness is in a state of continual change, and this may give rise to a feeling of instability, of lack of control, of what Whitehead called 'perpetual perishing', and thought of as the ultimate evil.[17] Perhaps if we could catch and hold onto one moment, never losing it, and never have it threatened by future loss, we could catch a glimpse of eternity, the timeless moment in which there is no loss, no grief, no haste, and no foreboding.

I wonder, however, whether this feeling is securely founded and fully thought through. If one had an experience in which there was no change at all, then even the contemplating mind could not shift the focus, intensity, or range of its contemplation. We would not have time to dwell on all the aspects of experience fully, since we would contemplate them unchangingly. Naturally, one would not get bored, since that too would be a change in consciousness. But would one be alive at all, locked into one unchanging mental state, without the possibility of anything new?

Perhaps it is not time as such which we feel to be unsatisfactory, but the particular way in which we usually react to our temporal existence. The present, as we experience it, is essentially asymmetrical. It is not 'pure present', as though everything in awareness was an immediate object of experience. Every present experience is interpreted in the light of past experience. We recognize objects only because we have seen them before. We name them because we have learned how to do so. Each experience builds upon what we have become and what we have experienced, placing the present in a uniquely individual context. Each present does not come to us as to a blank screen, to be passively recorded. It takes meaning for us as it enters into a complex conceptual world which we have constructed over time, and which makes it different for each experient. The past does not consist of elements which were once experienced, but have now simply ceased to exist. It consists of elements which have entered into our selves and which enter into our present experience to condition it and make it the sort of experience it is.

In a similar way, our present is projected towards a future. Of course the future does not yet exist; but it is a place of possibilities

[17] A. N. Whitehead, *Religion in the Making* (Cambridge: Cambridge University Press, 1927), 144.

which we envisage and can implement to some degree. The future too conditions present experience, but not as something changeless and unalterable. It is rather as something which is promise or threat, and which carries alternative paths. The present experience of 'the same' pain is quite different if it is part of a healing process from a terrible disease than if it is part of a process of torture which is just beginning. Thus our experience of 'presentness' is not a sort of foreshadowing of timelessness at all. It is essentially temporal, and would not at all be the same if it was not part of a flow from an unchangeable and constituting reality towards a partly open world of possibility. To eliminate these characteristics is not to open a window into a world of timelessness, but to eliminate conscious experience as we know it altogether.

THE REDEMPTION OF THE PAST

But are we to think of God as bounded by such human considerations? Of course not. That is not at issue. The question is whether there is something about time that makes temporal experience not fully real. I am suggesting that such experience is the only form of full reality of which we can form any conception. We do not form a conception of a fuller reality if we think of a timeless being. We only strip such a being of all the characteristics which make things real, as far as we can tell. We can, of course, conceive of timeless realities, such as mathematical entities and ideas of possible worlds or natures. But since these are clearly abstractions, it is hard to see in what sense they are more fully real than the world we see and touch and feel. If so, there is no advantage in thinking of God as more like such abstract entities than in thinking of God as bearing some admittedly remote analogy to temporal experience.

In fact, it is not too difficult to think of how the disadvantages which we feel with temporal experience could be eliminated, to provide some vague, but not wholly vacuous, idea of the temporal experience which a fully actual, self-existent being could possess. The past no longer exists, as something which can be changed or which is present to an experient as an inescapably apprehended reality. But we are familiar with a rather feeble ability to remember the past, to recall and relive it. One can imagine this memory ability vastly enhanced, so that none of the past is beyond recall, and such recall is perfectly comprehensive and detailed. The remembered past would still not be like the present, since we would be able to focus on it or not; to run over it all in various ways; and it would be located in a vastly extended range of experience which would include many of its consequences and its surroundings which were unknown at the time. Yet a perfectly remembered past would not be lost. If one had enjoyed an experience, one would be able to rest in that enjoyment again and again. On the other hand, if one had found great pain in an experience, one might be able to minimize that aspect of pain by placing the experience in a wider context which gave it a different feel and meaning. Selective forgetting would be a great advantage for a perfect temporal consciousness. Though the past would not be inaccessible, and thus would not be lost, one would be under no compulsion to experience it in the inescapably intense way in which one must endure present pain. One would have a control of focal awareness, so that the painful aspect could be marginalized. Yet the fact that it had been painful would be fully known. Further, since the experience would become part of the known background of present experience, it could be used to develop new forms of reaction and awareness. It would not be meaningless, or without point, since its past existence would enter into present experience, though one would not be compelled to relive its painful quality with its first intensity.

Past experiences can never be relived in exactly the same way in which they first occurred. Yet they are not lost. They can be recovered and made objects of focal awareness at will, and we have complete access to their experienced quality, as it enters into an ever-widening context of new experience. In this sense, the past is changed. It is not that it never occurred in a specific way, but that its felt quality, context, and meaning is changed by the extending context of experience and by the willed focal awareness of the experient. One begins to see what might be meant by the 'redemption of the past', as its consciously apprehensible existence as an element of a present experience, which has the precise quality it has because that past is what it was, and is now remembered by one who has responded to it in particular ways, and whose focal awareness reconstitutes it with a new meaning and significance.

The classical God of Augustine could never be conceived as redeeming the past in this way. God cannot remember, for nothing is past to God. God simply knows of everything that it exists at a particular time, which God causes to be as it is. In fact, God knows all times as they exist in the divine nature, since God's knowledge does not depend in any way upon the actual existence of particular things. There is no question of the past entering into the divine awareness and changing it in any respect. God is wholly unchangeable, so nothing that happens in time can make any difference to God.

THE OPENNESS OF THE FUTURE

The disadvantage with the future is that it is not under our control, so we are at the mercy of the unknown. Again, however, it is fairly easy to remove this disadvantage by a thought experiment of a similar sort to that just undertaken. Suppose that God is omnipotent, so that whatever happens is under the control of God. Then nothing can happen which does not happen either by divine decision or divine permission. There can be no threat that cannot be easily met. But is it not disadvantage enough that, even if God can control the future when it happens, God does not yet know what is going to happen? Such a God will be far from omniscient, it seems, since there will be infinitely many things God does not know. Moreover, divine knowledge will be continually growing as time passes, and so God will be constantly increasing in knowledge, and thus in perfection, which undermines the perfection one must ascribe to the divine being.

Theists usually do feel the force of Anselm's principle that God must possess every property which it is better to possess than not.[18] Since it is better to know more rather than less, a totally omniscient God, who knows every future state, is greater than a God whose knowledge is always growing, and is therefore limited at every point in time. Therefore God must know the future. I am disposed to accept Anselm's principle and to think that all theists should do so. So one has to ask, is it better to know every future state, or to know only some future states but not all, or perhaps even most of them? The answer can seem obvious, and the totally omniscient God wins—another strong support for the timeless God.

However, if one considers the nature of knowledge more closely, the answer may not seem so obvious after all. To know something is to know that something is the case. I know there is a chair in the

---

[18] Anselm, *Proslogion*, ch. 5: 121.

room only if it is the case, if it is true, that there is a chair in the room. I cannot know something that is not the case, though I may know what possibly could be the case; that is, what is not the case but might have been the case. It is possible, in principle, to know everything that is past and present, for all such states either have been or are the case. But the future is more tricky. Of course, if something will be the case, then I can know that it will be. But I obviously cannot know, of any future state, that it is now the case. All I could know would be that such a state will be the case. Now comes the problem. Can I know, at a given point in time, that something will be the case in the future? Only if it is true, at that time, that it will be the case. But it may not be true at that time that some future state will exist. It may only be true that one of a range of possible future states will exist. In other words, many future contingent statements may have no determinate truth-value. If so, I cannot, at any point in time, know them to be determinately true.[19]

What is in question here is nothing less than the nature of time. If the flow of time is real, then at any time there is much about the future that is indeterminate, much that will become true but of which it is not the case that it is now true, or now knowable that it will be true. On the other hand, if future contingents have determinate truth-values, then they can all be known in principle at any point in time, or (as in the classical view) timelessly. However, to assume that it is possible to know all temporal truths timelessly does necessarily presuppose a certain view of the nature of time. It presupposes that every point in time is determinate; that nothing is left undetermined or open; that the whole of time, from beginning to end, can be laid out on a determinate space-time grid in precise fashion.

That model of space-time, often called the 'block time' model, is much favoured by mathematicians and those who think easily in abstract terms. But it entails that time is symmetrical, that is, that there is no relevant difference between past and future, no direction in which time flows, from a mathematical point of view. And that of course is true. The question is whether the mathematical point of view gives insight into the real structure of reality, or whether it is an

---

[19] Richard Swinburne proposes a different solution, denying that if something will be the case, then necessarily it can be foreknown by some being (*The Christian God*, 133).

abstraction, useful for purposes of calculation, but misleading if taken as a model of reality. The real world, it might be said, is that of lived experience, and that must provide one's criterion of reality.

At this point, Platonism meets empirical realism head-on. If time is a wholly determinate set of relations, a timeless God is greater than a temporal God. But if time is essentially an extending set of asymmetrical relations 'in flow', changeless as to the past but open to the future, then the concept of timeless knowing is vacuous.[20] It cannot apply to anything, since it rests upon a basic misunderstanding of the nature of time. On a block view of time, Augustine's concept of God is superior, and omniscience must be interpreted as knowledge of what is true at every time, whether past, present, or future from our point of view. But on a dynamic view of time, omniscience will have to be reinterpreted. The greatest possible extent of knowledge will be knowledge of all past and present states of affairs, and knowledge of whatever future states are determined to be what they are either by past and present actualities or by God. Even the greatest conceivable being cannot logically have greater knowledge than that, if the dynamic view of time is correct.

On the dynamic view, God will not therefore increase in perfection as divine knowledge of what is actual increases. The number of things God knows to be actual will increase, because the number of things that are actual will increase. But at every time God will know maximally all that any being can logically know, and thus is as perfect in knowledge as any being can possibly be.

It follows from all this that God will, at any given time, lack many properties—the property of knowing all the things that have not happened yet, for instance. But is such a lack an imperfection? My first suggestion was that it is not an imperfection, since no possible being could possess those properties. But there is a more profound point still. That is, if God did not lack knowledge of what is not yet determinately true, then there would be nothing that was not determinately true. The future would not be open, and God would not be free to determine it in any number of different ways, according to deliberate decision. God could never make any new decisions, since everything would be decided in that one single act of creation which follows from the immutable divine nature. And one

---

[20] See David Pailin, *God and the Processes of Reality* (London: Routledge, 1989), ch. 5.

might wonder if such an act could properly be called a 'decision' at all. Only a temporal God can make new decisions or respond to things that happen in creation.

THE BEGINNING OF TIME

If God is temporal, must God have been acting without beginning? It baffles human understanding to think of a literally beginningless, and therefore infinite, number of divine conscious states having been in existence. The divine memory will have to contain an infinite number of items, which is however always enlarging. Since Cantor, however, the idea of larger and smaller infinities is quite acceptable. And the classical God may also be thought to have an infinite number of noetic items in its knowledge of all possible states—which must obviously be much larger even than the number of actual states the temporal God remembers. The idea of infinite knowledge is certainly hard to grasp; but that perhaps simply shows the limitations of human imagination.

Aristotle denied that there could exist an actually infinite number of things. He also believed, however, that time has no beginning, so that there could be an elapsed infinite time. Others have found difficulty with this idea. Suppose one makes an arbitrary interval of time and counts it as one unit. Then, if time had no beginning, an infinite number of such units must have existed at any point in time. But, it may be said, if some number of units has existed, it must be some specific number. If the number is said to be infinite, that simply means that, whatever number you select, there are more units than that. An infinite number is thus no specific number. So it may seem that there cannot have existed an infinite number of units of time.

This argument has been used, most famously by the *Kalam* philosophers in Islam, as a proof that the universe must have had a beginning in time, or, more accurately, that time must have had a beginning.[21] But it sounds suspiciously like one of Zeno's paradoxical arguments that, since any motion must traverse an infinitely divisible space, it can never be completed. There are a number of ways to counter the *Kalam* argument. Whatever interval of time one

---

[21] W. L. Craig, *The Cosmological Argument from Plato to Leibniz* (London: Macmillan, 1980), ch. 3.

selects, it is divisible into an infinite number of smaller intervals. It thus transpires that, even if time began, an infinite number of moments must have been actually traversed. If this is accepted, no objection to a beginningless time can be maintained on the ground that an infinite number cannot be traversed. One can also simply deny the claim that any number of things must be some specific number. For this is to make it a matter of definition that any number of things must be a finite number, so there cannot be an infinite number of things. Why should one not just postulate that there is an endless number of things? Admittedly, this beggars the human imagination. But, as Kant pointed out, so does the supposition that time began and will end. We are at the limits of conceivability here. It is important to stress that the view that time has no beginning does not confine God to time. God may still have a supra-temporal existence. The point is that God will also have a temporal existence, which is to say that, however far back in time one goes, God will have existed. However far forward one goes, God will exist. God is everlasting, without beginning or end—a good rendition of the Biblical terms '*olam*' and '*aiōnios*', respectively. Such an idea is not demonstrably incoherent, and it preserves as great a sense of the mystery and immensity of the divine being as one could wish. On this view of God, creation can be seen as the beginningless and endless generation of new actualities out of an unlimited store of divine potency. Alternatively, one might simply suppose that God's temporal activity, like the time of this physical universe, began. This would avoid the *Kalam* objection, and yet allow the divine activity to be endlessly infinite. Thus the notion of a temporal God is not undermined by unresolved arguments about the beginning of time.

DIVINE IMAGINATION

How far should one take the idea of potency in God? On a Leibnizian picture of God, all possibilities would actually exist in God, and the divine potency would consist in the ability to realize some of these at will (except that, for Leibniz, God would be morally compelled to realize the best of all possible worlds).[22] But one may take the idea of potency further than this, into the realm of possibles

---

[22] Leibniz, *Monadology* 53–5, trans. M. Morris and G. H. R. Parkinson (London: J. M. Dent, 1973), 187.

itself. At the beginning of this chapter, I appealed to the classical picture of God as containing in the divine mind the ideas of all possible universes. Suppose one discards the idea, derived from Plato's intelligible realm, that there is a fixed set of possible worlds which God surveys in its entirety. On that picture, God looks at every possible world, and chooses one of them, fairly arbitrarily, it would seem, from the subset of possible worlds which are more or less equally, or incommensurably, good. One seems forced into this picture by the thought that, if X is ever possible, it is always possible; so possibles must eternally exist. However, one may feel uneasy about supposing that merely possible X's somehow exist to be surveyed, even if one puts them in the mind of God.

But if possibilities do not exist, how can even God know what it is possible for God to do? The quick answer is that God can do anything; but how does God think of what God might do, if God has no possibilities to contemplate? If one begins from human experience, we speak of possible actions in a way which is parasitic upon actual existents. We know what we can do, because we know what we tend to do, and we learn the range and limits of our powers by exercising them. Possibilities are always extrapolations from experienced actualities, which are simply given to us in experience. We extrapolate by imagining things being different, by envisaging what might happen in the future.

We might envisage an actual divine experience which can function as the basis for a divine extrapolation of different sorts of actualities, different ways of expressing in finite form some image of the fullness of the divine life. There could be an unlimited number of such ways, as the divine mind images its own unlimited fullness in many forms. On such a picture, there is an infinite divine actuality of experience, which humans are wholly unable to envisage. This will contain general or indeterminate archetypes of created being, indivisibly part of the primordial unity of the divine life. There is also a divine imagination, which is able to envisage different particular ways of expressing this life in finite forms. It can envisage endlessly new particular forms of expression; but it does not have to envisage all of them at once. Indeed, if possible expressions are infinite, one might better think of endless creative conceptions of new possible states of affairs.

On this picture, God does not passively contemplate an array of given possible worlds. Rather, God actively and endlessly imagines possible finite expressions of the infinite divine life. Before God does so, such particular possibles do not exist, in any real sense. As God does so, they exist only as divinely envisaged, not as quasi-objective and strangely possible realities. God can actualize any envisaged possibility; and that actualization may in turn prompt new envisagements of new possible acts. This radically creative view of possibilities in the divine nature is similar to that proposed by Charles Hartshorne in developing the process philosophy of Whitehead. In *Process and Reality*, the primordial nature of God is described as 'the unlimited conceptual realization of the absolute wealth of potentiality'.[23] Here the Leibnizian picture of an envisaging of every possibility, of 'the entire multiplicity of eternal objects',[24] is espoused. Hartshorne, in response, insists that possibilities cannot be regarded as quasi-actuals, even in the mind of God. He holds that 'the distinction between possible and actual is that between the relatively indefinite and the relatively definite.'[25] There are no individual 'eternal objects', forming a realm of possibilities. Rather, there is a continuum without definite parts, which forms the basis of the creative and constructive activity of God. This 'indefinite continuum', which forms the primordial nature of God, is impossible for us to describe conceptually, but points to a form of reality which is unique to God, and perhaps is best caught by Boethius' haunting phrase, 'an unlimited ocean of being'.

God does not arbitrarily select some world from a range of broadly similar worlds. God does not even have to envisage a possible world as a whole, all at once in every detail, before its actualization. What happens is that God imaginatively generates, from the infinite actuality of the divine being, the idea of a possible world and actualizes it. God may envisage, and in this sense predetermine, the ultimate goal of a universe (say, the assumption of created rational beings to become vehicles of the divine life). God may determine many features of a universe, including its general character and probabilistic laws, the archetypes of its being. Yet God may leave many features open to genuinely creative choice, partly by creatures and partly by divine response to and providential guidance of their

[23] A. N. Whitehead, *Process and Reality* (New York: Free Press, 1978), 343.
[24] Ibid. 31.
[25] Charles Hartshorne, *Whitehead's Philosophy* (Lincoln, Nebr.: University of Nebraska Press, 1978), 32.

choices. This is not the selection of a universe from a range of pre-packaged alternatives. It is a creative self-expression of the divine being.

The answer to the question, 'Why did God create this universe?', is that God imaginatively envisaged it as a particular expression of divine infinite fullness. God could have envisaged other expressions, and no doubt did and will do again. It is, in other words, an ultimate contingency, but not an arbitrary one. On the contrary, it is generated by a wise, good, and intelligent creator, for the sake of its beauty and intelligibility and the valuable relationships it will make possible. If creativity is an intrinsic value, this is an ultimate form of explanation which cannot be reduced to necessity without undermining the structure of created being.

DUAL-ASPECT THEISM

It may seem rather alarming that God not only does not know the future, but does not even know what God might do next, or what possibilities are rooted in the divine nature. Apparently God not only lacks future knowledge, but lacks self-knowledge, too. Things are not quite as alarming as this, however. God, one must suppose, knows the divine being perfectly; and that is the only being there is, unless God creates others. When God creates others, God knows them perfectly, too. So what is it that God does not know? God does not know what God has not yet decided. It is not, after all, that God might decide absolutely anything; that God might be taken by surprise by the divine decisions; or that something untoward and quite unexpected might happen to God. God, in knowing the divine being absolutely, knows that all divine decisions will be in accordance with the divine nature, as perfectly wise and good. God cannot be surprised by divine decisions, since God will consciously make those decisions, and will know that their general character flows from, and is an expression of, the divine nature. If it is good for God to be able to make creatively new decisions, which express the divine nature in new ways, then it is necessarily the case that God cannot know what God decides until God does so.

God will be omniscient, in knowing the unlimited divine nature fully, in knowing all actualities fully, and in knowing all possibilities in so far as they are conceived by God (which is the only sense in which possibilities exist). There are no actual possible worlds for

God to know; so it is not that God fails to know something that is knowable. There is no depth of dark mystery in God which even God is unaware of. There is potentiality for new creative action in God, and God knows this potentiality fully. But it is precisely a potency for action, a dispositional property, and it does not somehow contain within itself a shadow or prefiguring of all the actual acts in which it might express itself. The classical view reifies possibles and makes them into quasi-actuals. Platonism still lives in the possible-worlds ontology of Leibniz and his logically acute successors, even if possibles are nowadays granted less, rather than more, reality than physical actualities. If we can exorcize it more completely, then one can see divine omnipotence as a power to do an unlimited number of things, all of which express something of the actual divine nature. Dispositions are not turned into occurrent states, so that the power to do anything becomes schematized into the occurrent state of having all possibilities in one's mind, and having either realized all of them (as in Spinoza and Schleiermacher) or the best of them (as in Leibniz) or an unchangeable sample of them (as in Aquinas).

The philosophical root of the classical idea is that possibles are more real than actuals, and the timeless is more real than the temporal. These ideas are connected, in that the realm of the timeless is precisely the realm of the possible. The theist can say that there is an actuality of the timeless, but must add that there is also the potentiality of the temporal, and that the timeless actuality is expressed in the unlimited creativity of the temporal. Time is the moving image of eternity. But the image has its own reality, and is not merely an inferior copy of what exists already and more fully in the timeless. The eternal generates uncountable images of itself, and in doing so it manifests itself in unlimitedly new ways, without changing its eternal character.

God is an infinite actuality and plenitude of being, changeless and beyond all time and distinction. This same God is also endlessly active, creative, and potent for ever-new futures. One can see this concept as one way of expressing the point that God is the wholly ineffable ground of all being, in whose nature there is a basic threefoldness. Phrased in Christian terms, the Father is the ground of all possibilities and power of all being, who gives being in archetypal power and receives it back in completed actuality. This same God is Spirit, searching the depths of the divine being, actively creating finite images of the divine glory, and integrating them into the divine life. It is also Wisdom, containing the archetypal possibilities of all created being and manifesting the divine being in particular intelligible forms of finitude. So God, remaining changeless in nature, endlessly creates images of eternity. God enters into them and unites them with the divine being, as the Divine Spirit both gives rise to the manifold forms of the finite and incorporates them into the divine experience. God creatively changes in willing fellowship with creation, and is responsively changed by uniting creation with the divine life. But in another and deeper aspect, God remains the unchanging source of this dynamic Trinitarian life, and the still centre of the infinite energies which create and consummate this, and every, universe.

In this way, a stress on the reality of the temporal, creative, and relational can complement the traditional stress on the eternity of God. This is not, after all, a rejection of the Platonic vision, but an extension of that aspect of it which sees the universe as a sacramental manifestation of eternity.[26] The major twentieth-century theologians I have considered from four religious traditions all seem to agree in this general reconstruction of the concept of God in a more dynamic and relational way. Thus it might fairly be seen as a distinctive reworking of the idea of God, partly in response to the rise of the natural sciences and partly occasioned by an increased realization of the possibility and importance of change and creativity in human existence. Within the Christian tradition, such a reconstruction can be seen as a way of taking seriously the ancient Christian insight that the eternal Word truly becomes flesh, in order that time itself might find its fulfilment in eternity.

[26] Plato, *Timaeus* 29.

Cosmology and the Trinitarian God

12
Creation and Modern Cosmology

I have considered the notion of God that is contained in four major scriptural traditions, and its interpretation by eminent twentieth-century theologians within those traditions. I have defended the possibility and necessity of making literally true statements about God, as a supernatural being of supreme power and value. I have developed a view of God as Creator, based on an analysis of the key divine attributes of creativity, wisdom, affectivity, beatitude, and love, which are common to the four traditions. Throughout, I have written as a Christian theologian, who is concerned to be open to the insights and criticisms of a range of religious traditions. It is clear, from what the four selected theologians have said, that the rise of the contemporary sciences has changed our view of the universe and of human life in important ways. These changes reverberate through and between religious traditions, making possible new forms of convergence and conversation. In the final part of this volume, my aim will be to make explicit a specifically Christian doctrine of God as Trinity, in the light of the new perspective on the universe which modern cosmology provides, and in response to the theological conversation which has shaped the preceding three parts. I hope in this way to show how positive conversation, far from merging everything in one dull uniformity, can enrich religious distinctiveness, while attenuating the exclusiveness, usually born of ignorance, which denies the important complementary insights of other traditions. Many religions are concerned with creation, and with the notion of a creator. The Christian tradition gives a distinctively Trinitarian shape to the doctrine of creation. By drawing together various strands of thought about God which have been considered in this volume, and placing them in the context of modern cosmological theory, I hope to suggest a way in which the Trinitarian shape of creation can be understood.

AUGUSTINE ON TIME

Physicists sometimes talk as though the question of creation is the question of whether the universe had a beginning. In modern physics the Friedmann-Lemaître-Robertson-Walker cosmological model has become standardly adopted. This is the model of the universe as expanding from a primal Big Bang, and it assigns a first moment of time to this universe. Some theologians take this to be a confirmation of creation by God. Robert John Russell argues that creation *ex nihilo* means ontological origination. That entails finitude. Finitude includes temporal finitude, and that includes past temporal finitude. If this is so, he argues, then any demonstration that the universe has a finite age will confirm the hypothesis of creation, and any demonstration that this is not so (like a 'Steady State' theory) will disconfirm it.[1] Others, however, think that scientific cosmologies are irrelevant to the theological assertion, which is one of ontological, not temporal, origination. Arthur Peacocke writes, 'Time, in modern relativistic physics . . . has to be regarded as owing its existence to God . . . It is this "owing its existence to God" which is the essential core of the idea of creation . . . Scientific cosmology . . . cannot, in principle, be doing anything which can contradict such a concept of creation.'[2]

The key point is whether finitude 'includes' past temporal finitude. Does the total dependence of the universe on God entail that the universe must be finite in space and time? One interpretation of Big Bang cosmology (the 'closed' interpretation) maintains that the universe will eventually collapse again, so that it is finite at both temporal ends. But this is not an entailment of the dependence of all times and spaces on God, and if one took an 'open' interpretation, that the universe will expand for ever, it would have no implications for the hypothesis of creation. Dr Russell may think that, if time began, that raises the probability that there is a creator, whereas, if there is always time, it looks more like an ultimate, brute, or even necessary, fact of itself. But it is not the case that a short extent of time is more in need of explanation than a long extent. *A fortiori*, a

---

[1] R. J. Russell, N. Murphy and C. Isham (eds.) *Quantum Cosmology and the Laws of Nature* (Notre Dame, Ind.: University of Notre Dame, 1993), 308.

[2] Arthur Peacocke, *Creation and the World of Science* (Oxford: Clarendon Press, 1979), 78 f.

long but finite extent is not more in need of explanation than an infinite extent. If time is susceptible of 'explanation' at all, its extent is irrelevant to the issue.

The classical doctrine of creation, in Jewish, Christian, and Muslim traditions, does not depend upon there being a first moment of time. To say that the universe is created is to say that it is brought about intentionally, that its existence is the expression of a consciously formed purpose. Theologians have usually stressed that the universe is not brought about in time, in the sense that there exists an uncreated time within which the physical universe comes to exist at a particular point. Augustine makes the point with particular clarity; and his discussion forms a classic statement of the theistic position. When Augustine asked the question, 'What made God create heaven and earth then, and not sooner?',[3] his reply was that 'no time passed before the world, because no creature was made by whose course it might pass.'[4] That is, as he understood it, time is a certain sort of relation between objects, and where no objects exist which are related by that relation, then the relation does not exist either. The temporal series extends back, as a relation, T, between objects, to an object which simply does not have T to anything preceding it. Since 'beforeness' is a relation between two objects, the first object is not related by 'beforeness' to anything. There is nothing 'before' the temporal universe, neither any objects nor any time. For Augustine, God brought about time and space as well as all the things that are in them. Just as God did not create space at a certain place, but non-spatially causes all places to exist, so God did not create time at a certain time, but non-temporally causes all times to exist.

Whatever reservations one may have about a doctrine of non-temporal causation, it does not seem self-contradictory to say that A wholly depends for its existence upon B, though there is no temporal relation between A and B. At any rate, this is a view Augustine is committed to. As far as this doctrine goes, there might or might not have been a first moment of time; both possibilities are consistent with the dependence of all times, however many there are, upon God. Like most classical theologians, Augustine did accept, on

---

[3] Augustine, *City of God*, bk. xi, ch. 4, ed. R. V. G. Tasker, tr. J. Healey (New York: E. P. Dutton, 1957), 314.   [4] Ibid. bk. xi, ch. 6: p. 3/7.

grounds of a temporal interpretation of Genesis 1: 1, that this universe had a beginning in time; though he also suggested that there might have been an infinite number of universes before this one, in which case, of course, time would have no beginning.[5]

If this is the case, it follows from the doctrine of creation that God, the Creator, is a non-spatio-temporal being. As the creator of the whole of space-time, God is beyond space-time. This is an important part of the traditional belief that God is transcendent. This statement, however, like most statements in theology, immediately needs to be qualified. God is not, for any standard theistic view, outside space-time in the sense that God is excluded from every space and time. On the contrary, God is omnipresent.[6] That is to say, every object or event standing in space-time relations only exists by the originating and sustaining power of God. Without such a divine activity of bringing into being and sustaining in being (these being simply different aspects of the same act in God), nothing could exist even for the smallest moment. That relation of *holding in being* is a relation of immediate and total origination, and it obtains between God and every created object, whenever it exists.

Thus it is wholly inadequate to think of God having created the universe at some remote point in time—say, at the Big Bang—so that now the universe goes on existing by its own power. This popular misconception, that 'the creation' is the first moment of the space-time universe, and that the universe continues by its own inherent power, wholly misconstrues every classical theistic tradition. The doctrine of creation *ex nihilo* simply maintains that there is nothing other than God from which the universe is made, and that the universe is other than God and wholly dependent upon God for its existence. Creation is, properly speaking, the relation which holds between every point of space-time and the Creator, such that each moment exists in total dependence upon the sustaining being and will of the Creator. In Aquinas' discussion of creation, he accepts that the word 'creation' is usually used to refer to the beginning of the universe.[7] But he makes it clear that there is only a logical, not a real, distinction between the divine act of beginning the time of the

---

[5] Augustine, *City of God*, bk. xii. ch. 5: 359.

[6] See Aquinas, *Summa Theologiae*, Ia q. 8 a. 2: 'As the soul exists wholly everywhere in the body, so God exists wholly in each and every thing' (Blackfriars edn.; London: Eyre and Spottiswoode, 1963–81).

[7] Ibid. Ia q. 45 a. 3.

universe and timelessly creating every moment of it from beginning to end. Creation is more properly spoken of as continuous than as one act at the beginning of this universe. God is not nearer to the beginning of time than to any other point of time.

For the classical view, as has been pointed out, God creates the universe in a single timeless act. Being timeless,[8] God contains no *internal* temporal relations—no 'before' and 'after', no past to be remembered or forgotten, and no future which is as yet undecided. And God has no *external* temporal relations—does not exist before, after, or at the same time as any other thing whatsoever.

The creation of the universe can then be represented as the total dependence of space-time, in all its parts from beginning to end (if time has a first and last moment), upon a timeless being, in whom there is no change, coming into being, or passing away. As Augustine put it, 'all that ever He created was in His unchanged fixed will eternally one and the same.'[9] Schleiermacher correctly drew the implication that one must not think of God wondering whether to create a universe, deciding it would be a good idea, choosing which one to create from a selection of possibilities, and then bringing it into being. Since God is in the strictest sense immutable, being wholly timeless, there is never a time when God has not yet decided to bring about a universe, or has not yet decided which one to bring about, or has not yet brought it about. 'It cannot be said of the original creation that it was created by the activity of foreknowledge prior to its actual existence.'[10] Schleiermacher, influenced by Spinoza, concludes that it is idle to think of God as existing without the created order, but that 'everything for which there is a causality in God happens and becomes real.'[11] Since God is wholly unchangeable, there is nothing in the divine being, and therefore nothing at all, which is truly potential but not actual. And since God is the only absolutely independent being, 'everything . . . is absolutely willed by God', and 'in willing Himself, willing the world is already included.'[12]

God timelessly brings the universe into being. There is, in the

---

[8] Ibid. Ia q. 10 a. 2.

[9] Augustine, *City of God*, bk. xii, ch. 17: 361.

[10] F. W. Schleiermacher, *The Christian Faith*, pt. I, sect. i, para. 41 (Edinburgh: T. & T. Clark, 1989; 1st pub. 1830), 154.   [11] Ibid. I ii. 54: 211.

[12] Ibid: 216, 217.

divine being, an immutable intention to bring precisely this universe into being, an intention which is actualized by the very same act by which it is formed. Everything is just as God wills it to be, and it is meaningless to think of a realm of possibilities from which God selects this particular universe, after due consideration. Schleiermacher thus presses to its logical extreme the idea of divine timelessness, not hesitating to draw consequences which are in acute tension with any ideas of real human freedom to affect God or to draw any free response from God, and with any ideas of a real choice made by God in the creation of the universe.

The main Catholic tradition has refused to draw these consequences, but it can be plausibly argued that it is really committed to doing so. As Aquinas put it, 'As the divine existing is essentially necessary, so also is the divine knowing and the divine willing.'[13] God's willing the universe is not something that God came to a new decision about; it is part of the immutable divine being from all eternity. It seems as though the classical doctrine of divine timelessness eliminates a strong view of both human and divine freedom.

The classical view of God's timelessness has been criticized and rejected in previous chapters. It is bound up, in theology, with a strong form of predestinarian or determinist theory, and in cosmology with the 'block view' of space-time which some physicists hold—the view that every point of space-time is in some sense existent, and that the sense of passage through time which is characteristic of humans does not point to a fundamental and irreducible characteristic of unobserved physical reality.[14] I have suggested, however, that there are general considerations about the nature of time which put the 'block view' in question. Even within physics the block time view faces severe conceptual difficulties. The laws of thermodynamics seem to give an irreversible direction to such factors as temperature and entropy, which provide an 'objective' measurement of temporal flow.[15] Quantum physics

---

[13] Aquinas, *Summa Theologiae*, Ia q. 19 a. 3.

[14] See the discussion by C. Isham and J. C. Polkinghorne, 'The Debate over the Block Universe', in Russell *et al.*, *Quantum Cosmology*, 135 ff.

[15] See Arthur Peacocke, *Theology for a Scientific Age* (London: SCM Press, 1990), 31 f. The Nobel Laureate chemist Ilya Prigogine has revolutionized much scientific thought with his insistence on the open creativity of time. See I. Prigogine and I. Stengers, *Order Out of Chaos* (London: Heinemann, 1984).

suggests that the future has an openness which is not characteristic of the past, and, on the most common interpretations, that without some external observer the transition from potential to actual cannot be effected.[16] It is true that, with the aid of sophisticated mathematical devices, such as the use of complex numbers, one can 'eliminate' the flow of time, by treating it as a quasi-spatial dimension. But whether, and in what sense, complex numbers could be 'mapped onto' reality is wholly unclear. Perhaps 'block time' is no more than a useful mathematical construction, which points to realms of conceptual possibility (one rather restricted set of 'possible worlds' in the mind of God?). What is certain is that such very theoretical considerations are not firmly enough established within physical science to counter more general philosophical arguments for the asymmetry of experienced time. Within theology, the strongest of those arguments, in my view, is that if God is creatively free, then there must in some sense be a divine future, and the 'flow' of time is thus real, even for God. God is temporal, though God transcends the physical space-time system of this universe.

CREATION AND COSMOLOGY

Even if God is temporal, this spatio-temporal universe may have had a beginning. As I have pointed out, the main reason theologians assigned a first moment of time to the universe was not abstract reasoning, but a certain interpretation of the first chapter of the book of Genesis.[17] But in fact the first words of the Hebrew Bible already pose major problems of interpretation: '*Bereshit barah elohim*': in the beginning, God created. In the beginning of what? By about the tenth century CE, it had become orthodox in Judaism and Christianity to say that time had a beginning, and that God created it 'out of nothing', that is, out of no prior matter. But other views had been, and continued to be, quite widespread. Levi ben Gershom is one of

---

[16] 'Each new act of measurement, by its radically unpredictable outcome, creates a new circumstance' (John Polkinghorne, *Science and Creation* (London: SPCK, 1988), 40).

[17] Aquinas, *Summa Theologiae*, Ia q. 46 a. 2: 'That the world has not always existed cannot be demonstratively proved but is held by faith alone'.

those[18] who argued that 'the waters' of Genesis 1: 2 were an uncreated, formless deep from which God fashioned the cosmos. Ibn Sina and Ibn Rushd, in the Muslim tradition, both held that creation was eternal, without beginning, so that there was no first moment of time. In the controversies that developed around these issues, it became usual to say that those who accepted the eternity of the universe believed not in creation, but in emanation, so that the world became necessary to God, and no divine purpose could be found in it.[19] There is no reason, however, why there should not be an endless number of divine purposes, each of them realized in some space-time system, and each such system freely willed. The 'necessity' of a universe, as I have argued, need not consist in its quasi-deductive unfolding from God. It can be a consequence of the nature of God, which naturally (essentially) overflows in goodness, but always in a free expression of that goodness, in infinite diverse forms. Perhaps the most natural thing to suggest is that *this* space-time did have a temporal first moment, so that one can say, 'in the beginning of this space-time'. But before it there may have been, without beginning, not a formless deep existing in independence of God, but a series of space-times, all of which depend wholly on the divine will for their existence, but which never leave God without some form of relational self-expression. This is consistent with the common rabbinic exegesis of the 'days' of creation as instances of logical, not temporal, ordering.[20] In that case, 'the beginning' would refer to the logical priority of the divine willing in the existence of any universe, and not to a temporal first moment. The question of whether or not this universe had a first moment of time is still not directly relevant to the question of whether it is created.

This may be clearer if one considers attempts to remove the initial singularity from cosmology by including it as a factor in a wider quantum-gravitational theory. In recent physics, this has been done in two main ways, by a quantum fluctuation theory and by the Hartle-Hawking model. On the quantum fluctuation view, matter originates by spontaneous quantum fluctuations in a vacuum (i.e. in

---

[18] Jacob Staub, *The Creation of the World According to Gersonides* (Scholars' Press: Chico, Calif.: 1982).

[19] Maimonides, *Guide For the Perplexed*, tr. S. Pines (Chicago: University of Chicago Press, 1963), bk. ii, ch. 21.   [20] Ibid. ii. 30.

the quiescent state of the background quantum fields). On this view, however, it is only matter that originates. What is presupposed as already existent is a background space-time, with quantum fields and laws of nature in operation. It is not, as is sometimes suggested, origination 'out of nothing', for space-time, quantum fields, and basic laws of nature remain as very definitely something, even if not material in the ordinary sense.

The Hartle-Hawking model goes further, in seeking to eliminate the background space-time, and generates the temporal process of this universe out of a wider timeless domain of three-spaces linked in 'fuzzy' ways. The model aims to resolve time, as we experience it, into a wider mathematically statable reality. This theory eliminates a 'beginning', and it led Hawking to say, 'So long as the universe had a beginning, we could suppose it had a creator. But if the universe is really completely self-contained, having no boundary or edge, it would have neither beginning nor end: it would simply be. What place, then, for a creator?'[21] It is very odd to suppose that, if the universe had such properties as those of having four basic forces, acting according to invariable laws, being mathematically structured, and having a first temporal moment, then God might explain its existence, whereas if it had all those properties except for having a first temporal moment, God would be superfluous. What is so special about temporal origin that a God might explain it, and what is so satisfying about being a highly ordered domain that a God would be quite unnecessary? The fundamental question remains exactly the same in both cases, namely, what causes these properties to be as they are? I would think it was even odder, if anything, to say that a highly ordered mathematical domain exists on its own than to say that a material universe just comes into being on its own. For the postulation of such a 'thing' as a four- (or more-) dimensional superspace, containing, among other components, imaginary time and probabilistic 'non-reduced' quantum fields (i.e. fields not reduced to actuality by some observation), seems remarkably like positing a purely conceptual reality as the ontological basis of material and ordinarily temporal reality. The theistic hypothesis is, in part, precisely that the material world originates from a more stable and enduring conceptual (or spiritual) realm. Hawking has

---

[21] Stephen Hawking, *A Brief History of Time* (London: Bantam Press, 1989), 141.

not made God superfluous; he has perhaps shown how the material cosmos can be understood as arising from a deeper, intelligible, beautiful, and non-material reality. This paves the way for a better understanding of God as a self-existent reality which generates the whole material universe. While the quasi-Platonic ontology of some mathematical physics does not *require* the postulation of a God, the natural place for conceptual realities to exist is in some supracosmic mind. From Philo onwards, Platonists have tended to locate the Forms in a divine mind.[22] And it is not wholly without significance that Hawking speaks, however ironically, of knowing the ultimate laws of nature as 'knowing the mind of God'.[23]

The theological import of the Hawking cosmology, as he seems to see it, is to eliminate the need for God as the initiator of the temporal process, leaving God with no explanatory role, a wholly superfluous hypothesis. The fundamental structures of the universe still need explaining, however. And those structures can no longer be seen as lying solely in some set of initial conditions and inflexible laws, from which every subsequent state of the universe will flow quasi-deductively. 'There is . . . an intrinsic openness to the future built somewhere into the structure of quantum theory.'[24] What quantum cosmology asserts, on the standard Copenhagen interpretation, is the non-deterministic nature of the micro-processes which underlie the fundamental laws of nature. God can no longer be banished to the beginning of the universe, as in eighteenth-century deism. If there is an explanation of events in the temporal flow, that explanation must be such that it governs emergent and non-determined processes at every point in time. Sensing this point, Hawking writes, 'If one likes, one could ascribe (quantum) randomness to the intervention of God, but it would be a very strange kind of intervention: there is no evidence that it is directed toward any purpose.'[25] He assumes here a picture and an evaluation of the universe which are both highly contentious.

The picture is that the universe is completely self-contained, so that God would have to intervene in it from outside to play any real

---

[22] Philo, *On the Creation* 16 and 20, tr. E. H. Colson and G. H. Whitaker (London: Heinemann, 1956), 14–19.

[23] Hawking, *A Brief History of Time*, 193.

[24] Polkinghorne, *Science and Creation*, 40.

[25] Hawking, *A Brief History of Time*, 166.

part in its nature. But if 'the pleromatic four-sphere' (to use a phrase of Prof. Isham[26]) is itself a reality in the mind of God, then God is not a separate reality 'outside' the universe. The physical universe is a state-reduction selected from a number of probabilistically quantified options. Both the selection of the original boundary conditions, which govern the emergence of a unique universe, and the reduction from probability to actuality suggest something analogous to an 'act of will' in the constituting of the universe itself.[27] As Thomas Torrance puts it, 'There is no intrinsic reason in the universe why it should exist at all, or why it should be what it actually is: hence we deceive ourselves if in our natural science we think we can establish that the universe could only be what it is.'[28] In other words, the universe is not 'self-contained', but is in fact contained in a mindlike reality whose creative act is not at some temporal beginning point, but coexistent with each temporal instant.

The evaluation Hawking makes is that there is no evidence of purpose in the cosmic process. Even on strictly physical grounds, one may question whether that is really true. However questionable some formulations of the anthropic principle may be, the features of the cosmos to which it draws attention do demonstrate a precise correlation of fundamental cosmic forces and their temporal development which is within the extremely narrow parameters required for the emergence of rational consciousnesses within the universe.[29] Again, that does not compel one to postulate a designing mind, since such a vastly improbable universe is perhaps no more improbable, a priori, than any other. Nevertheless, the postulate of a God who willed to relate to created conscious beings would render the existence of such a universe vastly more probable than it would otherwise be.[30] The demonstration of the amazing degree of elegant integration of the basic physical constants which is needed to

[26] C. J. Isham, '*Quantum Theories of the Creation of the Universe*', in Russell *et al.*, *Quantum Cosmology*, 78.

[27] Ian Barbour, *Issues in Science and Religion* (London: SCM Press, 1966), 285 ff.

[28] Thomas Torrance, *Divine and Contingent Order* (Oxford: Oxford University Press, 1981), 36.

[29] A number of definitions of the anthropic principle are given in John Barrow and Frank Tipler, *The Anthropic Cosmological Principle* (Oxford: Oxford University Press, 1986), 15 ff.

[30] See Richard Swinburne, *The Existence of God* (Oxford: Clarendon Press, 1979), 64 ff.

produce exactly this result is very good evidence for purposiveness in the universe. As Paul Davies says, 'In the case of living organisms, their existence seems to depend on a number of fortuitous coincidences that some scientists and philosophers have hailed as nothing short of astonishing.'[31] He goes further, and claims that 'science suggests that the existence of conscious organisms is a *fundamental* feature of the universe.'[32].

The fundamental physical constants and forces of nature seem to be precisely set up so as to produce conscious life. Even if they have not been set up that way by some designing mind, it is at least true that organic life is not some freak accident in the cosmos, as once may have been thought. The cosmos is not hostile or indifferent to life. On the contrary, its basic forces are such that life and consciousness are the natural development of its inherent potentialities. As Paul Davies puts it, the existence of finite minds 'can be no trivial detail, no minor by-product of mindless, purposeless forces. We are truly meant to be here.'[33] If conscious states of creating and appreciating value are themselves of great value, and if the many-billion-year history of the cosmos can be plausibly seen as a deep and complex process which naturally tends to issue in such states, this is certainly good evidence that the process is purposive. It is an efficient, self-regulating process, issuing in a valued state. While one cannot absolutely rule out chance as the origin of such a process, the existence of an intelligible, integrated, elegant process tending to produce states of value is far more likely on the hypothesis that there is a cosmic Mind which wills it to be thus.[34]

Within the perspective of modern cosmology, one might see God not as an intervener from outside a closed deterministic system, but as the total field which sets the fundamental constraints both of physical theory and of the actualization of actual events within such a theory, which sets the goal of the cosmic process and continuously influences events towards that goal. Wolfhart Pannenberg has suggested that one might think of the Spirit of God as such a 'total field' which environs the cosmos. In a number of essays,[35] he

---

[31] Davies, *The Mind of God* (New York: Simon and Schuster, 1992), 204.
[32] Ibid. 23, italics his.   [33] Ibid. 242.
[34] See Swinburne, *The Existence of God*, 290 f.
[35] Collected in Wolfhart Pannenberg, *Toward a Theology of Nature* (Louisville, Ky.: Westminster Press, 1993).

develops the idea of Spirit as a 'universal field of energy'[36] which engenders a process of creative unification, leading organisms to transcend themselves towards increasing complexity and structure.[37] He appeals to the work of Teilhard in developing this view, and also to Polanyi's idea of a morphogenic field, which may be an explanatory factor in individual development. The model suggests very well the way in which God's influence would not be either intermittent or confined to some initial act of origination. It would set the origin, the limits, and the goal of the process, being a constant presence and influence at every point.

What the Hartle-Hawking theory leaves unexplained is why the basic quantum fields, the boundary conditions of the cosmos, should be as they are, why the physical laws should be as they are, and how it is that the laws give the appearance of existing objectively and 'governing' the sorts of events that come into being. God has not been rendered superfluous by the theory at all. God has rather been integrated more fully with the created universe, as the ordainer of laws that could easily have been otherwise, which are elegant and intelligible, which make the universe predictable and trustworthy, yet which leave room for creativity, consciousness, and free action. God does not lay down these laws and then retire from the scene. Laws are simply the algorithmic compressions of observed regularities in the interactions of physical forces considered in isolation from influences from some wider causally efficacious field.[38] There is every reason to think that there is much in the observed world which is not so compressible at all (so-called 'chaotic' systems are common examples, as are quantum fluctuations at a sub-atomic level). It is almost absurd to speak of giving a complete description of the observable world which would consist solely of such compressions. In fact, quantum theory as presently understood requires that no complete description can be given which can enable wholly precise predictions to be made. 'The intrinsically statistical character of atomic events and the instability of many physical systems to minute fluctuations, ensures that the future remains open and undetermined by the present.'[39] On such a view, the way is open to conceive God as the supreme environing spiritual influence,

---

[36] Ibid. 132. [37] Ibid. 140.

[38] 'The entire scientific enterprise can be seen as the search for algorithmic compressions of observational data' (Davies, *The Mind of God*), 145.

[39] Ibid. 201.

drawing physical realities towards a goal which has been programmed as a possibility into their initial constitution, while leaving the details of its implementation to free and creative co-operative acts.

RELATIVITY AND SIMULTANEITY

It has been claimed that the special theory of relativity poses insuperable problems for the idea that God can act in this way as temporally co-creative with finite agents. For, it is sometimes said, the idea of simultaneity is itself relative. Whether one thing happens at the same time as another, or before it or after it, is relative to the position and velocity (the inertial frame) of the observer. One observer may register a flash of light and a sound as simultaneous, while another may hear the same sound as occurring long after the same flash of light (if the observer is at a distance from the observed events). What you see as simultaneous, and thus as constituting the present, depends on your own position. In general, every event, E, stands at the point of intersection of two 'light cones', one projected into the past, containing all events that can influence E, the other projected into the future, and containing all events that E can influence. The light cone is bounded by the upper limit of the speed of light, which sets parameters on the possible causal interactions between events (setting aside considerations from quantum theory which suggest exceptions to such a limitation on causal interaction). It seems that events outside a given light cone cannot be related by absolute simultaneity to E, since there is no preferential inertial frame within which this could be done. Thus there is no 'absolute present', and therefore God cannot know the present moment, as if it were one common temporal wave, flowing continually on throughout the whole universe from determinate past to open future. There is no such absolute present. Thus temporality cannot be real for God, as God has no absolute reference frame in which time can 'flow'.

This conclusion does not follow, however. Consider the analogous spatial case of two observers looking at two different towers, some distance apart. One observer, being near, sees them as very different in height. But the other observer, being far away, sees them as almost the same in height. One might conclude that the size of the towers is relative to the position from which they are observed, so that they have no real, 'absolute' size. But the truth is very simple.

The towers appear to be different relative sizes, depending on where they are observed from. The 'universal observer', God, would know just how they would appear from every possible location. God, being omniscient, will know how the towers look from every possible viewpoint, and will know which of those viewpoints, if any, are occupied. God would also have an absolute measure of their relative size in knowing how they would compare if they were laid alongside one another.

In the case of observing the temporal relations of events, these will naturally vary according to the position and velocity of the observer. God will know just how it will appear from every possible viewpoint. God will also know that there is an 'absolute' ordering, in that, for each set of events, at the place where they occur, there is an irreversible order of their occurrence. It is not possible for any observer to know an event in the future of P, where that event is an item of P's experience, before P does. Nor can it be the case that a later event in P's experience actually precedes an earlier event, from a certain frame of observation. It can only be the case that a later event in P's experience may *look* earlier, from a certain frame. That fact will in no way affect the quite determinate ordering of events in and for P. Relativity effects only come into play when great differences of distance or velocity are involved, and that does not affect the temporal ordering at each place. It is also false to suggest that the different temporal appearances cannot be temporally correlated in any absolute frame. Each event in the universe can be 'absolutely dated' by reference to the Big Bang, so there is a common reference frame of a quite general sort, set by that singularity and by the existence of causal processes governed by the laws of relativity and quantum physics.[40]

A further consideration is that, within each light cone, there is an infinite number of other events, each of which has its own light cone. These cones will overlap continuously, so that, if events are related in one space-time at all, every event can in fact be related to all others in ways precisely specifiable by such factors as the Lorenz transformations and the absolute speed of light from all locations. One may not be able to think of time as Newton did, as an absolute process which flows equably, whether or not there are events in it.

---

[40] See the discussion in Richard Swinburne, *Space and Time* (London: Macmillan, 1981), 181–202.

Time is a relation between events, by which they are ordered as one after another. If one thinks of time as the ordering of events in one experience (the experience of an 'observer'), then the same events will appear to be ordered differently for different observers. This may sound paradoxical, but there is nothing mysterious about it. Because light has a finite speed, we see light from distant stars many years after such light is emitted. If a distant star exploded thousands of years ago, we might see it exploding at the same time as a nearby star which only exploded last century. The explosions look simultaneous to us. It is the speed of light and the distance between the stars which both makes this appearance possible and which enables us to give an accurate temporal distance between the events. It is only 'what looks to be simultaneous' which is relative to observers, and that is entirely expected. The ordering of events at each location is irreversible. It is their appearance which varies, and the variance is not arbitrary, but is determined by absolute laws of nature. True simultaneity is given by such physical and irreversible factors as the rate of expansion of the universe and the speed of light. Knowing that, God can correctly locate the temporal flow from past to future of all events relative to others in the same space-time.[41] God, being omnipresent, is situated in every possible inertial reference frame. Knowing the laws of physics, God can correlate these in a unitary experience, to which our locally bound experiences offer only the remotest analogy. It is also part of the theistic hypothesis that God is not located at any particular point of space-time, so that God's temporal experience is non-physical. The preferred divine frame of observation is thus exempt from the purely physical constraints of relativity theory, and can give an absolute observed flow of time without contradicting the physical principle that, for spatially located observers, there is no absolute criterion of universal simultaneity for all phenomena in the cosmos. The relativity of simultaneity is a principle concerned only with the equivalence of inertial frames of reference with respect to such physical realities as electromagnetic phenomena. It does not, properly understood, rule out a supracosmic experient, God, who

---

[41] John Lucas argues for the coherence of the idea of a 'preferred frame of reference' set by the consciousness of God, which relativity physics can ignore, though there are no theoretical objections to it, in J. R. Lucas and P. E. Hodgson, *Space-Time and Electromagnetism* (Oxford: Oxford University Press, 1990), 117–21.

would have temporal knowledge of the universe, ordered in an objective way, even though that preferred ordering might be inaccessible to us or irrelevant to the special theory of relativity. The theory of relativity, as it applies only to finite observers acting under physical constraints, is quite consistent with God's knowledge of the universe having a universal temporal ordering, from past to future, which accurately reflects the temporal ordering that each finite set of events has in its own inertial frame.

A MODEL OF CREATIVE FREEDOM

If this is a plausible picture, then the best analogy for divine creative freedom may be something like the writing of a piece of music. This is an analogy which has been deployed effectively by A. R. Peacocke,[42] and the point of it is to suggest a form of causality which is neither wholly deterministic nor completely arbitrary. At any given point in composition, the note that is to come next is not *entailed* by any past or present note or any combination of them. A number of possible notes might exist but there is literally nothing which determines that one of them should. On the other hand, the note that will next exist is not arbitrarily assigned, as if a computerized random generator could do as well as Mozart. So what governs the choice of the immediately successive note? Simply the creative, directing activity of the composer, who generates musical patterns because of their beauty. It is important that there is an intentional activity at work; that is what prevents the process from being arbitrary. It is mind-directed or intentional. It is equally important that the intention is to create a unique and original form of beauty. It is concerned with the generation of order and sensory and affective appeal. So one has a mind concerned with the production of beauty, working to continue an unfinished pattern. Central elements of this situation are (1) the pattern itself, (2) the active concentration of a mind with certain skills and capacities, (3) canons of beauty and taste which can be modified but which provide models of creative activity, and (4) human pleasure in certain sorts of sensory pattern which form the basis of selected goals (i.e. realized states of value).

Deterministic models of causality work with a basically deductive scheme, for which the future can only unfold what is already

---

[42] Peacocke, *Creation and the World of Science*, 105.

contained in the past, given the unchanging set of laws of nature (one cannot have more in the conclusion of a deductive argument than there is in the premises). In cases of creativity one has what might be called a teleological model of causality. For such a model, the future builds on the past, by adding to it in a way which seeks to realize certain goals in the process of creation. At any moment of the temporal process, one has an incomplete pattern, a creative agency, and a general goal (itself emerging from the recognition of desires of certain sorts) setting the direction of creativity. It is consciousness which recognizes certain states as desirable, which accordingly sets certain goals of activity and which realizes these goals through continuing an apprehended process. At each moment its successor moment is generated by a directive agency informed by its apprehension of the past, endowed with characteristic skills and dispositions and oriented by its conception of values.[43] The threefold model of God as archetypal source of possibilities, realized value (or expressed Word), and creative Spirit, seems particularly suitable for articulating this as a basic form of causality at work in the cosmos.

What this means is that one cannot consider time as a series of quite discrete events, each complete in itself, one succeeding another either by some form of quasi-entailment or quite arbitrarily. At least as far as conscious and free agents are concerned, and as far as they are conscious and acting rationally, each temporal moment is filled with an awareness of the past and oriented towards a possible future, as part of a dynamic process in which future events are emergent—genuinely new and yet continuous with and to some extent developments of what has gone before. And this flow towards the future is essentially directed to the realization of values, which are what give the temporal process intelligibility.

Whitehead has, in my view, very helpfully emphasized the value of creative emergence and therefore of temporality, a value which gives a much more positive reason for the creation of a space-time universe than the traditional account provided. He has given creaturely freedom and creativity a much more important place in the explanation of how things have come to be as they are; and he has suggested a form of causality which fits the facts of human

---

[43] A. N. Whitehead has deployed these notions effectively in *Process and Reality* (New York: The Free Press, 1978), though I am restricting their range to conscious agents, as he does not.

experience quite well. It is a consequence of a Whiteheadian view that, where there are many developing sentient beings with limited knowledge, their aims will often conflict, and from such conflict suffering and destructive processes will flow. Some natural evil is inevitable in a world with this general structure. However helpful that may be with the problem of evil, many theists feel that a process view nevertheless undesirably limits the power and sovereignty of God. Whitehead was basically an atomist, believing that the real causal impulses of the world derive from its atomic constituents, the 'actual occasions'. He did give God a place as the 'poet of the world', or the lure towards greater harmony and beauty.[44] But he was not able to give a convincing account of how such conflict as there is could ever be overcome and the divine purposes ever be wholly fulfilled.

Process theology begins by rejecting the notion of substance as a permanent substratum of changing properties. Reality is composed of 'events' or 'actual occasions', linked together in a temporal process which is without beginning or end. Each actual occasion 'prehends', or is causally affected by, every other actual occasion in its immediate past. It organizes all these data from its own point of view, and in an act of creative synthesis, it continues the temporal pattern they form into the immediate future. As it does so, it perishes, giving rise to a new set of actual occasions in the process. This scheme derives from Leibniz's *Monadology*, with its infinite monads all reflecting the others from their own viewpoint. It differs from Leibniz in the stress laid on the transient and instantaneous nature of the actual occasions, and on the creativity of the temporal flow. Whereas Leibniz saw monads as substances, containing all their possible properties, and only appearing to be temporal, Whitehead reduced them to events and made temporality their essential property.

For Whitehead, actual occasions are layered in hierarchies of greater and lesser complexity. More complex actual occasions 'include' less complex ones—as the human mind includes all the actual occasions which make up the cells of the body, for instance. God is defined as the all-inclusive actual occasion, or infinite process of all actual occasions, forming one organic unity. Thus God includes all reality within the divine being. God literally prehends

---

[44] Ibid. 346.

every actual occasion, and so knows everything that any being can know. However, God does not know the future, since it is yet to come into being, as a result of an infinite number of creative acts by actual occasions. Since these acts are truly creative, and are not determined by the past or by God or existent in some supratemporal sense, even God cannot know what will happen in future.

Similarly, God is not omnipotent, in the sense that God can do anything, or be the ultimate cause of everything that happens. On the contrary, the actual occasions are the real causes of what happens, and God must simply prehend their activity; God cannot compel it. On this view, God is not an all-determining monarch; God is 'the fellow-sufferer who understands'.[45] God literally shares all experiences. Like all other beings, God is in continual temporal process. Yet God, unlike all other beings, is not wholly confined to the temporal process.

A crucial doctrine of process thought is that God is dipolar; God has a twofold nature. First, God has a 'primordial nature', which is, says Whitehead, abstract, without consciousness and 'deficiently actual'.[46] It is a sort of sum total of all possibilities or 'abstract objects', always deficient inasmuch as it contains a 'yearning after concrete fact—no particular facts, but after some actuality'.[47] God is, in a sense, the realm of Platonic Forms, 'the ultimate conceptual realization of the absolute wealth of potentiality'.[48] In that respect, God is changeless and eternal. But God is also lacking in concrete reality, for the real must be the concrete and particular, not just the abstract and universal.

This primordial nature of God contains all possible futures. The second pole of the divine nature is the 'consequential nature', by which God prehends all actual occasions, including their experiences, at every time. At any particular time, God prehends what is the case. From the primordial nature, God then provides each actual occasion with an 'initial aim', which is its best, most creative possibility. In this sense, God is 'the lure for feeling, the eternal urge of desire', 'the poet of the world'.[49] God does not compel things to happen, but persuades, by referring to the primordial nature, towards the best. However, actual occasions may not be persuaded; and God must

---

[45] Whitehead, *Process and Reality*, 532.   [46] Ibid. 521.
[47] Ibid. 50.   [48] Ibid. 521.   [49] Ibid. 522.

simply prehend whatever they freely decide to do. Whatever they do, however, God, who is infinitely patient, is finally able to integrate their choices into the all-inclusive harmony of the divine experience. Thereby things obtain an 'objective immortality' (not conceived as a real, independently enduring existence) by being taken into the unitary experience of God. In this sense, 'God is completed by the individual, fluent satisfactions of finite fact, and the temporal occasions are completed by their everlasting union with their transformed selves, purged into conformation with the eternal order.'[50]

God necessarily seeks some concrete temporal expression of the primordial nature; so the world is necessary to God. The world is a real temporal order in which creativity is an essential feature, which even God cannot obliterate. God can, however, 'lure' actual occasions towards the good. Having endless time, God will in the end increase the beauty and harmony of the world. In any case, the experience of God will be completed by taking the temporal process into the divine being and giving it there, in an ever-extending creative pattern, an eternal satisfaction.

Whitehead's philosophy picks up many elements of Hegelian thought—the stress on the necessity of the world; the stress on temporality; the idea of God as including all finite reality. He develops from it, however, a radically new metaphysical system, in which God has an important place. God is not, however, the impassible, non-temporal, simple Infinite of Thomism. Being dipolar, God does have such a nature, a primordial nature. But that nature is necessarily expressed in a consequential nature, which introduces possibility, temporality, and complexity into the divine being. To put it bluntly, the process God is not omnipotent or omniscient, and cannot ensure that the divine purposes will be realized, since God is limited to persuasion. This is a temporal God, who shares in the travails of the world, seeks to lure it towards greater good, and includes it, as so far completed, in the eternal memory of the divine awareness.

There are many possible variants of process theology, but they all share the general features of attributing to God dipolarity, all-inclusive infinity, temporality, creativity, and persuasive action. They usually deny or reinterpret the notions of omnipotence and

---

[50] Ibid. 527.

omniscience. They tend to see creation, not as a freely willed act of God, but as a necessary concretization of the abstract primordial nature of God, which endlessly proceeds by the free creative acts of many 'atomic' acts of actual occasions, not by direct divine ordinance. Process philosophy is a difficult, ambitious, and total metaphysical system, which is enough to make it suspect for many. Its stress on divine temporality, passibility, and persuasive action has influenced many theologians who might be suspicious of its general claims. In these respects it seems to show more affinity with the God of ordinary Christian belief than with the God of classical theism, who is never affected by the world and who therefore never really responds to free creaturely actions or is able to do anything radically new. The idea that God suffers, responds creatively to prayer, and seeks to persuade by love seems to fit quite well with the idea of an incarnate God. However, most theologians feel difficulty with limiting the divine power and knowledge, with accepting that God can never create a perfect heaven and the earth by free decision, and with the denial of individual resurrection or life after death.

Creativity and sensitivity are often thought to be qualities a perfect being should have; but it is not so clear that a perfect being should be conceived as being essentially dependent upon the world for actuality, as being limited in power and knowledge, or as being constantly developing and improving. The process concept of God remains controversial among theologians. It has, however, raised a challenge to the classical theistic position on a number of fronts. The basic idea of divine dipolarity, with its associated place for temporality and passibility in God, may survive dissociation from general process metaphysics, and may contribute to further discussion of the proper attributes of a being 'than which no greater can be conceived'.

On the account I am suggesting, human freedom and creativity remain basic constituents of the universe, but God has a much more active and positive role to play than in most versions of process thought. God is the master Creator, laying down the pattern, influencing creaturely choices towards a goal whose general nature is given by God but whose specific character is, in many respects, determined by creatures. God creates our capacities and influences them towards good. But we express them in specific ways. We can and should do so by free reliance on God, who will ensure that their potential for good is realized, though in a uniquely creative way that only we can specifically determine. To use another another analogy, that of the master chess player, used by Geach and Polkinghorne,[51] God enters into the game to ensure that it is concluded in the way that God desires. In this way, God ensures that all the evil caused by the misuse of creaturely freedom will finally be ordered to good, though the tragedy of its occurrence cannot be simply obliterated by anything God does.

NOMOLOGICAL AND AXIOLOGICAL EXPLANATION

In the light of this discussion, one might consider again the distinction made earlier[52] between the two complementary models of intelligibility by means of which one can understand a world containing free actions. They are the nomological—a model familiar to physicists—and the axiological—often found in the social sciences. For the first model, one understands the genesis of the new by appeal to general principles or laws of regular succession. That there are simple, elegant, and mathematically statable laws which describe the structures of the universe is a surprising and remarkable fact;[53] and their formulation enables scientists to understand and predict many of the processes of nature. For the second model, one understands the genesis of the new by appeal to values which are to be realized by beings of certain distinctive capacities and modes of awareness. This model does not provide general laws which facilitate prediction. It provides an idea of the values which are appropriate to beings of a certain nature and enables one to understand why such beings act as they do. The first model ends with the postulation of ultimate brute facts; the second with the postulation of ultimate values or desirable and worthwhile states.

The two models are not wholly disconnected, however. For the first model is strongly evaluative, in seeking the simplest, most elegant, and mathematically fruitful postulates. This is in fact an aesthetic criterion, answering the question about why ultimate brute facts are as they are by suggesting that they are the most beautiful

---

[51] P. T. Geach, *Providence and Evil* (Cambridge: Cambridge University Press, 1977), 59; John Polkinghorne, *Science and Providence* (London: SPCK, 1989), 98.
[52] Ch. 8, Sect. 3 ('The Value of Creativity').
[53] 'The physical universe is put together with an ingenuity so astonishing that I cannot accept it merely as a brute fact' (Davies, *The Mind of God*, 4).

(elegant or simple) set of facts which give rise to the interestingly complex universe we apprehend. One can say that it just happens that such a value—of ultimate mathematical beauty—is instantiated in our universe; or one can turn to the second model for intelligibility and say that such beauty exists because it realizes a state of great intrinsic value.

On the other hand, if one asks why the values that are realized in this universe should be just as they are—why these values are realized and not any others, which perhaps we cannot fully imagine—then one has to refer to the nature, capacities, and desires of beings within the universe. The values of sensitivity, creativity and freedom, wisdom, and justice which form the objective good of this universe are comprehensible as fulfilments of the natures of the sort of sentient social animals which have evolved in a physical universe of a particular structure. The values which this universe realizes are those states which unfold the potential implicit in its ultimate natural constitution. Thus to see what values this universe expresses one needs to discern the natural tendencies and capacities of beings in the universe, which in turn refer back to the ultimate brute facts of the universe. This insight is enshrined in the Semitic tradition that true human good is to be found in appropriate fulfilment of natural human inclinations; that goodness is rooted in the nature of things, and is not some sort of arbitrary decision or purely subjective expression of feeling.[54] If one asks why God created just this out of all possible universes, the answer lies in the creatively free choice to realize the distinctive set of values this world alone embodies. It lies in the will of God, not as an arbitrary fiat, but as a creative self-expression of the infinite divine being. No further, and no better, explanation can exist than this, if creativity is indeed a fundamental value and fact of being.

Ultimate brute facts and ultimate values are not disconnected. Using the first model of intelligibility alone leaves one with ultimate brute facts which are just there for no reason at all. Clearly many physicists are unhappy with this ultimate non-rationality, and have sought some sense of quasi-logical necessity which will remove the last trace of arbitrariness.[55] But they are thereby resorting to the

---

[54] 'Reason of its nature apprehends the things towards which man has a natural tendency . . . and therefore to be actively pursued' (Aquinas, *Summa Theologiae*, Ia-IIae q. 94 a. 2).   [55] See the remark of Steven Weinberg in Ch. 8, n. 9.

Principle of Sufficient Reason, which would make all things necessary implications of some initial state which is itself necessarily existent. For some quantum cosmologists, one can speak, albeit controversially, of an initial state (of quantum fluctuations in a vacuum) which is necessary, in that it instantiates the only set of states compatible with quantum theory.[56] But of course one still has to ask in what sense such a theory could be necessarily existent, or give rise to a physical instantiation of itself.

Theism comes surprisingly near to such a hypothesis, in holding that there is a being, God, which contains the basis of all possible universes, which exists necessarily, and which generates this universe as one contingent realization of the exhaustive set of possibles in its own being. The theistic model suggests how a mathematical theory could be existent (as conceived in the divine mind) and how a universe could be generated from it (by an intentional act); but it might be seen as simply a more pictorial way of putting the quantum cosmologists' proposal that this universe originates from a necessarily existent being, or is itself necessarily existent in its deep structure. However, although this cosmological model of intelligibility does eliminate arbitrariness from the universe, which is very satisfying for a physicist, it also seems to reduce the phenomena of freedom and creativity, of value-realization, to relative insignificance. One main advantage of introducing the concept of God is that it enables the aspects of necessity and creativity to be held together in one coherent, non-arbitrary, and yet non-deterministic form of explanation.

THE IDEA OF CREATIVE EMERGENCE

Thus the best possible intelligible explanation of the universe, its maximal explanation, is to be found, not in a set of physical brute facts and not in a form of 'personal explanation' which is rooted in the merely given nature of some personal being, but in a necessarily existent source of all possible and actual beings which creatively brings to be a universe in which creatures can co-operate in realizing a distinctive set of values. This source, this self-existent, supremely perfect, and freely creative being, is God. In this sense, theism is the completion of that search for intelligibility which characterizes the

---

[56] See the discussion by C. J. Isham in Russell *et al.*, *Quantum Cosmology* 49–89.

scientific enterprise. The universe can be seen as intentionally brought into being to realize a distinctive set of values, and the laws of nature are the general principles which set the conditions for the unfolding of natural tendencies which bring those values about through a temporal process of emergence. The discovery of the remarkable amount of 'fine-tuning' in the physical structure of the universe greatly enhances our view of the universe as one elegant and closely interconnected whole.[57] The universe is both rational and contingent; for necessity and freedom are both key characteristics of it, and require precisely that sense of creative but non-arbitrary emergence which is the mark of the divine creative act itself.

This model of causality is different from the classical philosophical model of sufficient causality—the entailment model, which fails completely to account for the fact that the universe, as we know it, contains qualities which did not exist in its primordial constitution. And it is different from the Humean regularity model, which sees laws of science simply as statements of observed regularities between events. It is a model of *creative emergence*, accounting for the existence of things by seeing them as creative realizations of envisaged intrinsic values (states valued for their own intrinsic qualities, not their consequences or effects).

The doctrine of creation cannot be construed properly by either the sufficient causality model or the regularity model. At least for orthodox belief, the universe does not flow from God as a quasi-deductive entailment of the divine being. And there is certainly no regular observable succession between Gods and the production of universes. But it could be construed by a creative emergence model, according to which this universe is a novel imaginative expression of specific intrinsic values. The particular values chosen are a subset of the many values which exist eternally in God, and they are chosen precisely by the sort of creative spontaneity in God which it is itself a very great value to possess. This universe exists for the sake of the values it can realize and it is a realization of those values in ways which have not previously existed, which might have taken a different particular form, but which partly because of their novelty and individuality are of inherent worth. Rational creatures may reasonably be seen on this model as co-operating in the creative

---

[57] Polkinghorne, *Science and Creation* 22–33.

emergence of the natural order. They are subcreators with specific roles in the general creative pattern which issues from God.

Recent findings in cosmology should not be interpreted as 'proving' the existence of God, yet they are very important for assessing the coherence and plausibility of a doctrine of God as creator of the universe. What modern cosmology does is to show the elegant structure and the parameters of natural necessity, the unity and necessity of nature. It makes plausible a general view of the universe as a creatively emergent holistic system. Revelation claims to show the purpose of this holistic and intelligible natural order, construed in the Christian tradition as the creation of a community of love which is also a participation in the divine love. Thus modern cosmology and the central assertions of revelation can be seen as illuminating each other, disclosing an intelligibility and purpose inherent in the structure of the universe which point to its possible foundation in a deeply interfused spiritual reality.

The laws of the physical universe should not be set in opposition to God, as inviolable general rules which God, as an external power, would have to violate in order to act. The laws give the structure within which the purposes of God are brought to realization; and the structure provides many points at which there is the possibility of a creatively free initiative or response both for creatures and for God. One may think of God as having the universe-long intention of bringing conscious beings into a community of freely chosen loving relationships. This intention will shape the initial laws of the universe and the emergence of more complex possibilities within it. It seems reasonable to suppose that such influence will take the form of the maximum influence for good which is compatible with the preservation of the relative autonomy of nature and its probabilistic laws, and the freedom of creaturely acts, a freedom to reject love and thus cause suffering as well as to accept it and so bring happiness. As creatures become able to apprehend and co-operate with the divine intention, more specific divine acts will express the divine presence and purpose for them. Revelatory acts will disclose God's presence, character, and purpose to those who are receptive to them. They may often take the form of acts of judgement or blessing, as creatures either reject justice, love, and mercy, or pursue them and turn away from self-regard.

Many of these particular divine acts, though not all, may be termed 'miracles'. They are not violations of immutable laws of nature—a picture which makes one think they are both immoral (instances of law-breaking) and irrational (since the laws should have been better designed in the first place).[58] They are law-transcending events which manifest the basis or goal of the physical world in a wider spiritual realm. They show the power of Spirit to relate matter to itself so as to transcend normal material patterns of interaction, and establish a new interaction between the material and the spiritual.[59]

For Christians, the key example of a miracle is the resurrection of Jesus. It did not violate a law that dead people do not appear in bodily form. It showed a higher principle, that matter can be united to God to become a sacrament of divine life. When it is so united, it is immune from decay and dissolution. It is transfigured into a perfectly receptive vehicle of the divine will. Thus the body of Jesus disappeared from the physical world, and a new transfigured body showed the goal of the whole physical process to be the transformation of the physical into an incorruptible vehicle of divine Life.[60] The Resurrection is not an arbitrary breaking down of the physical process. It is the foreshadowing, at one point in human history, of the goal of material evolution, and thus a proleptic fulfilment of the physical process.

In miracles, God does not 'interfere' in a closed physical process. God perfects the physical process, showing what the ultimate divine purpose is. Every authentic miracle has such a disclosive function, transforming matter to be a sacrament of spirit. In the New Testament phrase, it is a *sēmeion*, a sign of God's purpose. It occurs only when that purpose needs to be declared or guided in a new way. Thus miracles will not upset the order of nature—as though God could well perform them all the time, to order. They have the function of showing what the basis and purpose of the order of nature is. They will occur rarely, in contexts in which great spiritual teachers have prepared the way for a new declaration of the divine will, and in ways which the cultures and histories of those teachers are ready to understand.

---

[58] Cf. David Hume's vastly popular definition of miracle as 'a violation of a law of nature' in 'Of Miracles', *Enquiry Concerning Human Understanding*, sect. 10 (1st pub. 1748).

[59] 'The possibility of miracle is part of the openness of creation to its Creator' (Polkinghorne, *Science and Creation*, 80).   [60] 1 Cor. 15.

In overturning old mechanistic and deterministic models of laws of nature, modern science helps towards a more satisfactory formation of a conception of divine action as the creative realization of purposes potential in the physical structure itself, not as interferences from some alien power wholly outside the system. Not all potentials can be realized, so there remains much scope for creative choice. Nor are potentials realized in a wholly predetermined way, so there remains much scope for imaginative elaboration and specification. Yet the model of the universe as directed towards a future which is partly open to creative choice is very different from the mechanistic model of it as predetermined in every detail, and it allows of divine and human action in much more intelligible and specific ways.

Modern cosmology may lead one to see the physical cosmos as an emergent value-oriented totality which is the optimal solution of a highly ordered and elegant set of boundary conditions. To the extent that it does so, it is consistent with and even suggestive of the belief that the physical universe is intentionally brought about by a self-existent being of supreme value. It may well suggest that the maximal form of explanation is that postulated by theism, and it helps to show the way in which the universe can be understood as the creative act of God. In these ways theism can be seen as sharing a common fundamental axiom of intelligibility with science, and the pursuit of scientific understanding may be seen as converging upon the religious quest for self-transforming knowledge of God rather than as being opposed to it. As modern science sprang from the context of Christian belief, so now it seems to many to be leading back to its roots, the apprehension of the physical cosmos as the visible expression of the mind of God.

13
Creation and the Trinity

Theologians have tried in various ways to articulate the basic idea of a reality of supreme power and value, thought to reveal its nature in a special way in their own religious traditions. They broadly agree on the supreme perfections that are ascribable to God. Power, wisdom, knowledge, bliss, and compassion are ascribed to God in both Indian and Semitic traditions. There have nevertheless been many different ways of spelling out what such perfections imply, and how they relate to the universe. A common theme has been the desire to exclude from God any hint of imperfection or limitation. This has led to a concept of God which is strongly distinguished from time, finitude, suffering, ignorance, and passibility. God must be absolutely beyond change by any created being, an untouched and immutable reality. Yet in various ways, all religious traditions have had to account for change, suffering, development, and ignorance in the universe.

The Buddhist schools, which have not been treated in this volume, in so far as they accept the existence of a pure reality of wisdom and compassion beyond space and time, make the strongest demarcation by denying any causal relation between such a reality and the realm of *samsara*. This world exists because of desire, and it is by the cessation of desire that the realm of changeless bliss will remain in its purity. Such a view preserves perfection in inviolable purity, though it excludes from the idea of the origin of the universe any action of a personal being.

The Vedantic schools involve Brahman in time as the inner Self of all. In some manner, Brahman enters into finitude, ignorance, and suffering. Yet in itself it remains unchanged, and the goal of religious life is to realize one's inner unity with that unchanging reality. Aurobindo gives to the temporal process a positive role, as the expression of the relational and emergent being of Brahman.

Thus Brahman has a dual reality, being both infinite and time-transcending and temporally emergent. The relation between them is that the temporal necessarily manifests the timeless. The Vedantic view shares with neo-Platonism and with Hegelian philosophers a vision of the finite universe as eternally emanating from the timeless One. Where Brahman is the sole reality, suffering and ignorance must in a sense be properties of the Supreme itself, though they are somehow sublated in the completed and timeless experience of the One.

Theologians in the Semitic tradition began from a much firmer distinction between God, as Creator, and the created universe. They were thus inclined from the first to attribute suffering and ignorance to the finite created realm alone, and exclude it from the being of God. This tendency was strengthened by the influence of Greek philosophical ideas of divine perfection, which tended to separate the material world from the divine mind, as two distinct forms of reality. Jewish, Christian and Muslim philosophers classically developed a concept of divine perfection which saw it as timeless, immutable, simple, impassible, and untouched by suffering or real relationship to the created order.

I have suggested that belief in creation was always in tension with such a radical distinction between creator and creatures. The tension is seen at its sharpest in Islam, where, as Fazlur Rahman has put it, 'The theory of the eternity of the world is the hallmark of all Muslim philosophers except al-Kindi, while all theologians in Islam are voluntarists and place their entire weight on the side of God's power and will.'[1] An eternal emanation of the universe from God makes it possible to see the world as a sort of 'overflow' from the divine being, which leaves God truly unchanged. A contingently willed creation of space-time, however, introduces an active and contingent element into the divine being which suggests that the existence of the world makes a difference to God. The 'theologians', of course, did not admit such a contingent element in God, as they were, ironically, influenced by the philosophers to the extent that they could not see divine perfection as allowing any change (thus any temporality) at all. If the theologians had emancipated themselves further from the

---

[1] Fazlur Rahman, 'Ibn Sina's Theory of the God–World Relationship', in D. B. Burrell and B. McGinn (eds.), *God and Creation* (Notre Dame, Ind.: Notre Dame University Press, 1990), 51.

classical Greek philosophers, they might have achieved a rather different view of divine perfection.

A number of twentieth-century theologians, including those I have considered here—Iqbal, Heschel, and Barth—have sought precisely such a further emancipation. They stress, in different ways, a real relationship of God to creatures, in an empathetic and responsive fellowship with created persons. Such a stress, well rooted in the Semitic scriptures, makes possible a reconception of perfection as essentially involving creativity, affectivity, and relationship. The perfect is not the immutably solitary, excluding all finite limitations, but a supremely creative and affective reality which both includes and transcends all finite goods. Its infinity is not a sheer boundlessness whose emptiness of content excludes every particular good, but an endlessly creative and universally inclusive infinity of values. Suffering and ignorance do not have to be ascribed to God, since they may be properties of created beings, to which God can relate in appropriate ways without being subject to them, as creatures are. Of course, the theist must give some account of how suffering arises, and of how a supremely perfect being will respond to it.

In the Semitic traditions, suffering is in general attributed to a failure or corruption of created wills, and God, while permitting it for the sake of an end which is good, will eventually eliminate it from creation to enable the purpose of creating finite goods to be fully realized. Judaism, Christianity, and Islam propose diverse views of how God, as perfect being, responds creatively to the corruption of created wills, and of how such corruption can be overcome. Contemporary theologians in each faith, however, are much more open than were classical theologians to seeing God as permitting real creaturely freedom, as responding affectively, in sorrow as well as in delight, to created beings, and as exhibiting a co-operative creativity in working out the divine purposes for good in the world.

THE NECESSITY OF CREATION

A Christian theologian might find that such a more dynamic and inclusive idea of divine infinity and perfection is particularly well suited to articulate the distinctive Christian idea of God as Trinity. For the Christian gospel is that God enters into time ('becomes incarnate'), shares in human suffering so as to liberate human wills from corruption, and continues to act inwardly and by the persuasion of love in order to make human persons sharers in the divine being, and to make human lives the vehicles and mediators of the divine life. God is manifest in Christ as redemptive love, and that must be the central image which governs Christian reflection about the divine being.

It may be an essential part of the divine nature to be loving. If that is so, it will be essential to God to create beings other than the divine self, with which God can enter into fellowship, as a way of realizing the divine nature in creative and relational action. This is no lack in God, but it is to say that the divine nature is essentially self-expressing—which means that it is essentially other-creating and unitively loving. If it is better for God to be actually loving than to be merely capable of loving, it will follow that this is the case.

Paul Helm, in commenting on a previous book of mine, attributes to me the view that God must create a universe if God is to be loving, together with the view that there is no necessity for God to create the universe.[2] He suggests that this is a contradictory position; but it is not, as long as one holds that God is contingently loving. My way of construing this was to hold that God is essentially good, but, since creation is contingent, that divine goodness should relate to others in love is contingent.[3] God would have been good without any universe, but could only be loving with one. It is good that God is actually loving; and, of course, in a sense, God would be eternally loving, namely, in the sense that God would love the divine self wholly and, if God created a universe, would relate to it in love. But God was under no compulsion to realize that disposition, and thus would not be called actually loving with any degree of plausibility, just because God had the capacity to love under unrealized circumstances.

As Helm points out, we do not complain at the thought that God has to be good or wise or happy, that it is part of the divine nature to be so. So should it be a defect to create by necessity of one's nature? 'God eternally chooses this universe as the expression of his nature,' says Helm.[4] I suppose the hesitation is connected with a desire to give God as great a sovereign freedom as possible. If God restricts

---

[2] Paul Helm, *Eternal God* (Oxford: Clarendon Press, 1988), 193.
[3] K. Ward, *Rational Theology and the Creativity of God* (Oxford: Basil Blackwell, 1982), 85 ff.   [4] Helm, *Eternal God*, 193.

the divine self in creation—by not knowing the future, by suffering?—then God must at least voluntarily do so. Perhaps it is also the thought that God must be self-sufficient without any universe, that God cannot depend upon us in any ultimate sense; so God could remain God without a universe.

I do not now think these arguments very strong. If God is not free to be evil or non-existent, why is it important that God be free not to create? As God is essentially good, so God may be essentially a loving creator; and one might expect that God would be, if God is the greatest conceivable being, and loving creativity is one of the greatest perfections. Nor does God's necessarily creating some universe render God not self-existent. It is only that the divine self-existence would naturally, essentially, overflow into other forms of existence, and there is no defect in that, but a plenitude of actuality. Thus I am now inclined to think—though with a hesitation prompted by my reluctance to say that I really understand the divine nature—that some creation, and some disposition to creative activity and loving fellowship, necessarily actualized at some time, is necessary to God being what God is.

It need not be true that God always has to be related in love to creatures, as though there must always be non-divine sentient beings in creation (though angels have sometimes been so interpreted). For God is not necessitated to exercise all divine properties maximally— if this notion of a 'maximum' even makes any sense with regard to God's possible relations with creatures. It is rather that God's disposition to give the divine being in love, if it is a genuine disposition, must be actualized to some degree and in some way. It is the same with the divine creativity, which need not be unceasingly exercised, but must be exercised in some way. As far as this point is concerned, then, this may be the only universe God relates to in self-giving love, or there may be many or even an unlimited number. Naturally, we know of only this one, but perhaps we should not limit the divine being in thought, either by assuming it to be the only one, or by asserting categorically that God had to create, and love, beings just like us.

It may be that the specific kind of relational, suffering, reconciling love manifested in this universe is not an essential property of God, but something like a supererogatory power—one that it is good, but not essential, to manifest. However, if Christ is taken to disclose God as God truly is, as self-diffusive love, it seems reasonable to assert that some universe is a necessary expression of divine love, which will involve real relationship to what is other, sympathetic knowledge of the feelings of others, and creative response to the acts of others. It will therefore involve passibility and temporality as essential features of divine love.

THE IDEA OF A SOCIAL TRINITY

Classical theology accepts that love is an essential characteristic of God, but has often concluded that the Trinity provides the possibility of loving relationship within God, without having to posit the necessity of creation.[5] Yet it is obvious that, within the Trinitarian being of God, there is no real creation of another, and no unitive reconciliation of that other to God. For all the *hypostases* are one God. There can be no real otherness and no need of reconciliation. The Trinity may indeed reflect or prefigure in the nature of God itself those aspects of perfect being, other-creation and unitive reconciliation which will characterize the divine actions in the universe. But there will still be no actual redemptive love of the other unless there is some created universe. A fully Christian view of perfection might show it to be, not a self-contemplating unalloyed and unaffected bliss, but a loving, passionate, and relational creativity.

Much contemporary Trinitarian thought deploys the notion of a 'social Trinity', thinking of God as a society of persons in loving relationship. One of the most persuasive accounts of such a 'plurality model' of the Trinity has been given by David Brown.[6] He proposes that we think of the persons of the Trinity as 'three distinct centres of consciousness, each with its own distinctive mental content'.[7] They act in necessary, indivisible, and full co-operation, and thus cannot conflict with one another. Each is an omnipotent, omniscient individual, though some have forms of action (e.g. the Spirit acts internally in human souls) and forms of experience (e.g. Jesus experiences suffering as human) that the others do not. This model enables one to think of God as a communion of persons, each of

---

[5] See Richard of St. Victor, *De Trinitate*, bk. ii, ch. 14, ed. J. Ribaillier (Paris: Librairie Philosophique J. Vrin, 1958), 149.

[6] David Brown, *The Divine Trinity* (London: Duckworth, 1985).

[7] Ibid. 289.

which is self-giving and constituted by relation to others. So one can think that 'God is Love', even without any relation to created reality. Relationships of giving, receiving, and sharing love exist within the divine being itself, whether or not there is any creation.

Richard Swinburne develops a rather similar account, suggesting that there is a compelling reason, in the essential divine property of love, for the existence of a Trinity.[8] A loving being must create another to love, which should be of the same perfection as itself. Since it is the nature of love to share, those two divine individuals must generate a third. 'Love must share and love must co-operate in sharing',[9] so there is a good reason why there should be three and only three divine souls, which in their indivisibility constitute the being of God. For these views, there are three omnipotent, omniscient individuals, and together they enable God to be thought of as truly loving, even without any universe.

Attractive as this model seems, it has grave drawbacks. It seems to conflict with what Jesus selected as the most important commandment: 'The Lord our God, the Lord is one.'[10] As Brown concedes, his view could be put by saying that there are three gods, bound together in indivisible unity of action and purpose. This is very much like a form of polytheism; indeed, a rather cosy and harmonious polytheism. The model it relies upon is a community of rational persons, inextricably bound together in mutual love. For this model to work, each person must be an individual, with a distinct consciousness and will of the same sort, yet each must have distinguishing characteristics which make them different persons. This already distinguishes the model from the traditional view that the 'persons' differ only in their relation to one another, and not in any substantial property.[11] It is very hard to say just what love between two persons consists in; but it must include a concern to help the other, an interest in the acts and distinctive characteristics of the other, a co-operation in using complementary gifts to achieve shared actions and experiences. If one is thinking of two (or three) persons who are omnipotent and omniscient, none of them can need

---

[8] Richard Swinburne, *The Christian God* (Oxford: Clarendon Pres, 1994), ch. 8.
[9] Ibid. 178.   [10] Mark 12: 29.
[11] The Council of Florence (CE 1439) asserted that '*in Deo omnia sunt unum, ubi non obviat relationis oppositio*' (H. Denzinger (ed.), *Enchiridion Symbolorum*, 23rd edn. (Frieburg: 1963), no. 1330.

help from the others, nothing can be hidden from the others, and no action or experience can be shared which is not already enacted or known by each person anyway. Brown says, 'Though they have separate powers, to know the mind and will of one is to know that of all three.'[12] The persons have diverse mental contents. The Word has, as part of its unique mental content, the experience of human suffering. The Father does not have that experience. But, as omniscient, he may know *that* the Word has the experience. In a similar way, every experience of every divine person is completely known by the others.

The divine persons can also have distinctive forms of activity. The Father is the only one whose creative acts are wholly underived from another. The Son is the only one who suffers and atones. The Spirit is the only one who strives within creatures to conform them to the pattern of the Son. It is unavoidable that the three 'persons' have diverse forms of awareness and action. Each may respond to knowledge of the other persons in their own way, by sympathy and encouragement. One may think of a continual interplay of actions and responses, in which each has its own awareness and activity, and all are fully aware of the consciousnesses of the others.

Yet there is something uncomfortable in the thought that one has here three distinct individuals (what Swinburne calls souls), each with its own independent centre of consciousness. Is it not true that, as Rahner puts it, 'There exists in God only one power, one will, only one self-presence'?[13] Is it not the *same* God who creates, who suffers and dies, who guides and sanctifies? What that seems to require is that there is one ultimate subject which possesses three distinct forms of action and awareness. Bernard Lonergan puts it succinctly: 'The three subjects are aware of each other through one consciousness which is possessed in a different way by the three of them.'[14]

One view posits three divine souls who always act indivisibly and know each other completely, and the other posits one divine subject with three forms of consciousness. A problem with the 'three souls' view is that it seems to require a principle of the necessary unity of

---

[12] Brown, *The Divine Trinity*, 293.

[13] Karl Rahner, *The Trinity*, tr. J. Donceel (London: Burns and Oates, 1979), 75.

[14] Bernard Lonergan, *De Deo Trino* (2 vols.; Rome: Gregorian University Press, 1964), ii. 193).

the three which is superior to the three themselves. How does it come about that the three are necessarily indivisible, omnipotent, and omniscient? It must be more than a fortunate chance, but wherein can such a necessity lie? The obvious move, which Swinburne makes, is to make the Father the ingenerate cause and the root of unity between the three. Wolfhart Pannenberg, in commenting on a similar sounding Cappadocian proposal, points out that this seems inevitably to lead to subordinationism.[15] For the Father cannot create another being with exactly the same divine properties as he has.

Suppose the Father tries to create another essentially divine being with the same divine properties, namely, the Son. At least one divine property cannot be thus created, the property of being the unoriginated cause of everything other than itself. The Son will owe being wholly to the Father, and will thus be dependent for existence in a way the Father is not. The Son will have no causal power over the Father that the Father does not give to the Son. The Son's action will necessarily have to be compatible with the Father's existence and actions. As Swinburne admits, this will have to be achieved by the Father initiating a plan to which the Son will, as perfectly good, assent. Thus the Father has a clear causal, volitional, and executive priority. It is implausible to suppose that the Father causally depends upon the Son in the way that the Son depends upon the Father. The upshot is that these two beings do not share the same divine properties. The Son is more like an archangel, after all, than like another god.

Pannenberg's own way to avoid subordinationism is to find the desired principle of divine unity in love which, as 'the power that manifests itself in the mutual relations of the Trinitarian persons, is identical with the divine essence'. The divine essence is 'the power and fire of love glowing through the divine persons, uniting them and radiating from them as the light of the glory of God'.[16] However, this also seems uncomfortably to depersonalize and hypostatize love, as a force superior to the persons in which it is actualized. The divine essence is not an abstract property, even as high-sounding as love, which actualizes itself in precisely three individuals. Love is the disposition of a being to create and delight in goodness, to create

[15] Wolfhart Pannenberg, *Systematic Theology*, tr. G. W. Bromiley (2 vols. Edinburgh: T. & T. Clark, 1991–), i. 321.   [16] Ibid. 427.

other subjects who can do so, to co-create and co-experience with them, and to care for their well-being and proper fulfilment. It is a power, but it is essentially the power of a personal subject, and must be embodied in a particular subject. Pannenberg's proposal does not really solve the problem of the divine unity, since one has to ask why the power of love should be embodied in three co-equal subjects, especially when one of them (the Father) is admitted to be the real *archē*, or origin, of the other two. Either love is the underived property of the Father, given derivatively to Son and Spirit, which reintroduces the sort of subordination which Pannenberg feels uneasy with, or love must be the property of the Trinitarian God, who must therefore be seen as one subject. Certainly, in the idea of the Trinity one transcends the idea of self-centred or solitary individuality, but not by positing a society of similar divine souls. In the idea of coinhering willing and knowing one has the root of love as delight, giving, receiving, sharing, and co-operating. Yet God is love, not as three loving individuals, but as a unity of three coinherent modes of action of one supreme being. That is to say, God does not contain within the divine unity a true otherness, a plurality of similar and relatively autonomous subjects. As Rahner puts it, 'Within the Trinity there is no reciprocal "Thou".'[17] Again, 'There is properly no mutual love between Father and Son.'[18]

When we say that 'God is love', we do not mean that God is one objective person standing in a relationship of love to other persons. As the primordial depth of love, God is the ultimate basis of all the forms of goodness we hope to share. As such, God stands infinitely beyond us, though relating to us in loving-kindness as the source of good. As love manifest, God takes on the form of a person like us, and we can relate to him in devotion and a certain kinship. Yet here also, God has a cosmic dimension which transcends our humanity, being the pattern of all creation and the final unity into which we hope to grow. As the power of love, God works creatively within us to transform us into the image of love manifest as person. So we live in the power of the Spirit, on the pattern of the Son, in total dependence on the Father. Love relates to us as unbounded goodness, as self-emptying personal being, and as inward unitive power. This threefold form of love is the form of one divine subject in three distinct subsistences, forms of awareness and activity.

---

[17] Rahner, *The Trinity*, 176 n.   [18] Ibid. 106.

I do not think that it is possible to construct such a view of God simply from reflection on what love as such is. One may however find in many theistic traditions, as I have tried to show, a sense that a simple understanding of God as a loving person misses some of the complexity of an adequate account of the Divine as Creator. The Christian claim is that by reflection on the person and role of Jesus, a profound understanding of divine and therefore of true human love can be formed. As Sarah Coakley has suggested, Christian experience of prayer suggests a basis for Trinitarian thought, for which the Trinity 'is the graced ways of God with the creation, alluring and conforming that creation into the life of the "Son".'[19] But such prayer itself depends for its precise form on acceptance of the role of the Spirit as the one who 'intercedes for us with sighs too deep for words',[20] and who is sent as 'Comforter' by the Son.

The problem of incipient tritheism arises from thinking of the persons of the Trinity as separate minds, which have intra-divine relations, apart from any relationship to created reality. Jürgen Moltmann, who also develops a social view of the Trinity, evinces some reservations about this model. He does insist that 'Father, Son, and Spirit are in fact subjects with a will and understanding.'[21] They are not, he insists, 'modes of being' of a single divine subject. The main reason he gives is that, if one begins from a biblical perspective, the Father, Son, and Spirit seem to be treated as different subjects, the Son praying to the Father, the Father grieving over the suffering of the Son, and the Spirit glorifying both. So Moltmann asserts that 'the Trinity supersedes theism.'[22]. At the same time, he qualifies this social model by suggesting that the three hypostases of the Trinity are not of the same kind at all.[23] 'No subsuming generic terms may be used in the doctrine of the Trinity', he writes, which must mean that the 'persons' cannot properly be conceived as three mental beings after all.

Moltmann seems to me entirely right to insist that all talk of the Trinity must be rooted in the biblical history of salvation. But when he says that Father, Son, and Spirit do not belong to some common

---

[19] Sarah Coakley, 'Why Three?', in S. Coakley and D. Pailin (eds.), *The Making and Remaking of Christian Doctrine* (Oxford: Clarendon Press, 1993), 37.

[20] Rom. 8: 26.

[21] Jürgen Moltmann, *History and the Triune God*, tr. J. Bourden (London: SCM, 1991), 84.　　　　　　　[22] Ibid. 24.　　　　　　　[23] Ibid. 88.

genus, he provides the best reason for denying that they are all independent subjects of the same kind, with will and understanding (the genus of 'person'). New Testament exegesis very rarely, if ever, comes up with an analysis of the texts which suggests that there are three divine individuals in continuing conversation throughout the Gospels. It is usually agreed that the idea of the Trinity only exists embryonically in the Gospels, and that what needs to be worked out is the exact relation between Jesus as Lord, God as Creator, and the Spirit as life-renewing and inspiring power in the early Church. Such working out is a complicated and delicate task, but I judge that Moltmann is mistaken to say that 'Those who begin from this salvation history begin . . . with the recognition of these three indivisible and different subjects and their one, unique collaboration in their history.'[24]. They begin, as the Apostles began, from belief in the one God of monotheism, who is somehow mediated to them through Jesus and intimately present in the power of the Spirit. The idea of the Trinity does not supersede monotheism; it interprets it, in the light of a specific set of revelatory events and experiences.

A plurality model of the Trinity has not been accepted by the main traditions in the West. The main alternative model, largely adopted, with some amendments, by Anselm and Aquinas, is that of Augustine's *De Trinitate*. As is often pointed out, the psychological analogies appealed to by this model again seem to commit one to thinking of God as a cosmic mind, though this time not three minds but one mind, operating in three different ways. If one thinks of the Trinity as something like the *memoria, intelligentia*, and *voluntas* of a human mind,[25] and one thinks of the many ways in which mental activity can be analysed, this might, as David Brown says, 'make one doubt what it could mean to say that a mind might have internal divisions that are non-arbitrary'.[26] Augustine interpreted intradivine love as a delight in one's own perfection; but that cancels out the social aspect completely, and makes divine love a matter of self-contemplation. While it has some appeal to think of Father and Son as lover and beloved, it is quite unsatisfactory to think of the Spirit as the love which binds them together, since that depersonalizes the Spirit, perhaps helping to give rise to the rather mechanical theories

---

[24] Ibid. 83.
[25] Augustine, *De Trinitate*, bk. ix, ch. 1, tr. E. Hill (New York: New City Press) 271. [26] Brown, *The Divine Trinity*, 275.

of the operations of grace which permeate late medieval theology. What makes both plurality and unity accounts seem unsatisfactory is their determination to think of God as a sort of disembodied mind, or triumvirate of minds, coupled with their separation of the timeless intra-divine life of God from the economy of salvation in which Trinitarian talk was originally rooted.

Catherine Lacugna has argued that 'the divine processions, "being begotten" and "being breathed", are inconceivable apart from the divine missions: the life and ministry of Jesus and the sending of the Spirit to his followers.'[27] The basic Christian perception about God is that God never existed as a solitary figure. 'God is ecstatic, fecund, self-emptying out of love for another, a personal God who comes to self through another.'[28] The 'social Trinitarians' are quite right to try to explore this insight. But this cannot be done by making the communion of divine persons somehow intra-divine, which retains a slightly extended self-absorption in the divine being, after all. Any model of love within the Trinity must be, in the end, simply the love of God for the divine self, and not the love of another who may pose a real otherness and distance, and in some sense an opposition, to the lover, and who may then stand in need of reconciliation. 'The communion of divine life is God's communion with us in Christ and as Spirit.'[29] Thus 'an ontological distinction between God *in se* and God *pro nobis* is, finally, inconsistent with biblical revelation.'[30]

To take such a view is not to reduce the Trinity to a merely economic role, as though it was a matter of different ways in which God acts towards creation, while the *theologia*, the inner being of God, remains non-Trinitarian. One can insist—indeed, one can insist with increased emphasis—that the economic Trinity, God as known to us historically through Christ and in the power of the Spirit, gives an insight into what God truly is. It is our only access to what has been called the immanent Trinity, the inner Trinitarian being of God, and such access is authentic and reliable. What one cannot do is to take the hypostases of Father, Son, and Spirit out of all historical relations and present them as internal goings-on within a wholly self-contained and self-sufficient Godhead. That would, ironically, betray precisely the fundamental insight into God's ecstatic, overflowing goodness into a realm of genuine otherness,

---

[27] Catherine Mowry Lacugna, *God For Us* (San Francisco: Harper, 1991), 6.
[28] Ibid. 15.   [29] Ibid. 15.   [30] Ibid. 6.

responsiveness, and dynamic creativity. The Divine threefoldness is a real quality of God *in se*. But that '*in se*' is not existent out of relation to creation. It is manifested in its true and essential character in creation and in the return of creation to God, a *Patre ad Patrem*, which is always through Christ and in the power of the Spirit.

This should not be interpreted to mean that there is no immanent Trinity, that God is only Trinitarian in relation to creation. It means that the intra-Trinitarian being is given to us only in revelation. Our speaking of it is a conceptual abstraction and inference from the revelation in Christ, not an independent metaphysical hypothesis. In this restricted sense, 'Rahner's Rule', that the economic Trinity is the immanent Trinity,[31] can be endorsed. It is not that there is no more to God than what is revealed to us, nor that we know exactly what God's inner being is like when we speak of the Trinity. It is rather that God essentially is such as to be authentically revealed as a Trinitarian God. Nonetheless, the Christian theologian must beware of reducing the infinite divine being to the compass of any human mind, however inspired, and also of constructing a speculative theory of the divine being in itself which makes human history and divine relation to it virtually irrelevant. God is what God is in relation to creation, a God of self-giving, suffering, redemptive and reconciling love. God remains for us, of course, a mystery hidden in uncreated light, but is, Christians claim, revealed for human understanding in a threefold—ecstatic, incarnate, and unitive—form. The doctrine of the Trinity is not founded on pure speculation, but on the belief that God has truly revealed the divine self in the life and teaching of Jesus and the advent of the Spirit at Pentecost.

THE BASIS OF TRINITARIAN DOCTRINE

The doctrine of the Trinity is firmly rooted in the apostolic experience of Jesus as the one who makes God present and who inaugurates the rule of God in the world. The Gospels suggest that some at least partly misunderstood Jesus' message and role during his lifetime, expecting him to rule over a liberated Israel in a new historical era.[32] But Jesus inaugurated a spiritual, not a political,

---

[31] Rahner, *The Trinity*, 27.   [32] Luke 24: 21.

kingdom.[33] He did proclaim the inauguration of the Kingdom of God, and he claimed by his deeds that he was the King who was to rule in a new Israel and a new era.[34] That rule is foreshadowed by the outpouring of the Spirit upon the young Church community. It is too crude, however, to see the expectation of the Kingdom as belief in an end of history in the near future. It is truer to the subtlety of apocalyptic and eschatological imagery to see the Kingdom as something which remains always future to every historical time, though it is always imminent at every historical time, as each temporal moment is integrated into the eternal life of God. The 'end of history' is imminent at every time, as its inner purpose and intended consummation. Yet it does not put a stop to history, wherein the Spirit continually makes present its foreshadowed realization, by making the Christ who was present in Jesus present again in the community of the Church.

Jesus comes to be seen as himself the end or goal of history, and his death and ascension to God unveils the inner meaning of the whole historical process, the drama of conflict with evil, victory by self-giving, and union with God in which the whole human race participates. Though he is the exemplar of perfected humanity, he is not only a paradigm of human life. He is also the temporal image of the eternal love of God, embodied in a human life, as the word of grace which invites all earthly beings into communion with God. In the early Church community, God comes to be seen primarily as the Father of Jesus Christ, the one who sends the Spirit to empower Jesus' life with grace, who remains the object of Jesus' prayers and obedience, and who is the final goal, to union with which Jesus leads all earthly beings. Jesus is the obedient Son, who, in perfectly obeying the Father's will to make him the King of the redeemed earth, becomes the visible image of the invisible God. Together with the Father, Jesus sends the Spirit upon those who follow him, to make them holy and incorporate them into a life of indivisible community with one another and with God.

In the first four centuries of the Church's existence, these new strands of religious thought were gradually woven into an elaborate doctrine of God as Trinity. But the simple historical source of this doctrine is the apostolic experience of God as loving Father, Jesus as the obedient Son, the Father's image on earth, and the Spirit as the

[33] John 18: 36.   [34] e.g. Mark 11: 1–10.

one who makes Jesus present to every time and place, and unites all in him. The experience of new life, the foreshadowing of salvation, came to the Christians from the Father, through the Son, and in the Holy Spirit. That experience began with the acceptance of Jesus as Lord, of his testimony that God was his Father, and of the Spirit as the inner power which he sent in a sort of spiritual baptism upon their community.

There is here a sort of simple primitive Trinity, preceding the formulae of later Church councils. The Father is God the transcendent Creator of all, who loves creation so much that God calls Jesus to be the express image of Divinity and to manifest redemptive love on earth. Jesus is God in Wisdom, embodied in a human life, revealing the mystery of redemption, which is the uniting of all things in the Spirit. The Spirit is God working within the heart, realizing a redemptive purpose and bringing humans to wholeness of being. Father, Son, and Spirit picture God the transcendent Creator, beyond all history; God the redeeming Saviour, manifesting the divine being decisively at one historical time to inaugurate the rule of the Spirit; and God the empowering Spirit within, present at every earthly time to prepare and complete the process of redemption.

THE DEVELOPMENT OF TRINITARIAN DOCTRINE

In one way, Christian belief in the Trinity need never move beyond this fairly simple picture. It captures what is essential in the distinctively Christian view of God. Yet it soon became clear that Christian thought could not remain content with a purely historical, and therefore relatively local, account of the God who had become known in a new way in and through Jesus. From the earliest times, Jesus was naturally interpreted in the context of the ideas of God which can be found in the Hebrew Bible. God the Father was not only the Father of Jesus. God was the Father of Israel, creator of heaven and earth, making a covenant with humanity to bring it into a relationship of love. The Spirit is not only the new power known in the apostolic community. Spirit is the power of creativity, courage, and vision who had rested upon the prophets of Israel and who moved over the waters at creation. Jesus himself cannot be seen just as a man who is empowered by God. He manifests the Torah, the Wisdom of God, which had existed before all time, and who as such expresses the pattern for all creation and the final goal towards which all things move. In the rabbinic tradition, the attributes of God were often hypostasized to become virtually distinct spiritual beings. One key text is found in Proverbs 8: 22 ff., which makes Wisdom into a personal being, the 'child of God': 'The Lord created me at the beginning of his work, the first of his acts of old.'[35] This Wisdom was identified with Torah by some rabbis, and with the *cosmos noētos* by Philo. It is that through which the universe was created, which delights in creation, and which is itself the first delight of God. It can easily be identified with that primal creative word of God by which all things came into being, when 'God said', and things came to be.[36]

For Christians, the idea that this primal Word or Wisdom was created, and was thus different in being from God, was ruled out after the defeat of Arianism. There is good conceptual reason for ruling it out, since it is odd to speak of the Wisdom of God as something created by God, as though God had no wisdom before God created it, and so must have created it unwisely. On the other hand, it also seems odd at first to speak of Wisdom as a personal reality, instead of simply as a property of the divine being. One can think of wisdom, in one way, as the content of the divine thought. Wisdom, as in part the plan of this universe or the archetypal model of true humanity (the eternal Torah), might be created, in the sense of being conceived in the mind of God by a creative act of thought. A standard account of the 'days of creation' in Jewish thought was that they did not provide a temporal ordering, but a logical ordering.[37] Thus to say that Wisdom was the 'first' divine act does not have to imply that it came at the first moment of time, but only that it is logically the primary turning of God towards a created order, or towards the conception of such an order. In that way, Wisdom can be an eternal thought of God, engendered by something analogous to a creative act of intellection, though not coming into being when once it was not. In so far as Wisdom is in the mind of God, it is not different in being from God. In fact, it can intelligibly be said to form an essential part of what God is, so that without it, God would not be God, an intellective agent. The divine thought could be called 'consubstantial with' God, since it is part of the one divine substance, without which that substance would lack something essential to its existence.

[35] Prov. 8: 30.   [36] Gen. 1: 3.   [37] See Ch. 12.

Yet neither as a disposition of God nor as the eternal content of divine thinking is Wisdom a person, which can 'delight in' creation or be with God like a little child. It is significant, nonetheless, that rabbinic thought did hypostatize Wisdom,[38] and that the sense in which Wisdom is created by God is very different from the sense in which the universe is created, since the former, but not the latter, may well be said to be necessary to the divine being and to be part of the divine mind rather than a separate or distinct consciousness. The Christian view of Wisdom obviously requires that it not be considered as simply a passive content of the divine thinking, but as a reality which has some form of conscious relationship to its *archē*, or creative source in the divine nature. At this point the neo-Platonic tradition of emanations within the divine nature inevitably comes to mind. In Plotinus' influential version, the ultimate source, the One, generates from itself the intellective world, *Nous*, which in turn generates the World-Soul. From this triple being the universe emanates, as a sort of overflowing of being, down to the last dim echo of positive reality, infected with unreality, fading into nothingness.[39]

Such an emanationist view qualifies any straightforward account of God as a divine person, containing thoughts (Wisdom) and bringing things into being by creative fiat (so that 'the Spirit', too, is just a term for the creative activity of one divine person). The concept of a divine person is, in the end, too restrictive for the infinity of the divine reality—an infinity and mystery which, as has been noted, Jewish thought is very keen to stress. One might then think of the Wisdom of God as possessing its own proper form of intellective activity, with its own mode of acting and its own generative nature. Wisdom was hypostatized by the rabbis partly because it was not seen as a purely passive content of thought in the mind of a divine subject. It was seen as an active and substantial intelligible principle, though one which received its form of being from a reality beyond itself.

What seems to be essential to such a development of thought

[38] See Solomon Schechter, *Aspects of Rabbinic Theology* (New York: Schocken Books, 1961), ch. 9.

[39] Plotinus, *The Enneads*, v. i. 3–12, trans. S. MacKenna (Harmondsworth: Penguin, 1991), 350–60.

about God is that the Creator and Wisdom are not to be conceived as two things of the same sort (e.g. as two 'persons' in anything like the modern sense). Nor are they to be conceived as a person and one of its activities. They must be conceived as two distinct forms of existence within the divine reality. There is the primal source of all being, the 'depth of being', which is almost wholly beyond our conceptual grasp. And there is the relatively concrete, 'formed', active intellectual being which, as intelligible, generates the structures of this universe on the pattern of its own reality. Wisdom is hypostatized because it is dimly grasped that the intelligible Lord and pattern of this universe is itself grounded in an infinite reality which is beyond human comprehension. In neo-Platonic thought and in the Hebrew wisdom tradition, belief in the infinity of the divine being led to various hypostatizations or emanations from the ultimate divine source, which could connect it to this universe by a sort of chain of intermediaries. The hymn to Wisdom in Proverbs 8 leaves the status of Wisdom indeterminate, a creature and yet a child of God. In Plotinus, the hypostases of the Divine emanate from greater to lesser. Plotinus holds that 'the offspring is always minor',[40] but the Council of Constantinople (CE 381) condemned the view that Son and Spirit are subordinate to the Father. It is analytically true that, if the Father generates Son and Spirit, and if effects are always subordinate to their causes, then in one way Son and Spirit are subordinate to the Father. What the Council condemned was the view that the Father freely creates Son and Spirit as different beings. The most plausible view of the Christian tradition on this issue is that Son and Spirit are generated necessarily, as ways in which the one God exists. Divine omnipotence is necessarily and only exercised by Father, Son, and Spirit together. The Father can be called omnipotent, but only with the proviso that his power is exercised through the Son and in the Spirit, as essential aspects of the one divine being.

Thus in Christian theology, Wisdom became fully consubstantial with God, not created but procreated or 'begotten', a distinct active and substantial source (an hypostasis), receiving its reality from the imageless origin of all. The letter to the Colossians contains what is thought to be an early hymn, saying of Christ, 'He is the . . . first

---

[40] Plotinus, *The Enneads*, v. i. 6: 354.

born of all creation; for in him all things were created . . . through him and for him.'[41]

Christians added a third form of being to the divine nature, again prompted primarily by reflection on the impact of Jesus on the apostolic community and modelled on concepts suggested in the Hebrew Bible. In Genesis, the Spirit of God moved over the face of the waters,[42] and throughout the Hebrew Bible the Spirit inspires and gives life, as a dynamic power. If one may think of the Divine Wisdom as an 'active intellect' within the divine nature, one may perhaps think of the Spirit as the creative energy of God. This energy, as a creative Power or hypostasis, has its source in the 'unoriginate One' and finds the forms which direct and pattern its activity in the Divine Wisdom. The Spirit is not simply an inchoate energy. It works according to a particular form and pattern, and it works to generate new particular forms, realizing the divine archetypes in new particular ways. Spirit requires Word to give it form, and Word requires Spirit to give it life. They are bound together, as an infinite generation of living forms, originating from one source generating self-expressive order and creative bliss in their dynamic harmony. Such a notion lies beyond the reach of human thought. It is simply an extrapolation from the triadic model of God which is rooted in the human experience of Jesus, through the Spirit. It stumblingly affirms that in the God beyond thought and time there is that which is the true and authentic ground of the God who endlessly relates in love to creatures. God is not adequately thought of as a solitary cosmic mind. Neither should God be conceived as a society of similar beings, inextricably bound together. The nearest human imagination, prompted by revelation, can get is to say that God is the infinite and boundless ocean of being, within whom there is both intelligible contemplation and creative life. Far beyond both individual mind and any society of finite beings, the divine nature may be conceived as the archetypal perfection of both individual and communal personal being. In a triadic unity of being, creativity, and intelligible form, that changeless and perfectly actualized reality exists which is the sole foundation of every created universe. Thus Cyril of Alexandria could say that '*Everything* is from the Father, through the Son, in the Holy Spirit.'[43]

---

[41] Col. 1: 16.   [42] Gen. 1: 2.

[43] Cyril, *Contra Julianum*, 3, in *Patrologia Cursus Completus*, ed. J. P. Migne, Series Graeca (Paris, 1957–66), lxxvi. 649.

At the end of this process of reflection on the mystery of God revealed in Jesus, one may speak, in the most fundamental and yet in the most abstract way, of a Triad of the depth of being, the power of being, and the manifestation of being. The depth of being is that beyond all words, the ground of all beings, the infinite potency of all things which is also a wholly and unimaginably unrestricted actuality, beyond conceptual grasp. The power of being is the creative activity which expresses the divine being, actualizing from the abyss of potency endless particular forms, without end in its creative energy. The manifestation of being is the archetypal pattern and the completed image, the matrix and completion of creative activity, fully apprehended and appreciated within the divine life. These are not three distinct subjects of awareness, but three forms of the being of God, in each of which its whole being is expressed in a different manner. 'The one God subsists in three distinct manners of subsisting.'[44]

As triadic being, God can be said to exist from the divine being alone, without dependence on any other thing. God is the supreme self-knower, seeing the divine self as truth in the divine image.[45] God is supremely creative, a principle of energy and life, not of static aloofness, yet without having any lack or discontent which needs to be remedied by action, moving in *ek-stasis* out from itself to express itself in creativity.

In the terminology developed in the fourth century, the Trinity is three hypostases in one *ousia*. On the account just given, the best way of interpreting this rather vague description is to say, using the term suggested by Barth, that there are three modes of being of the one omnipotent and omniscient will and awareness who is God. The primal being, the manifested being, and the creative being are all ways in which the one God experiences and acts. All of these coinhere, forming one Subject in three centres of awareness and will, indivisibly co-acting and experiencing, each in its own way, and with its own form of awareness of the other centres. Each hypostasis of the same consciousness and will interpenetrates the others, being aware of them in its own appropriate mode and willing with them in its own distinctive modality.

---

[44] Rahner, *The Trinity*, 109.

[45] Athanasius, *Contra Arianos*, i. 20–1, ed. W. Bright (Oxford; Oxford University Press, 1873).

THE THREEFOLD GOD

It can now be seen how this developed doctrine of God as Trinity has strong and sometimes unexpected points of resemblance with views of God in other religious traditions, while it remains quite distinctive. Heschel, Iqbal, and Aurobindo all speak of God as an ineffable and infinite source of all being. They all hold that, though in one sense that source is self-existent and in need of nothing, yet it does not remain alone and self-sufficient. It makes itself known in particular forms of relation to created reality, and thus constitutes itself in some way as a personal reality, though that personal relationship does not change or detract from the infinite nature itself in any way. So, for Christian Trinitarian thought, the Father is the incomprehensible abyss of being, which is also ecstatic being, going out through the internal generosity of love to the creation of other forms of goodness. God manifests the primal divine reality as the Lord and Bridegroom of Israel and as the Father of Jesus Christ, entering into responsive and personal relationship with creatures. God also receives all things into the divine self, as God delights in the completed experience of redeemed creation.

Iqbal speaks of God as the Cosmic Ego, realizing its character in the progressive unfolding of history, and Aurobindo speaks of God as the Supermind, which expresses itself in the temporal evolution of the universe. The Christian idea of the Son or eternal Wisdom of God, as an intelligible agent who conceives the particular forms of created being in archetypal form, the *Nous Haplos*, expresses part of that notion. Christians do not quite see the whole process of history as realizing the archetypal pattern present in the Divine Wisdom, since individuals frustrate and deflect the primal divine plan to some degree. Nevertheless, that Wisdom is manifested in one perfect exemplar, Jesus of Nazareth, who incarnates the pattern of human loving responsiveness in time. Thereafter the destiny of creation is to be united in Christ,[46] so that Christ might in that sense be seen as the Cosmic Mind or Self in which the universe is completed and reconciled. All finite realities are to be included in the Christ, and it is in that all-including life that they are offered to the Father, the ultimate source of all and goal to which all things must return.

Iqbal speaks of God as co-operating with creatures in bringing

---

[46] Eph. 1: 10.

new forms of reality into being. Aurobindo speaks of *Shakti* as the primal energy of emergent creation, and of *Sachchidananda* as emerging through time to realize its inner potentiality. One can find here echoes of the Christian idea of the Spirit of God as the immanent creativity of God, projected as the creative energy which forms this space-time universe, as the co-operative and inner power who forms Christ in the lives of believers, and as the one who actively unites all things in Christ, making them whole and bringing them to the fullness of the stature of mature humanity.

The Christian idea of the Trinity is thus not wholly at odds with the sorts of reflection that take place in other religious traditions. But it does articulate the concept of God in a way which is most unlikely to have taken the exact form it has without a dependence upon what is taken to be a decisive divine self-disclosure in the person of Jesus. Once posited, this concept may be thought to have a coherence that provides a rationale for Christian devotion and suggests a fruitful basis for understanding the structure of created being and history. It can be seen as developing logically in a fourfold form, which expresses the eternal-primordial, originative-expressive, historical-responsive, and eschatological-unitive character of the divine being as it is revealed in Jesus Christ.

The timeless and primordial pure actuality of being, creativity, and form, which is the immanent Trinity, remains unchanging and unchanged in an active and self-sufficient perfection. It is the primordial aspect of the divine, the source of all beings, the absolutely unoriginated, possessing indivisible unity and self-existence. It is not, as in Whitehead, an unconsciously envisaged conceptual realm of abstract objects,[47] but an objectless intelligence (having its own activity as object), an unchanging activity and a completeness of being that must remain hidden from human comprehension in inaccessible light. Nor is it, as in Neo-Platonic thought, an undifferentiated One,[48] since even in its primordial character it retains an internal richness and complexity which Christian reflection expresses in triadic form. The infinite and primal depth of being, through the timeless exercise of the power of being, will actualize a supremely valuable set of states which manifest supreme beauty. It will do so by the actualization of value

---

[47] A. N. Whitehead, *Process and Reality*, (New York: The Free Press, 1978), 521.
[48] Plotinus, *Enneads*, v. i. 7: 355 f.

from the intelligible pattern of being which is, logically, its first self-expression.

Thus one may think of the depth of being (the Father) generating an intelligible self-expression and pattern of being (the Son), with its own form of consciousness of all possibilities. Together, they generate, through the power of being (the Spirit), with its own actualizing and evaluating consciousness, a set of supreme values, which forms the changelessly completed awareness of the Father.

So there is, in the Trinity, a giving of primal being, expressing itself in an objectified form of consciousness, and taking that back into primal being as realized experience, by the power of an evaluating, actualizing, and unitive form of consciousness. This is not a temporal process, but an always completed and immutable relational unity in which infinite depth, intelligible expression, and unitive creativity are bound together in blissful communion of being.

This account has unmistakable echoes of the Hegelian explication of Absolute Spirit as being in-itself, for-itself, and consciously in-and-for-itself.[49] Hegel has, in my view, illuminated the way in which one may give temporality a real function in the self-expression of God, while retaining a notion of the ultimate transtemporal reality of God. It should be borne in mind, however, that accepting the usefulness of this terminology does not commit one to the philosophy of Absolute Idealism. In particular, a Christian may wish to stress the otherness of God and the autonomy of creatures more than Hegel did, and to insist that to talk of an immanent, timeless Trinity is not to disclose the philosophical truth of which religious doctrines give only a pictorial representation.[50] It is rather to accept the religious insight that the divine being has a timeless, fully actual, and perfect aspect as well as a temporally expressive aspect. Further, the doctrine of the economic Trinity, while it is the starting point and substance of Christian prayer and practice, will be reflected in the immanent being of God, though in a form which all human concepts must fall far short of representing adequately. The doctrine of the immanent Trinity is not a speculative philosophical basis for Christian belief. It is a stumbling attempt to say what the primordial

---

[49] Hegel, *Phenomenology of Spirit*, trans. A. V. Miller (Oxford: Oxford University Press, 1977; 1st pub. 1807), 465.   [50] Ibid. 463.

aspect of God may be, if the economic revelation of God as Trinity is an authentic self-disclosure of the Divine.

The primordial being of God gives rise to the origin of worlds in a distinctively threefold pattern. The ecstatic abyss of potentiality engenders the archetypal intellect which forms the pattern for a particular universe, and the power of creativity which embodies that form materially. The world is created through the Divine Wisdom, the Christ, in the power of the Spirit. 'In him were all things created . . . through him and for him.'[51] In a movement beyond the divine being itself, through the power of the Spirit which moves over the waters of chaos, and through the intelligible forms of beauty which are inherent in the image of the Son, the universe is brought into being by the will of the Father. The Spirit proceeds from the Father in creative energy, and proceeds from the Father and the Son together as the Spirit shapes particular created things into the image of the archetypal Son. This is the creative aspect of the Divine, the dynamic infinity of the self-existent, as it manifests the divine being by an overflowing of its goodness. This creativity leaves the primordial nature unchanged, yet classical Thomist accounts of the Divine fail fully to acknowledge the reality of this changing and creative aspect of God, a reality which does not impair the divine perfection, but extends its scope.

Throughout the process which is the history of the universe, the primal source constitutes itself in relation to the world as Father, as transcendent Judge and Deliverer. This Father calls a particular people into fellowship. God becomes known as a transcendent but loving presence, who calls a particular people into covenant relationship. God sends the Spirit to inspire the prophets and make known the divine will. The divine being is embodied, first in Torah and then in the person of Jesus, as the incarnation of the cosmic image upon which all things are patterned. The Christ is incarnated on earth as the particular historical image of divine love, responsive to created human beings, whom he guides and teaches. The Spirit, in relation to the historical process, becomes the one who makes the love of Christ present within creatures. 'God has sent the Spirit of his Son into our hearts.'[52] This is the responsive aspect of the Divine, which interacts with created beings to check tendencies to disintegration and guide them actively towards perfection. This is the aspect

---

[51] Col. 1: 15.   [52] Gal. 4: 6.

which Whitehead most markedly fails to deal with, reducing the guiding function of God to that of a 'lure', which is only ambiguously responsive at best.[53]

Finally, as creation returns to its source, the Spirit sanctifies, reconciles, and unites all things within the perfected and actualized form which is the cosmic Christ. In the Spirit and through Christ, all things return to the Father, and all the values of temporal existence are conserved in a completed experience, in which all sentient creatures can share in an appropriate way. 'His purpose is . . . to unite all things in him, things in heaven and things on earth.'[54] At the end of this historical time, all created life which is responsive to God's call is taken into fellowship with the life of God, who will be all in all. The goal of all things is the *apokatastasis*, the return of all created things in the Spirit, through Christ as the body of the completed cosmos, to the Father. This is the consequential aspect of the Divine, incorporating into its being all the completed realizations of value which comprise the history of the universe, purged of evil and corruption. Process theology has great difficulty in thinking of a final elimination of evil from the unending process of reality, in which finite 'actual occasions' may always conflict. Where creativity is placed more firmly in the omnipotent being of God, and the laws of this space-time are given a finite duration, it becomes possible to think of a final triumph of the divine will, in a 'new heaven and earth', which is the transfiguration of present physical reality by its completed union with the Divine. 'Then comes the end, when he delivers the Kingdom to God the Father . . . that God may be everything to everyone.'[55]

CONCLUDING REMARKS

This volume began by outlining four twentieth-century doctrines of God as the creator of the universe, each claiming to be an authentic yet original exposition of the scriptures of Judaism, Christianity, Islam, and Hinduism, respectively. Abraham Heschel expounded the Jewish, 'prophetic', concept of God as that of a passionate,

---

[53] This problem in Whitehead is pointed out and discussed in J. Cobb and D. Griffin, *Process Theology* (Philadelphia: Westminster Press, 1976), ch. 4, and a more positive responsive role is given to God.   [54] Eph. 1: 10.
[55] 1 Cor. 15: 24.

morally demanding, responsive, and liberating power which underlies the processes of history. Karl Barth drew from the New
Testament an idea of God as essentially self-giving love, creating
others, entering into their alienated condition, and uniting them to
the divine life. Mohammed Iqbal elaborated a Muslim idea of God as
dynamically creative, and of the universe as the self-unfolding of a
Cosmic Self, guiding a community of finite selves into final union
with Itself. Aurobindo Ghose developed the Upanishadic doctrine of
Brahman to show the universe as the evolving, dynamic self-
expression of Brahman, and its goal as the full manifestation in time
of the divine life. Heschel, Barth, Iqbal, and Aurobindo all modify
their classical traditions by stressing the affectivity, creativity,
relationality, and temporality of the Divine. For all the differences of
their scriptural sources, they agree in seeing the Supreme Being as
creatively powerful, wise, expressing goodness in relational love,
affectively knowing, and blissful. Those five essential characteristics
modify, but do not replace, the traditional theologians' idea of God
as a timeless and self-sufficient reality. They do, however, clearly
make creation central to the being of God, and claim, not only that
the character of God makes a difference to the sort of universe this is,
but also that creation makes a difference to the sort of reality God is.

In Part 2, the coherence and plausibility of speaking about God as
Creator was defended. It was argued that non-realist theologians are
right in seeing theism as primarily a way of expressing and evoking
attitudes such as those of awe, gratitude, and hope, grounded in a
basic search for self-transformation in the realization of supreme
value. But they are wrong in thinking that such a form of life can be
appropriate without a metaphysical commitment to beliefs about
what the universe is like in its general nature. It was also argued that
there must be some literal, if analogical, statements about God, and
that theistic speech cannot coherently be regarded as wholly
symbolic or metaphorical.

In Part 3, an exposition of the five essential characteristics of God,
brought to light in Part 1, was offered. Though written from a
Christian viewpoint, the exposition tried to take the range of views
considered in the first part into account. It aimed to produce a
doctrine of God as Creator which would be broadly acceptable to all
four traditions (and to others, not mentioned here), and which has
learned from each of them. It is, however, not uncontroversial, and
will be contested by defenders of more classical interpretations of

their traditions. Nevertheless, it is defensible on scriptural grounds in each tradition, and provides a coherent and theologically fruitful account from a theistic perspective of the nature and purpose of creation.

Anselm's definition of God as 'that than which no greater can be conceived' was accepted as suggesting a helpful way of setting out the notion of a being of supreme power and value, which is at least implicit in all four scriptures. A supremely powerful being, it was suggested, would be the one and only creator of everything other than itself, though it could limit the exercise of its power so that other beings could exercise a limited autonomy. The most valuable aspect of power is creativity, which is itself a great value. Divine perfection is not the complete coexistence of all values in one being—a dubiously coherent idea—but the endless creative realization of many sorts of goodness, which is the supreme exercise of power. Power is a necessarily possessed dispositional state which issues in infinite contingent realizations of creatively envisaged possibility. Divine power is thus better conceived as divine creativity, and this in turn is an expression of divine love.

The wisdom of God is shown in the intelligibility of the universe. God is an absolute explanation of the universe, as the depth of being, the ontological foundation of all possibility; the power of being, not deriving its existence from another; and the manifestation of being, actualizing a set of possible states for the sake of their goodness. God is not just a sufficient cause of the universe, as though it flowed from a changeless, purely actual being by pure necessity. God freely and intentionally creates the universe out of infinite potentiality. The universe is intelligible, both in the elegance and economy of its basic laws and as an expression of free creativity for the sake of goodness.

The goodness of God follows necessarily from the fact that a powerful all-knowing being will choose maximally desirable states for itself, and will create what is desirable to others and to itself. God's goodness is inherently self-diffusive, sharing action and experience with others. In that sense, the creation of some universe may be necessary to God, as an expression of the divine nature as love. The creation of a community of rational agents who can share in creating and appreciating goodness increases the quantity and variety of the forms of existent goodness, and so flows from the divine nature as a free expression of self-diffusive love. Expressive creativity and relationship are both great values, which can be possessed by the divine being as it brings created persons into existence and relates to them in an ever-growing community of being.

The affectivity of God consists in that experiential knowledge by which God finds delight in goodness and beauty. But in a world of free agents, God will also feel compassion for suffering and revulsion from evil. Thus God's knowledge will be fully responsive and affective. It will express a real relationship to creatures, and will partly depend on the free actions of creatures. It follows that God will not have a complete knowledge of a future which is truly open, but God will still be omniscient, as knowing everything it is logically possible for any being to know at any time. However, the future is not wholly unknown to God, since God orders all things to good, wills that all creatures should find a proper fulfilment, and determines that evil will finally be eliminated and goodness fully realized. This is what is meant by speaking of God's predestinating knowledge and efficacious grace.

God is supremely blissful, since the being of God itself contains infinite actualized perfections, and since all created evil will be turned to good or eliminated. Sorrow will exist in God, but it is redeemed by its integration into a wider experience of goodness and beauty. There is an immutable and transtemporal divine perfection and bliss. But that primordial aspect of the divine being is expressed in the temporal process of value-creation which is the history of the created universe. By the *kenosis* and *koinonia* of love, by divine self-giving and sharing in fellowship with creatures, God is supremely affected by creation. But God ensures that creation will find fulfilment in supreme beatitude, and the creative, affective, relational, and unitive acts of God impart a character to the joy of the divine being which only the creation of communities of free co-agents and experients could realize.

Part 4 sought to locate this general concept of God in relation to the picture of the physical universe which modern cosmology provides. It also sought to show how the Christian doctrine of God as Trinity has many complex overlaps with elements of non-Christian traditions, while taking a distinctive form as it is shaped around the mystery of God revealed in Jesus Christ.

The universe disclosed by modern cosmology is a non-mechanistic, highly interconnected, emergent whole whose boundary conditions are highly ordered and finely tuned for the genesis of sentient life.

The universe seems to be a contingent but efficient and mathematically elegant process issuing in states of intrinsic and distinctive value. The theistic claim that the purpose of this universe is the creation of a community of love takes on plausibility as one sees the whole process as one of creative emergence, in which the material order becomes gradually self-aware and self-directing. God sets the basic parameters of the universe and continuously influences it towards the goal of communal sentient life, ensuring that finally a transformed material order will become a luminous sacrament of spiritual being.

In the final chapter, a number of strands of thought which had emerged throughout the volume were gathered up to provide a Christian doctrine of God as a Trinitarian being, the depth and pattern and power of love. The primordial depth of being (the Father) moves outwards in love to generate creatures and to respond to them in loving-kindness and judgement, through the archetypal pattern of Divine Wisdom (the Son), which takes particular form in human history, and in the power of the creative Spirit, which makes that form present throughout history. Then the Spirit gathers up and unites all creation in the completed form of the cosmic Christ and returns it to the Father as the transfigured fulfilment and goal of the original creative purpose.

This concept of the Trinitarian God is a Christian description of the idea of a creator of the universe, and it is given its distinctive form by reflection on the life and person of Jesus as an authentic revelation of God. It is one of many traditions which interpret the suprasensory reality with which the religious life is concerned in terms of a being supreme in power and value, the creator of everything other than itself. I have examined the idea of creation in four such traditions, and the way in which those traditions have been reinterpreted in the light of developments in scientific and historical knowledge. Such reinterpretations involve a stress on the creative, relational, and unitive involvement of God in the temporal structure of the created universe, and on the importance of that temporal structure to the self-expression of the divine being. These reinterpretations show how each tradition may hope to preserve the main elements of its own distinctive witness, while engaging in positive interaction both with other traditions and with developments in scientific views of the universe. This volume is written from within the Christian tradition, illuminated and deepened by the teachings of a number of revelatory traditions, and by recent advances in the physical sciences. As such, it has aimed to present an intelligible and defensible doctrine of creation, which can enable one to see the physical universe as the expression of the mind and heart of God. With such an understanding, religious faith, in its theistic form, may be understood, not as an irrational leap into the unknown, or as a satisfaction of some purely emotional needs, but as a reasoned commitment to seek personal union with a reality of supreme value and power, which gives to the universe and to sentient lives within it objective purpose and significance.

AUTHOR INDEX

SUBJECT INDEX